THE BATTLECRUISER HMS
HOOD

THE BATTLECRUISER HMS
HOOD

An Illustrated Biography
1916–1941

BRUCE TAYLOR

B.A. *Manc.* D.PHIL. *Oxon.*

Illustrations by
THOMAS SCHMID

Seaforth
PUBLISHING

In memory of
His Majesty's Battlecruiser

Hood
1916–1941

'A glorious ship, a great ship and a happy ship'

Half title:
The sealed pattern of *Hood*'s badge, designed by Major Charles ffoulkes and approved by the Ships' Badges Committee on 6 September 1919. The badge is derived from the crest of Admiral Viscount Hood (1724–1816) and shows a Cornish chough (*Pyrrhocorax graculus*) holding a golden anchor. Beak and legs should be bright red. The motto *Ventis secundis* is also Viscount Hood's, meaning 'With favouring winds'. The date 1859, usually omitted, alludes to the first major ship of the name, the 80-gun *Edgar* converted to screw propulsion and launched in that year; she was renamed *Hood* in January 1860. The badge, less the Navy crown, was used to adorn the ship's boats and guns (in the form of tompions) along with other artefacts and areas of the ship, including the Commander's lobby. The largest version, over 22 inches in diameter, was set on the bridge.

Frontispiece:
Officers and men on the forecastle of HMS *Hood* as she passes through the Pedro Miguel Locks, Panama Canal, 24 July 1924.
Illustrated London News

Death closes all: but something ere the end,
Some work of noble note, may yet be done,
Not unbecoming men that strove with Gods.
The lights begin to twinkle from the rocks:
The long day wanes: the slow moon climbs: the deep
Moans round with many voices. Come, my friends,
'Tis not too late to seek a newer world.
Push off, and sitting well in order smite
The sounding furrows; for my purpose holds
To sail beyond the sunset, and the baths
Of all the western stars, until I die.
It may be that the gulfs will wash us down:
It may be we shall touch the Happy Isles,
And see the great Achilles, whom we knew.
Though much is taken, much abides; and though
We are not now that strength which in old days
Moved earth and heaven, that which we are, we are;
One equal temper of heroic hearts,
Made weak by time and fate, but strong in will
To strive, to seek, to find, and not to yield.

TENNYSON, *Ulysses*, ll. 51–70

Text copyright © Bruce Taylor 2004
Colour illustration copyright © Thomas Schmid 2004

This paperback edition published in Great Britain in 2015 and reprinted in 2021 by
Seaforth Publishing,
Pen & Sword Books Ltd,
47 Church Street,
Barnsley S70 2AS

ISBN 978-1-84832-248-6

First published by Chatham Publishing 2004

Typeset and designed by Roger Daniels
Printed and bound in India by Replika Press Pvt. Ltd.

Contents

Author's Note

In preparing the pages that follow I have been confronted with the problem of presenting frequent citations from disparate sources in a consistent yet intelligible manner. Every effort has been made to preserve the character and intent of the originals but spelling errors have been corrected and punctuation inserted or adapted for clarity. The reminiscences of Boy Fred Coombs (1935–8) deposited in the Imperial War Museum (91/7/1) proved particularly challenging in this respect, much confusing detail and grammar having to be stripped away without sacrificing the qualities that make it such a unique memoir.

In order to help orientate the reader dates are provided after names to indicate an individual's period of service in the ship. Similarly, a man's rank or rating is usually indicated where appropriate. The variety of forms resulting from the use of this system seemed to me balanced by the value of the information imparted in what is a thematic rather than a chronological study, and in what was a highly stratified community. Readers will decide how effective this has been.

It may be helpful to remind readers of the traditional currency of the United Kingdom before decimalization in 1971: there were twelve pence to a shilling (known as a 'bob') and twenty shillings to a pound (also known as a sovereign or a 'quid'). Among the many coins engendered by this system was that known as 'half a crown', worth two shillings and sixpence.

The epigraphs at the head of each chapter are of course from William Blake's 'The Tiger' of *c*.1789. Citations from documents in the Public Record Office are Crown Copyright. The copyright of much of the remainder rests either with their authors or their descendants. Credits are given after each photograph where it has been possible to establish either the source or the copyright with certainty. Extensive efforts have been made to locate copyright holders in the remaining cases and these are invited to contact the author with proof of copyright. Citations from books and articles are acknowledged by means of a reference in the footnotes.

Abbreviations

AB	Able Seaman
ACQ	Admiral Commanding Battle Cruiser Squadron
AFO	Admiralty Fleet Order
APC	Armour-Piercing Capped (shells)
BCS	Battle Cruiser Squadron
B.E.M.	British Empire Medal
CAC	Churchill Archives Centre, Churchill College, Cambridge
Capt.	Captain
C.B.	Companion of the Order of the Bath
C.B.E.	Commander of the Order of the British Empire
Cdr	Commander
CERA	Chief Engine Room Artificer
C.O.	Commanding Officer
CPC	Common Pointed Capped (shells)
CPO	Chief Petty Officer
(D)	Dental
DNC	Director of Naval Construction
D.S.C.	Distinguished Service Cross
D.S.M.	Distinguished Service Medal
D.S.O.	Distinguished Service Order
(E)	Engineering
EA	Electrical Artificer
EOOW	Engineer Officer of the Watch
ERA	Engine Room Artificer
(G)	Gunnery
HA	High Angle
HACP	High-Angle Control Position
HACS	High-Angle Control Station
HMAS	His Majesty's Australian Ship
HMCS	His Majesty's Canadian Ship
HMS	His Majesty's Ship
HMS/M	His Majesty's Submarine
IWM	Imperial War Museum, London
IWM/SA	Imperial War Museum, Sound Archive
KCL	King's College, London
LHCMA	Liddell Hart Centre for Military Archives, KCL
LS	Leading Seaman
Lt	Lieutenant
Lt-Cdr	Lieutenant-Commander
Mid.	Midshipman
M.M.	Military Medal
MS	Manuscript
(N)	Navigation
NAAFI	Navy, Army, and Air Force Institutes
NCO	non-commissioned officer
NMM	National Maritime Museum, Greenwich
NWC	U.S. Naval War College, Newport, Rhode Island
OA	Ordnance Artificer
OD	Ordinary Seaman
OOW	Officer of the Watch
OSig.	Ordinary Signalman
OTel.	Ordinary Telegraphist
PO	Petty Officer
PRO	Public Record Office, Kew
p.s.i.	pounds per square inch
QO	Qualified Ordnanceman *or* Qualified in Ordnance
R.A.N.R.	Royal Australian Navy Reserve
R.A.N.V.R.	Royal Australian Naval Volunteer Reserve
RBS	Capt. Rory O'Conor, *Running a Big Ship on 'Ten Commandments' (With Modern Executive Ideas and a Complete Organisation)* (Portsmouth: Gieves, 1937)
R.C.N.	Royal Canadian Navy
R.D.F.	Radio Direction Finding
RFA	Royal Fleet Auxiliary
R.I.N.	Royal Indian Navy
R.M.	Royal Marines
R.M.A.	Royal Marine Artillery
R.M.L.I.	Royal Marine Light Infantry
RMS	Royal Mail Steamer
R.N.	Royal Navy
R.N.D.	Royal Naval Division
RNM	Royal Naval Museum, Portsmouth
R.N.R.	Royal Naval Reserve
R.N.V.R.	Royal Naval Volunteer Reserve
R.N.Z.N.	Royal New Zealand Navy
r.p.m.	revolutions per minute
RPO	Regulating Petty Officer
SBA	Sick Berth Attendant
s.h.p.	shaft horsepower
Sig.	Signalman
S.O.D.S.	Ship's Own Dramatic Society
SS	Steamship
Sub-Lt	Sub-Lieutenant
SWWEC	The Second World War Experience Centre, Horsforth, Leeds
(T)	Torpedoes
Tel.	Telegraphist
Temp.	Temporary
TS	Transmitting Station
UP	Unrotated/Unrifled Projectile/Projector
U.S.N.	United States Navy
USS	United States Ship

Foreword

by Vice-Admiral Sir Louis Le Bailly, K.B.E. C.B. O.B.E.

I SUPPOSE I MUST BE the last of HMS *Hood*'s ship's company to have served in part of each of her four final commissions between August 1932 and November 1939. From Cadet through Midshipman, Sub-Lieutenant and Lieutenant, I gazed with reverence at Admirals James, Bailey, Blake, Cunningham, Layton and Whitworth. And I served Captains Binney, Tower, Pridham, Walker, Glennie, and Commanders McCrum, O'Conor, Orr-Ewing, Davis and, in the Engineering Department, Commanders (E) Sankey, Berthon and Grogan, the last of whom went down with the ship. Each one in his own way was a great man; some greater than others.

Few can have been so consistently lucky as I at being permitted to watch such a posse of inspirational leaders. I did not recognise it, of course, but history was being made. As a result of failures in the First World War the Royal Navy, led by poor Boards of Admiralty, reversed much of Lord Fisher's work, ruthlessly discharged officers, and by inept handling of pay cuts created in 1931 the first major naval mutiny since 1797. The officers under whom I was so lucky to serve, together with Kelly, Chatfield, Henderson, Backhouse, Ramsay, Drax, W.W. Fisher, Fraser and dozens of others I never knew, led the Navy and all its intricate elements spiritually from its nadir at Invergordon to war readiness only eight years later. It was they who made it such an unconquerable element of our fighting forces as its numbers rose from 161,000 in 1939 to 750,000 in 1945.

Crowned as the greatest warship ever built, HMS *Hood* was an icon. For two decades from her cradling at John Brown's until 1939 she was used unsparingly in all her beauty and power as a political pawn sustaining the Pax Britannica before two years of war took her to a silent grave. It was when she was called on to fulfil her fighting role and ride the stormy northern seas as the backbone of the fleet in the winters of 1939 and 1940 that her company suffered such unspeakable hardship. *Hood*'s peacetime role had denied her the refit that would have made her watertight and the reconstruction that would have made her proof against plunging fire. And so when battle was joined she was gone within a few minutes leaving just three of the 1,418 men whose equable spirit had defied the elements since she left Portsmouth for the last time in August 1939, three weeks before the Admiralty made that general signal TOTAL GERMANY.

With the losses in the Battle for Crete mounting by the hour and the *Hood* sunk, May 1941 was probably the worst month for naval casualties in the whole war. The three Dockyard Towns of Portsmouth, Devonport and Chatham, already reeling from air bombardment, became very quiet as summer drew near and many tears were shed. 'Stick it out. Navy must not let Army down. It takes three years to build a ship but three hundred to build a tradition' signalled Cunningham in the Battle for Crete as one after the other the carrier, battleships, cruisers and destroyers of his fleet were lost or damaged by air attack. Though none could have foretold it, it was this simultaneous naval, land and air battle stretching from Greenland to the Eastern Mediterranean in May 1941 which cost Germany the war. In the West it was the sinking of the *Bismarck*, at the expense of the *Hood*, which put an end to German surface operations in the Atlantic. In the Eastern Mediterranean it was the resistance of British and imperial troops in Greece and Crete, of pilots who flew what aircraft could be found against the might of Axis air power, and of the Royal Navy which, at terrible cost in ships and men, delayed the inevitable and decimated Hitler's only complete airborne division. The removal of the Atlantic surface warship threat gave safe passage to a million Americans to their D-Day jump-off position in Britain. The battles for Greece and Crete caused Operation 'Barbarossa', the German attack on the Soviet Union, to be postponed by six weeks. 'Barbarossa' planned to destroy the Soviets by first taking Moscow but the Germans, like Napoleon, failed to reach the city before the terrible Russian winter set in.

HMS *Hood* lies 9,000 feet at the bottom of the Denmark Strait and through the marvels of technology her wreck has been filmed and shown to a worldwide audience. Nevertheless, the cause of her disintegration remains shrouded in mystery. Perhaps in another decade or so closer inspection will determine how came the end. There have been many books about HMS *Hood* but until man can exist and move 9,000 feet down on the ocean bed I doubt if there will ever be such a history, such a biography, such an obituary as Bruce Taylor has written. The astonishing volume of research he has managed to achieve brings alive not only *Hood*'s irreplaceable years of service in the cause of peace, but also the neglect to update her fighting potential and the pattern of her operations in war that led to almost unbearable conditions for her gallant company who somehow kept her going against all odds.

It has been a privilege watching Dr Taylor knit together a vast and varied theme into what must surely be, for many years to come, the definitive account of an awe-inspiring piece of Britain's naval history.

St Tudy, Cornwall
St Valentine's Day, 2004

Introduction

THIS BOOK HAS BEEN WRITTEN to address two longstanding needs in the field of British naval history. First, to give due treatment to the greatest warship to have hoisted the White Ensign since the *Victory*, one that explains how she acquired her exalted status, why her loss temporarily shattered the morale of the British people; why, perhaps, she retains the hold she does over the imagination of those who never knew her. Second, in doing so, to provide a new perspective on the genre of ship biography, one that for the first time marries the technical reality and operational career of a vessel with the experience and mentality of those who breathed life into her, made her what she was in all her vast complexity. To provide, in short, the first integrated history of one of the great capital ships of the twentieth century, the ultimate expression of a nation's power, the summit of technology and innovation, and the most evolved community in military society.

Any historian attempting a 'total history' of a warship must gird himself for prolonged research among widely scattered sources in many fields. As with most recent ships in the Royal Navy, the fabric and structural history of HMS *Hood* has been the subject of considerable investigation. This is just as well since naval history requires of its practicants an unusually firm grasp of the immediate physical and technical environment of their subject if they are to do it justice. Indeed, it is hard to imagine how the present volume would have evolved without the benefit of John Roberts' remarkable 'Anatomy of the Ship', published in 1982.[1] But the fabric of a ship is one thing, her operation quite another. To be afforded a plan or photograph of a 15in turret is not, alas, to be given any significant idea of its functioning, much less the impact it had on those who worked in it. Indeed, to study the *Hood*'s engine spaces in particular is to be made aware that certain items of equipment acquired a character all their own, one intimately associated with those given responsibility for serving or maintaining them. Can any member of the Engineering Department have thought of the boiler room fan flats without thinking also of Chief Mechanician Charles W. Bostock? For the *Hood*, which had the rare distinction of being the only ship of her class, this becomes an important consideration, one which among other things implied extended periods of service for a core of specialist ratings. Equally, while the *Hood*'s career is either well known or readily traced in official sources, the tenor of her shipboard life—hitherto largely unstudied—is far harder to follow or reconstruct. For here lies a near-insuperable challenge to any who would write the social history of a warship: where they survive at all the overwhelming majority of documents are in private hands, though increasing numbers are becoming available to researchers in one form or another; long and richly may this flow continue. In times past it was common for naval writers to exhort their readers to join the Navy League; this one will confine himself to exhorting his readers to entrust their documents or memoirs of service to the Imperial War Museum.[2]

However, the richest source for the life and being of the ship has come through personal contact with the dwindling band of survivors of her successive commissions. In this the *Hood* is, numerically at least, much less well provided than other vessels of comparable size. On 24 May 1941 she was lost with over 99 per cent of her company and perhaps 70 per cent of those who had sailed in her since the outbreak of war, including many who had given her five, ten or even 20 years of service. A high proportion of those who knew her best therefore succumbed either in the Denmark Strait or to the savage attrition suffered by the Royal Navy during the conflict as a whole. Nonetheless, the author has been able to uncover significant information from surviving crewmen dating as far back as the 1933–6 commission. The atmosphere of the 1931–3 commission, which comprehended the Invergordon Mutiny, has been reconstructed mainly from oral histories along with the testimony of a single veteran. For obvious reasons the World Cruise of 1923–4 is a well-documented interlude in the history of the ship but the scythe of time has deprived this writer of any truly detailed or first-hand information on the four commissions of the 1920s. Further investigation would no doubt attribute this not only to generational factors—it was the 1970s before the preservationist movement set in—but to the poor morale among both officers and men that increasingly characterised the Navy as the 1920s wore on.

For the material that survives, in whatever form it is transmitted—letters, diaries, memoirs, oral histories or direct contact with veterans—further obstacles and pitfalls remain where its interpretation is concerned. To read the memoirs of an officer and a rating of the same commission is to appreciate the gulf-like gap in outlook and prospects separating the two sides. There was mutual respect, collaboration and comradeship in adversity, but to pretend that HMS *Hood* was 'of one company' is to ignore the fundamental realities of service afloat. Both then and since, the opinions voiced are invariably bound up in the assumptions and realities of class which continue to characterise British and particularly English society generally. The views range from those of Boy Fred Coombs, frequently marked by a morbid bitterness and disgust, to those of officers such as Admiral Sir William James in which a supposition is made of harmony and satisfaction which existed among only a small proportion of ratings. Between these extremes are memoirs offering penetrating insights into the life and atmosphere of the ship, among which those of LS Len Williams and Vice-Admiral Sir Louis Le Bailly stand out. Nor are these the only considerations. The war years are much the best documented period in the history of the ship but, with a few notable exceptions, censorship at the time and restraint thereafter have conspired to make this material comparatively less candid and valuable than that from earlier commissions.

Some 15,000 men served in the *Hood* between 1919 and

[1] John Roberts, *The Battlecruiser* Hood [Anatomy of the Ship] (London: Conway, 1982).
[2] Department of Documents, Imperial War Museum, Lambeth Road, London SE1 6HZ.

Some 15,000 men served in the *Hood* between 1919 and 1941 and this book is based on the partial records of 150 of their number—a mere 1%. Inevitably, citations are often made which reflect the very decided opinion or agenda of their author, either at the time or later. In the pages that follow the present writer is careful to draw a distinction between opinions purely those of their author and those which can be taken as representative of the views of a wider community of men; between those written at the time and those the product of memory, more reasoned and ordered in their perceptions but less accurate in their detail or emotional tone. Then there is the matter of confidentiality and withholding of information alluded to just above. The 'Silent Service', whose members set down and publish their memoirs rather less frequently than those of the other armed services, yields its secrets only with the greatest reluctance. The sense of a world apart which only those who lived it can share or understand remains strong. Beyond this, service in a ship usually implies a bond of loyalty and attachment to be broken only by death. In preparing this volume the author has become aware how much information about the *Hood*—inevitably concerning her less agreeable aspects and episodes—is known but neither revealed nor admitted. This of itself has something to say about the mentality of those studied in this book, about the values of the community in which they served and about the self-perception of the Navy of the time and since. The following pages therefore contain many stark revelations about life aboard, particularly in wartime; many more are no doubt passing into oblivion. Personal enormities of one sort or another are part and parcel of any large community but the general condition of the ship, both structurally and in terms of her morale, is another matter. The *Hood* was undeniably in a state of advanced dilapidation by 1939 and her crew were to suffer for it in the months and years to follow. Many British warships required their men to serve in conditions similar or worse, but few were as hard-pressed as she while at the same time operating under the rigours and discipline of big-ship life. The morale of the ship was never broken but it is clear that by late 1940 and early 1941 many were finding the strain of war service intolerable. Naturally, some men bore their lot easier than others. If the view offered in Chapter 8 alters the prevailing impression of 'the Mighty *Hood*' then it is fair to her last company that it should be written, as it would have been written had she survived to be scrapped and they to enjoy the fruits of peace. Commemoration cannot be allowed to efface reality. The achievement is the greater for the suffering endured.

The ultimate end of historical research is to understand a society or community with the same clarity and richness with which we grasp our own. On that criterion the present volume must be regarded as falling some way short. Nonetheless, with its limitations, this study offers a vision of the *Hood* and her world which goes far beyond anything previously available for this vessel, or any other for that matter. Moreover, it offers a tentative methodology and approach upon which others might build if warship history is to progress beyond the uninhabited corridors of technical data and conjectural analysis in which it is now largely conceived. Above all, these pages cannot fail to demonstrate that the culture and community of a capital ship was even richer and more imposing in its order and design than the structure which enclosed it. If nothing else, they demonstrate that those wishing to grasp the essence of a ship must approach her first and foremost through her people. It was iron men not steel ships that made the Second World War the swansong of the Royal Navy, victorious in terrible adversity. Let that never be forgotten.

Hood alongside the South Mole at Gibraltar in 1937 or 1938. Lengthy interludes in Mediterranean waters kept her from the reconstruction she so desperately needed.
HMS Hood Association/Percival Collection

1 Genesis, Design and Construction

Did He smile His work to see?
Did He who made the lamb make thee?

T HE BATTLECRUISER HMS *Hood* was the fine flowering of a shipbuilding industry that had lead the world in technology, capacity and innovation since the early nineteenth century. Above all, she was born in the crucible of war and in the context of the greatest naval building race in history. Despite the tragic fate that awaited her, the *Hood* remains a monument to an era of naval and industrial organisation then reaching the height of its powers. How she came to be built and readied for service is the subject of the following pages.

The immediate origins of HM battlecruiser *Hood* can be traced to a note sent by the Controller of the Navy, Rear-Admiral Frederick Tudor, to the Director of Naval Construction, Sir Eustace Tennyson d'Eyncourt, in October 1915.[1] In it Tudor requested designs for an experimental battleship based on the successful *Queen Elizabeth* class but incorporating the latest advances in seakeeping and underwater protection. Central to the Admiralty's brief was a higher freeboard and shallower draught than previous construction, features that would not only permit more effective operation under wartime loads but lessen the threat to the ship posed by underwater damage. Between November 1915 and January 1916 d'Eyncourt evolved five designs, the most promising of which had a greatly enlarged hull and beam in order to achieve the necessary reduction in draught. However, these studies were rejected in a lengthy memorandum by Admiral Sir John Jellicoe, the Commander-in-Chief of the Grand Fleet. Whereas the Royal Navy had a marked superiority in battleships over the High Seas Fleet, it had no answer to the large Mackensen-class battlecruisers then under construction for the German Navy. Accordingly, six more designs were produced in February, based on the earlier studies but emphasizing speed over protection. Of these one was selected for development, resulting in a further pair of designs in March. It was the second of these, Design 'B', which received the nod from the Admiralty Board on 7 April 1916 and upon which the ship that came to be known as HMS *Hood* was based. The final studies had been evolved under d'Eyncourt's supervision by E.L. Attwood, head of the Battleship section of the Royal Corps of Naval Constructors, assisted by S.V. Goodall.

What did this design consist of? On a standard displacement of 36,300 tons—over 5,000 tons more than any other ship in the Royal Navy—Design 'B' promised a speed of 32 knots through the use of the lighter small-tube boiler. A length of 860 feet—approaching the length of two and a half football fields—meant that there would only be three graving docks in Britain capable of accepting her, those at Portsmouth, Rosyth and Liverpool. There were to be eight 15in guns in a modified turret design along with sixteen of the new 5.5in mountings. An 8-inch main armour belt was believed to offer better protection than the 10

inches of the *Queen Elizabeth* class thanks to the introduction of a sophisticated arrangement of sloped armour. However, horizontal protection showed no improvement on earlier designs, being restricted to a maximum of 2.5 inches, and that only on the lower deck; elsewhere it was no more than 1.5 inches. On 17 April orders for three ships were placed by the Admiralty, one, eventually called *Hood*, at John Brown & Co. of Clydebank.[2] Then came Jutland.

On 31 May and 1 June 1916 an action was fought 100 miles off the Danish coast which was to have far-reaching consequences for the Royal Navy. Of these only one need concern us here: the fate of the British battlecruisers, three of which blew up under German shellfire. The battlecruiser was a product of the fertile mind of Admiral Lord Fisher, the mercurial genius who transformed the Royal Navy in the years before the First World War. Fisher's intentions are not readily divined, but he evidently recognized that a *guerre de course*, a concerted campaign on British merchant shipping, would form a key element of German naval strategy in the coming war.[3] To counter this he took the principal innovations of his other brainchild, the *Dreadnought*, and created the battlecruiser, a ship which married the size and fighting power of a battleship with the swiftness of a cruiser. However, ship design is a science based on compromise and in order to attain speeds in excess of 25 knots major sacrifices in armour protection had to be made. The first generation of battlecruisers therefore represented a risky and prodigiously expensive solution to the problem of commerce-raiding and cruiser warfare, but the expenditure was vindicated first at the Battle of the Falkland Islands in December 1914 and then at the Dogger Bank in January of the following year. In the first action the main units of Vizeadmiral Graf von Spee's *Deutsche Südseegeschwader* were sunk by *Invincible* and *Inflexible* 8,000 miles from Britain, thus ending German hopes of a sustained offensive against imperial trade. In the second the armoured cruiser *Blücher* was overhauled and crushed by weight of fire from Vice-Admiral Sir David Beatty's battlecruisers. However, there was another side to Fisher's concept, that of fast scout for the battle fleet, and for this role the battlecruiser was to prove significantly less well equipped. Inevitably the moment came when the battlecruiser began trading salvoes with ships of similar firepower and at ranges which presented a severe danger to her thin horizontal protection. The First World War, it turned out, was fought over ranges far greater than had been anticipated by ship constructors when they designed the armour layout of their ships. Whereas most capital ships had been optimized to absorb shells fired from 4, 6 and 8,000 yards, the ranges at which Jutland in particular was fought—10, 12 and 14,000 yards—brought shells to target on a far steeper trajectory than their protection had been designed to resist. This was particularly true of the British battlecruisers, much of whose horizontal plating was no more than 1.5 inches thick.

[1] See Northcott, *HMS Hood*, pp. 1–14, Roberts, *Battlecruisers*, pp. 55–62, and Brown, *The Grand Fleet*, pp. 98–100.

[2] The other two were *Howe* (Cammell Laird, Birkenhead) and *Rodney* (Fairfield, Govan). A fourth was ordered on 13 June: *Anson* (Armstrong Whitworth, Newcastle upon Tyne).

[3] The battlecruiser debate is framed by James Goldrick in 'The Problems of Modern Naval History' in John B. Hattendorf (ed) *Doing Naval History: Essays Toward Improvement* (Newport, RI: Naval War College Press, 1995), pp. 15–19.

The construction of the *Hood* had proceeded with little fanfare and a fair degree of secrecy. Her keel-laying in September 1916 seems not to have been accompanied by the ceremony usually accorded these occasions but it was wartime and such events were in any case more subdued in commercial shipbuilding than they were in the Royal Dockyards of Portsmouth, Devonport and Chatham. The launching in August 1918 was another matter but even this was tinged with sadness. On the Western Front the Allies were defeating the German army but the previous four years had cost Britain and her empire the lives of a million men. Among the dead was Rear-Admiral the Hon. Sir Horace Hood, killed at Jutland in the battlecruiser *Invincible*, whose American widow performed the launching ceremony. The name *Hood* first appears in a communication from the Admiralty to John Brown on 14 July 1916. She was intended as the lead ship of her class, to include *Howe*, *Rodney* and *Anson*, four great admirals of the eighteenth century. The man after whom the subject of this book was named was a vicar's son of Thorncombe in Dorset, Samuel Hood (1724–1816). In a career spanning 55 years Hood acquired a reputation as a master tactician, making his name at St Kitt's, Dominica, Toulon and Corsica before being granted the title of Viscount Hood of Whitley in 1796. Nor by any means was he the last member of his family to distinguish himself in naval service. Samuel's brother Alexander (1726–1814) also made his career in the wars against the French, becoming Viscount Bridport in 1801. Then came their nephews Alexander (1758–98) and Samuel Hood (1762–1814), the former killed leading the *Mars* in a desperate action with the French *Hercule* and the latter one of Nelson's captains at the Nile in 1798. Others followed, including Admiral Lord Hood of Avalon, First Sea Lord from 1885–9.

The Hood family therefore had a record of service going back 175 years and the selection of the name for Britain's latest battlecruiser may have owed something to Rear-Admiral Hood's sacrifice at Jutland. However, it was his great-great grandfather the first Viscount whose name, device and motto she bore. The badge was of an anchor supported by a Cornish chough, the rare coastal bird of the crow family with a popular reputation for fire-raising. The motto was *Ventis secundis*, 'With favouring winds'. The *Hood* was not the first ship to carry the name. In 1797, just two years after he had hauled down his flag, the Navy commissioned a fourteen-gun vessel named *Lord Hood* which, however, was stricken in December of the following year. It was not until 1860 that the name was revived, in this case when the 80-gun *Edgar* was converted to screw propulsion during the naval scare of the late 1850s. Rendered obsolete by *Warrior* and her successors, the *Hood* spent a dismal career in the reserve and then as a barracks ship at Chatham before being sold out of the Navy in 1888. The next *Hood*, however, was a first-rate unit, launched in 1891 as the eighth and final member of the *Royal Sovereign* class of battleships. Though designed by Sir William White, a naval architect of genius, the ship was marred by the insistence of her namesake, the First Sea Lord Admiral Sir Arthur Hood, that she carry enclosed turrets rather than the open barbettes of her half sisters. These not only made *Hood* the Royal Navy's last turret ship but greatly reduced her freeboard and consequently her effectiveness in anything other than a flat calm. In 1914, to the delight of later generations of scuba divers, she

was expended as a blockship at the entrance to Portland Harbour as a measure against German submarine attack. If the name *Hood* had a ring to it this therefore owed more to famous men than famous ships. But all that was to change.

At five minutes past one on Thursday 22 August 1918 Lady Hood shattered a bottle over the ship's bows and the *Hood* slipped stern-first down the ways and into the Clyde. The act of launching came at the end of a lengthy process of work and calculation dating from before the laying down of the ship.[12] During construction the weight of the hull was borne on massive baulks of timber and shored up under the bilges with numerous beams and wedges. In order to launch the ship a continuous platform of 'ground ways' was laid on either side of the keel. Resting on these was the 'sliding way' and atop this two wooden cradles or poppets, one at the point where the 5-inch armour belt ended approximately 75 feet from the bows and the other abreast the brackets of the outer propellers. The purpose of the cradles was to carry the weight of the hull as the stern entered the water and until such time as the ship had come to rest in her own element. As the hour of launching approached the sliding ways were greased and supports withdrawn until only the locking of the hull to the fixed ground ways held the ship in place. By this time, too, a launching platform had been built before the bows to accommodate the dignitaries attending the spectacle. The tradition of a lady christening the ship seems to date from the time of the Prince Regent and the ceremony performed by her was usually in three parts. Having wished good fortune on the ship and all who sailed in her, she smashed a bottle against the bow and then pressed a button knocking out the securing trigger of the last cables securing her to the land. With this the band struck up *Rule Britannia* and the *Hood* began to slide down the ways in a crescendo of sound, of smashed timber, roaring chains and cheering spectators. It was required of those planning the launch to afford the ship sufficient motive force to reach the water but never so much as to render her uncontrollable once she got there. To restrain this movement enormous drag chains were fixed to the hull so as to check her way and bring her up sufficiently for the dockyard tugs to take charge of her. Since the *Hood* had a launch weight of 21,920 tons it can readily be understand how exacting this task was. In the event, the launch passed off without a hitch.

12 Talbot-Booth, *All the World's Fighting Fleets*, 3rd edn, pp. 59–61.

The forepart of the hull ready for launching in the autumn of 1918. To the left is the port side of one of the cradles or poppets on which the ship will slide down the ways on launching. The small ovoid shape nearer the camera is that of the port submerged torpedo tube. The bulge is complete but the belts of 5-, 7- and 12-inch armour will not be fitted until she is launched.
National Archives of Scotland, Edinburgh

Above: The *Hood* dominates John Brown's East Yard on 21 August 1918, the day before her launch. The hull is complete except for the armour. Boilers are fitted but not turbines.
National Archives of Scotland, Edinburgh

Right: Twelve-inch barbette armour for 'B' turret being hoisted aboard in the fitting-out basin at John Brown's towards the end of 1918. Armour was tongue and grooved on its butt edges to interlock with adjacent plates and then secured on its inner face by an arrangement of bolts. Note the protective cover to keep the weather out of 'A' turret.
National Archives of Scotland, Edinburgh

Above: *Hood* thunders into the Clyde on 22 August 1918, the Union Flag flying from the jack staff and the John Brown company flag from the stump of the conning tower.
National Archives of Scotland, Edinburgh

Below: *Hood*'s first 15in gun, the right-hand barrel of 'X' turret, is swung into position on 9 August 1919.
National Archives of Scotland, Edinburgh

Above: *Hood* in the final stages of fitting out on 2 December 1919. The 15in guns of 'A' and 'B' turrets have been installed but the plating has yet to be completed. The armoured director is missing its hood and the aloft director remains to be fitted.
National Archives of Scotland, Edinburgh

Right: The conning tower and bridge structure seen on 9 January 1920, the day the *Hood* departed for Greenock under her own power.
National Archives of Scotland, Edinburgh

Above, right and centre: Three views of *Hood* preparing to leave the fitting-out basin at John Brown's for the last time, 9 January 1920. The photographs were taken from the West Yard's 150-ton cantilever crane.
National Archives of Scotland, Edinburgh

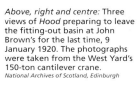

Above: Four tugs haul the *Hood* out into the Clyde on 9 January 1920. There is no particular fanfare but a good crowd has gathered on the edge of the East Yard to see her off.
National Archives of Scotland, Edinburgh

Hood as the public first knew
her: running trials off the Isle of
Arran in March 1920.
National Archives of Scotland, Edinburgh

Even after her launch the *Hood* retained a remarkably low profile. As the *Dumbarton Herald* noted on 15 January 1919, 'very few people have hitherto been aware of her existence, and yet the *Hood* is a far more wonderful vessel than the Hush! Hush! ships which made such a sensation [*Glorious, Courageous* and *Furious*]'.[13] However, the ship received the wrong sort of publicity on 19 May when a build-up of gas in an airtight compartment exploded, killing two men and injuring six more. It was therefore in a curiously muted atmosphere that John Brown's last major warship contract for several years left the yard under her own power on 9 January 1920. Things were different at Greenock later that afternoon where the *Hood* received the first of many rapturous welcomes from crowds lining Customs House Quay and Prince's Pier. Already advance parties of stokers and sailors had been arriving from the battlecruiser *Lion*, the ship whose company would eventually commission her. The Executive Officer, Cdr Lachlan MacKinnon, arranged for numerous signs to be put up to help them find their way round. Twenty years later MacKinnon would have the misfortune of being Commodore of Convoy SC7, the first to be subjected to the *Rudeltaktik*, a massed attack by U-boats. For now he had to cope with a different order of chaos as the *Hood* began the long process of becoming a commissioned ship in the Royal Navy. It had been decided to finish the work at HM Dockyard Rosyth so as to clear John Brown's fitting-out basin for the urgent completion of merchant contracts.[14] The voyage round Scotland was to give the crew an early taste of the *Hood*'s seakeeping quali-

ties as a Force 8 gale buried her forecastle and quarterdeck and vibration made life in the spotting top unbearable at speed. Once at Rosyth the ship had to wait six days before wind and current permitted her to be drawn into No. 2 Dock for the fitting out to be resumed. Before the *Hood* departed an experiment was carried out to establish her final displacement, revealed as 46,680 tons at deep load and 42,670 tons at full load—1,470 tons above the final 1917 legend and no less than 17.5 per cent above the original 1916 design, most of it armour.

After preliminary testing of her torpedo armament the *Hood* returned to Greenock in early March for full builder's and gunnery trials. These, as both d'Eyncourt and Rear-Admiral Sir Roger Keyes were aboard to confirm, were a conspicuous success. All the innovation of her design now stood revealed.[15] Advanced boiler and turbine technology permitted the *Hood* to develop over a third more power for the same weight of plant than the *Renown* class completed in 1916. During full-power trials off the Isle of Arran the *Hood* reached a speed of 32.07 knots on 151,280 s.h.p., making her by some distance the most powerful ship in the world. At this speed the four propellers—20 tons of forged manganese bronze apiece—were making 207 r.p.m., giving her a margin of several knots on any foreign capital ship. However, this margin of speed could only be obtained with an extremely high fuel consumption. The *Hood*'s oil capacity was 3,895 tons of which over 70 needed to be burned each hour for her to maintain 32 knots. On the other hand, only 7 tons per hour were required

[13] Cited in Johnston, *Ships for a Nation*, p. 166.
[14] Northcott, *HMS Hood*, pp. 14–19.
[15] Sir Eustace H.W. Tennyson d'Eyncourt, 'H.M.S. *Hood*' in *Engineering* [London], 109 (January–June 1920), pp. 423–6.

on by Royal Marine attendants serving food from an enormous buffet, the admiral either dined alone or in the company of up to 45 guests. Heated by two coal fires and lit by a pair of scuttles and four square ports, an impressive venue could be created for entertaining guests, but for all the comfort and amenity a visitor had only to glance up at the unadorned trunking and cabling to remember that he was in a ship whose principal business was war. Still, with tables and chairs cleared away it was possible for Vice-Admiral Andrew Cunningham to have two eightsome reels going at one time during his St Andrew's Night celebrations at Malta in 1937.[11] A single door aft led to the admiral's day cabin, a large triangular room overlooking the quarterdeck which the admiral could decorate as his tastes or pocket dictated. Pelmets and chintz cretonne curtains and fender covers (in a poppy design in Keyes' case), desks and chairs of several kinds, side tables awash with silver-framed photographs and china along with the occasional potted plant constituted the usual décor, never too masculine nor too modish. The cabin was presided over by a large mantelpiece and coal fire making it one of the few truly personal spaces aboard. As Cunningham, who occupied them in 1937–8, was to remember,

> To one who had spent most of his life in small ships my quarters in the *Hood* were palatial, large, airy cabins on the deck above the quarterdeck with great windows instead of the ordinary portholes. Even my cabin in the *Rodney* was small in comparison.[12]

Top right: The immense quarterdeck dominated by 'X' and 'Y' turrets; autumn 1940. The Officer of the Watch and his men are on duty on the starboard side. The open hatch leads down to the officers' cabin flat.
Bibliothek für Zeitgeschichte, Stuttgart

Above: Vice-Admiral Field's dining room during the World Cruise of 1923–4. Note the large buffet on the right and the ventilation trunking at the deckhead.
Illustrated Tasmanian Mail

Above: Vice-Admiral Field's day cabin, *c.*1924. Pelmets, curtains, potted plants and a club fender round the coal fire.
Illustrated Tasmanian Mail

Left: Royal Marines passing a quiet dog watch in the starboard battery, one of the main thoroughfares of the ship, in the late 1930s. A game is under way beside Starboard No. 6 5.5in gun. Above them someone has slung a hammock. Odd bits of dhobeying are hanging out to dry. The structure between the pillars is the head of the dredger hoist serving the gun.
HMS Hood Association/Higginson Collection

[11] Cunningham, *A Sailor's Odyssey*, p. 187.
[12] Ibid., p. 182.

Deck Plans

The plans that follow show the *Hood*'s internal arrangements in the 1920s. The interior of the ship was never substantially altered but the uses to which spaces—especially messdecks—were put varied as time passed, particularly after the outbreak of war. The numeration of the spaces is approximately that of the route of the tour on each deck, which is indicated by a line of arrows. These plans owe much to John Roberts' 'Anatomy of the Ship' volume, to which acknowledgement is hereby made.

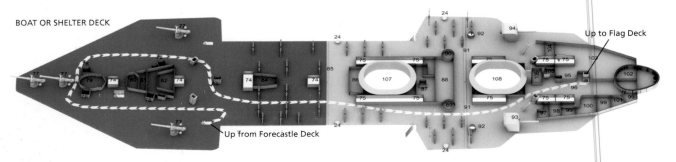

BOAT OR SHELTER DECK

Up to Flag Deck

Up from Forecastle Deck

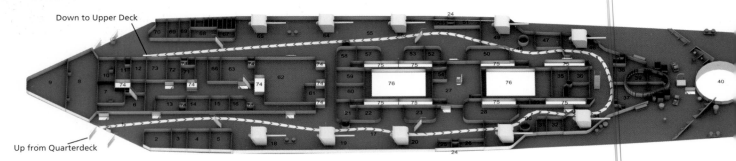

FORECASTLE DECK

Down to Upper Deck

Up from Quarterdeck

FORECASTLE AND BOAT OR SHELTER DECKS

1 Commander's lobby	24 5.5in Officer of Quarters	44 Capstan	67 Subordinate officers' heads	88 Coppersmith's house
2 Commander's cabin	position and hood (on Boat	45 Hawsepipe	68 Commissioned officers' heads	(Midships searchlight
3 Gunnery Officer's cabin	Deck)	46 Port No. 1 5.5in gun	69 Squadron commander's cabin	platform above)
4 Gunner's ready-use store	25 Urinal	47 Gunner's ready-use store	70 Paymaster Commander's cabin	89 Starboard 5.5in director
5 Billiard room (converted by	26 Potato store	48 Support of Port No. 2 5.5in	71 Chief of Staff's bathroom	90 Port 5.5in director
1931)	27 Main galley	gun (on Boat Deck)	72 Chief of Staff's sleeping cabin	91 Forward expansion joint
6 Admiral's lobby	28 Drying store	49 Port No. 3 5.5in gun	73 Chief of Staff's day cabin	92 Emergency signal tube
7 Admiral's pantry	29 Starboard No. 3 5.5in gun	50 Cooks' kitchen	74 Engine Room vent	93 Starboard No. 2 5.5in gun
8 Admiral's dining room	30 Support of Starboard No. 2	51 Ready-use oilskin store	75 Boiler Room vent	94 Port No. 2 5.5in gun
9 Admiral's day cabin	5.5in gun (on Boat Deck)	52 Gunroom kitchen	76 Funnel hatch	95 Foremast
10 Admiral's sleeping cabin	31 Boatswain's ready-use store	53 Gunroom galley	77 4in Mk V high-angle gun	96 Bridge lobby
11 Admiral's bathroom	32 Gym gear store	54 Air compressor compartment	78 4in ready-use ammunition	97 Signal house
12 Admiral's spare cabin	33 Paravane gear store	55 Port battery	lockers	98 Signal officer's cabin
13 Secretary's cabin	34 Starboard No. 1 5.5in gun	56 Port No. 4 5.5in gun	79 Torpedo control tower and	99 Watch officer's cabin
14 Secretary's clerk's office	35 Bakery	57 Officers' drying room	15-foot rangefinder	100 Navigating officer's cabin
15 Engineer Commander's cabin	36 Bread-cooling room	58 Wardroom kitchen	80 Marines' store	101 Chaplain's cabin (alternative)
16 Surgeon Commander's cabin	37 Electrical Artificers' workshop	59 Wardroom galley	81 Oilskin room	102 Conning tower (at Signal
17 Starboard battery	38 Gyro compass adjusting space	60 Admiral's galley	82 Night defence control station	Distributing Office level)
18 Starboard No. 6 5.5in gun	39 Conning tower (at	61 Wardroom pantry	83 Mainmast	103 Reading Room
19 Starboard No. 5 5.5in gun	Intelligence Office level)	62 Wardroom	84 Secondary battery room	104 Library
20 Starboard No. 4 5.5in gun	40 'B' turret	63 Wardroom anteroom	85 After expansion joint	105 Wire rope bin
21 Admiral's kitchen	41 'A' turret	64 Port No. 5 5.5in gun	86 Disinfector house	106 Watchkeeper's store
22 Beef screen	42 Paravane house	65 Port No. 6 5.5in gun	87 Blacksmith's shop	107 After funnel
23 Warrant Officers' galley	43 Torpedo embarkation hatch	66 Flag Lieutenant's cabin		108 Forward funnel

The *Hood* raising steam before leaving her builders, John Brown & Co., Clydebank for the last time on 9 January 1920. Heavy black smoke, as here, suggests insufficient draft or too much oil on the boiler burners.
National Archives of Scotland, Edinburgh

The *Hood's* boat deck seen at John Brown, Clydebank on 9 January 1920. The ship's two 50-foot steam picket boats (or pinnaces) sit on crutches to starboard of the main derrick, their funnels hinged back. On the other side the 36-foot sailing pinnace is nested inside the 42-foot sailing launch, which was equipped with an auxiliary motor. Further forward a 32-foot cutter hangs on its davits abreast the funnel. Carley floats in two sizes await stowage in the foreground. The structure beneath the derrick is the after vent of the Forward Engine Room.
National Archives of Scotland, Edinburgh

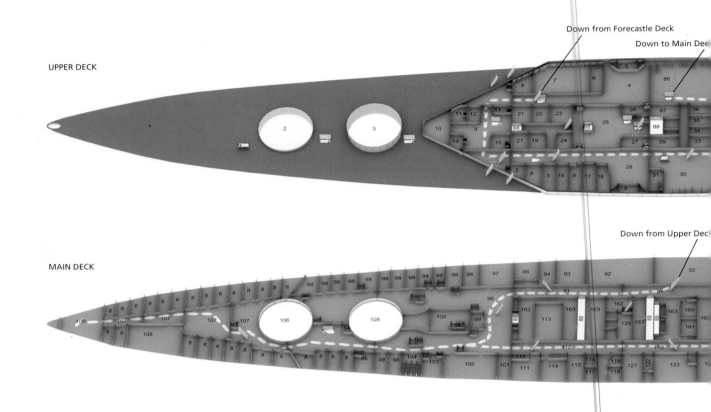

UPPER DECK

MAIN DECK

Down from Forecastle Deck

Down to Main Dec

Down from Upper Dec

UPPER AND MAIN DECKS

1 Quarterdeck
2 'Y' turret
3 'X' turret
4 Port torpedo adjusting space and tubes
5 Armoured torpedo warhead box
6 Gunroom pantry
7 Gunroom
8 Officer's cabin
9 Captain's lobby
10 Captain's day cabin
11 Captain's sleeping cabin
12 Captain's bathroom
13 Confidential book store
14 Captain's pantry
15 Captain's office
16 W/T officer's cabin
17 Senior Engineer's cabin
18 Chaplain's cabin (alternative)
19 Gunnery office

20 Torpedo office
21 Secretary's writers' office
22 Telegraph office
23 Ship's office
24 Printing office
25 Main derrick hoisting compartment
26 Gunroom and Warrant Officers' stewards' mess
27 Post office
28 Starboard torpedo adjusting space and tubes
29 Admiral's stewards' and cooks' mess
30 Marine barracks
31 Marine Sergeants' mess
32 Topmen's messdeck
33 Chief Petty Officers' mess
34 Wardroom stewards' and cooks' mess
35 Ship's police office

36 Master-at-Arms' and Secretary's writers' mess
37 Scullery
38 Topmen's messdeck
39 Canteen
40 Cooks' lobby
41 Fox'lemen's messdeck
42 Regulating Petty Officers' mess
43 Engineers' store
44 Issue Room flat
45 Chaplain's office
46 Issue Room
47 Hammock stowage
48 Conning tower (at level of Auxiliary Coding and 3rd W/T offices)
49 Petty Officers' mess
50 Barber's shop
51 Stokers' messdeck
52 'B' turret

53 Cooks' and Supply Branch messdeck
54 Magazine flooding cabinet
55 Petty Officers' pantry
56 Canteen staff's mess
57 'A' turret
58 Sick Bay flat, spare messdeck
59 Bookstall
60 Dispensary
61 Sick Berth Attendants' mess
62 Torpedo embarkation hatch
63 Sick Bay
64 Isolation ward or 'Rose Cottage'
65 WC
66 Flag Lieutenant's cabin
67 Ablution cabinet
68 Operating theatre
69 Examining room
70 Shipwrights' working space
71 Cable locker

72 Shipwrights' ready-use store
73 Chief and Petty Officers' heads
74 Main heads
75 Watertight compartment
76 Stoker Petty Officers' pantry
77 Stoker Petty Officers' mess
78 Chief Stoker's office
79 Chief Petty Officers' and Artificers' pantry
80 Chief Petty Officers' and Artificers' mess
81 Engine Room Artificers' pantry
82 Engine Room Artificers' mess
83 Chief Stokers' and Mechanicians' pantry
84 Chief Stokers' and Mechanicians' mess
85 Torpedomen's messdeck
86 Quarterdeckmen's messdeck

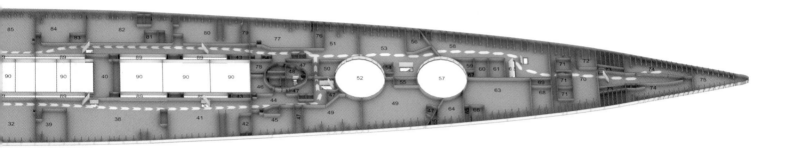

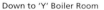

Down to 'Y' Boiler Room

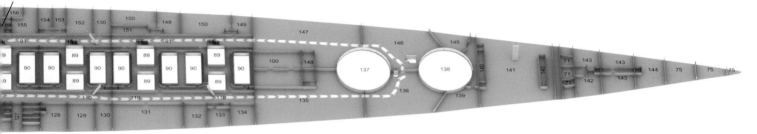

87 Ship's cooks' mess
88 Engine Room vent
89 Boiler Room vent
90 Funnel hatch
91 Port ammunition passage
92 Engineers' workshop
93 Subordinate officers' bathroom
94 Subordinate officers' dressing room
95 Secondary light store
96 Warrant Officers' flat
97 Midshipmen's chest room
98 Warrant Officer's cabin (single or double)
99 4in ammunition working space
100 5.5in ammunition working space
101 Warrant Officers' pantry
102 Warrant Officers' mess

103 Warrant Officers' bathroom
104 Warrant Officers' heads
105 'X' turret
106 'Y' turret
107 After cabin flat
108 Chapel
109 Midshipmen's study
110 Starboard ammunition passage
111 Commissioned officers' bathroom
112 Commander's bathroom
113 Central store
114 W/T store
115 Engineers' ready-use store
116 Admiral's steward's cabin
117 Admiral's cook's cabin
118 Wardroom steward's cabin
119 Captain's steward's cabin
120 W/T office
121 Engineers' office

122 Electrical Artificers' ready-use store
123 Electrical Artificers' workshop
124 Ordnance Artificers' workshop
125 Armourers' workshop
126 Band instrument room
127 Cells
128 Canteen store
129 Coal bunker
130 Emergency signal station
131 Seamen's bathroom
132 Marines' bathroom
133 Chief Petty Officers' bathroom
134 Petty Officers' bathroom
135 Fox'lemen's messdeck (Stokers by 1931)
136 Boys' messdeck
137 'B' turret

138 'A' turret
139 Awning room
140 Torpedo body lift
141 Torpedo body room
142 Lamp room
143 Clothing issue room
144 Paint room
145 Diving gear store
146 Spare messdeck (for Seamen by 1931)
147 Stokers' messdeck
148 Searchlight transmitting station
149 Stokers' dressing room
150 Stokers' bathroom
151 Boys' bathroom
152 Stoker Petty Officers' bathroom
153 Stoker Petty Officers' dressing room
154 Stokers' urinals

155 Chief Stokers' and Mechanicians' bathroom
156 Chief Stokers' and Mechanicians' dressing room
157 Engine Room Artificers' bathroom
158 Engine Room Artificers' dressing room
159 Boiler Room lift
160 Enginesmiths' shop
161 Auxiliary spare gear store
162 Coding office
163 Engine Room fan vent compartment

The forecastle and bridge structure seen from the eyes of the ship. The stripes painted in red, white and blue on 'B' turret date the photograph to 1937 or 1938. 'A' and 'B' turrets are trained to port, along with the armoured and aloft directors. The capstans, anchor cables and hawsepipe covers have been painted.
HMS Hood Association/Percival Collection

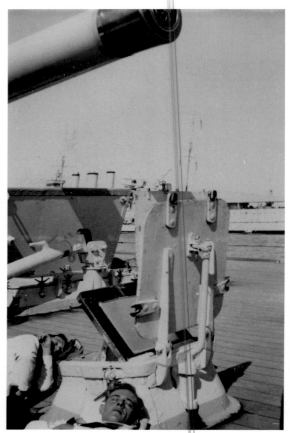

A kip on the forecastle in the late 1930s. The hatch leads down to the Sick Bay flat on the upper deck. The box-like structure beyond is the torpedo embarkation hatch with its attendant crane. A County-class cruiser is obscured by the forward breakwater.
HMS Hood Association/Clark Collection

[13] KCL, LHCMA, Aston 1/10, p. 57.
[14] 'At Sea in the "Hood"' in *The Navy*, February 1920, p. 13.

The admiral's suite was completed by his sleeping cabin and bathroom and by a pantry fitted with an electric hot-cupboard and sink for washing-up. Round about were the cabins of his staff. On the seaward side moving forward lay the Commander's cabin from where in 1933 Rory O'Conor had initiated his celebrated 'open-door' policy of greater accessibility for ratings. Adjacent to it was the Gunnery Officer's cabin and two doors down the officers' billiards room where Aston was instructed in the finer points of five-ball 'Scoff' by members of the wardroom one night in January 1926.[13] Beyond the Surgeon and Engineer commanders' cabins the passage opened out onto the Starboard Battery where until 1940 stood three 5.5in guns of *Hood*'s secondary armament. Inboard were the ship's galleys, including the main galley between the funnels and the bakery just forward, issuing its warm aroma. As much as anywhere in the ship, it was in the galleys that the innovation

of *Hood*'s design and equipment could be appreciated:

In the first place, she is the first big ship in our Navy to be fitted with oil-burning kitchen ranges. There are three in the men's galley on the forecastle deck, immense things, stretching half across the beam of the ship and capable of cooking 1,400 meals at a time. There are also great steam-heated boiling and stewing pots for the making of soups, boiling vegetables and so on, and one interesting new feature is the hot water boiler specially fitted for the making of tea, coffee or cocoa by the cooks of the messes on the mess deck. The kitchen, which adjoins the galley, is fitted with all modern labour-saving devices, such as potato peelers and choppers, sausage-makers, bacon slicers, and so on. And presently, I am told, there will be a 'fish and chips' range added to the equipment.[14]

Navy food remained of doubtful quality even with the benefit of every modern convenience, but few complained of the bread, over three-quarters of a ton of which was produced in five bakings each day. Indeed, during the visit of the Spanish royal family at Málaga in March 1928 Queen Ena had occasion to savour a bun in the bakery along with a spoonful or two of soup in the galley.[15] History does not recount what impression this *dégustation* made on her. Among a host of ancillary compartments was the beef screen, which, under the charge of a Royal Marine butcher, refrigerated several days' supply of meat. Another was the ship's potato store from which 1,500 pounds were drawn daily. Having passed the gun crews' urinal and the large drying room provided for laundry or the use of men coming off watch in foul weather, a bulkhead door would then be crossed to reveal the Starboard No. 3 5.5in gun and a fleeting glimpse of the forecastle. Next came the Boatswain's ready-use store stacked with the shackles, marline-spikes, serving hammers and the other equipment he and his men used to carry out their many duties around the ship. Beyond lay Starboard No. 1 5.5in gun and from here a good view of the 350-foot forecastle, the eye moving past the paravane stowed on the bridge screen, past the enormous conning tower, the forward turrets and the pair of breakwaters flanking them, and on to the capstans, cables and hawsepipes up to the eyes of the ship where the Union Flag fluttered from the jack staff. Beneath it crewmen were to gather amid the cable shackles to sing and hear speeches during the Invergordon Mutiny of September 1931. But under a canvas awning the forecastle could also be the most restful of sleeping places. AB Leonard Williams recalls unforgettable nights at Malta in the summer of 1937:

> On nights we were not ashore, Doug and I slept on the upper deck under the huge forecastle awning. We both had camp beds and we would lie and watch the signal lamp, high up on the mast of the Castille Signal Station, flashing its messages to the fleet lying in the Grand Harbour. It was the limit of our vision before the awning blotted out the stars. It was pleasant lying there, listening to the bells of the horse-drawn carozzins or gharries, as we usually called them, and watching the lights of the waterfront bars and cafes ashore and the bobbing lights of the dghaisas going about their business. We would talk until the lights ashore began to go out one by one, and soon we ourselves would grow tired and fall asleep.[16]

Turning left, Aston moves athwart the vessel, passing the bread-cooling room adjoining the bakery and, in the lee of the conning tower, the Electrical Artificers' daytime workshop and the adjusting space for the gyro compasses. Here he would encounter Port No. 1 5.5in gun and, stepping through another door, begin moving aft along the port side of the ship to find himself once more in the officers' quarters. A series of lavatories, hierarchically arranged for commissioned and subordinate officers, was followed by cabins for the Paymaster Commander and two staff officers. The officers' heads caught the attention of Lt-Cdr Ernest M. Eller, the U.S. Navy's official observer in *Hood* in the spring of 1941:

> The head was equally unique. It was out on a sponson just outside the wardroom, hanging over the side. [...] Instead of being on deck level, though, you walked into this 'throne room' as the British call it, and then you walked up two steps. They were sitting well up high, up to six feet above the deck...[17]

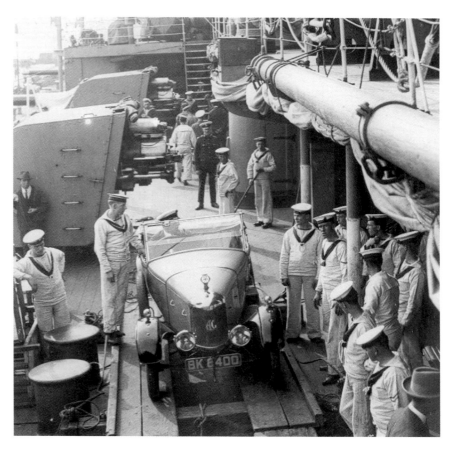

Nearby was the admiral's guest cabin where another U.S. Navy observer, Lt-Cdr Joseph H. Wellings, was accommodated over Christmas and New Year 1940–1. Beside it was a hatch descending to the upper deck where much of the ship's company lived.

Reaching the upper deck, Aston finds himself outside the midshipmen's gunroom and, further forward, the Port Torpedo Tubes, identifiable from outside the ship by the pair of heavy mantlets fitted to the hull. Inboard was a large compartment containing the hoisting engine for the ship's derrick on the boat deck. Turning aft, Aston makes his way into the Captain's quarters overlooking the quarterdeck. Like the admiral's directly above, these reflected the extent to which his life was spent apart from the wardroom officers. The Captain's lobby, reached through a pair of arched openings and guarded day and night by a Royal Marine sentry, was a marvel of gleaming paint and polished brightwork. Here the captain sat in judgement over the most serious cases of crime and indiscipline in the ship. Among the fixtures were two magnificent models of the ship in 1:64 scale, each over thirteen feet long. On one, produced in time for the Jubilee Review of 1935, the detailing extended to a likeness of Cdr O'Conor's West Highland terrier, but neither was to survive the war. Landed just before *Hood* sailed north in August 1939, they were lost in the Portsmouth Blitz of 1940–1.[18] Also kept in the lobby were a pair of benches used for divine service on Sunday mornings and now preserved at the Church of St John the Baptist at

The port battery looking forward some time between 1925 and 1927. Capt. Harold Reinold's AC Tourer sports car lies near Port No. 4 and No. 5 guns. The requirement to keep officers' private property not only clean but also in good repair was a source of some resentment before Invergordon.
HMS Hood Association/Reinold Collection

[15] Dreyer, *The Sea Heritage*, p. 288.
[16] Williams, *Gone A Long Journey*, p. 123.
[17] Eller, *Reminiscences*, II, pp. 463–4.
[18] I owe this detail to Vice-Admiral Sir Louis Le Bailly, letter to the author, 23 November 2001.

[19] Rea, *A Curate's Egg*, p. 120.
[20] Cited in Coles & Briggs, *Flagship Hood*, pp. 10–11. January 1920.
[21] Halpern (ed), *The Keyes Papers*, II, p. 26.
[22] *The Navy*, February 1920, p. 13.

Boldre in the New Forest. Here too in glass-fronted cases were the keys to the vital compartments in the ship including the magazines and transmitting stations. Radiating off the lobby were the captain's office, pantry and the Confidential book store where orders, ciphers and other material of a sensitive nature were locked away for safekeeping, all weighted with lead for the day they might have to be ditched over the side. Then came the extensive day cabin in which the captain dined and entertained his guests. The suite was completed by a sleeping cabin (for use in harbour only) and a bathroom.

Exiting the lobby on the starboard side, a door led forward to the administrative heart of the ship in the shape of a cluster of offices lying off the passageway. Here was the Secretary's writers' office, the Telegraph office and the Ship's office itself, and then those concerning her armament: Gunnery and Torpedoes. Finally there was the Printing office where, among other things, *The Chough*, the ship's magazine, was produced. Further along was the Post Office manned by the Royal Marines which daily in harbour collected letters from nine boxes distributed around the ship and sorted all incoming mail, the record haul of which appears to have been the 57 bags *Hood* received when she reached Sydney in April 1924, seven months into the World Cruise. Sorted mail was collected by the duty men from each mess and distributed to their companions; letters to crewmen stated his name, his mess number and finally 'HMS *Hood*, c/o GPO London'. Opposite, on the seaward side, was a row of cabins including that of the Senior Engineer, who here found sanctuary from the infernal din of the engine spaces, and that usually occupied by the ship's Chaplain, though in 1936 the Rev. Edgar Rea managed, with some controversy, to obtain an adjoining pair in the bridge structure, 'One to sleep in during the night and one to rest in during the day' as one of his messmates unkindly described them.[19]

Moving forward past the Starboard Torpedo Tubes, Aston

The ship's Canteen on the upper deck amidships in about 1924, stacked high with supplies and provisions to augment the sailor's diet and cater to his day-to-day needs. A NAAFI canteen assistant stands by.
Illustrated Tasmanian Mail

The Canteen

now stepped into a world exclusively of artificial light and forced ventilation. The space in question was the flat or messdeck containing the Royal Marine barracks, 70 feet long and 30 across, the deckhead supported by three slender pillars and a column of ventilation trunking ten feet high. It was home to perhaps 160 men, their possessions and much of their equipment, stowed between the frames marking the ship's side. To a landsman the messdecks would appear cramped and oppressive, but in the early days the chief impression was one of spaciousness, though for some at least size came at a price. AB L.E. Brown:

> Even though she was still in dockyard hands and not properly clean, the *Hood* was a delight. I had just come from a coal-burning cruiser, grimy with dust, dingily lit, with restricted headroom and overcrowded. Now I found myself in a roomy, clean ship in which you could get lost. She was so big that notices giving directions to the upper deck were posted.[20]

His admiral, Roger Keyes, though delighted with his own quarters, would not have agreed with Brown's assessment:

> These cabins are palatial and I feel ashamed to have so much space while the men are so appallingly crowded.[21]

Though *Hood*'s is still the largest hull in the history of British naval construction, it also contained some of the bulkiest engineering plant ever fitted in a British warship, with a consequent loss of crew living-space. The labyrinth of whitened passages and sealed compartments festooned with trunking and wiring evidently took some getting used to, but there can be little doubt that after the coal-fired veterans of the Grand Fleet or the slums of industrial Britain, the *Hood* of 1920 was a miracle of comfort, space and amenity. In this, as the correspondent of *The Navy* recognised in February 1920, she was quite unprecedented:

> …In the past I think we have always been too prone to dwell in the material side of the Navy and to ignore the personnel. The design of the *Hood* marks a change in that respect as in many others…[22]

In the corner of the Marines' flat lay the first of the small enclosed messes for senior ratings and NCOs, the Sergeants of Marines' mess. Moving forward, a bulkhead door opened onto another equally large mess where the bulk of the *Hood*'s Topmen were quartered. In one corner stood the ship's canteen, a general store providing the men with cigarettes, tobacco, newspapers, toiletries, medications, stationery and such supplements to the General Mess diet as fruit and confectionery. Here too and in sub-bars around the ship were dispensed the non-alcoholic sodas and cordials the men derisively called 'goffers', a term of abuse for anything soft or inadequate. Operated by the NAAFI and staffed from 1921 by civilians of the Naval Canteen Service, merchandise was sold tax-free and the profits mostly ploughed into the Ship's Fund administered by the Canteen Committee. Lying between the funnel uptakes inboard was the Cooks' lobby to which food for the messes was conveyed in lifts from the galley above and kept warm in steam-heated cupboards until it was ready to be served. Through this system the entire ship's company could be served within half an hour. Aft was the mechanical scullery, another miracle of labour-saving technology where plates and utensils from the messes were cleaned in electric washers and then stowed in preparation for the next meal.

A third mess on the starboard side, that of the Fox'lemen, led via a bulkhead door into a passage which curved round past the Issue room (from where the daily rations of tea, sugar, milk, margarine and butter were drawn at 12.30 p.m.), the Chaplain's office, past the first of two adjoining Petty Officers' messes and on between the lowest stage of the conning tower and the trunk of 'B' turret to the port side of the ship. Here, amid several hammock-stowage compartments, was the barber's shop where Stoker Bill Stone plied his trade for 4d. a cut between 1921 and 1925. At this point the narrowing of the ship towards the bows and the obstruction created by the trunks of the forward turrets prevented the continuation of any passageway forward. The forward compartments were therefore reached by passing directly through a succession of messdecks on the port side, beginning with one for stokers, then that of the Cooks and Supply Department and finally the Sick Bay flat. The Sick Bay, described elsewhere, consisted of a large suite of rooms on the starboard side forward of 'A' turret.[23] The *Hood*'s company increasingly looked to reading as one of its main recreations and by 1926 the nearby bookstall was selling over 400 volumes each cruise.[24] The bookstall also provided stationery and the various guides, postcards, mounted photos and trinkets which are among the few tangible links to survive from the ship.[25] Clearly, some found the prices cheaper than others. Whereas Aston 'spent about 13/- on knives, ashtray, matchbox, a book about *Hood*' in 1926, two years earlier neither S.M. Ghani nor his Malayan schoolfriends had felt able to stretch to any of the goods on offer.[26] A further bulkhead door gave access to the Shipwrights' working space and store, into which three large cable lockers intruded. It was from here that the 'chippies', as shipwrights continued to be known, undertook the endless maintenance of hull, masts, yards, pumps, paint and woodwork. A final door opened onto the heads, the main toilets aboard, whose presence had been announced on the insalubrious air breathed below decks in the *Hood*. Against this odour none of the ventilation systems installed during her career were to prove adequate.

For time out of mind ship designers had placed the heads in the forepeak of their vessels and, excepting the watertight compartments, those in *Hood* occupied the forwardmost space in the ship. Presided over by the 'Captains of the Heads', the amenities offered reflected the privilege of rank aboard. Thus, while senior ratings were afforded the privacy of a full steel door, their juniors had to make do with half ones. Ted Briggs:

> My most anxious moments were going to the lavatory— the 'heads'. I found it embarrassing to sit on the throne with only my genitals covered by the tiny cubicle doors and being able to see over the top the straining faces of my shipmates, squatting in long rows like roosting birds. I was too shy to have discussion with other matelots, which was the general practice, and in heavy weather tried to contain my motions, otherwise one risked a sudden dowsing of urine from a neighbouring lavatory as the ship rolled.[27]

However, things could get even worse. OD Jon Pertwee, who later found fame as an actor, has left the following graphic account from his time aboard in 1940–1:

> In these lavatories, to prevent the sea flowing back up the soil pipes when she dipped her bow down deep, non-return flaps were fitted under the water-line. Unfortunately, in North Sea waters, we dipped so deep, and so rapidly, that the flaps were lifted instead of closed, allowing the water to surge back up the pipes. So if you were one of the uninitiated, the following would happen. You entered the doorless loo, sat upon the seat, and with trousers around the ankles, did your business. The ship would then commence its downward plunge, causing the sea to by-pass the retaining flap and surge up into the bowl. The water level would then rise, until before you knew it, your offering had been deposited into the unsuspecting trouser below. This disaster caused riotous laughter from the cognoscenti, who would then instruct you in the ancient art of 'dodging'. For this method, you advanced trouserless and under-pantless to the bowl, hovered over its port or starboard side, until the water level had begun to subside, swung your buttocks quickly over the porcelain to make your deposit, then whipped the bottom back again out of immediate danger. This procedure could be continued as required and when all was done, the defecator would dart for safety.[28]

Though urinals were sited around the ship, these were the only heads available to seamen and a visit at sea could often be a tiring and somewhat lengthy undertaking. The heads thus viewed, Aston's path takes him aft through the two messes by which he has come and then along the port side of the upper deck past the enclosed messes and pantries of the Stoker Petty

[23] See ch. 5, pp. 125.
[24] KCL, LHCMA, Aston 1/10, p. 61.
[25] Ibid., pp. 60–1.
[26] www.forcez-survivors.org.uk/schoolboy.html.
[27] Coles & Briggs, *Flagship* Hood, pp. 134–5.
[28] Pertwee, *Moon Boots and Dinner Suits*, p. 150.

An unusual record of dinner in one of the petty officers' messes, perhaps that of the Chiefs on the upper deck amidships, *c*.1924. The austerity of the surroundings is apparent. Despite the ventilation trunking above, the sides and bulkheads were often running with condensation.
Illustrated Tasmanian Mail

Officers, the Chief Petty Officers and Electricians, the Engine Room Artificers, Ordnance Artificers and Shipwrights and finally the Chief Stokers and Mechanicians. Though similar to the open messdecks in most respects, these were much less crowded and generally more comfortable with their curtained-off wardrobes and easy chairs gathered in a lounge area at one end. At this point the passage along which he is moving ends in a bulkhead door opening onto another large mess, that shared by the Quarterdeckmen and the Torpedo ratings. In the corner of this flat lies a hatch, its armoured cover opened and closed on a pulley system. Through it he descends to the main deck.

The main deck was the first to run the whole length of the ship and the lowest on which members of the crew were quartered. Alighting from the ladder, Aston finds himself outside the Engineers' workshops, turns aft and passes the Central Store and the Gunroom Officers' bathroom where, bent double over the ejector pump, Mid. Blundell received a dozen cuts for 'insolence' from the Sub-Lieutenant of the gunroom in 1923.[29] Here he comes to a bulkhead door patrolled day and night by an armed sentry of the Royal Marines, an infallible sign that officers' accommodation lay on the other side. Beyond it a large lobby running beneath the quarterdeck gave access to both sides of the ship. Between here and the stern were quartered the balance of the *Hood*'s officers, despite the fact that her low freeboard made it one of the least comfortable parts of the ship. The Rev. Edgar Rea explains:

Most of the officers slept under the quarter-deck where, only in harbour and under the most favourable conditions at sea, they were able to carry their scuttles. This meant that all the air for their cabins had to be sucked in from the inboard passages. This was quite a satisfactory solution so long as it was possible to keep the air in the inboard spaces fresh but at sea this was often impossible. In even a mildly disturbed sea the water came splashing over the quarter-deck with the inevitable result that the ventilators providing the fresh air for the officers had to be covered with thick canvas to prevent the water from finding its way below. As a result the air, both in the cabins and the compartments, became unspeakably foul at times and every bad smell in the ship seemed to drift aft and make it worse.[30]

Coupled with this was the severe vibration experienced aft when the ship went on to full power. Boy Frank Pavey:

At high power she would throb like the devil. I felt sorry for the midshipmen because their flat was right aft—the very after part of the ship, right above the screws. So they had a massage every time they turned in, I should think![31]

The first compartment on the port side was the midshipmen's chest flat, designed for smaller numbers than were usually borne. Beyond this stretched a dozen warrant officers' cabins, the last demarcated by the 4-inch bulkhead running between 'Y' turret and the ship's side. On the starboard side, across a flat dominated by the enormous trunks of 'X' and 'Y' turrets, lay the Warrant Officers' mess, pantry, bathroom and lavatories together with a further range of cabins. The only means of getting aft was through a door piercing the armoured bulkhead to starboard of 'Y' turret beyond which a number of officers' cab-

ins, the ship's chapel and, right aft, the midshipmen's study lay grouped round a succession of lobbies. Near the chapel was an armoured hatch leading to the steering compartment two decks below. Shut at sea in wartime, it could only be opened by the Damage Control parties from above.

Retracing his steps, Aston moves forward until, passing through another door guarded by a Marine sentry, he reaches the starboard ammunition passage, running almost 300 feet amidships. The ammunition passage, of which there was a second on the port side, owed its name to the 5.5in shells which were transferred along it for the hand-worked guns on the forecastle and boat decks, the ordnance being raised by a series of six dredger hoists in each passage. The inboard spaces were largely absorbed by funnel uptakes and vents from the boiler and engine rooms, but on the seaward sides an array of compartments contained many of the principal working, administrative and ancillary spaces in the ship. The first of these was the Commissioned officers' bathroom, fitted with a private compartment for the Commander who had nonetheless to descend two decks from his cabin to use it. Unlike the men, who were limited to showers, this consisted principally of 'long baths' filled with water heated by a steam main. Lt-Cdr Ernest M. Eller U.S.N., who spent a fortnight in the *Hood* in the spring of 1941, has left this description of the Officers' bathroom and the etiquette for using it:

They had a huge bathroom. It must have been 30 feet across. In here were great enamel tubs. Every officer had a bath every morning, I think. If you wanted a bath, your man would draw it at, say, 7:15. So this tub was yours at this particular time. You would go in and see all these bodies lying in scalding hot water. Everybody would just lie there saying nothing. After soaking a while, they would get out these loofa sponges, big rough sponges used in cleaning boilers to some degree. They would scrub with these till they were several degrees pinker than they were already from the heat. Then they would come out, rub themselves vigorously with the towel, and go to breakfast, never saying a word.[32]

A number of workshops, offices and stores followed, including the Engineers' office of which Vice-Admiral Sir Louis Le Bailly has left this memorable description:

This small emporium contained a desk for the Commander (E), a slightly smaller one for the Senior Engineer, quite a large one for the Engineers' Office Writer, Chief Stoker Biggenden [...], a small spot for me (part of my department was 'The Office') and nothing at all for the other seven watchkeepers. Whatever space remained was occupied by a repository for the ship's drawings, two telephones and the important boiler- and feed-water testing chemicals and impedimenta. Overhead there was a large bookshelf with a series of enormous tomes in which my many predecessors, like me, had had to enter the details of every examination and repair to each of the 1,000 or so machines, ranging from dough mixers to main turbines, for which the Commander (E) was personally responsible.[33]

Three compartments forward was the Ordnance Artificers'

[29] IWM, 90/38/1, vol. III, no. 3, p. 3.
[30] Rea, *A Curate's Egg*, pp. 119–20.
[31] Cited in Mearns & White, *Hood and Bismarck*, p. 12.
[32] Eller, *Reminiscences*, II, p. 463.
[33] CAC, LEBY 1/2, MS of *The Man Around the Engine*, ch. 12, p. 1. Chief Stoker W.J. Biggenden was lost with the ship in May 1941.

workshop where spare parts for the ship's gunnery installations and equipment were produced on an array of lathes, power drills, grinding and milling machines. A couple of doors away was the storeroom in which the Royal Marine band kept its instruments. Adjoining it were the ship's cells, five in number, where offenders could be incarcerated under Marine sentry for up to fourteen days. Sets of keys were kept both in the Regulating Office and in a glass-fronted case in the cell flat itself for a timely escape in the event of underwater damage. Each prisoner was allowed a Bible in his cell and the ship's chaplain might well take the opportunity to relieve his boredom with such morally improving titles as *Your Better Self, Religion in Plain Clothes* and *As Man to Man*.[34] Inboard and accessible only from the upper deck were two of the most sensitive compartments in the ship: the Coding office and the main W/T office.[35]

Continuing along the passage, Aston passes a row of ratings' bathrooms before entering the first of two large seamens' messes along the starboard side, that of the Fox'lemen and, forward of it, the Boys' messdeck where Ted Briggs first slung his hammock in the summer of 1939. A complementary pair lay to port, first the Stokers' messdeck and then a spare flat used as overflow accommodation. All four were designed round the massive trunking of 'A' and 'B' turrets. Forward of these Aston cannot go, the remaining stores and compartments—including the Torpedo body room—having vertical access only. He therefore turns aft and, passing the Searchlight transmitting station and the ammunition working space of the 5.5in guns, enters the port ammunition passage. Almost its entire length was taken up with bathrooms and dressing rooms of one kind or another, all of them fitted with lobbies and secondary doors and most destined to lose their tiles when the *Hood* was bombed in the North Sea in September 1939.

Passing the bathrooms Aston reaches the two main Engineers' workshops from whence he started. From here there is no way down save by one of the four electric lifts lining the passage along which he has come. Entering one via an air lock, he presses the 'go' button on a brass panel and descends to the lower deck proper, the domain of the Engineering Department. If the main deck was the first to run the full extent of the ship it was also the last that could be traversed readily along the greater part of its length. Not so the lower deck which was largely taken up by boiler and engine spaces that could only be reached from above. So it is that, stepping out at the first stop of the lift, he finds himself in an enclosed space running 50 feet athwartships, the fan compartment of 'Y' boiler room which supplied air to the boiler furnaces. All about were vast pipes clad in heavy white lagging taking saturated steam to and from the surrounding spaces. If the ship were lying quietly at anchor then perhaps only the stifling atmosphere and incessant noise of high-pressure fans might impress itself on his senses. But if she were under way then the heat would be unbearable, the din indescribable and the air pressure several inches above atmospheric as vibration shook every dial, cylinder, wheel and panel. At full power the fans sent a gale of wind into the working spaces though with no great improvement in the temperature. Returning to the lift, he descends to the upper stokehold and his first clear view of the six boilers of which 'Y' boiler room was composed, these facing each other in rows of three. The upper stokehold consisted of a pair of platforms to allow monitoring of the water

levels in the upper section of each boiler. A few steps down a ladder or another ride in the lift brings him to the lower platform and the stokehold itself, filled with a confusion of pipes, pumps, gauges, dials and oil sprayers serving the boilers. This arrangement was replicated in each of the four boiler rooms lying fore and aft for 170 feet amidships.

Further aft and, again, accessible only from the main deck, were the ship's three cavernous engine rooms occupying four decks along 125 feet of their length. Of all her internal spaces none were more impressive. The view from the ladders descending from the main deck was of a bewildering accumulation of machinery, of pumps, turbines and condensers intertwined with elephantine tubes and pipes of every dimension. From these spaces, against the high-pitched whine of fourteen geared turbines, four propeller shafts up to 300 feet long drove the vessel at over 30 knots. The two outer shafts were driven by a pair of turbines in the forward engine room, the middle room containing the inner port unit and the after room the inner starboard. The minutiae of life in the *Hood*'s engine spaces is discussed elsewhere, but for now Aston has experienced all he cares to and gratefully returns via a series of steep ladders to continue his tour from the main deck.

From the main deck numerous hatches gave access to the machine and storage compartments which filled the lower deck aft. Among them were the dynamo and turbo-generator compartments for electricity, the hydraulic engine rooms which supplied power to the main armament, along with a variety of stores, including those of the captain and admiral. Several of the machine spaces extended down to the platform deck which, again, could only be reached from above. On this level were the Spirit Room where the ship's rum was kept under a double lock, the steering compartment over the rudder and the magazines and handing rooms for 'X' and 'Y' turrets. Then came the hold where the shellrooms for the 15in guns were laid out between turret trunking and revolving propeller shafts. Here, 25 feet below the waterline, Aston completed his descent into the lower reaches of the ship. Beneath him was the ship's double bottom with its sturdy box construction,

[34] Beardmore, *The Waters of Uncertainty*, p. 54.
[35] The latter is described in ch. 4, p. 93.

An exceedingly rare view inside the *Hood*'s upper conning tower, c.1924. The main steering position stands before a beech grating. Orders were transmitted to the helmsman through the voicepipes in front. Other voicepipes and telephones can be seen all around. Slender viewing slits offered limited light and vision.
Illustrated Tasmanian Mail

[36] *RBS*, p. 134.

her first and chief defence against the ocean.

Forward of the boiler rooms and, again, reached from hatches on the main deck flats beneath the forecastle, was a similar arrangement of decks and compartments. Those on the lower deck included a pair of motor generator rooms extending down to the platform deck, the main electrical switchboards, and the exchange for the ship's 380 telephones. The telephone exchange, kept permanently manned by at least one operator, was nonetheless in Cdr Rory O'Conor's view a somewhat undertaxed amenity, a result of the reluctance to use modern equipment where traditional means were readily to hand:

> The ship's telephone service is not always used to the full extent to which it might be. If fuller use were made, much running backwards and forwards by messengers could be avoided, and perhaps the number of messengers reduced. […] For everyday use there are about fifty numbers that matter in a big ship, and an increased use of the telephone might result from these being issued in a small frame to hang by the telephone.[36]

Here also were the transmitting rooms for the *Hood*'s torpedo and 5.5in armament. Directly beneath them on the platform deck was the 15in Transmitting Station where a crew of 28 provided aiming instructions to the main armament. Descriptions of the TS are few and far between but, the Dreyer Table apart, there was one feature which no visitor was likely to forget: a bicycle to provide motive power for the fire-control table in the event of an electrical failure. Also on the platform deck, forward of the magazines and handing rooms for 'A' and 'B' turrets, were a pair of submerged torpedo tubes destined to be removed in 1937. As aft, the deck arrangement was completed with the shellrooms and shell bins in the hold and lower platform.

The tour of the lower decks complete, an exhausting climb up four ladders is now required to regain the main deck and the 5.5in ammunition working space abaft the trunking of 'B' turret. From here, and here alone, could access be gained to the *Hood*'s great armoured citadel, the conning tower or 'Queen Anne's Mansions' as the men called it. The conning tower consisted of an ovoid cylinder rising in seven stages from the upper deck to a point level with the Admiral's bridge. Crowned with an armoured director and pierced by viewing slits of sinister aspect, the tower, though faired into the bridge structure, was not accessible from any part of it. Built of increasingly massive sections of curved armour plate ranging from 3 to 10 inches thick, the entire structure weighed 600 tons. The purpose of the conning tower was to protect the ship's most critical battle functions in a casing impervious to all except a catastrophic internal explosion. Accordingly, the first stage at upper deck level was taken up by the Third W/T and Auxiliary coding offices. Next up was the Intelligence office followed by the Signal distributing office at boat-deck level. It was in the former that German and Italian signals were first intercepted during the Spanish Civil War. Then came one of the torpedo control positions, the first level to be lit with viewing slits. Above this was the split-level upper conning tower containing, in concentric circles, the admiral's tower and telephone exchange, the 15in control position and, on an immaculate beech grating, the steering position that gave the structure its name. Over it all sat a revolving director protected by an armoured hood.

The conning tower explored, Aston retraces his steps to the main deck where he follows the port ammunition passage to the Warrant Officers' flat aft. Emerging through a hatch forward of 'X' turret, he reaches the quarterdeck and inhales his first lungful of fresh air in several hours. Thus revived, he returns up the ladder on the starboard screen to the forecastle

The port side of the boat deck in 1923. An assortment of boats and floats can be seen nested and on crutches while a 32-foot cutter hangs on its davits. To the left is Port 4in Mk V High-Angle gun. Opposite is the Night defence control station with its viewing slit and beside it a ready-use ammunition locker for the 4in gun. Just forward is the port tripod support of the mainmast along with an exhaust pipe from the after diesel dynamo on the platform deck.
Cribb

deck before taking another to the open boat deck occupying the middle third of the vessel. Stepping out he finds himself overlooking the starboard battery a deck below. Looking up the view is dominated by the two funnels and, forward of these, the bridge structure and fore top. Behind him, the after section of the boat deck is presided over by the mainmast, at 150 feet the ship's tallest and the place from which, in war, the White Ensign flew from the gaff. It fell to boy seamen, trained on the famous 120-foot mast at HMS *Ganges* or its counterpart at *St Vincent*, to retrieve a lost halyard or strike the main or fore top whenever the ship passed beneath the Forth Bridge. Ted Briggs describes an excursion up the latter:

> The masts were not difficult to scale, and only the last six feet of the main one, which was a sheer pole, had to be shinned up. One day when a halyard had been blown away on the starboard forward upper yardarm, I was ordered to go up for it. I had inched my way to the end of the yardarm to retain the Inglefield clip when the safety valves in the engine-room were blown. A large cloud of steam swirled up towards me. I clung on grimly but decided that, if the white mist spiralling upwards was hot, I would let go and drop into the sea. I preferred drowning to being boiled alive. But by the time it immersed me the steam had turned into a cold shower.[37]

Against the mainmast was rigged the ship's derrick, operated on a pulley system secured in the hoisting compartment two decks below. It required 80 men on four guy ropes to work, and only the cry of 'derrick topping' as the arm neared the perpendicular to provide a ripple of amusement to an otherwise exhausting evolution.[38] Boy Jim Taylor of Portsmouth (1939–40) remembers the drudgery:

> …the *Hood* was a bit old fashioned in that she did not have a proper crane. Everything that came aboard had either to be brought on board by hand or by means of the main derrick. Christmas 1939 sticks in my mind as we had lots of crates of turkeys to hoist aboard four at a time and it took half the night to get them all aboard.[39]

Abaft the mainmast was the Night defence control station and over it the Searchlight control position with its four lights (reduced to two in the 1930s). Aft again was the torpedo control tower, capped with an armoured rangefinder. Nearby sat a quartet of 4in high-angle gun mountings destined to be removed in 1940, and the skylight over the admiral's sleeping cabin through which a prankster shoved Bill, the ship's goat mascot, one day in the summer of 1921. If the starboard side of the quarterdeck was the Captain's domain, then the starboard after end of the boat deck was the Admiral's, his to use and enjoy without fear of interruption. Around the Secondary battery room and a series of large engine-room vents were ranged the *Hood*'s flotilla of boats, never less than fourteen strong. Then came the funnels themselves, 50 foot high and each capable, so the ship's guide book said, of accommodating two London tube trains abreast. Between them sat the Midships searchlight control platform, largely dismantled in 1939. Nestled about the after funnel was the Sick Bay's Disinfector house, the Coppersmith's and Blacksmith's shops and outboard a pair of 40-foot derricks for hoisting the small-

Above: The after superstructure draped in splinter protection in September 1938. The newly installed Mk II pom-pom director sits between the two 32-inch searchlights; its mounting can be seen further aft. To the right is the mainmast with one of its tripod supports on the left. Between them is the main vent of the Middle Engine Room. This area of the boat deck was the object of close scrutiny by the Boards of Enquiry investigating the loss of the ship in 1941.
HMS Hood Association/Fotheringham Collection

Left: The boat deck seen from the spotting top in the late 1930s. The Midships searchlight control platform lies between the funnels. Visible on the mainmast halyards are the two helm signals, a green ball to starboard and two red cones to port. Beyond is the after superstructure and the quarterdeck. A steam picket boat is being attended to on the right. See the photograph on p. 212 for a wartime comparison.
HMS Hood Association/Percival Collection

[37] Coles & Briggs, *Flagship* Hood, p. 136.
[38] See ch. 4, p. 104 for an explanation of this.
[39] HMS *Hood* Association archives.

40 IWM, 90/38/1, vol. III, no. 3, p. 2.
41 *The Chough*, April 1936, p. 14.

er boats stowed forward. It was in the Coppersmith's workshop that a kindly artisan sat up all night to repair the funnel of Mid. George Blundell's picket boat after he had snapped it off against the ship's boom in a heavy swell off Sierra Leone in December 1923.[40] The blacksmith, meanwhile, enjoyed a reclusive existence surrounded by his anvil, forge and bellows until the moment came for the ship to secure to a buoy. Then for a few minutes he became the most important member of the ship's company, for none could get ashore until he had hammered the retaining pin into the shackle of the mooring buoy. The boat deck ended with a 5.5in mounting on either side of the forward funnel, thus completing the ship's twelve-gun secondary armament.

It is perhaps with some trepidation that Aston now contemplates the bridge structure and fore top, rising in stages up an immense tripod 100 feet above the boat deck. However, he presses on and enters the open lobby of the bridge structure in the lee of the conning tower. Along the starboard side lay some

of the best-lit and most agreeable cabins in the ship, including those of the duty watch, navigating and signal officers, the latter connected by a small hatch to the Signal Distributing Office, one of the most critical compartments in the ship. The port side was largely taken up by a spacious Reading Room, the first of its type to be fitted in a fighting ship of the Royal Navy. Lit by five scuttles and open to all ranks and rates, the Reading Room was evidently one of the most popular spaces aboard. In 1936 it was the subject of the following atrocious doggerel by 'Rosslynite', one of the ship's bards:

Re. improvements to the Reading Room, everyone agreed
That the more important items should be carried out with
    speed.
Tiddley tables, chairs and curtains and lots of Pusser's baize,
Where re-entries can lay their weary bones and lie of bygone
    days.[41]

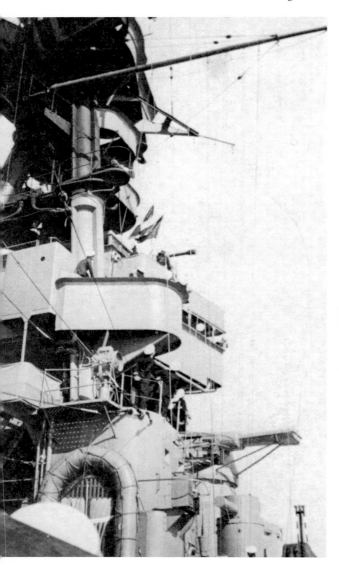

Left: The starboard side of the bridge structure in the spring of 1936. The photograph is taken from the level of the flag deck. The signalling searchlight visible above it is on the Admiral's bridge. The projecting tub is part of the Fore bridge and the edge of the Compass platform can be seen further forward. Next up are the Foremast searchlight platform (removed in the autumn of 1936) and the Torpedo lookout platform (removed in 1941), and finally the spotting top itself on its starfish base.

Above: The *Hood*'s bridge structure and conning tower seen from the air off Hawaii in June 1924. The flag deck and its saluting guns are protected by an awning. A semaphore and the aerial trunk from the Auxiliary W/T office can be seen on the Conning tower platform. An officer waves at the camera from the door of the compass platform. Above him are the Foremast searchlight platform and the Torpedo lookout platform with one of the range clocks for concentration firing just visible. The mass of voice pipes connecting the various levels can be seen in the centre of the picture.
U.S. Naval Historical Center, Washington

Leading off it was the Subscription Library, another amenity catering to the increasingly educated men of which *Hood*'s crew was composed. On commissioning the *Hood* was provided by the Admiralty with a library of some 700 books 'consisting in great part of the standard classical novels of the past and present'.[42] By the 1930s this stock, which was kept in the Schoolroom off the Warrant Officers' flat, was clearly regarded as somewhat stodgy fare and Cdr Rory O'Conor applied his characteristic zeal to the launch of a Ship's Subscription Library.[43] Beginning with a £50 loan from the Canteen Committee, the Subscription Library purchased 500 new books and then charged borrowers a penny per volume for a week's loan. The scheme was an instant success and by the end of the commission, two years after its inception, the Library boasted 5,000 titles with an average weekly issue of over a thousand books. As for the men's tastes, these ran to the following: 40 per cent Westerns, 25 per cent crime, 25 per cent general fiction, 10 per cent military.

A ladder beside the Reading Room takes Aston up to the first level of the bridge structure, the Flag deck. Isolated in the centre was the admiral's sea cabin and forward of it, abutting the conning tower, was the Signal House. From a range of lockers on each side of the platform signalmen hoisted the flags that controlled the movements of ships in company. Also here were the director towers for the 5.5in guns, repositioned from the spotting top in 1934. The next level was the conning tower platform, taken up by the captain's and chief of staff's sea cabins. Further up was the enclosed Admiral's bridge, extended in 1939 to wrap around the control tower and containing his chart and signal houses. Here, on decks kept immaculately clean by the bridge sweeper, a peacetime admiral might direct his ships in tactical exercises, operations and manoeuvres. However, battle would likely find him in its main command centre, the Fore bridge, surrounded by his flag captain and staff.[44] Reached by a ladder from the Admiral's bridge, the Fore bridge consisted of a compass platform, chart house, W/T office and Admiral's plotting room connected via numerous voice pipes to the conning tower and engine rooms. These two levels were the subject of considerable rearrangement between 1929 and 1931, the aim of which was to improve all-round vision and eliminate the appalling draught that swept through the Fore bridge whenever the rear doors and forward windows were open, as they had to be to avoid being shattered by the ship's own salvoes. However, if the letter written by Vice-Admiral Geoffrey Blake to the Controller of the Navy, Admiral Sir Reginald Henderson, is anything to go by, then little had been done to rectify this by 1936.[45] Nor could it have been without a complete reconstruction and Blake had to content himself with the installation of armoured glass and clear-view wipers at Malta the following year.

Set above the Fore bridge was the searchlight control platform, transformed to an air-defence position in 1936, with the Torpedo control position added in 1927 aft. The next stage, reached by a precarious set of rungs on the main tripod support, was the foremast searchlight platform, removed in 1936. Above this was the slender and enclosed shape of the Torpedo lookout platform, reclassified as the Searchlight manipulating platform after 1927 and destined to be removed during the *Hood*'s final refit in 1941. Last came the large and imposing structure of the control or spotting top, crowned by a 15-foot director rangefinder 120 feet above the waterline. Reaching it

could be something of a trial at sea. Boy Jim Taylor:

> Whilst I was in *Hood* my action station was in the aloft director. This was right at the top of the foremast above the spotting top. What a journey it was to get up there. Normally one would have to climb up the ladders on the outside of the mast struts. These could get very hot indeed from the gases coming from the funnels. On one occasion I remember that the hood of my dufflecoat blew down off my head and the back of my neck was singed. Of course, apart from the risk of burning there was the problem of staying on the ladder. Anyone who served in *Hood* will tell you how the ship pitched and rolled. I can testify to how bad that was when you were towards the top of the mast. Sometimes I would make my way up the inside of the mast struts. There were numerous electrical cables, wires and iron junction boxes in there as well as the internal structure of the mast to get round. Having arrived at the spotting top I had to get through its roof to finally arrive at my action station.[46]

Once there severe vibration and the exaggerated motion of the ship often made life hellish for many of those who had it as their station. But for others, with perhaps only the ocean and its birds for company, there was no more invigorating place aboard. Two such were Fred and Frank Coombs (1935–8) of Sheffield, boy seamen and twin brothers:

> Whether it was an attempt to take some of the cockiness out of us as the motions of the ship are exaggerated up the mast, we could not know, but the job suited us and we found it [so] exhilarating that we stayed up there for the dog watches too, helped by one of us nipping down to our mess at teatime for a plentiful supply of corned beef sandwiches.[47]

An enclosed triangular structure set on a large star-shaped support, the spotting top contained some of the principal gunnery direction and control equipment in the ship. From here the Gunnery Officer commanded the monstrous weapons that were his ship's principal *raison d'être*. Over it, high above the 15-foot rangefinder, stood the fore top mast bearing the admiral's flag.

Where her internal design was concerned, the *Hood* was therefore laid out on lines that had become traditional for big ships in the Royal Navy, though with a somewhat ungenerous allocation of living space where the men were concerned and, being a battlecruiser, a deck less than the battleships. The elongated plan that resulted meant that whereas battleships accommodated their senior officers on the main deck aft, in *Hood* they resided in considerably greater comfort beneath the boat deck and in the bridge structure. The Marines occupied their traditional buffer space while the balance of the ship's company messed on the upper deck amidships and forward, with the exception of stokers and boys who were accommodated on the main deck. Meanwhile, the *Hood*'s sea-keeping qualities meant that the majority of officers lived in only moderate comfort on the main deck aft. On completion in 1920 she enjoyed amenities unmatched by any save the latest American battleship designs, but as the years passed and the peculiar conditions of life aboard began to assert themselves these received less fre-

42 *RBS*, p. 154.
43 Ibid., pp. 153–4.
44 Vice-Admiral Sir James Somerville was an exception, usually retiring to the conning tower in action; Simpson (ed), *The Somerville Papers*, p. 120.
45 NMM, HMS *Hood*, ship's cover, III, no. 35, Gibraltar, 23 December 1936.
46 HMS *Hood* Association archives.
47 IWM, 91/7/1, p. 47; 1935–8.

quent or favourable comment. For senior officers, however, conditions remained unequalled in every respect but one: the *Hood* had no stern walk from which the admiral and his guests might contemplate the ship's wake in serene privacy. This relic of an earlier era only *Queen Elizabeth*, *Warspite*, *Barham* and *Revenge* would take with them into the Second World War.

Four hours after it began Aston's tour is over. In penetrating both above the compass platform and below the upper deck he has already departed from the ship's standing orders which, in addition, expressly barred visitors from entering the conning tower, torpedo flats and other sensitive compartments. The complete tour of the engine spaces and the internal arrangements of the main armament will have to wait. For now, nursing a bruised head and a pair of barked shins from failing to stoop or step smartly enough through the dozens of door-frames and coamings he has passed, he retires to his cabin for a bath and a change of clothing before repairing to the wardroom for the Navy's staple pick-me-up: the brandy and ginger ale concoction known as a Horse's Neck.

Guns and Engines

Warships are defined by two irreducible elements: weaponry and mobility. Since its refinement during the sixteenth century the capital ship had emerged as a vessel capable of asserting its power and that of the nation she represented on a worldwide stage. The tactical and technological apogee of the wooden warship came during the French Revolutionary Wars when the British Navy gained command of the sea, broke Napoleon's Continental System and laid the foundation for his defeat on land. Within a few decades, however, the ship of the line had been swept away by another revolution which replaced her sails, timber and cannonballs with steam, steel and shellfire. For all this, the fundamental role of the battleship, that of a mobile gun platform, remained unaltered and by the early twentieth century two elements of her design had become critical to the full realization of that purpose. The first, which the Navy had occasionally neglected but never ceased to recognise, rested in the enormous power of her guns and the ability to use them with consistent speed and accuracy at long ranges—to 'hit first, hit hard and keep on hitting' as Admiral Fisher bluntly put it. The second, the full permutations of which it took the Service rather longer to embrace, lay in mechanised propulsion, in the ability of a ship to reach her station and then keep the seas long enough for her tactical or strategic purpose to be accomplished. A ship's guns might be a marvel of power and technical precision but they were meaningless unless the Engineering Department could deliver them to her fighting officers at the decisive moment. On these two elements a great ship's effectiveness depended, both as a fighting unit and as a tool of diplomacy. Deprived of one or the other she was nothing.

Propulsion

In *Achtung! Panzer!*, the revolutionary tract on mechanised warfare he published in 1937, Colonel Heinz Guderian impressed on his readers the need to regard the engine of a tank as a weapon no different from its gun.[48] An engine is not perhaps the first thing one associates with a tank, any more than it is with a battleship. On the contrary, to visualise a cap-

ital ship is to see, in V.C. Scott O'Connor's words, 'her colossal turrets, the long straining muzzles of her guns…, her tiers of decks' and her hull coursing through the water.[49] Though the smoke issuing from her funnels might serve as a reminder, the engineering plant is frequently neglected when the fighting power of a capital ship comes to be assessed, too often reduced to the bare bones of speed, power and range. In its own way, this state of affairs reflects the view long held in the upper echelons of the Navy, that the Engineering Department, battened down in its hellish domain, was best kept out of sight and out of mind. Not until the 1950s was it finally recognised that the fount of a warship's strength, endurance and flexibility lay in her engine spaces. On them rested that ability to project their power and symbolism which distinguishes warships from all other engines of war. For much of her career two things above all set the *Hood* apart from other capital ships: her speed and her appearance. From a tactical point of view, it was speed alone that distinguished her from such unregarded mastodons as *Resolution* and *Malaya*, from *Lorraine*, *Wyoming* and *Hyuga*. It was speed that kept the *Hood* in the vanguard of the Royal Navy in peace and war, that made her what she was. That speed came from her engine spaces and the 300 men who worked in them.[50]

The basis of the *Hood*'s propulsion rested in her 24 Yarrow small-tube boilers, a design first fitted in the 'large light cruisers' of the *Courageous* class. These were carried in four boiler rooms set fore and aft in the middle section of the ship and offered 30 per cent more power for the same weight of plant than the large-tube models. Each boiler, 17 feet wide, 16.5 high and 13 deep, contained a large furnace fed by eight oil sprayers, the fuel being drawn from tanks adjacent to each boiler room by a system of pumps and heaters. Since the stability of the ship depended on a uniform distribution of oil in the tanks, dials were monitored to verify that she was on an even keel and adjustments made as necessary, a highly responsible job since these had in turn to be filled by more distant ones. The requisite furnace temperature was reached under forced draught from six 90-inch supply fans in compartments over the boilers. The resulting inferno heated water supplied from the four main feed tanks in the engine rooms to a working pressure of 235 p.s.i. From this came the saturated steam which, by means of four 19-inch pipes, provided power to the geared turbines in the engine rooms aft. Each of these sets was attached to one of the 24-inch shafts on whose propellers the ship was powered through the water. Rather than the Parsons turbine fitted in most dreadnoughts before the Great War, the *Hood* was equipped with a modified version of the American Curtis design for which her builder, John Brown of Clydebank, held the British licence. Each set consisted of one high-pressure and one low-pressure turbine, an astern turbine and, in the case of those in the forward engine room, a cruising turbine for each of the two outer propeller shafts. Single reduction gearing was used to harness the revolutions of the turbine shaft to the optimum rate of the propellers. In *Hood* this entailed reducing the 1,500 r.p.m. of the HP and 1,100 r.p.m. of the LP turbines to a shaft speed of about 210 r.p.m. at maximum power of 32 knots. Geared drive of this sort depended on Michell-type bearing blocks to carry the thrust of the shaft. The supply of steam and therefore the speed of the ship was controlled from platforms in each of the three engine rooms as well as by nozzle valves on the turbines themselves.

[48] This section owes much to the advice and assistance of Vice-Admiral Sir Louis Le Bailly.

[49] O'Connor, *The Empire Cruise*, p. 37.

[50] 'H.M. Battlecruiser *Hood*' in *Engineering* [London], 109 (January–June 1920), pp. 397–9.

Once it had passed through the engines the steam was exhausted into a condenser fitted beneath each of the low-pressure turbines. The purpose of the condenser was to improve the efficiency of the turbine by increasing the pressure differential between the incoming and outgoing steam. This it accomplished by creating a vacuum in which the exhaust steam was cooled by being passed over a series of pipes bearing sea water drawn into the condenser by a pair of pumps. The by-product of this process, a condensate of distilled water, was then transferred to the main feed tanks from where it returned to the boilers, thereby repeating the process. Needless to say, this cycle used rather more water than was eventually returned to the feed tanks, the shortfall being made good by the evaporators and the 110-ton reserve feed tanks which resided under each of the *Hood*'s four boiler rooms. The evaporators, of which *Hood* carried three, used a honeycomb of tubes filled with exhaust steam to boil sea water, a process which yielded up to 240 tons of distillate per day. Most of the distillate was reserved for boiler feed, the rest—though never more than 70 tons—being allocated for washing and drinking in the living spaces. But it was in the reserve feed tanks and above all in the condensers that the *Hood*'s Engineering Department faced a critical problem from the mid-1930s. Louis Le Bailly, an engineer officer between 1937–9, explains the situation:

The other nightmare affecting the ship's mobility was the feed water's worsening impurity which corroded our boilers. The tubes in the ship's main condensers under the great turbines were aged and rotting. Salt sea water drawn by vacuum into the condensing steam contaminated the water on its way back to the boiler, a constant problem in ships during World War One known as 'condenseritis'. In addition the reserve boiler feed water tanks in the double bottoms were leaking at their seams, causing more contamination. And these two problems fed on each other. When the boiler water became contaminated it was necessary to ditch it and replenish supplies from the evaporators which were sometimes of insufficient capacity to cope with the amount needing replacement. Then water, probably contaminated, had to be pumped from the reserve tanks.[51]

At the best, if permitted to continue, such salt contamination would damage the boilers; at the worst. 'priming', the passage of water droplets in the steam, would cause damage to steam joints leading to further loss of boiler feed water and sometimes explosions in steam valves, with fatal results to those nearby. In either case, the only remedy was to ditch the contaminated water which would somehow have to be replaced by evaporating machinery or the provision of a water boat or some other conveyance with distilled water.[52]

Problems of this magnitude left the Engineering Department with little margin for equipment failure and the severe damage done to the *Hood*'s dilapidated condensers by the bomb hit of 26 September 1939 came close to leaving her dead in the water. Though few have survived to record it, it took heroic efforts on the part of her engine room staff to bring their ship into harbour and then make her seaworthy.[53] Indeed, Sub-Lt (E) Brian Scott-Garrett was to spend most of the nine months he served

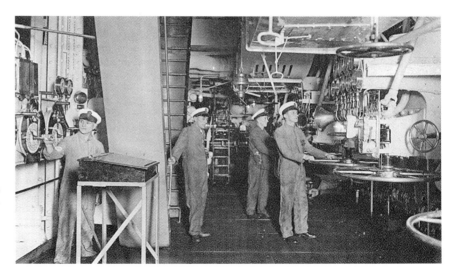

Four engine room artificers on the control platform of the After Engine Room, *c*.1931. Two are on the throttles (ahead and astern) controlling the revolutions of the starboard inner shaft. The desk on the left houses the engine-room register, written up hourly. By it are the telegraphs to the Forward and Middle Engine Rooms and from the Forward Engine Room and the bridge. The latter reads 'Full', 'Half', 'Slow' and 'Stop' (Ahead and Astern). The structure dimly seen in the background is an evaporator. The oil lamp in the centre is for emergency lighting. *Sellicks*

in the *Hood* between 1940 and 1941 working on nothing else but her corroded condenser tubes.[54] This problem had a long-term effect on the crew at large since the need to draw on the evaporators for boiler feed not only reduced the amount of fresh water available for washing and bathing, but prevented operation of the ship's leaky steam heating, the haemorrhage of water being too great in view of critical shortages elsewhere.[55] Even during the 1933–6 commission bathing water was rationed when the ship was at sea, while the wartime *Hood* was fated to spend two winters in northern waters with unheated messdecks.

The events of 26 September 1939, related in detail elsewhere, provide a grim snapshot of life in the *Hood*'s engine spaces as her career drew on.[56] At the best of times the engineer's world, particularly at sea, was one of deafening noise from fans and turbines, ear-popping air pressure and brutal heat, reaching 140°F in places. Such conditions made it very hard for men to give of their best over long periods of time, a fact overlooked by the majority of the ship's company who never ventured into the engine spaces. In December 1940 a damage-control exercise took Mid. Philip Buckett to the control platform of the forward engine room. As he subsequently noted in his journal, 'I soon realised their difficulty to work properly in such terrific heat and foul atmosphere'.[57] Apart from the nature of the work carried on there and despite the provision of extensive ventilation systems, these conditions were often due to basic flaws in engineering hardware. Louis Le Bailly:

…The change to oil-fired installations opened the way to higher pressures and steam temperatures [but] lagging techniques and heat removal had not kept pace nor had jointing techniques, so steam leaks were frequent. Heat and humidity below, always bad, had worsened so that heat stroke and exhaustion were common. To lead in such conditions required superlative fitness.[58]

But leaders there were aplenty among both engineer officers and the long-service stokers, mechanicians and artificers who kept the ship steaming come hell or high water.

How was this machinery controlled and operated? The

[51] Le Bailly, *The Man Around the Engine*, pp. 49–50.
[52] Id., *From Fisher to the Falklands*, p. 23.
[53] See ch. 8, pp. 191–2.
[54] IWM/SA, no. 16741, reel 1.
[55] See, respectively, *RBS*, p. 210, and Le Bailly, *The Man Around the Engine*, p. 54.
[56] See ch. 8, pp. 191–2.
[57] RNM, 1998/42, 10 December 1940.
[58] Le Bailly, *The Man Around the Engine*, p. 32.

[59] Letter to the author, 11 January 2004.
[60] Le Bailly, *The Man Around the Engine*, p. 44.

Hood's engine rooms can be divided into four levels. The lowest of these, with a clearance of no more than five feet, was the 'dungeon' in which maintenance was performed on the air and lubrication pumps serving each turbine set. Above these, on the lower platform, rose the bulk of the high- and low-pressure turbines themselves, each connected to the gear casing which drove the propeller shaft. High above, flights of ladders and lofty gangways in the vault of each space gave access to valves on the steam mains which periodically needed to be opened or closed with an immense three-foot wheel spanner. Built into the deckhead itself were large exhaust fans drawing heat up from the engine rooms and venting it out onto the boat deck, but temperatures in the upper reaches could still approach 140°F. Spanning these levels were lengths of vast bulbous tubing bringing steam to the machinery below. The critical level from an operational point of view was the control or starting platform lying against the forward bulkhead of each engine room and overlooking the lower platform from a height of about fifteen feet. From here the various turbines were each regulated by a pair of throttles ('Forward' and 'Astern') which were turned in response to orders received from the bridge via the engine room telegraphs. In the case of the forward control platform there was a third throttle for each set, that for the cruising turbine. These throttles took the form of large handwheels operated by an engine room artificer, though the increased reliance on auxiliary machinery required stokers to be trained for this duty after the outbreak of war. Presiding over the entire operation was the

Engineer Officer of the Watch on the forward control platform, the nerve centre of the *Hood*'s propulsion. The EOOW (in the shape of a commissioned officer) was required to translate bridge orders into appropriate instructions for each turbine, these being rung through to the control platform in question and entered in the engine-room register. To him also fell the duty of operating the boiler room telegraph so that the oil sprayers could be regulated accordingly. Demanding as it was, his task was greatly complicated when sudden bursts of speed were required in action or when entering harbour. In the following passage Louis Le Bailly draws a comparison between the *Hood* and the light cruiser *Naiad* (to which he transferred in November 1939) which gives an idea of the judgement, foresight and composure required to handle a big ship:

> When a dive bomber started its dive the Captain would order 'Full Speed' (emergency) and put the helm hard over port or starboard. In the engine room on receiving the order 'Full Speed' (and hearing the pompoms start firing), I would ring through to Boiler Room who would put on all sprayers; BUT I would count to ten slowly before allowing the throttle watchkeepers to swing open the throttles as fast as they could. That was to make sure that the steam pressure was rising BEFORE the throttles were opened. Otherwise the open throttle would take steam away from the boilers too fast; all dynamos would slow down or stop and a whole series of disasters would occur, perhaps losing steam altogether as fans would slow down and steam fall back. In a ship like *Hood* all this would be much slower. But steam always had to be going up when the throttles were to be opened, and sprayers taken off when Bridge ordered 'Slow'.[59]

Almost as fraught was the operation of the boiler rooms themselves, a task entrusted to a Chief Stoker, his PO Stoker assistant, and a stoker for each of the six boilers under the overall control of the Boiler Room EOOW. Louis Le Bailly:

> The chief stoker was 'orchestral' conductor in a boiler room usually at a temperature of 90°F–100°F, dimly lit by shockproof lamps and the flickering of furnace flames. Fans supplying air for combustion made normal conversation impossible and ears popped badly with 10 inches or more of varying air pressure. While controlling the steam to the fans, the chief stoker would keep his eye both on a periscope to watch for funnel smoke, and the steam to the oil fuel pumps whose speed was related to the number, up to eight, of sprayers on each boiler. This he would orchestrate by hitting a shell case with a spanner to attract each boiler operator's attention and manually indicate whether to open up and flash further sprayers or shut them and close the air flaps. Incorrect operation by a single stoker… could cause smoke to billow from the funnels; or if sprayers were shut slowly as the turbine throttles were closed, the safety valves would lift with a roar…[60]

A look through the boiler room periscope would soon tell him how he was doing, white smoke if too much air in proportion to the oil supply and black if too little.

Naturally, there were risks inherent in operating high-performance plant of this sort. The possibility of a dangerous

A detail of the throttles and gauges of the Forward Engine Room showing the ship's chough badge. Throttles for each propeller shaft were opened and closed in accordance with the desired speed and helm of the ship and the supply of steam power from the boiler rooms. An exceedingly delicate balance. The horn-like objects are voicepipes through which instructions were passed to the engine room artificers controlling the throttles.
HMS Hood Association/Sait Collection

oversupply of water or oil to the boilers kept a Leading Stoker 'Water Tender' busy on each gallery of the upper stokehold:

> Those who have boiled over milk in a saucepan are only too aware of the froth that spills onto the stove. Similarly, automatic valves regulate the water level when more sprayers are opened and heat is applied (as water level rises so supply is cut off) or sprayers are shut and heat reduced (water level falls so supply opens up). There was one watchkeeper to every three boilers by the water gauge glasses, as any failure of the automatic water regulators required an instantaneous changeover to hand operation or a major disaster, with casualties, would ensue.[61]

Then came the arduous labour of cleaning and repairing boilers and condensers. Thanks to the refusal of successive Engineers-in-Chief at the Admiralty to sanction the addition of chemical compound to the feed water, the *Hood*'s Engineering Department, like those of every ship in the Navy, was condemned to a regime requiring each boiler to be cleaned after 21 days' steaming. Louis Le Bailly describes the undertaking:

> To prevent corrosion of boiler drums and tubes it was frequently necessary, depending on sea time, to remove all heat-insulating lagging, open up each boiler, clean and blacklead the internal fittings and then, through a small manhole, perform the same rites inside each of the three boiler drums, brushing through every tube. By dropping carefully counted balls down each of several thousand individual tubes we ensured that there was no blockage which, when steaming, could inhibit the water's circulation and cause the tube to melt and explode into the furnace with probable casualties. Leading Stoker bricklayers with their unskilled mates would be breaking up damaged fire brick walls in the furnace and removing the rubble before building and cementing new ones. Yet another gang would be inserting 10ft saws between the tubes to remove soot and clinker and sweeping down and oiling the inside of *Hood*'s huge funnels. Meantime artificers and mechanicians would be refitting steam, water and oil valves, repairing steam leaks, resetting safety valves and refitting associated auxiliary machinery. Finally, each boiler would be pumped up to its working pressure and tested for leaks. With 24 boilers in four boiler rooms this job was never ending. Asbestosis had not been heard of and we all lived for long hours in a fog of brick dust, asbestos fibre and soot. Work went on round the clock in six- or eight-hour spells, depending on the heat and urgency, until completed.[62]

A day of steaming, it should be noted, was defined as any during which feed water had been admitted to the boiler for however long or short a period. Even between cleanings the boilers required constant attention to remove the soot which gathered on the water drums and clear the clinker accumulating around the oil sprayers.

Although fitted with straight water tubes to facilitate cleaning, the *Hood*'s small-tube boilers therefore paid for their improved capacity and reduced weight and volume with increased maintenance. On the other hand, the Brown-Curtis geared turbine proved to be a superb design whose output of

144,000 shaft horsepower in *Hood* was not exceeded in British construction until the completion of the carrier *Eagle* in 1951. Propeller shaft bearings would occasionally run hot during prolonged bursts at speed or, as during the pursuit of the *Strasbourg* after Mers-el-Kebir, one or more turbine wheels would be stripped of its blades requiring it to be shut down and steam from the boilers redistributed. But this was rare and the *Hood*'s engine plant stands among the finest of its era.

The work of the Engineering Department was not limited to propulsion. In his capacity as Chief Engineer the Commander (E) was responsible for over 1,000 machines in the ship, ranging from meat slicers in the galley to the CO_2 compressor on the lower deck and the hydraulic engines supplying power to the main armament. To take one major example, the basis of the ship's electricity-generating plant consisted of eight 200kW dynamos, their output controlled by the Torpedomen on the main switchboard but each operated and maintained by the Engineering Department. In addition there were dozens of smaller dynamos driven by electric motors to supply power for guns, searchlights and fire-control installations etc., many with one or more stokers in attendance. There were also pumps of every size and description, ranging from the 50-ton model served by Stoker Ken Clark in the base of 'X' turret to the 1,000-ton turbo bilge pump fitted in each boiler room.[63] Even when the ship was in harbour the need to maintain such essential services as the production of water and electricity required boilers to be permanently lit and tended by the Engineering Department. Then there was the matter of oil, the consumption of which was strictly rationed in the cash-strapped 1930s. It was one of Chief Stoker Biggenden's unwritten tasks to ensure that, whatever the reality, as far as Their Lordships were concerned HM battlecruiser *Hood* never exceeded her stipulated allowance. Louis Le Bailly:

> Chief Stoker Biggenden slaved away with two registers in the stuffy engineer's office, one recording, *inter alia*, the actual oil consumption and the other the permitted consumption. The latter, kept uniquely for the inspection of the fleet engineer officer showed, mysteriously, that we abided strictly by the rules, whatever the true facts. How the books were reconciled was neither sought nor divulged.[64]

Part of the problem was that the *Hood*'s fans could not always provide sufficient draft to burn the oil sprayed into the boilers, particularly if the thicker Western Hemisphere fuel were being used instead of the premium-grade Arabian crude for which they had been designed.[65] This design fault could well result in vast quantities of smoke roiling out of her funnels, a tactical disadvantage at sea and an embarrassment in harbour. Clean as she was in comparison with the coal-fired dreadnoughts of the Great War, it still fell to the men of the Double Bottom Party to perform the filthy job of cleaning her oil tanks with rags and buckets for an extra 6d. a day. The task required the supervising officer to make a very careful head count of those entering and exiting in case any were overcome by fumes. Stoker Ken Clark:

> Once the oil tanks were empty they had to be cleaned by the stokers. Men would go inside the tanks and clean them up with cotton rags. There was a special kit for this duty—

[61] Ibid., pp. 44–5.
[62] Ibid., pp. 43–4.
[63] HMS *Hood* Association archives. 1938–40.
[64] Le Bailly, *The Man Around the Engine*, p. 39.
[65] Vice-Admiral Sir Louis Le Bailly, letter to the author, 24 December 2002.

rubber suits and clogs—but the suits leaked and many men felt that they were better off without them and would go into the tanks naked to clean them.[66]

For such occasions one hopes there was sufficient hot water in the Stokers' bathroom to wash themselves clean when their work was done. Nor was this the worst of it. Occasionally severe damage to boiler brickwork caused by high furnace temperatures would require relays of men in wet asbestos suits to enter the very maw of hell to effect repairs for as long as they could stand it before collapsing. To be sure, an engineer's was often an unenviable existence. The following description of a typical day in harbour by Sub-Lt (E) Peter Stokes of the *Howe* could stand for any capital ship in the Royal Navy:

In harbour, the Engineer Officer of the Day has unparalleled scope for involvement in chaos—a turbo-generator will trip (all lights start dimming), a 'Red Alert' will require the flashing up of an extra boiler, the laundry machinery will 'fall over', the firemain will develop a leak, the possibilities are endless. The day will culminate in Engineer's Rounds which, if carried out according to the book, will involve visits to every space manned by the Department, concluding with the writing up of the register. It is after such exertions that testing the Wardroom gin for purity, instead of the boiler feed water, will provide a brief relaxation before the Duty Picket Boat is towed in with a damaged propeller. Despite the hazards lurking in the Harbour Machinery Room, it's really more peaceful being at sea…[67]

The implications of this labour in war are to be imagined. Unlike the *Hood*'s seaman complement which kept a two-watch system, the Engineering Department worked in three eight-hour watches. With regular boiler cleaning this meant somewhat more than an eight-hour day even in peacetime in harbour. But in war it translated into a daily sea routine of not less than eight hours

on Steaming Watch and eight at Damage Control or Ammunition Supply Stations, quite apart from the dawn and dusk action stations that required every man in the ship to be at his post.[68] The return to harbour heralded not a few days' comparative rest but the resumption of boiler cleaning in the most overworked capital ship in the Navy. No wonder the *Hood*'s stokers apparently came close to mutiny in December 1940.[69]

Evidently, it took a special type of man to endure this regime. Until the Invergordon Mutiny the *Hood*'s stokers were drawn largely from the mining communities of the British Isles. However, by the mid-1930s this sort of man had little interest in a naval career and the Admiralty even less in exposing the Navy to the militant politics he threatened to bring with him. The Admiralty therefore began to recruit teenage stokers from the traditional forcing grounds of the Navy in southern England. Despite concerns for the poor standard of education among recruits no steps were taken to improve the literacy of the new intake. Rather than the year or more that boy seamen spent under training in one of the shore establishments, stokers received no more than eight weeks' drill followed by two months' mechanical instruction before being drafted for sea service as Stoker 2nd Class. Progression to Stoker 1st Class came by means of a test to demonstrate competence in handling various types of machinery. For the ambitious a three-month period as an Auxiliary Watchkeeper was followed by an examination which, if successful, would grant him a certificate and the chance of further training ashore. Others would take advantage of the Mechanician Scheme which allowed stokers of above-average ability to specialise in equipment maintenance with the prospect of warrant rank. But, her eight (E) officers and three warrant engineers apart, the key figures in the *Hood*'s Engineering Department were the 35 engine room artificers, men who entered the Navy after a challenging written examination and spent no less than four years under training before going to sea. Louis Le Bailly, then a Sub-Lieutenant (E), has this unforgettable reminiscence of his first visit to the *Hood*'s engine spaces on rejoining the ship in May 1937.

On my first morning the Senior [Engineer] took me into all the machinery spaces including numerous glory holes known as cabooses, mostly housing ventilation machinery. But throwing open one caboose door he let me take a glance at five whey-faced elderly men in blue overalls, each holding a glass. 'Those five chief engine room artificers (Ch ERAs), Maycock, Bradfield, Edmiston, Snell and Hemmings,' he said, 'are among the most senior skilled men we have. I know, and they know, they have no right to be drinking prairie oysters of rum and raw eggs in the forenoon but they would give their lives for this ship. If we had to go to sea in an emergency it would be their skills on which we would depend. Listen to them, learn from them and never mind asking them anything. If, after six months, when you come to get your watchkeeping ticket, you know a quarter of what they do about this ship, you will have done well.'[70]

The Engineering Department was distinguished from others in the *Hood* by the fact that its personnel frequently gave very extended periods of service to the ship, men who over time became indispensable in their work and indivisible from her character. In the late 1930s there was Mechanician Chilvers of

[66] HMS *Hood* Association archives.
[67] Cited in Coward, *Battleship at War*, p. 95.
[68] Le Bailly, 'Rum, Bum & the Lash', p. 56.
[69] See ch. 8, p. 195.
[70] Le Bailly, *The Man Around the Engine*, pp. 38–9. The Senior Engineer was Lt-Cdr (E) Lancelot Fogg-Elliot. Reginald F. Edmiston, John Snell and Bertie Hemmings were lost with the ship in 1941.
[71] Details in this paragraph from ibid., p. 39, HMS *Hood* Association archives (Stoker George Donnelly, 1936–8) and Vice-Admiral Sir Louis Le Bailly, letters to the author, 12 July 2002 and 1 February 2004. Apart from Watson the following were lost on 24 May 1941: John E. Binnie, Sydney S. Stoyles, Charles R. Bostock and Walden J. Biggenden.
[72] Le Bailly, *The Man Around the Engine*, p. 82.
[73] Bradford, *The Mighty* Hood, p. 112.

Members of the Double Bottom Party pose by Starboard No. 1 5.5in gun, *c*.1938. Stoker Ken 'Nobby' Clark on the left.
HMS Hood Association/Clark Collection

meagre income. In the way of this or any other navy, its work co-existed with the lives of those who made it what it was.

The chief purpose of the working chamber was to transfer the shell and cordite cartridges from the main hoisting cage to the gun-loading cage which would take them up to the gun house. On arrival the cordite was automatically tipped out into a waiting position while a bewildering concert of flashtight scuttles opened and closed about it. Once the gun-loading cage was ready the cordite was forced in by a pair of rammers, to be followed by the shell itself which again occupied the lower stage. The cage operators' ability to perform these actions was controlled by some of the 37 interlocking systems which governed the operation of the entire turret. These arrangements, which took the form of mechanical obstructions to the operating levers, were designed to regulate the passage of shells and above all cordite from magazine to breech and so minimise the possibility of a disastrous explosion in the event of a hit or accident. At a given moment there could never be more than three shells in the system for each gun, only two of them accompanied by their propellant during the clearing phase of the operation. The *Hood's Gunnery Guide* spelt it out in bold type:

No charge is to be taken from the Magazine until it is required for loading in the Main Cage, and the Main Cage is not to be brought up with a new round until the preceding round in the Gun Loading Cage is required at the gun.[88]

Thus, when the order 'Load' was passed, the first round was sent up to the gunhouse, the second was brought up to the working chamber, and the third loaded onto the main hoisting cage once it had returned to the base of the turret trunking, the cordite joining it in the hoppers above. We are following the progress of the first round which now travelled up the rails of the gun-loading cage, through another flashproof scuttle and so into the turret itself.

A 15in gun turret had a crew of around 20 men under the command of the Captain of the Turret. Four of them occupied the control cabinet behind the guns: the range taker at his 30-foot rangefinder should the turret pass into local control, a periscope observer, a communications rating with headphones and the turret captain himself, protected by an additional layer of 3-inch plate. The rest worked the guns under the Second Captain of the Turret. Each gun was served by a gun layer seated against the 15-inch face plate to the left of the barrel, his eyes glued either to an electric pointer in the case of director control or to a telescopic sight adjusted for range and deflection by the sight setter in the event of independent firing. By turning a brass handwheel he caused the barrel to be elevated or lowered on its trunnions by an immense hydraulic cylinder beneath the gun. The sights were individually calibrated to the ballistic characteristics unique to each gun. On the right of the gunhouse sat the trainer who operated the hydraulic swash-plate engines which traversed the turret by rack and pinion at a speed of two degrees per second, so smoothly that few of the turret crew were ever aware of it. Under director control, however, training of the turret was carried out from a position in the working chamber, the operator 'following pointers' transmitted remotely. The gun crew consisted of a pair of loading numbers, the ram operator, a breech worker and an ordnance artificer in the event of

mechanical failure, all supervised by the Captain of the Gun. There was also an interceptor operator whose job it was to break the circuits of the gun in the event of a local emergency, isolating it from director control until it was ready to resume operation. Others like LS J.R. Williams (1939–40) stood by with emergency generators in the event of any failure in the circuits themselves.[89] The turret was dominated by the usual warship smell of oil and metal, often cold and dank and always poorly lit by lamps in steel enclosures against the turret roof and sides.[90] Few spaces in the ship were more dominated by steel and machinery, the men hemmed in by sloping plating and dwarfed by the monstrous weapons before them. Around the breech slender mesh barriers kept them from the gaping hole of the gun well into which the cage guide rails disappeared. To all this was added the squelch and hiss of the hydraulics, the racket of the cages and the dreadful concussions of the loading process once the turret came into action. It was no place for claustrophobia.

The shell has now come level with the breech of the gun. A pull on a lever activated a hydraulic chain rammer which thrust it along the loading tray and into the breech until the copper driving bands around its rim bit deep into the rifling of the barrel. The driving bands not only settled the shell into the chamber but activated the fuse on the explosive. Another lever brought half the cordite charge onto the tray, this also being forced into the gun by the ram operator. Seconds later the remaining 214 pounds were on their way into the barrel. A single problem was sufficient to stall the entire procedure from magazine to breech, and it only took a cordite cartridge with its red igniter pad facing the wrong way for precious seconds to be lost in the rhythm of firing the guns. Occasionally, too, the operator's failure to reduce the length of the rammer stroke after the shell had been loaded caused the cordite to be crushed into the base of the projectile on the next ram, the ensuing mess bringing the entire turret to a halt. But otherwise the process was well nigh complete and the breech block would now be closed with a mighty slam, the interrupted screw turning to engage the barrel lining against the enormous energy that would shortly be unleashed against it. The loading process was completed by the breech worker inserting a small firing tube into the lock of the gun. At this the gun layer and trainer, following pointers from the remote director, fixed the target on their instruments. Once they were both 'on', the electrical circuits were closed and the weapon reported as 'Ready!', a light burning before the layer in the aloft director to indicate this. The moment had come. A shrill 'Ding! Ding!' on the fire gong warned the ship to brace itself for what was to follow. With a shudder and a blinding flash the shell was hurled out of the barrel at a speed of over 2,400 feet per second as a sheet of flame engulfed the decks. In the turret the explosion was felt more than heard. The pressurised atmosphere of the gun house kept the sound to a muffled roar but the concussion of the firing created a momentary vacuum that emptied the lungs of many in the ship. In salvo firing the passage of a few seconds would bring a further assault as the left-hand gun thundered into action, the barrel recoiling on its cradles deep into the gun well. The recoil was absorbed by a recuperator controlled by a set of recoil cylinders, the barrel then being returned to its starting position on a pneumatic run-out system unique to the Mk II mounting. The breech, lately exposed

[88] *Gunnery Guide*, p. 12.
[89] HMS *Hood* Association archives.
[90] Though white in peacetime, the turret interiors were repainted in dark grey on the outbreak of war. The reason has presumably to do with the need to reduce light emanating from the sighting ports.

'X' turret at the limit of its firing arc, 1926. The right-hand gun is at maximum elevation of 30 degrees. The tall structure on the left is the wireless trunking from the Second W/T office on the lower deck. *Repulse* astern.
U.S. Naval Historical Center

[91] The *Hood*'s turrets did, however, suffer from a number of early teething problems; see the journal of Mid. Robert Elkins, NMM, Elkins/1, 29 September 1921.
[92] IWM/SA, no. 22147, reel 2. HMS *Excellent* on Whale Island, Portsmouth Harbour, was the Navy's principal gunnery school.
[93] Sumida, *In Defence of Naval Supremacy*, p. 153.
[94] Padfield, *The Battleship Era*, p. 185.
[95] Sumida, *In Defence of Naval Supremacy*, pp. 79–80. The interpretation of the development of fire control in the Royal Navy offered in these paragraphs relies heavily on Dr. Sumida's work, to which acknowledgement is hereby made. It should be noted, however, that many of Dr. Sumida's interpretations are challenged in John Brooks' forthcoming *Dreadnought Gunnery: Fire Control and the Battle of Jutland* (London: Frank Cass), to which Dr Brooks was kind enough to give the author access.
[96] Sumida, *In Defence of Naval Supremacy*, pp. 208–15.

to pressures of almost 20 tons per square inch, was now subjected to a blast of compressed air from bottles stowed in the turret trunking in order to extinguish any remaining fire. With this the block was opened, the turret filling with acrid cordite fumes while jets of water played over the breech in readiness for the next shell. For a trained crew, working like automata on equipment of proven reliability, the process from magazine to firing would take less than a minute.[91] With three shells in the system at any one time this gave a firing rate of approximately 30 seconds for each gun.

Thus was *Hood*'s main armament fired. But how did her guns acquire their target? The answer takes us back to the revolution in naval gunnery at the close of the nineteenth century. Until the 1890s the firing of naval guns had no more direction than that afforded them by the intuition of the gun layer and the orders of his officer. However, from this time on the adoption of larger and more powerful guns on correspondingly fewer mountings began to lead the technically-minded officer and his civilian counterpart to consider how the accuracy and impact of the new weapons might be improved over longer ranges. Out of these concerns came a number of innovations on which the development of naval gunnery in the twentieth century was to be based. One of these was the rangefinder, the first practical example of which was a 4½-foot model introduced by a Professor Barr of Glasgow University in 1892. Operating on the coincidence principle, the Barr rangefinder required the observer to align two separate images of the target by means of a pair of mirrors and a set of prisms, the result of his adjustments permitting the range to be read off a scale on the instrument. The calculation of range was derived by measuring the parallax angle of the object relative to the point of observation once the image came into focus or alignment. The Barr design and its longer-base successors were to provide the British with an effective means of establishing the range of a

target, but they did not compare in range, speed and accuracy with the stereoscopic models produced for the German Navy by Carl Zeiss of Jena. Though requiring highly-trained operators with superb vision, initially at least the Zeiss model left comparatively little to the range taker once he had slotted his individual lenses into the instrument, the data being simply read off from numbers in his field of view. The Barr & Stroud model, on the other hand, required constant adjustment on the part of the operator to fix the point of coincidence, though prolonged trials after the Great War convinced the Admiralty that the effectiveness of either system had more to do with base length and prevailing conditions of light than any fundamental design element. Be this as it may, by the 1930s there seems to have been little doubt in the Royal Navy—even in the hallowed precincts of HMS *Excellent*—as to which side had the better rangefinding equipment.[92]

By 1900 a new breed of gunnery officer nurtured by Capt. Percy Scott was beginning to address the problem of accurately engaging targets whose range and bearing were subject to constant alteration. The first step towards solving this came in 1902 when Lt John Dumaresq produced the trigonometrical calculator which bears his name. Provided with own ship's speed, course and bearing to the target along with the estimated speed and course of the target, the Dumaresq would produce rates of change for both target range *and* target bearing. To this was added the Vickers Clock into which both the range and rate of change of range were fed, the mechanism at length producing an update to the indicated range and deflection based on the *predicted* rate of change. This data permitted salvo firing to be maintained without any more than periodic reference to the rangefinder, though with variable results. The system that made the transfer of this data to the guns and then their firing as one unit possible was Capt. Scott's own innovation, Director Firing, which he devised in 1904.[93] The essence of Scott's idea was that the laying, training and firing of the guns should all be controlled and synchronised by a device called a 'director' operated by a single observer high above the fracas of battle. Here the aiming instructions would be set on a master sight and transmitted to the guns by means of a 'converger', the broadside being fired by an electrical signal triggered by the director observer once the guns were correctly laid. The director firing system has been called 'the most vital single gunnery invention of the twentieth century' but its potential could not be made good until the fire-control instruments on which the guns depended for their accuracy had proved equal to the vast problem in spherical trigonometry implied by engaging a moving target at sea.[94] It was this, along with entrenched opposition in the Admiralty, that delayed the installation of director firing in the British fleet until 1913.

The answer to the problem of accuracy in long-range naval gunnery lay in the shape of the 'Argo Clock' produced by a designer of genius: Arthur Hungerford Pollen.[95] The Dumaresq devices had greatly extended the range at which ships might be engaged but accuracy could not enjoy similar improvement until gunnery officers were supplied with a continuous reading of the *relative* rate of change of the target. In 1904 Pollen addressed this problem by designing a plotting table, gyroscopically stabilised against the motion of the vessel, capable of generating a constant readout of the relative positions of ship and target.[96] This it accomplished by means of a moving roll of paper, aligned and powered to correspond with the ship's course and speed while a fixed pencil inscribed a line on the plot to match the movement of the firing vessel. Simultaneously, observed ranges and bearings sent by electrical signal from the latest rangefinding equipment were added to the plot in coloured inks to provide a record of the target relative to the firing ship. This permitted the helm and revolutions of the ship to be adjusted to match the course and speed of the target, thereby presenting the gunnery officer with a consistent range and deflection at which to engage the enemy. Alternatively, the relative bearings given by the plot allowed a prediction to be made of the future position of the target and the guns aimed accordingly. Together with a gyromounted rangefinder designed by Pollen, the final variant of the Argo Clock, the Mk V Course and Speed Plotter of 1913, offered the Royal Navy the holy grail of fire control: helm-free gunnery, the ability to compute ranges and bearings even while the firing ship was executing a turn. But it was not to be. Already in 1908 a prominent gunnery officer, Lt Frederic Dreyer, had produced a rate plotter which, though of limited use, recommended itself to the Admiralty in that it was based on existing instruments and thus more readily assimilated than the Pollen design. In 1910 Dreyer followed this with the first model of the fire-control table that took his name, a development of the earlier rate plotter but with several critical features heavily plagiarised from the Argo Clock. The Dreyer Table was the product of considerable ingenuity but suffered from flaws both of design, conception and construction which greatly limited its effectiveness under battle as against practice conditions. In the event, Dreyer cribbed the Argo Clock in virtually every respect except that in which its advantage might have proved decisive: automatic as against manual range plotting. Because of shifting politics and allegiances in the Admiralty and the traditional suspicion of outsiders, it was the Dreyer Table that the Navy adopted and with which the Grand Fleet sailed for its fateful encounter off Jutland on 31 May 1916. Though the Pollen system was never fully tested in combat, its rejection may have had serious implications both for the accuracy of the Navy's gunnery and indeed for the *Hood* herself, which was completed with the Mk V model of the Dreyer Table and retained it to the end of her days.[97] The final variants of the Dreyer Table provided a reasonably effective fire-control system under ideal conditions but without the advanced capability of the Pollen design, and it was not until 1925 that the Navy received the helm-free gunnery promised it by the Argo Clock almost fifteen years earlier. Even then, financial constraints prevented the Admiralty Fire Control Table being fitted in any save the *Nelson* class battleships and those vessels subsequently completed or reconstructed. The *Hood* was not of course among them but, ironically, it was during the design process of her Mk V Table that the first concerted objections were raised to the Dreyer system as a whole, and the Admiralty committee formed which led to its replacement.[98]

Of what, then, did the *Hood*'s main fire-control system consist? How did it function? First came target selection, made by the captain or one of the gunnery officers and transmitted to the directors by means of an Evershed bearing indicator. The aiming process began in the aloft director, perched on the spotting top 120 feet above the waterline. The chief instruments were a pair of gyroscopically-stabilised gun sights through which the director layer and trainer acquired and held their target. As the trainer turned his handwheel, so the director traversed to follow the target regardless of the heading of the ship. Through a system of electrical circuits, each adjustment of these two gun sights actuated pointers on dials which, once aligned manually with the previous settings of bearing and elevation, provided the ship's fire-control calculator with the change of bearing and elevation of the target. Meanwhile, continual estimates of enemy speed and inclination were being transmitted via earphones to the same calculator, 140 feet below. To this data the range of the target was added by the ship's master rangefinder, a 30-foot Barr & Stroud model fitted in the armoured director atop the conning tower. As with the gun sights, the minute alterations made by the range taker in bringing the image of his target into coincidence were automatically registered on a dial which, aligned with earlier settings, provided the change of range. This equipment permitted range calculations to be issued at intervals of approximately 20 seconds, the results being plotted by a typewriter arrangement on the fire-control calculator. The armoured director was also home to a Dumaresq which delivered the rates of change for target speed and course when fed with estimates of its speed and inclination (that is, the angle of its course relative to the observer's line of sight). The resulting data was all sent electrically to the Transmitting Station, the nerve centre of the *Hood*'s fire-control system.

On the platform deck directly beneath the conning tower lay the 15in Transmitting Station, perhaps the most important single space in the ship. Lying abaft the forward magazines and encased in the same thickness of armour, it was here that a firing solution was computed for the ship's main armament. The TS was manned by the seventeen musicians of the ship's Royal Marine band under the overall command of a gunnery officer. Assisting him was the Warrant Ordnance Officer, a Chief Ordnance Artificer in the event of mechanical breakdown, and a handful of plotters, telephonists and messengers making a total crew of 28. The centrepiece of the *Hood*'s TS was the Dreyer fire-control table in its Mk V variant.[99] The Dreyer Table was essentially an enormous mechanical slide rule which worked by cross-checking theoretical data with actual observations to produce a continuous range and bearing plot; a machine that, in C.S. Forester's words, 'looked into the future yet never forgot the past'.[100] This data was extrapolated by differentials, geared adding machines churning out a constant stream of range and bearing calculations for the fire-control table. Fed with target range and bearing, estimated speed and inclination of the enemy along with own speed and course; with readings for barrel temperature, outside air temperature, barometric pressure, wind speed and direction; and with compensation for drift of shell and the rotation of the earth relative to the ship's heading, the Dreyer Table generated calculations of the rate of change of range. The key to the fire-control table was the range clock or 'integrator', known colloquially as the 'potter's wheel'. This device, heavily but imperfectly plagiarised from the Pollen Argo Clock, consisted of a ring disc revolving at a constant speed. Travelling across it were ball bearings which moved in accordance with the range of the enemy. The movement of these bearings actuated a screw to which a pencil was attached. The line thus drawn on the moving plot permitted a comparative calculation to be

[97] Ibid., pp. 315–6.
[98] Ibid., p. 312.
[99] See William Schleihauf, '*Hood*'s Fire Control System: An Overview' on www.hmshood.com.
[100] C. S. Forester, *The Ship* (Harmondsworth: Penguin, 1949; 1st pubd 1943), p. 114.

made which yielded the rate of change of range of the target. The resulting plots and data permitted the *future* range and bearing of the target to be deduced, the results being transmitted to the turrets in the form of corrections to the elevation and training of the guns. These signals, sent via electrical circuits, were immediately acted on by the gun layers and trainers, each nudging his handwheel to align pointers on the master dial before him. The order to fire therefore dispatched a projectile which, though aimed at an empty patch of sea, would hopefully reach the end of its trajectory to find it filled with the bulk of the enemy. At ranges of approximately 10,000 yards this flight would last around 15 seconds, and over a minute at the maximum effective range of 30,000 yards.

The Dreyer Table was capable of computing data not only from the two director control towers but from all four turrets simultaneously, and the following account by a young officer stationed in the armoured director of HMS *Valiant* gives some idea of the constant exchange of information upon which the system relied:

Down below in the Transmitting Station,… was a much larger Dumaresq and the rate it was showing was connected to a pencil which drew a line on the plotting paper on which the ranges of the target were being plotted as they came in. If then my rate produced a line which coincided with change of range shown by the mean of the rangefinder's plot, then my 'guesstimation' of the speed and inclination of the target must be fairly good. […] To enable me to chat back and forth to the Dreyer plot, I had a direct and personal telephone to the Midshipman who could make suggestions to me, guiding my guesstimations from what he deduced from his plot. I was seated immediately alongside the 15in Control Officer, so I could ask his opinion of the inclination and speed and if, from his fall of shot, it seemed that my rate was not working right, he could quickly tell me so.[101]

But, for all its vast complexity, the Dreyer system suffered from several major flaws which made it rather less than the sum of its parts. In relying on estimates of rate of change of range derived from manually-operated as against automatic instrumentation, the Dreyer Table introduced an element of human error into the results of its calculations which severely compromised its accuracy, particularly over longer ranges. Not only that, but the absence of the gyroscopic stabilisation which would have allowed the Dreyer Table to produce a consistent plot of the relative rate of change of range also deprived it of the ability to generate accurate data when the ship was firing under helm. The Dreyer system was incapable of making good these deficiencies and it was the 1920s before the infinitely variable speed drive and automatic range plotting of the Pollen Argo Clock at last gave the Navy a truly effective system of directed firing. However, these developments came too late for the *Hood*, which for reasons unexplained was left to struggle on with her inadequate Mk V calculator. The 1935 edition of *Progress in Naval Gunnery* reported that 'A method has been evolved in *Hood* by which the rate [of change of range] is applied automatically to the transmitting clock', but this could hardly compensate for the limitations described above.[102] This regrettable state of affairs was not lost on Lt-Cdr Joseph H.

Wellings, the U.S. Navy's official observer in the *Hood* over the winter of 1940–1:

I remember clearly my surprise, as I inspected the *Hood*'s Gunnery Department on December 17, 1940, when I saw the antiquated equipment in the plotting room—heart and brains of the main battery fire control system! In my opinion, the range keepers, for example, were not as modern by far as were those in the battleship *Florida* (when I was a plotting room officer in 1928). Our battleships *West Virginia* and *Colorado* had far superior plotting room equipment.[103]

The intricacies of all this were of course well beyond the ordinary matelot. OD Jon Pertwee's action station in 1940–1 appears to have been in the High-Angle Control Position on the platform deck. His description of his duty runs as follows:

My battle station was down in the bowels of the ship winding a small wheel. Somehow with the aid of other wheel-winders our mutual endeavour enabled *Hood*'s gunnery to reach a greater state of accuracy.[104]

But however detached from its permutations, no crewman could abstract himself from the reality of naval gunfire. As each gun was made ready the closing of an interceptor switch caused a lamp to be ignited on panels in the aloft and armoured directors. Once all were lit the director layer would place his hands on the master pistol grip, the target still firm in his sights. It was a moment of high excitement, even for a convinced sceptic of naval gunnery like Admiral Sir Andrew Cunningham:

Never in the whole of my life have I experienced a more thrilling moment than when I heard a calm voice from the director tower—'Director layer sees the target'; sure sign that the guns were ready and that his finger was itching on the trigger.[105]

Inside the director layer's telescope was a gyroscopically-stabilised prism which kept the viewer's eye on the target irrespective of the motion of the ship. The gyro also controlled an electrical gun-firing circuit which, though the layer pulled the trigger, did not close until the ship was on an even keel. Finally the moment came. The sound of the fire gong announced the pulling of the trigger and seconds later the combined efforts of 400 men bore fruit in a convulsion of fire, sound and smoke.

The impact of full-calibre firing defies accurate description. Boy Signalman Reg Bragg, who joined the ship in 1922, believed the end of the world had come when 'A' turret first opened up. The turret crew were largely spared the effects of noise and blast but others would be momentarily lifted from the deck and those caught in the open had their faces slapped as if by a wet cloth. The Rev. Edgar Rea, ship's chaplain between 1936 and 1938, has this impression of what Wilfred Owen called 'the monstrous anger of the guns':

Always they fascinated me, though at first they terrified me. There was the tremendous bang and burst of fire, followed by a shudder from stem to stern and the uncomfortable sensation of having been struck in the midriff with a heavy pillow. Soon, however, I got over the terror and was able to

[101] Cited in Coward, *Battleship at War*, pp. 40–1.
[102] *Progress in Naval Gunnery, 1935* (restricted circulation, Admiralty, 1936), p. 100.
[103] NWC, Wellings, *Reminiscences*, p. 73.
[104] Pertwee, *Moon Boots and Dinner Suits*, p. 149.
[105] Cunningham, *A Sailor's Odyssey*, p. 332, referring to the Battle of Cape Matapan.

Above: An important view showing the state of *Hood*'s secondary armament in the latter half of 1938. 'Sammy', the Mk V pom-pom mounting installed on the starboard side of the boat deck, is about to go into action. Forward of it is the recuperator cylinder of one of the 4in Mk V High-Angle mountings fitted in place of the boat-deck 5.5in guns at Malta that summer; just aft is one of a second pair installed over the 5.5in batteries in the autumn of 1937. These were no more than temporary measures until the twin 4in Mk XIX mountings could be fitted the following year. The bell-shaped structure with its lid propped open in the foreground is one of the emergency signal tubes, part of a system that allowed signals to be hoisted from a station on the main deck in the event of the flag-deck crews being wiped out. Visible between this and the pom-pom is one of the two expansion joints fitted athwart the boat deck to allow for the flexing of the hull in a head sea. The large structure on the right is one of the 5.5in director towers.
HMS Hood Association/Percival Collection

A quadruple 0.5in machine-gun mounting of a type not dissimilar to those fitted in *Hood*, *c.*1940. Each water-cooled barrel was fed by its own ammunition drum.

the UP (Unrotated or Unrifled Projectile) launcher.[143] The quirks of this device and the trials of using it are discussed elsewhere; suffice to add that ready-use projectile stowage for this weapon brought the number of ammunition lockers ranged on the *Hood*'s boat deck to over 40.[144]

The *Hood*'s final secondary armament was therefore something of a hotchpotch, greatly improved from her pre-war outfit but still inadequate for the tasks she was likely to encounter. The installation of her Type 279M air-warning radar seems to have been completed before she left Rosyth in pursuit of the *Scharnhorst* and *Gneisenau* on 18 March 1941 but may never have become fully operational. It was no doubt felt that the long-awaited reconstruction which would overhaul all her fittings could not be delayed much longer. But time had run out for HMS *Hood*. As Lt-Cdr Eller noted in a different context, she couldn't stick it out, couldn't last long enough to win her second chance.

Belting 2-pounder pom-pom ammunition in the port battery, *c.*1935.
HMS Hood Association/Willis Collection

[143] Roskill, *Churchill and the Admirals*, pp. 295–6.
[144] Ch. 8, p. 205.

3 Glory Ship

In what distant deeps or skies
Burnt the fire of thine eyes?

O N 29 MARCH 1920 the *Hood* commissioned to full complement at Rosyth in the Firth of Forth. That a high proportion of her 1,150 officers and men should have come from the battlecruiser *Lion* was no accident. Under Vice-Admiral Sir David Beatty the *Lion* had become the most famous ship in the Royal Navy, the bloodied veteran of Heligoland Bight, the Dogger Bank and Jutland. Now that she was passing into the reserve there could be no more fitting vessel to receive her mantle than the *Hood*, the promised flagship of the post-war Navy. Before the year was out the *Hood* had assumed that mantle in full and in doing so had traced the pattern of her next twenty years. As *Lion* had been a great ship of war *Hood* was to prove herself the great vessel of peace.

On 15 May the *Hood* weighed anchor at Rosyth and steamed south for the first time. Pausing in Cawsand Bay to hoist the flag of Rear-Admiral Sir Roger Keyes, the hero of Zeebrugge, she made her way up Plymouth Sound to her home port for the next decade. No sooner had the *Hood* reached Devonport than she was assigned the first in a long succession of diplomatic missions on which her peacetime reputation would be built. The Bolshevik revolution in November 1917 had made Allied intervention first in Russia and then the Baltic essential for strategic, commercial and humanitarian reasons. Where the Royal Navy was concerned this entailed landings at Murmansk, Archangel and elsewhere on Russian soil along with a significant presence in the Baltic from 1918, operations which stretched its resources and tested its resolve to the limit. Despite the effort expended by Britain and her allies, by 1920 the Soviets had gained the upper hand against the White Russians and the forces of intervention. As the outcome of the Russian Civil War became apparent the policy of the British government became one of preserving the sovereignty of the Baltic States and maintaining its interests and presence in that region. To this end, the Admiralty ordered Keyes to take the *Hood*, the battlecruiser *Tiger* and nine destroyers into the Baltic to alert the Soviet fleet at Kronstadt of the consequences of any offensive activity that summer. In the event, the easing of tensions with the Soviets and ongoing negotiations with her neighbours restricted the Battle Cruiser Squadron to the agreeable cruise of Scandinavia which had been planned as cover for the operation.

In retrospect, the Scandinavian cruise seems very much the beginning of a new era of naval diplomacy which, while it lasted, found no greater emissary than HMS *Hood*, the velvet fist of British sea power. Nearing Denmark on the evening of 31 May Capt. Wilfred Tomkinson held a memorial service on the *Hood*'s quarterdeck for the dead of Jutland over whose graves they were then passing. It was four years since an earlier generation of battlecruisers had met disaster under German gunfire. But the guns were still now and Keyes' squadron was given

a rapturous welcome in Scandinavia. Gunner 'Windy' Breeze, Royal Marine Artillery (1920–2), has this memoir of it:

> We were the first British ships to visit these countries after the war and what a welcome we got. The first stop was Christiania (now Oslo), up the fiord... with many near stops to negotiate the bends, and finally into a wide open basin with the town built all round—a most splendid sight, the land of the midnight sun. We had many ceremonial guards of honour etc. King Haakon and Queen Maud came aboard; the Queen was a sister of our King George V. Free parties ashore and entertainment aboard—one whole round of festivities. Next on to Kalmar for the visit to Stockholm: we had to anchor as only the destroyers could get to Stockholm, and we went by train with a wood-fired engine with plenty of stops for fuel. Now on to Copenhagen for the final visit. Tivoli Gardens was the highlight of this visit with all the free parties and entertainment, and here we had thousands of visitors coming aboard, including the King and Queen of Sweden and the King of Denmark. [...] The quarter-deck was always rigged for dancing with the awning spread and the Marine band playing.[1]

The *Hood*'s midshipmen had a field day. Lt-Cdr Douglas Fairbairn (1920):

> All that evening the ship was surrounded by the youth and beauty of Oslo in motor-boats and canoes, while big sailing yachts with parties on board passed close by. The snotties had the time of their lives fishing for 'mermaids' out of the stern ports: by means of chocolates balanced on the blades of oars they lured the fair Norwegian damsels in their canoes close to the ship, and made them promise to come on board and dance after dinner. The British Consul had rashly said that he would be able to provide at short notice at least fifty Norwegian ladies who could dance. We kept him at his word, and within a few hours of our arrival they and the 'mermaids' were dancing on our quarterdeck.[2]

Beautiful as the landscape and people were, there was little doubt that the *Hood* was making an equally lasting impression on all who saw her. Fairbairn describes the passage up Oslofjorden:

> A few miles farther on comes the narrowest part, a strait nearly ten miles long and but half a mile wide, with 600 feet of water under the ship's bottom. With the wooded shore slipping past on either side, the *Hood* pursued her stately way through this narrow channel. At each little village we passed were crowds of cheering Norwegians, some of whom even swam out towards the ship. At every white flagstaff among the trees the Norwegian flag was

---

[1] HMS *Hood* Association archives.
[2] Fairbairn, *The Narrative of a Naval Nobody*, pp. 234–5.

flying, and dipped in salute to us as we went by: this continued for a whole hour. It was a wonderful welcome, and to those ashore the mighty *Hood*, the largest warship in the world, winding her way through those land-locked waters must have been a magnificent sight.[3]

As a visible symbol of a nation's power the *Hood* can scarcely ever have been equalled.

For the Navy the *Hood*'s role as its flagbearer was matched only by her reputation as the premier sporting ship in the fleet and it was for this that many of her men would remember her. The view is summarised by a member of the 1933–6 commission:

> What a ship! Efficient. Fast. Happy. Beautiful lines. Good at sport. Football. Running… Good at everything. COCK OF THE FLEET![4]

Already on her maiden voyage south in May 1920 the foundations were being laid for a great athletic tradition, men being selected to represent the ship in each of the main sports competed for in the Navy. The emphasis on sport was one of the key elements of the Royal Navy between the wars, though ironically it was a product not of peace but of war. During its vigil at Scapa Flow the Grand Fleet had turned to organised sporting activity as one of the few outlets for its men in their long confinement. After the war a pinched economy, reduced opportunities for training and the increasing acceptance of the need for physical activity to maintain health and morale led to organised sport being placed on a permanent footing for the benefit of all ranks and rates.[5] In March 1920 the Royal Navy and Royal Marines Sports Control Board was formed as an adjunct of the Admiralty's Physical Training and Sports Branch to provide financial and other support, and with this sport in the Navy never looked back. A year later the *Hood* received her first Physical and Recreational Training Officer. For the Navy, par-

ticularly after the Invergordon Mutiny of 1931, it was a case of *Mens sana in corpore sano* and sporting activity was pursued with increasing vigour as the 1930s unfolded.

The basis of shipboard sport was the inter-part competition, the organisation of games by Division, Watch, Branch or Department, in *Hood*'s case usually seamen, Marines, stokers, artificers and artisans, Supply and Communications ratings. These teams competed in several sports and from them were drawn the sides that represented the ship in fleet events. The organisation of each sport at both inter-part and fleet level was entrusted to an officer and on his zeal and the morale of his men depended the ship's chances of victory. Among the most popular was football, played both in organised competitions ashore and as a gesture of goodwill at home and abroad. During the coal and rail strikes of 1921 the *Hood*'s seamen had eased tensions with rioting miners at Cowdenbeath near Edinburgh by challenging them to a game.[6] The result of the match is not on record but there were certainly some upsets during the *Hood*'s long sporting career. At Vancouver in 1924 her team was defeated by the Royal Canadian Mounted Police by an undisclosed margin. However, the Battle Cruiser Squadron went down only 7–2 to Brazil's national side in 1922 and Santos, Pelé's future team, they beat 2–1…[7] By the 1930s the *Hood* was able to field a dozen sides for inter-part football from which the ship's team was selected for the King's Cup, the fleet trophy competed for each year. Another important sport was cross-country running in which ships provided teams of 30 men for the Arbuthnot Trophy, known as 'The Bronze Man'. As Rory O'Conor, Commander of the *Hood* from 1933–6 and the driving force behind her sporting success, noted,

> Running is a healthy exercise possessing the great advantages of needing no special pitch and of being unaffected by bad weather. It is not everyone's idea of fun, but it has an ever-increasing number of adherents.[8]

Hood glides into Devonport wearing the flag of Rear-Admiral Sir Roger Keyes, c.1920. The lattice structure abaft the after superstructure appears to have been a prototype W/T set.
Bibliothek für Zeitgeschichte, Stuttgart

[3] Ibid., pp. 233–4.
[4] HMS *Hood* Association, Newssheet No. 2 (c.1975).
[5] On this see the essays and debates in *Naval Review*, 7 & 8 (1919 & 1920).
[6] Coles & Briggs, *Flagship* Hood, p. 19.
[7] Brazilian details from Connor, *To Rio and Back*, p. 19.
[8] RBS, pp. 149–50.

There was certainly no shortage of adherents in the *Hood* which won the Arbuthnot Trophy three years running between 1933 and 1935. However, as O'Conor indicated, cross-country running was something of a trial and with this twin brothers Fred and Frank Coombs (1935–8) would certainly have agreed. It is the autumn of 1935:

> …To make a change, we took the opportunity to get ashore by taking part in a cross-country running race. It was a mistake to be regretted for a long time. All the runners were landed on Weymouth Pier to wait the start and, unfortunately, found a nice fresh water tap which was nectar compared with the flat, stale water aboard, so took in a bladder full which was a mistake as a toilet could not be found before the start. After a lot of milling and pushing about 150 of us set off… but we soon became separated. Frank thinking that Fred was up in front increased his pace and Fred thinking that Frank was behind slowed down and we never did meet up till it was too late… Frank, seeing that he had caught up with the… well known figure of Leading Steward Barnes, the Navy runner, in front, decided that if he stuck near them there was more chance of stopping to relieve himself when the country bit was reached. Unfortunately that bit was never

reached and he was still suffering from the effects of a bladder full of beautiful tap water when the finishing line was reached. Also, unfortunately, seeing a sign for toilets he was encouraged to make a sprint for them and in doing so passed a Leading Seaman, Potts, a promotion-seeking experienced runner who took offence at being pushed into 5th place by a common Boy and was heard to be casting parental doubts on a crafty Boy… Frank, on returning aboard, attended the Sick Bay where he was found to have a temperature and was kept in. On being visited by the Doctor he was told that he had strained his stomach muscles and was confined to bed for a few days.[9]

Running was one of the activities in which officers competed alongside the men but others like cricket, golf, squash and polo remained very much the preserve of the wardroom. However, rugby was increasingly played by ratings of the Devonport Division after the Great War, many of whom no doubt saw it as the perfect opportunity to get some of their own back on officers. In this they were not alone. Mid. Ross Warden (1940–1) recalls a physical match between the *Hood*'s wardroom and gunroom officers in the autumn of 1940:

> This was a golden opportunity to settle any outstanding scores. Anything goes was our motto, but alas we found our senior officers more than able to return elbows, knees and (when the referee was not looking) the occasional fist. Twice our Commander, who was referee, threatened to call a halt. However, there were no fatalities, and a good time was had by all.[10]

The Navy had a great tradition in rugby and in 1933 there were no fewer than 50 living members of the Royal Navy and Royal Marines Rugby Union with international caps, among them W.J.A. Davies, Constructor Commander in the *Hood* in 1937–8 and still regarded as one of the game's finest players.

The other sport offering the chance of beating hell out of an officer was of course boxing. AB Fred Copeman, Invergordon mutineer and champion pugilist:

> Mind you, I was a bit of a boxer and a footballer. I was all sport. And I was well known in the Navy, you see, especially in [the championships]. And I was lucky because in the… championships I always met a big fat commander. And there's nothing better than the thrill of thumping an officer. And I used to thump them good and proper. I really had a good one there. I used to take a pasting, you know. But once I got that on they didn't last. And they always used to wait for old Fred. 'Right. Up we go!'[11]

But it wasn't one-way traffic by any means. Cdr (G) E.H.G. 'Tiny' Gregson, lost in the *Hood* in May 1941, won consecutive heavyweight boxing titles between 1925 and at least 1931. Regrettably, this was another sport in which the Coombs twins came unstuck. Malta in the spring of 1937:

> Between us we brought the crowd to its feet when it was Fred's turn to go in the ring. The fights were being staged in the Corradino Canteen in Malta, which was packed with the normal complement of sailors on shore for their

Below: Hood's athletes pose at Malta in the winter of 1938–9 with the Arbuthnot Trophy for cross-country running, probably the last major sporting competition she ever won. One of the ship's liferings hangs from a length of ventilation trunking beside 'X' turret. Capt. Harold Walker in the centre.
Mr John Haynes

Right: The captain of Hood's victorious 1926 Battle Cruiser Squadron Cup football team poses with Capt. Harold Reinold on his left and Rear-Admiral Cyril Fuller on his right. They are on the starboard side of the Night defence control station, its viewing slits closed off with louvre shutters.
HMS Hood Association/Reinold Collection

[9] IWM, 91/7/1, p. 46.
[10] Warden, 'Memories of the Battle Cruiser H.M.S. "Hood"', p. 84.
[11] IWM/SA, no. 794, reel 12. Copeman did not serve in *Hood*.

usual few pints… and a lot of boxing enthusiasts ashore to see the fights. At that time Service boxing was pure amateur with no fancy boots or gum shields. The only difference being that the boy from the red corner tied a red sash round his waist and the other wore green. Other than that it was navy blue socks and white blancoed gym slippers below the ordinary white sports shorts and vest up top. There was no need for a boxer's hair cut as our instructors and the ship's barber made sure that we still had the Boys' hair cut of short back and sides which could mean nearly bald. As in amateur boxing, no shouting or cheering was allowed when the fight was taking place, this being reserved for in between round breaks. There was a fair buzz went up when the difference was seen between the two boys' sizes. Most of the support was for Fred as the underdog is always the favourite but, as usual in boxing, a 'good big 'un' will always beat a 'good little 'un'. After the success of his first fight in going in under a bigger lad's guard he had been advised to do the same and was getting away with it and we thought he was ahead on points in the first round. Whether his opponent from the battleship *Barham* had used his first round to practise in was not known but half-way through the second round… saw Fred still keeping out of his way with long left jabs and, occasionally catching his opponent with what we colloquially described as 'hitting him in the shitlocker' and getting away with it. He did it once too often and, as he went down and under with his right the other lad went up and over with his short left timed nicely to catch Fred's chin going down as his left came up and sitting Fred on his backside. The whole hall was deathly silent as Fred sat there trying to move his head to find out if it was still on his neck. At the back [I] broke the spell by shouting 'Gerrup, Fred!'… Fred was not listening but all the rest heard it and proved that pathos is next door to humour by breaking out into uncontrolled laughter, leaving just Fred and [I] with tears in [our] eyes. That finished the twins' boxing career as hard hitters. We found that there was always someone who could hit harder but it stood us in good stead and we proved that there was more in our make-up than the ability to get into trouble.[12]

Like rugby and football, boxing was one of the few organised sports to survive the onset of war in 1939. On the evening of 29 July 1940 a match took place in the *Ark Royal* at Gibraltar with *Hood's* men in the green corner and their hosts in the red. The *Hood* won by six bouts to four.

Other sports included tug-of-war, fencing, shooting, field hockey, tennis and water polo. The latter enjoyed considerable popularity and games are recorded against the battleship USS *Maryland* at Gibraltar in March 1922, against the Mayor of Hartlepool's XI in September 1932, and against a Yugoslav naval side at Split five years later which swam out to the ship, thrashed the *Hood's* team and then swam back to shore after tea on the messdecks.[13] Then there was bayonets, a form of fencing in which the *Hood* excelled under O'Conor, her men carrying off the Home Fleet's Palmer Trophy between 1934 and 1936. However, the blue ribband events were the sailing and particularly the pulling regattas. On these much of the ship's energies were expended as spring turned into summer.

From the moment of her commissioning in March 1920 rowing was a sport in which the *Hood* had a head start on the competition. Among the men bequeathed her from *Lion* was the cutter crew which had triumphed in the inaugural challenge for the Rodman Cup in 1919. Needless to say, they had little difficulty in repeating the performance at Portland that autumn, or in winning the Battle Cruiser Regatta at Lamlash on the Isle of Arran in August. Enormous prestige was attached to the Silver Coquerelle, the trophy which awaited the victor in the fleet pulling regatta in June each year. Rory O'Conor, Commander of the *Hood* between 1933–6, explains why:

The Pulling Regatta is the principal sporting event in the Fleet, and for good reason. Eleven men only can represent their ship at football, and at cross-country running the largest team is thirty, but in a big-ship Regatta a team of nearly three hundred officers and men goes forth in the boats to do battle for their ship, and it is no wonder therefore that the Cock is the most highly prized of

Top: Boys boxing in an improvised ring on the forecastle, c.1935.
HMS Hood Association/Willis Collection

Above: Hood's marksmen pose with their trophies and weapons on the quarterdeck at Portsmouth, c.1935. With them is Capt. F.T.B. Tower, Cdr Rory O'Conor and Judy, O'Conor's West Highland terrier. Notice the brass tompions with the ship's chough emblem decorating the muzzles of 'Y' turret.
HMS Hood Association/Clark Collection

---

[12] IWM, 91/7/1, p. 59.
[13] Ibid., p. 70.

trophies; it is the reward of arduous training and of massed effort on a grand scale. […] There is nothing in this world to surpass the heartfelt satisfaction and delight of a ship's company when the Cock comes on board—it is a moment worth living for and worth working for.[14]

Victory, as O'Conor demonstrated in 1935, required an enormous organisation: a large committee chaired by the Commander; an officer in charge of each of the twenty boats; picked racing coxswains to drive the men to the limit; a stockpile of oars, and above all weeks of arduous training. Fred and Frank Coombs were among O'Conor's oarsmen:

> At that time… our only worry was that we had been caught up in the hard work of training to meet the needs of the Boys' cutters' crew. We did not mind the hard work of going out in a cutter at varied times during working hours,… but [having to spend] at least one hour of each day, in our own time,… pulling on our length of oar handle to raise the weight was sheer unadulterated hard work, particularly when the Instructor was walking round us giving us the occasional clip across the shoulders with a short length of knotted rope or stonnicky as it was called to encourage us. […] After what seemed hour upon hour of boat pulling in practice and on the exercise frame came the honour of being named as bowmen in the Second Boys' Cutter's crew… Almost every single hour of daylight was spent by some crew of the different divisions out in a pulling boat, practising and practising for the big day which seemed never to come.[15]

The gunroom also had its part to play. Vice-Admiral Sir Louis Le Bailly recalls the regatta campaign of 1933:

> Admiral James and Captain Binney… set out to imbue the ship's company with the idea that the *Hood* should win the forthcoming fleet regatta. The gunroom soon discovered that we had a vital role to play in this. Traditionally the fleet gunrooms raced gigs for the Battenberg Trophy the day before the main regatta. A win by *Hood*'s gunroom would be taken as a good augury for the following day. Failure however would be regarded as a bad omen against the ship becoming Cock of the Fleet. Then short and lean I was, I suppose, the obvious choice for coxswain. But for those who were to undertake the hard work we gathered a formidable crew; Beckwith as stroke, Thurstan, Wainwright, Charles, MacFarlan and Gray. […] But we were young and enthusiastic and how we trained. The chaplain, the Rev J C Waters, himself a notable oarsman was in charge and the new sub, Aylwin, urbane and highly civilised, also took a hand. Even the messman's food improved (subsidised by the wardroom I heard many years later). We practised at dawn and dusk and some afternoons too. I found my duties involved taking charge of the methylated spirit for blistered hands and bottoms. Gig's thwarts, however well polished, were not far removed from sandpaper.[16]

Both attempts were rewarded with victory. Le Bailly:

> *Hood*'s gunroom won the Battenberg Trophy: and next day

we raced again and won again. Much money changed hands as *Hood* became Cock of the Fleet. That evening Captain Binney sent down a case of champagne to the gunroom. Later I have a faint recollection of an invading posse of midshipmen from one of the battleships carrying me forcibly to our wardroom and casting me through the door, when I knew no more. The next morning I awoke with the first in a lifetime of hangovers, recovering sufficiently to go over with the rest of the crews to HMS *Nelson* to receive our trophies from the great John Kelly himself.

Fred Coombs:

> When [the day finally came] it was soon over but the taste of success and jubilations as we… proclaimed to the whole Fleet that the Mighty *Hood* was now Cock of the Fleet was to be tasted for a long time.[17]

Equally, to surrender the Cock was the greatest of disasters. On 19 October 1921 the *Hood* lost the Battle Cruiser Cock to *Repulse* at Scapa Flow. Two days later it was handed over in a funereal atmosphere, the Marine band leading a procession consisting of the ship's goat mascot Bill and a party of midshipmen bearing the trophy, all to the strains of Chopin's *Death March*. However, once Capt. Dudley Pound had received the Cock on behalf of the *Repulse* he was piped over the side to the Squadron's own air, *The Battle-Cruisers*.[18]

Also very popular were the sailing regattas though not as much prestige attached to these as to their pulling equivalents. They were Francis Pridham's reigning passion during his tenure as captain of the *Hood* in 1936–8. His description of a race at Gibraltar in March 1938 reveals the skill, hazards and excitement which attended these occasions:

> During an assembly of the Home and Mediterranean Fleets at Gibraltar for a 'Stand Easy', the *Hood* created a record by taking all three places in the Gibraltar Cup Race, an annual event. The race was sailed in a full gale, and was full also of excitement, since boats were being dismasted and were capsizing all round the nine-mile course. At one time my White Galley was the only boat of eighty-two competitors not reefed down. I had faith in my fully trained crew and good rigging. But my luck was out. I had taken an extra hand in the boat as 'live ballast', much needed until the gale eased. This otherwise excellent man, being strange to racing with me, failed to hold himself tight up the windward when we were hit by a heavy squall. He fell down to leeward causing the boat to heel over and ship water nearly up to her thwarts. At that time we were well in the lead, but now fell behind while we bailed out for dear life and got going again, steadily catching up all those boats which had passed us, except two. At the finish, Orr-Ewing was first in a cutter, Admiral Cunningham was second in his galley and I was third in my White Galley. A fine enough performance, but oh! if only I had not got half swamped and had held on to my lead, it would have been even better. I had been keen to beat the Admiral, a renowned boat-sailer, and was within an ace of doing so.[19]

The sailing regattas had a particular hold on those who prized

[14] *RBS*, p. 141.
[15] IWM, 91/7/1, p. 44.
[16] Le Bailly, *The Man Around the Engine*, p. 26. Mids. Richard Beckwith (1933–4?), R.P. Thurstan (1933–4?), R.C.P. Wainwright (1933–4?), Paymaster Mid. J. Charles (1932–3?), Mids. T.J. MacFarlan (1932–4?), A. Gray (1932–4?) and Sub-Lt C.K.S. Aylwin (1933–4?).
[17] IWM, 91/7/1, p. 44.
[18] NMM, Elkins/1, Journal, 21 October 1921.
[19] Pridham, *Memoirs*, II, p. 162. Cdr David Orr-Ewing, Executive Officer of the *Hood*, 1936–9.

Left: A water polo match in the Mediterranean in the late 1930s. Among the boats at the starboard boom are a whaler and one of the ship's steam pinnaces with her crew.
HMS Hood Association/Percival Collection

Left: Bayonet practice on the quarterdeck, *c.*1935. The Marine detachment was always represented in the *Hood*'s bayonet teams. Notice the decorative brass plaque on the screen door.
HMS Hood Association/Willis Collection

Above: The conclusion of a race in the 1934 Home Fleet Regatta, during which *Hood* lost the Cock to *Nelson*, seen opposite.
HMS Hood Association/Willis Collection

Left: Capt. Reinold poses with one of his boat crews in the *Hood*'s successful challenge for the title of 'Cock of the Fleet' in 1926, the first of three consecutive victories in the Atlantic Fleet Regatta. The Silver Coquerelle sits before him. The commander to his left is presumably Arthur J. Power, *Hood*'s Executive Officer from 1925–7 and later a distinguished admiral. Behind them is Port 4in Mk V High-Angle gun.
HMS Hood Association/Reinold Collection

The Chuffiosoarus, *Hood*'s mascot for the 1935 Regatta campaign. The name is a pun on 'chough' and 'oar'. The diminutive figure below is George, spirit of the *Hood*'s sporting accomplishments. These two caricatures show the unmistakable influence of Cdr Rory O'Conor.
Mrs Nixie Taverner

[20] Arnold-Forster, *The Ways of the Navy*, pp. 116–7.
[21] Dreyer, *The Sea Heritage*, p. 276.
[22] *RBS*, p. 149.
[23] *The Chough*, April 1936, p. 25.
[24] See ch. 6, pp. 163–4.

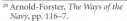

'Not Eleven—Eleven Hundred.' Spectators from the *Hood* complete with cheerleader and banner before a football match against the *Barham*, c.1938.
HMS Hood Association/Clark Collection

shiphandling as the truest test of seamanship and who felt a profound nostalgia for the lore of sail just as it was disappearing from the life of the Navy. Rear-Admiral D. Arnold-Forster, writing in about 1930, captures the sentiment perfectly:

In a really stiff freshening breeze a boat-sailer with confidence in himself and his crew will 'carry on' to the utmost limit before shortening sail, despite the solid water which is almost lapping over the lee side. With an eye glued on the 'luff' of the sails, the sheets firmly tended by the most experienced men of his crew, and eased slightly to the heavier puffs, he hangs on to the straining tiller, and steers so as to ride at an easy angle over any particularly nasty wave that would overwhelm the boat if taken direct. The wind often drops to a gentle breeze before the end of the race, and the midshipman of a boat may see their hated rival, whom they have outsailed fairly and squarely, creeping up with a local slant of wind. Nothing could be more exasperating. Every eye in the boat scans the surface of the sea for ripples marking the approach of a puff of wind. The sheets are trimmed and everything done to make the most of every breath: the midshipman whistles softly to encourage the wind to come his way, whilst the foremast hands scratch the mast and stick knives into it— an old sea superstition. It is not unusual to see two rival ships' cutters drifting down between the columns of ships towards the finishing line, each with twelve clasp-knives stuck like hedgehogs' quills in their masts![20]

However, there were many who believed that athletic excellence was being bought at the expense of fighting efficiency. One of them was Rear-Admiral Frederic Dreyer who flew his flag in *Hood* from 1927–9:

We carried out excellent and instructive practices by day and night, in which we did very well. But we would have done even better if there had been *competition* not merely in each Fleet but for the whole Navy. It seemed to me so odd to say, 'Yes, we will have a terrific competition in our Bisley rifle meetings, but we will not have all-Navy competition for guns of larger calibres as were carried out

with great advantage before the First World War.' The Royal Artillery were better advised—they went on with their annual competition firings with coast-defence guns.[21]

It should be noted that Dreyer's tenure coincided with a hat trick of Cock and Rodman Cup victories for the *Hood*'s oarsmen between 1926 and 1928. Rory O'Conor, as can be imagined, took quite a different view in *Running a Big Ship*, the manual on ship husbandry he produced in 1937:

It is easy to decry as pot-hunting the efforts of the enthusiastic to lead their ship to victory in sporting events, but those who say these things are often the ones who lack the spirit of leadership, or the ability to organise, and the will to carry things through. It is in many cases a facile excuse for slackness or indifference. Opportunities to prove ability to lead are too few in times of peace for any to be neglected. Can there be any reasonable person who would sooner be in a dull and apathetic ship as far as sport goes, as compared with being in one who is always keen and spirited? A good ship is one who is always 'there or thereabouts' in the achievement of anything to which she puts her hand. There is no substitute for going all out for your ship whether in work or in play, unless, of course, you are prepared to toddle complacently towards your pension.[22]

More impressive even than his results was the enormous spirit O'Conor was able to instil in his ship's company. No stone was left unturned. The embodiment of this spirit was 'George', a caricature in singlet and shorts who made his first appearance in the run-up to the 1935 Regatta. Here he is a year later in his footballing persona:

GEORGE

George is the spirit of the *Hood*. Everyone in the ship carries a little bit of him and therefore he is only able to go full steam ahead when all the *Hood*s are present in support. Only eleven men can play for us on the field (not counting the Referee), but eleven hundred can support them! **'Not Eleven—Eleven Hundred'** is the *Hood*'s motto, and when all hands are manning the touchline, George will be there too.[23]

O'Conor's first campaign for the King's Cup in the autumn of 1933 was accompanied by a chough mascot on a pole, borne at all matches. Ties were produced in the ship's colours for officers to wear ashore, green with the chough emblem. To this O'Conor added preferential treatment for his players, the *Hood*'s football team being assigned a separate mess with specially designed kit lockers. By the time it was all over George had been transmogrified into a taxidermal chough in a glass case, taking his place in a Commander's lobby awash with trophies. For all this, it is clear that by the late 1930s sport had done its work in healing the wounds of Invergordon and as war clouds gathered far greater emphasis was needed on fighting efficiency. O'Conor's prescriptions for sporting victory would die with him in the bitter waters of the Mediterranean but the spirit which infused them lived on.[24]

Operational demands caused severe disruption to the Navy's sporting calendar as the 1930s wore on, though the mantle of victory was one the *Hood* shrugged off only reluc-

tantly. Patrol duty off Spain prevented her competing for the Cock at Alexandria in 1938 but the record of trophies accumulated during her career outshines that of any other ship. Between 1920 and 1938, the last full year of competition, the *Hood* won the King's Cup once, the Rodman Cup at least four times, the Arbuthnot Trophy on at least four occasions and was Cock of the Fleet on no less than five. During the 1933–6 commission she won virtually every competition in the Home Fleet at least once. This success engendered enormous pride in her ship's company. AB Len Williams (1936–41):

> She was probably the best loved ship in the service, and I, her latest, and very humble torpedoman, was very proud to be of her company.[25]

However, as the premier ship in the fleet the *Hood* had always been given a more than even chance of succeeding in anything she set herself to. As Pridham recalled when assuming command in 1936,

> I well remembered how Portsmouth had been cleared of all the best runners, boxers and footballers in order that the *Hood* should excel in any sports.[26]

But favoured she was from the very beginning. In November 1920 the *Hood*'s Marine detachment was called on to supply the guard of honour at the burial of the Unknown Warrior in Westminster Abbey on Armistice Day, the men lining the Mall with bayonets fixed as the body passed on its way. As can be imagined, this did not go down well with the rest of the battlefleet which looked on the *Hood* as the only vessel in its ranks to have escaped service in the Great War. A few pints in the canteen ashore and certain men would be passing loud opinions on which was the best or worst ship in the fleet as the liberty boats cleared the jetty. Cdr Neville Cambell was a cadet in *Hood* in the 1920s:

> When I was returning in a launch at Cromarty, an egg was thrown and burst at my feet. Then a voice yelled from a nearby ship: 'Yah! And what did the Mighty *'ood* do in the bloody war?'[27]

Frequent brawls reflect a degree of resentment and no doubt the swagger of men who believed their ship to be a cut above any in the Navy. As AB Bob Tilburn (1938–41) put it,

> The majority of people who joined the *Hood* believed they were slightly above average because it was the flagship of the fleet.[28]

However, much of this rivalry was essentially good-humoured in nature, the result of high spirits, a release of tension and the competitiveness that always existed between ships of different home ports. After months of arduous wartime service *Hood* and *Rodney* viewed each other as 'chummy ships' but this did not prevent a good measure of ribaldry between the crews at Scapa Flow, and not just because the one was manned from Portsmouth and the other from Devonport. Over the winter of 1940–1 a rating in the *Rodney* was court-martialled for committing an enormity with a sheep, an event which naturally

Above: Hood and *Admiral Graf Spee* about to meet on the football field at Tangier in September 1938. *Hood*'s team colours consisted of green shirts and white shorts; they won 4–1.
HMS Hood Association/Clark Collection

Left: A team of stoker dart players triumphant at Malta, 1938. Darts was a popular messdeck activity and keenly contested in inter-part competition.
HMS Hood Association/Clark Collection

persuaded the crew of the *Hood* that, *faute de mieux*, his shipmates all indulged the same proclivity on the windswept braes of Orkney. OD Jon Pertwee (1940–1):

> That night in the company of a phalanx of boozed-up *Hood* shipmates, I was weaving down the jetty prior to boarding our liberty boats, when we spied fifty or sixty liberty men off the *Rodney*, waiting to be picked up by their boats. 'Let's see if the sheep-loving bastards can swim,' cried a primed torpedo-man. With unanimous agreement we linked arms and advancing slowly, systematically swept the poor unfortunate men straight off the end of the jetty into the sea. Inevitably a few of us up front went in the 'oggin' with them, as the pushers at the back couldn't differentiate in the dark between *Rodney*'s crew and ours and didn't know when to stop. The drop from the end of the jetty was some fifteen feet and the resulting shouting and general hubbub from the tumbling men was tremendous. Apart from that the water was freezing and we realised that if we didn't get out quick, someone was going to drown. Suddenly the feud was forgotten, albeit temporarily, and everybody started helping everybody else to safety. Strange how immersion in cold water will kill off passion, in *all* its forms. The serio-comic end to the foray was that quite a few of the more drunken participants being capless and therefore

[25] Williams, *Gone A Long Journey*, p. 116.
[26] Pridham, *Memoirs*, II, p. 146.
[27] Cited in Coles & Briggs, *Flagship Hood*, p. 47.
[28] IWM/SA, no. 11746, reel 1.

unidentifiable, ended up in the 'Lions' Den' by finding themselves aboard the wrong ships. From that night on the crews of *Rodney* and the *Hood* were understandably never allowed ashore at the same time.[29]

All this should of course be taken with a grain of salt but there was one rivalry which assumed a more serious dimension, that between *Hood* and another battlecruiser, the *Renown*. The *Hood* might be the greatest ship in the Navy but only *Renown* could claim for herself the attribute of a royal yacht. In 1919, 1920 and again between 1921–2 the *Renown* had carried the Prince of Wales on his wildly successful cruises of North America, Australasia and finally India and the Far East. In 1927 she took the Duke and Duchess of York on a state visit to Australia, making her at least as eligible as *Hood* to the nickname 'Cook's Tours' which had attached to the latter during the World Cruise of 1923–4.[30] Though relations were never particularly close, this did not prevent the Battle Cruiser Squadron being welded into a unit of formidable morale and efficiency during the tenure of Rear-Admiral William James (1932–4). However, the great falling out came in the spring of 1935 when *Hood* and *Renown* collided following an inclination exercise off the Spanish coast. The incident, which is covered elsewhere, reflected badly on James' successor, Rear-Admiral Sidney Bailey, who took a thoroughly partisan line in his attempts to exculpate himself and the *Hood*'s officers of any responsibility in the affair.[31] This was quite naturally resented in the *Renown* which felt itself the injured party yet had to carry the can at the subsequent courts-martial. As James later put it, 'After the courts-martial would have been just the moment for the Admiral to have gone on board *Renown*… and shown a big, generous spirit', but it was not to be and the incident served to rekindle the age-old rivalry between Portsmouth and Chatham, which *Renown* had as her home port.[32] In the event, the Admiralty dissented from the findings of the courts-martial and shared the blame among them but the damage was done and ill-feeling prevailed between the two ships until *Renown* was taken in hand for reconstruction in the summer of 1936. The falling out expressed itself in various ways, from *Renown*'s failure to offer congratulations to *Hood* on her regatta victory in June 1935 to the petty animosity that developed between the two ships' companies. If the *Hood*'s wartime company decided that *Rodney* had a taste for sheep then those of her 1933–6 commission concluded that *Renown*'s men had a penchant for each other. Boy Fred Coombs (1935–8) recalls an incident in spring of 1936:

…The big laugh was to come later on when we tied up astern of the *Renown* on the North Mole at Gib. Our crew had to march past the *Renown* to go ashore and after a few leave-takers had gone ashore a party fell in for inspection. Their station cards were taken and straight away mixed up so that nobody could be identified as to have been in that particular party, which made us think that some senior rates had something to do with it. Some of us were advised to watch the proceedings which meant that there was plenty on the forecastle looking over the side when the leave-takers went over the gangway. Ashore, they were marched smartly past the ship by a killick but when they came to the *Renown*'s quarter deck, he gave another order

and they all started a slow, knee-high trot with one hand clasped firmly over their duck run. They kept it up all the way past the *Renown* then they broke into an ordinary double march and kept it up till they had got out of the dockyard gates. They got a big chuck up from us aboard but not from the *Renown*, where signals were flashing and telephones rung to complain, but the culprits were ashore and out of it. Our officers must have had a laugh about it too but all we got was a warning notice on the notice board and after fruitless enquiries as to who had been in that particular party, it was forgotten.[33]

However, rivalries of this sort were not confined to the Navy. In the early 1920s the conclusion of the Washington Treaty and the realization that the Royal Navy had lost the predominant position she had held for over a century was the cause of much tension between it and the United States Navy. To this was added the jealousy of the British matelot for the superior pay of his American counterpart, flaunted now in ports all over the world. Rear-Admiral Hugh Rodman U.S.N. may have presented the cup which bore his name in recognition of the 'ties of friendship and brotherhood which have been formed and ripened into maturity between the officers and men of the British and American Navies in the Grand Fleet' but the Grand Fleet was no more.[34] Already in January 1921 the Combined Fleet exercises off Gibraltar had pitted the Royal Navy against the 'American Battle Fleet', and not for the last time either.[35] Now in September 1922, just seven months after the signing of the Treaty, the centennial celebrations of Brazilian independence at Rio de Janeiro provided both navies with an opportunity to show which was the first among equals.[36] The first indication that *Hood* had been selected to represent the Navy came during a visit to the ship by King George V at Torquay in July. Soon after it was announced that she and the battlecruiser *Repulse* would be sailing to Rio where a sports competition would be held for the attending navies. Throughout much of July and August preparations went on at Devonport which made it clear that this was to be rather more than a goodwill cruise. National prestige was at stake and neither expense nor effort was spared to equip the Battle Cruiser Squadron for the voyage or to strip the fleet of her finest sportsmen.

On 14 August *Hood* and *Repulse* sailed from Devonport, reaching Rio by way of Gibraltar and Cape Verde on 3 September. On 29 August the *Hood* crossed the Equator for the very first time, celebrating the fact with time-honoured relish. Not even Bill the ship's goat was spared the attentions of Neptune's court. W. Connor:

As we were due to cross the Equator on this portion of our journey, preparations were made for carrying out the ceremony of 'Crossing the Line.' Various meetings were held by those responsible, though the details were shrouded in mystery, and the novices, of whom we carried a good few, began to get somewhat nervous as the time approached, due principally to the exaggerated rumours which were flying about as to the 'punishment' they would receive. Four days after leaving St. Vincent we arrived at the Equator, crossing the 'line' at nine p.m. A short time previous Father Neptune, accompanied by Amphitrite and their 'court,' assembled on the fore end of the ship, which was shrouded in darkness;

[29] Pertwee, *Moon Boots and Dinner Suits*, p. 158.
[30] HMS *Hood* Association archives, memoir of Stoker Bill Stone (1921–5). The joke alludes to the package tours for holidaymakers introduced by Thomas Cook in the 1850s.
[31] See ch. 6, pp. 165–8.
[32] NMM, Chatfield/4/1–3, ff. 57r–60r, James to Chatfield, Churt, Surrey, undated but c.February 1936; f. 60r.
[33] IWM, 91/7/1, p. 68.
[34] *Royal Navy and Royal Marines Sports Handbook 1933* (Royal Marines Sports Control Board, Admiralty, 1933), p. 263. The citation is from Rear-Admiral Rodman's letter of donation, USS *New York*, Scapa Flow, 10 October 1918.
[35] NMM, Elkins/1, Journal, 21 January 1921.
[36] See W. Connor, *To Rio and Back with H.M.S.* Hood (London: The Westminster Press, 1922).

the lower deck was cleared, and the guard and band paraded to receive them. Suddenly the look-out on the bridge reported 'Line right ahead, Sir'; the Captain gave the order, 'All hands clear away the "line"'. Engines were stopped; a voice was then heard on the fo'csle hailing the ship, searchlights were switched on, and Neptune and his court were discovered on board in full regalia. After asking the name of the ship, whither bound, the entire court, escorted by the band, marched in stately procession to the quarter-deck, where they were received by the Admiral. Greetings were exchanged and officers were presented to Father Neptune, who announced to all and sundry that he would return on board the following morning and hold his court, when various honours would be presented and all novices were to be ready to be initiated in the 'Order of the Bath.' Neptune and Amphitrite, the latter leaning on the arm of the Admiral, then departed. Punctually at nine a.m. the next day Neptune and his court again appeared and proceeded to the quarter-deck, where an investiture was held, the Rear-Admiral, Captain, and other officers receiving various decorations, after which Neptune gave orders that all novices, irrespective of rank or rating, who had not previously 'crossed the line' should be at once initiated; for this purpose a huge canvas bath had been erected. The candidates lined up and were inspected in turn by Neptune's Physician and his assistants. After swallowing some extremely vile 'medicine' they were passed to the barbers, who lathered them with soap and flour applied with a whitewash brush, finally being 'shaved' with a large wooden razor. Whilst this portion of the operation was in progress the 'victim' would suddenly find himself canted on to a greasy slide which led to the bath, where some twenty lusty 'Bears' gave him a severe ducking, after which he was received by Neptune and presented with a certificate. This was carried out throughout the whole of the day without interruption; no one escaped the ordeal, even the ship's pet, a somewhat hefty goat, being the final candidate.[37]

Already at Rio were the battleships *Minas Gerais* and *São Paulo* of the Brazilian Navy, three cruisers of the Imperial Japanese Navy led by the elderly *Idzumo*, and a pair of sloops representing Portugal and Mexico. Then on the 5th the American representation arrived in the shape of the battleships *Maryland* and *Nevada*. Mid. Robert Elkins' journal conveys the bellicose mood of the *Hood*:

> The *Maryland*, which is one of the most modern battleships afloat, looked very small compared to ourselves and *Repulse*. She was also very dirty.[38]

The *Hood* seems to have crossed swords with *Maryland* once already, at Gibraltar in March when the Americans had referred to her as 'some fine picket boat'.[39] So there were evidently a few scores to settle. The first opportunity for getting even came on the 7th when each ship landed a naval battalion for a parade through the city, Elkins declaring *Hood*'s to have been 'by far the smartest'. Though no points were at stake, Elkins also judged the Battle Cruiser Squadron to have provided the best illuminations that night 'since we were the only ships which darkened ship before switching on the circuits'. So

to the athletics and on the 8th a day of triumph for the British. Elkins could barely contain himself:

> In every race our competitors walked through, the Japanese and Americans being nowhere. That is the sort of thing which raises British prestige, which has suffered here just lately at the hands of the Yanks.

During a review of the assembled fleet by President Pessoa of Brazil on the 9th only the British Navy 'cheered ship'. And so on. However, on the morning of the 10th came the first setback for the Squadron. In a result that in retrospect could surprise no one, the Brazilian Navy defeated the British 2–nil in the football final. Worse was to come. In the Regatta that afternoon the Brazilians won the skiffs and, of all humiliations, the Americans took the seamen's cutter race, though a measure of pride was salvaged by the midshipmen's cutter. Things were different in the athletics finals on the 11th, the Squadron winning nine of fifteen events and, crowed Elkins, 'knocking the Yanks into a cocked hat. The tug of war was an absolute walkover.' But it was the boxing competition that brought the 'Naval Olympics' to a truly memorable climax. That same evening 4,000 British and American matelots crammed into a marquee pitched on the outskirts of the city. There were eight bouts on the programme and on its outcome depended overall victory in the Games. By the final bout the British were leading by four wins to three. The Squadron had reason to be confident since their last boxer was none other than the Navy and British Amateur champion, Stoker Petty Officer Spillar of the *Hood*. Mid. Gerald Cobb (1921–3?) takes up the story:

> Spillar advanced to touch gloves with his rival—as all boxers in previous bouts had done—when the American immediately struck Spillar with a straight left, followed by a right hook. Curtains for Spillar. Uproar![40]

Only prompt action by Rear-Admiral Walter Cowan, who stepped into the ring and ordered his men to give three cheers for the US Navy, prevented the situation turning ugly. In the event, the bout was declared null and void, Cowan's counterpart apologised and the Squadron won the tourney, but it had been, as they say, a close-run thing. The following day *Maryland* weighed anchor and left for New York, cheered as she went by the *Hood*'s company, though what they muttered under their breath is anyone's guess. On the quarterdeck that night the *Hood* hosted a Grand Ball attended by President Pessoa and the cream of Rio society, probably the most sumptuous event ever celebrated in her. The centre-piece was a huge fountain surrounded by a grove of palm trees hung with coloured lights. As Elkins wrote in his journal, 'Preparations were on a most lavish scale and must cost hundreds of pounds'. The following day, having collected three magnificent trophies for their sporting achievements, the Squadron took part in the closing act of the centennial celebrations, an illuminated water pageant in Botafogo Bay in which the *Hood*'s Chief Painter played the part of Britannia. In all the *Hood*'s career, in all her great voyages, there can have been few spectacles to match this. On 14 September 1922 the Squadron swept out of the anchorage and into the Atlantic leaving a flotilla of Brazilian destroyers trailing in its wake.

For all its splendour the Brazilian cruise was only a taste of

37 Ibid., pp. 12–13. The admiral and captain referred to were Rear-Admiral Sir Walter Cowan and Capt. Geoffrey Mackworth.
38 NMM, Elkins/1, Journal, 5 September 1922 and successive entries.
39 HMS *Hood* Association archives, memoir of Gunner 'Windy' Breeze, R.M.A. (1920–2).
40 Cited in Coles & Briggs, *Flagship Hood*, p. 25.

41 PRO, ADM 116/2219, ff. 5–6, Leo Amery to Admiral of the Fleet Earl Beatty, 24 April 1923.

42 PRO, ADM 116/2219, ff. 9r & 24r.

43 PRO, ADM 116/2219, ff. 29–30.

44 PRO, ADM 1/8662, Capt. John K. Im Thurn to Vice-Admiral Sir Frederick Field & Rear-Admiral the Hon. Sir Hubert Brand, HMS *Hood*, Devonport, 8 November 1923.

45 Extracts from Diary of World Cruise, 1923–4, p. 4.

46 The main published sources for the cruise are O'Connor, *The Empire Cruise, passim*, C.R. Benstead, *Round the World with the Battle Cruisers* (London: Hurst & Blackett, 1925?), Bradford, *The Mighty* Hood, pp. 64–88, and Coles & Briggs, *Flagship* Hood, pp. 28–42.

things to come. On 29 November 1923 a squadron of ships embarked on the greatest circumnavigation undertaken by the Royal Navy since Commodore Anson's heroic feat of 1740–4. The World Cruise of the Special Service Squadron as it came to be known was first mooted in the spring of 1923. At the Imperial Conference called for that autumn the Admiralty intended not only to emphasise the dependence of the Dominions on British sea power, but to encourage them to participate in its maintenance through the creation of their own naval staffs and by contributing to regional and trade defence with money, ships and base facilities. The World Cruise had therefore a far more overtly navalist agenda than the three cruises made by the Prince of Wales in the *Renown* between 1919 and 1922 which preceded it. It was also far larger and more ambitious than these, to which the First Lord's proposal to Beatty, the First Sea Lord, in April 1923 bears witness:

> I am considering the desirability, pending the proposed redistribution of Fleets, of sending a really representative Squadron of our most modern ships round the Empire (a) in order to follow up any agreements for co-operation made at the Imperial Conference by creating Dominion interest and enthusiasm so that such agreements may be really carried out; (b) to let the local forces in Australia and elsewhere not only see our standard of work etc. but have an opportunity of doing joint exercises etc., and getting in touch generally, as a prelude to some more permanent system of interchange and co-operation; (c) to give our own ships more experience of long distance cruises and of waters practically unvisited by the Navy at large for nearly 20 years. [...] My present idea is that the Squadron composed say of *Hood* and *Repulse* and a Squadron of modern light cruisers should during or immediately after the Conference, say some time in November, go (1) to South Africa, staying there three or four weeks; (2) India—Bombay or Trincomalee—stopping for a few days only; (3) Singapore (4) Australia and New Zealand where they should spend say two or even three months doing joint exercises etc.; (5) Vancouver (6) Panama Canal, and W. Indies and Bermuda; (7) Eastern Canada and Newfoundland for say a month before returning home. I should like you to consider the possibility of... taking an Australian cruiser with our Fleet

to Canada and W.I.—this not only as experience for Australians but in order to show Canada what the Australians are doing. There is also the question of paying courtesy visits en route at San Francisco and Seattle on the U.S. West Coast and one or more U.S. east coast ports.[41]

With a few alterations this indeed proved to be the itinerary of the main units of the Special Service Squadron, which was to sail over 38,000 miles in ten months. It remained to carry out the immense organisation needed to make the cruise possible: assessing the safety of over 30 anchorages in the season in question; verifying the availability of oil and provisions; arranging events and entertainments in concert with local authorities; above all, budgeting for the enormous cost of sending half a dozen ships and 4,600 men around the world. At an economical speed of 11 knots the squadron's fuel requirement was assessed at 110,000 tons at approximately £3 per ton.[42] Total *additional* expenditure of refitting, fuel and stores above ordinary service including a generous £8,000 allowance for shipboard entertaining was calculated at £239,000.[43] There was to be a Squadron 'At Home' laid on by the *Hood* at every major port of call while her companions were to host children's parties, dances and other entertainments at any location visited longer than a week.[44] Sports events were to be participated in ashore. As before the Brazilian cruise two years earlier, the *Hood* was taken in hand for refitting at Devonport, first in August and then in November 1923. The final act was the landing of known troublemakers before the battlecruisers sailed without fanfare on the morning of 27 November. For most it was the beginning of an unforgettable adventure, the zenith of the peacetime Navy. For others like the newly-married Lieutenant (E) Geoffrey Wells (1923–4) it was a desperate wrench:

> We were casting off the wires and by 07.30 hrs we were clear of No. 6 wharf, Keyham Dockyard. As the engines started I felt a pang of realization of the fact that I was here, Inez in London and that realization only grew greater as we steamed past Plymouth Hoe and turned seawards. Just to think of 10 months ahead, 30,000 odd miles steaming! I can't.[45]

The Special Service Squadron consisted of *Hood*, *Repulse* and the 1st Light Cruiser Squadron under Rear-Admiral the Hon. Sir Hubert Brand, including *Delhi*, *Dauntless*, *Danae* and *Dragon*. With them sailed HMS *Dunedin*, on passage to join the New Zealand Division of the Royal Navy. In overall command of the Squadron was Vice-Admiral Sir Frederick Field flying his flag in *Hood*. Field's reputation rests on his disastrous tenure as First Sea Lord during the Invergordon Mutiny but his tact and diplomacy during the World Cruise earned him the headline 'Freddy Field Proves Reg'lar Guy' in San Francisco in July 1924 and he was to prove an inspired choice for this command. A truly gifted speaker, Field's skills as a conjurer (he was a member of the Magic Circle) were guaranteed to break the ice at any dinner party. The initial stop on the cruise was Freetown, Sierra Leone where the *Hood* received a silver-mounted elephant's tusk, the first in a succession of big-game curios which were to enliven her wardroom for the next fifteen years.[46] Then came Cape Town where the pattern for the rest of the cruise was set: an official reception ashore; the landing of the Squadron's naval

Ten months and 38,000 miles: the World Cruise of 1923–4 showing the routes taken by the Battle Cruiser Squadron and the 1st Light Cruiser Squadron.
Empire Photographic Publishing

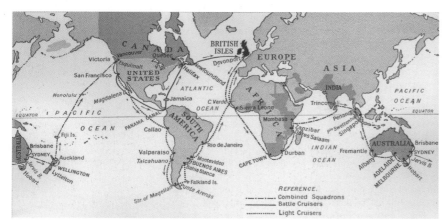

REFERENCE.
- - - Combined Squadrons
——— Battle Cruisers
·········· Light Cruisers

battalion for a march through the city with fixed bayonets; banyan parties and excursions into the hinterland; an outpouring of generosity and patriotic fervour reciprocated with tours of the ship and lavish entertainments aboard. Introductions made, gifts exchanged, engagements sealed. It was here, too, that the Squadron suffered the first of over 150 desertions, but the cruise as a whole upheld the British matelot's reputation for good behaviour in foreign climes.

After South Africa came the British protectorate of Zanzibar. A small island off the mandated territory of Tanganyika, the Sultanate of Zanzibar was perhaps an unlikely destination for the Special Service Squadron but the Royal Navy had something to exorcise in these waters. On 20 September 1914 the small cruiser *Pegasus* had hauled down her colours under heavy fire from the German light cruiser *Königsberg*. Not only was it the first occasion in over 100 years that a British ship had surrendered, but her humiliation had played out in full view of the citizenry of Zanzibar. The *Königsberg* had been dealt with on the Rufiji River in Tanganyika in July 1915 by monitors sent out from Britain but the Admiralty no doubt felt that prestige needed to be restored. Besides, the Sultan had loyally stood by Britain in a territory just 50 miles off German Tanganyika. Reaching Zanzibar on the morning of 12 January 1924 the Squadron was received by the Sultan Sayyid Khalifa ben Hamid in his yacht with a string of war canoes in tow. Not for the first time the 3-pounder saluting guns on the *Hood*'s flag decks boomed out, 21 guns for the Sultan and then fifteen in reply to the light cruiser USS *Concord*, also in harbour.[47] A landing party of Royal Marines and field guns was put ashore for a ceremonial march-past and there was instruction for non-swimmers in the Zanzibar Channel. There were trips to the orchards from which 75 per cent of the world's cloves came or, in the case of Lt Wells, a futile attempt to repair the Sultan's electric generator.[48] The Squadron refuelled from a waiting oiler and *Hood* was in receipt of twelve tons of fresh meat and vegetables. Then on the 15th the Sultan arrived aboard for lunch in oppressive heat, the crews of the saluting guns busy once more. The following day he led the

Squadron out to sea in his yacht and, after hearing another 21-gun salute, watched it disappear over the horizon.

Next came the tropical splendour of Trincomalee in Ceylon and then Malaya where officers gagged down a Chinese banquet in Kuala Lumpur while their men toured the rubber plantations. Then Singapore where, in token of its broken alliance with Japan, the Navy wanted to build a fortified base for its ships in the event of war. Off the same coasts seventeen years later *Repulse* would herself be a victim of the catastrophic failure of British planning in the East. On 17 February the Squadron weighed anchor and embarked on a ten-day voyage down the east coast of Sumatra, through the Sunda Strait where the *Exeter* would likewise meet her fate at the hands of the Japanese Navy in March 1942, past the extinct cone of Krakatoa and at length to Fremantle in Western Australia. In Australia and New Zealand awaited the greatest reception for the Special Service Squadron. At Fremantle there was a new mascot, Joey the wallaby. At Adelaide the Squadron received nearly 70,000 visitors, at Melbourne 486,000. Lieutenant (E) Geoffrey Wells:

> We remained at Melbourne for seven days and enormous crowds besieged us. Numbers unprecedented percolated into every place in the ship. Women fainted on the gangways which almost gave beneath the weight. To get ashore became a feat of no mean skill and elbow power. The *Repulse* also suffered. The little boys of the crowd fared best, they could squeeze where their sisters could not and could deal more rapidly with the ladders.[49]

Half a million people lined Sydney Harbour to watch the Squadron glide in on 9 April. But here, amid the hysteria, sports and festivities, came a major setback for the Navy: the announcement in London that the Singapore base would not be built. Nonetheless, the Australian government ordered a pair of heavy cruisers from British yards and detached the light cruiser *Adelaide* to join the Squadron along with ten midshipmen from the Naval College at Jervis Bay. After eleven days of

47 Details from PRO, ADM 53/78914, deck log of HMS *Hood*, January 1924.
48 Diary of World Cruise, p. 21.
49 Ibid., p. 29.

Another open day at Melbourne, March 1924.
HMS Hood Association/Mackie Collection

Two of the *Hood*'s four 3-pounder Hotchkiss saluting guns in action on the flag deck, *c.*1935.
HMS Hood Association/Willis Collection

'A' turret's guns at maximum elevation, Wellington, April or May 1924. The Squadron was exhausted by the time it reached New Zealand.

sport and entertainment Field's battlecruisers sailed for Wellington, their crews exhausted. Mid. George Blundell:

> I was running a picket boat, which meant solid work from 6 a.m. to 2 a.m. or midnight. And on my day off it meant entertaining visitors or being entertained ashore. The shore entertainment was a terrible duty. The official dances were a nightmare at which one had to stay until about 1 a.m. Sometimes I could hardly stand up, having had little sleep for several days. The job of laundering and keeping our clothes spotlessly clean was also a nightmare.[50]

A trying passage of the Tasman Sea left officers and men so drained that all civic functions in Wellington had to be cancelled. However, time and energy was found for one of those shipboard children's parties for which the Navy was famous. Perhaps it was the prolonged separation from their own families, but sailors always went to enormous lengths to entertain children aboard. Merry-go-rounds rigged on the main capstan; slides swishing down from the bridge to a cushioned landing below; a 'flight' in an improvised gondola dangled from a derrick; the Marine band in full swing; 'Aunt Sally' in the form of a bluejacket dodging missiles being hurled at him from all quarters; tours of the ship and vast teas served out on deck by matelots dressed up as pirates. On 8 May Earl Jellicoe, now Governor-General of New Zealand, joined the *Hood* and, hoisting his flag beside Field's, volunteered to ease the burden by taking the Middle watch (midnight–04.00) on the bridge

for the run to Auckland.[51] Here another 78,000 visited the *Hood* but as Geoffrey Wells noted, the ship's company had had enough of the World Cruise by the time she sailed for Fiji:

> It is very noticeable on board that now passed New Zealand everyone seems to be getting bored with the cruise. I certainly am. Going round the world is alright. In fact being paid to go round and under such circumstances as this is great but one needs a fortnight's holiday at home in the middle of it. Everything moves at such a pace.[52]

Spirits were no doubt revived with draughts of kava, the intoxicating drink of Fiji, and then by the Polynesian beauties of Western Samoa where *Hood* dropped anchor for a few hours on 29 May. But by the time the Squadron reached Hawaii on 6 June a gradual suspension of the issue of alcohol had left Field's ships 'dry' in deference to the Prohibition laws of the United States. Still, a dance for 1,100 guests given by the *Hood* at Honolulu, though it toasted the King and President Coolidge in water, was remembered as the finest of the cruise. Then to British Columbia and perhaps Field's most important remit, to encourage Canada to maintain a pair of cruisers on each coast, a suggestion which raised a storm of protest in Ottawa. At San Francisco the Squadron was given a truly remarkable reception, though it must have proved a great disappointment to the apostle of air power, Brigadier-General Billy Mitchell. Learning of a plan to use an aircraft to drop a symbolic floral key 'to unlock the Golden Gate' onto *Hood*'s quarterdeck, Mitchell

[50] Cited in Coles & Briggs, *Flagship Hood*, p. 36.
[51] Lt (E) Geoffrey Wells, Diary of World Cruise, p. 35.
[52] Ibid., p. 39.

Above: The *Hood* anchored off Honolulu, June 1924. This photo shows the distinct flare of her hull, designed to lessen the angle at which a shell might strike her side. She is moored with both her bower anchors, their cables joined with a mooring swivel.
Author's Collection

Left: Vice-Admiral Field's flag superimposed by the Stars and Stripes at San Francisco in July 1924. This photo provides a particularly good view of the rig of the foremast. What appears to be the Church Pendant is triced up to the starboard signal yard. Above this on spurs projecting from the starfish and fore top roof are pairs of manoeuvring lights. Rigged to the fore topmast is the 40-foot signal yard supporting further halyards and the four 'flat roof' aerials for long-range wireless communications. Stepped to the fore topmast is the flagpole on which the ship wore the admiral's flag. On the right is Starboard 4in Mk V High-Angle gun.
U.S. Naval Historical Center, Washington

Below: The *Hood* approaching Honolulu on 6 June 1924. Men off watch are formed up by divisions and the cable party is fallen in on the forecastle ready to drop anchor. Not a drop of alcohol had been served since midnight on the 5th.
U.S. Naval Historical Center, Washington

took the controls himself intent on making a further demonstration of the vulnerability of the capital ship to air attack.[53] However, his efforts resulted only in the key pitching unceremoniously into the bay as the guns of Fort Scott boomed out in welcome. It was the first time in 40 years that a British squadron had dropped anchor in American waters and Field's ships made a lasting impression not only on the city but on relations between their two countries. As Mayor James Rolph put it,

Your presence with us today will, we trust, make a pact between the British-speaking races even closer. We take a pride in your magnificent ships, which we feel will never be used except in the defense of the world's peace. We surrender our city unto you. We capitulate.[54]

Meanwhile, it was quite clear that the Squadron's efforts to adhere to Prohibition greatly outstripped those of their hosts ashore. Geoffrey Wells has this memory of the Bohemian Club in San Francisco:

'I guess you boys will have a drink' said one of our hosts producing, as the conjurer does the rabbit, a bottle of whiskey which he passed to the bar attendant who therewith dispensed whiskey and sodas. We received sympathy for our stocks on board being locked up and it became apparent that the only dry community in the district was the British ships. There were some that did not believe we were dry and could not understand that we had no bottles in our cabins. Our reason for not having any was that it was not allowed. This absolutely baffled the American mind![55]

On 11 July the *Hood* began the longest leg of her journey, the 3,440 miles that separated San Francisco from Balboa and the navigation of the Panama Canal. Almost immediately the 1st Light Cruiser Squadron parted company with *Hood*, *Repulse* and *Adelaide* and steered for Callao, the first stop in a lengthy tour of South America. Field's ships reached Balboa on the 23rd, took in mail and a few stores and then proceeded towards the Canal which *Hood* would become the largest vessel to traverse. Here is Lt (E) Geoffrey Wells' commentary of the passage through the Pedro Miguel Locks, which afforded *Hood*'s bulges a clearance of only 30 inches on each side:

The rule of the road being 'au droit' we entered the starboard lock. In each case there are two locks and the centre wall runs out some 1000 feet clear from the outer gates either end. We approached with our bow well towards this wall and as we closed a small boat brought ropes which we hauled in to get the ends of the wire hawsers from each of four electric mules. These four mules then spread out, one well forward, two between and one abaft midships. They took orders from the pilot which were given by hand signal. Wires from the outside wall were then brought to the ship which still made steady way while her bow, well toward the centre wall, was slowly centred. Thus we glided into the lock. On either beam lookouts were stationed on overhung wooden platforms—they had flags to indicate the clearance twixt ship and lock while the position in which the flag was held showed whether that clearance was opening or closing. Under 1 foot a red flag came into use. We had not much to spare but we

sure had a great pilot. '1 foot closing—red flag' was shown by the port lookout. The little man of unassuming airs in a small grey suit just waved a hand to one of the mules and whispered down a voice pipe 'half ahead starboard'. Then he rolls his cigar round his mouth. The lookout hovers with the flag ready to drop it if we touch. There is barely an inch. Then, quickly to the voice pipe, the little grey man says 'amidships—stop starboard'. A wave to another mule and a wire becomes taut. One foot is indicated, then the bow slides slowly back to the centre line off which it had deviated in order to keep our quarter clear. By this time we were up to the safety chain which runs across the lock to protect the gates from any ship that might rush at them. The double gates behind us closed and a similar safety chain rose below our stern. Then the sluices opened and we rose rapidly for, being a large ship, little water was required to lift us 31 feet. Our decks now well above land, the lock level with the water in the Galliard Cut, the inner gates opened and the chain dropped beneath the water. We gave a kick ahead and the mules led us out into the cut.[56]

The pilot, for his part, commented on the skill with which the *Hood*'s engines had been handled in the locks. The following morning the Squadron set off down the eight miles of the Culebra Cut, the greatest feat of civil engineering in history. Wells:

We tried main engines at 5.30 am and half an hour later we cast off from Pedro Miguel and started down the Culebra Cut. A tug assisted. The Senior [Engineer] and I took turns to nip up on deck to see the cut. In fact we so arranged it that not one man in the engine room failed to see one part or another of this great excavation. We proceeded at four knots which meant slow and stop alternately all the while and the cut is not straight. At one part, a sharp bend to the right, where it passes Gold Hill, it is a truly magnificent sight with high banks of either side but a few feet away made even a 42,000 ton ship feel small so close to solid land.[57]

Having passed through the Gatún Locks the *Hood* at last reached the Caribbean. The cost of her passage to the Admiralty was $22,399.50 at 50 cents per ton plus towing fees—a little over £5,000 in the currency of the day.[58] In *Hood* 'General subdued cheers were lead by the Constructor Commander on sighting what he described as the same sea as our wives see' but there remained stops at Jamaica, Nova Scotia and Quebec before the *Hood* could return down the St Lawrence to Newfoundland and make for home.[59] At Halifax, Nova Scotia Field had to deal with the consequences of his earlier remarks in Victoria, B.C. but on 21 September the *Hood*, *Repulse* and *Adelaide* finally quit Topsail Bay, Newfoundland to the longed-for strains of *Rolling Home*. A week later and with exquisite timing they were reunited with Brand's cruiser squadron off the Lizard before Field took his ships into Cawsand Bay and thence to Devonport. In his diary Lt Wells wrote

Joy such as this is too great to describe by words alone. Ten months ago I left my new possession and now I am with her again.[60]

[53] Gruner, *Blue Water Beat*, p. 72.
[54] Cited in Bradford, *The Mighty Hood*, p. 85.
[55] Diary of World Cruise, p. 50.
[56] Ibid., pp. 51–2.
[57] Ibid., p. 54. The Senior Engineer was Engineer Lt-Cdr Ernest C. Plant.
[58] *The Panama Canal Record*, 17 (1924), no. 51, pp. 731–2.
[59] Diary of World Cruise, p. 54.
[60] Ibid., p. 60.

efficiency. For conduct in war he is guided by the articles of war, which enjoin that he shall 'use his utmost exertion to bring his ship into action, and during such action, in his own person encourage his inferior officers and men to fight courageously.' Here you will see that two of his responsibilities, the safety of his ship and the taking of her into action, must be balanced one against the other. [...] In as much as he must take every decision himself, and has to bear full responsibility for it, he is completely alone. The ship is moving through the water at whatever speed he alone has ordered. The guns' crews are all at their stations. When he gives the order they will open fire. When they fire, whether they hit the enemy or not will depend upon the training he has ensured these crews have had, and whether the whole enormously complex mechanism of fire control and guns has been maintained to produce its maximum efficiency at this moment. And lastly he has to consider the moment ahead when the enemy's shells will burst on board his ship. How his ship's company will react to that almost inevitable moment, how much or how little it will affect their morale, will depend upon things almost indefinable, upon 'all their yesterdays,' upon the spirit that he has instilled throughout the ship. The loneliness of high command accompanies him wherever he may be, on board, at sea or in harbour, in peace and in war. He lives alone in fact as much as in spirit.[7]

It was the Commander's duty as Executive Officer to deliver into the captain's (and implicitly the admiral's) hands a ship capable of meeting every demand that circumstance and tactical necessity might make of her. To this every facet of her life and the life of every man embarked in her was subordinated.

The ship commissioned, the first full muster of 'Divisions' heralded the stirring of her routine and organisation. If the captain and his officers were the head of this organisation then its heart was the divisional system. By it the *Hood*'s crew was separated into thirteen divisions based on their trade and the part of the ship for which they were responsible, each numbering about 100 men. Seamen were gathered into three divisions—Forecastlemen, Topmen and Quarterdeckmen—each of which manned one of the ship's 15in turrets, the fourth being crewed by the Royal Marine detachment which formed a division in its own right. There were separate divisions for Torpedo and Communications ratings, along with those for Boys, Engine Room Artificers and Mechanicians, the Supply Department and another for Miscellaneous ratings including artisans, Ordnance and Electrical Artificers, cooks and Sick Berth Attendants. Like the seamen, the stoker complement was split into three divisions, in their case by watches: Red, White and Blue. And in war a fourteenth division was added: Hostilities-Only Ratings. Each division was placed under a lieutenant or lieutenant-commander who was charged with its discipline, training, clothing and organisation, and who in turn placed the greatest reliance on the chief and petty officers who made up the heart of the *Hood*'s company. On this system turned the organisation of the entire ship and its ultimate purpose as a fighting unit of the fleet.

So it was that early afternoon on Commissioning Day found much of the crew mustered once more on the quarterdeck and in the port and starboard batteries. At the bugle call they laid aft to hear the Captain's address. AB Len Wincott, who served in *Hood* in 1926, recalls the anticipation which always attended this occasion:

It was an event which set the tone for the future life of the ship's company. 'To be or not to be' was the question, and in this case a much more worrying one than the young chap from Denmark ever faced. The point at issue was whether this would, or would not, be a 'happy ship'—the alternative to which was a 'hell ship'. True, that term was generally reserved for the merchant service and naval ratings rarely used it; but that did not stop them from thinking it.[8]

[7] 'Life on Board a Battleship' in Bacon, ed., *Britain's Glorious Navy*, p. 25.
[8] Wincott, *Invergordon Mutineer*, pp. 75–6.

Hood alongside at Portsmouth in early September 1933. On 30 August she had recommissioned under a new Captain and a new Commander, Rory O'Conor.
Bibliothek für Zeitgeschichte, Stuttgart

9 The ship's routine described in these paragraphs is based on the revised schedules laid out in *RBS*, pp. 229–34 which obtained during the 1933–6 commission; see Appendix IV.
10 Wincott, *Invergordon Mutineer*, p. 76.
11 Ibid.

Reassured or otherwise, the Cooks of the Mess would then draw their comrades' 'mess traps' or utensils from one of the storerooms and hasten to serve the first meal aboard: tea at 15.30. Afterwards the Commander would likely drill his men in such evolutions as 'Collision Stations' or 'Fire Stations'. If the ship were already fully ammunitioned then the only call on the Gunnery Department would be to assume the duty of recording the magazine temperatures. Otherwise the crew would begin the dangerous task of ammunitioning ship from an assortment of barges and lighters loaded with shells, torpedoes, cordite cartridges and detonators. But this was unusual and for most the last official act of Commissioning Day would be a medical inspection of all new ratings in the Sick Bay. Then to the messdeck and animated discussion over supper on the prospects for the new commission with messmates or with those remaining from the old. For some 'Pipe Down' at 22.30 would confirm their choice or fortune of hammock berth. For others, bumped by heads or tormented by lights or ventilators, the night would provide a somewhat different realisation.

Shortly after 05.00 a bugle call would herald the beginning of the first full day of the commission.[9] By 05.30 the duty petty officers were passing through the messdecks bellowing the old refrain 'Wakey, wakey, rise and shine. Sun's scorchin' yer bleedin' eyes out' under decks lashed with rain or caked with snow. A mug of 'ky' inside them, 05.45 found the Duty Boys of the Morning watch hard at work, to be followed at 06.00 by the bulk of the ship's company fallen in to 'Clean Ship'. Over the next hour or so the entire quarterdeck would be scrubbed down from the stern forward to the aft screens and the brass bollards and other brightwork polished to a brilliant sheen. In the engine spaces, especially on the control platforms, this took the form of cleaning the steel deck plates, white-washing the more prominent stretches of lagging and polishing the array of brass voice pipes, steel ladders, dials and indicators which filled every space. If, as was often the case, the ship was emerging from a period of refitting then the greatest call on the time and energy of the crew was in getting her to an acceptable degree of cleanliness. Under certain circumstances this might require special measures on the part of the ship's officers. AB Wincott:

Now, to achieve the high degree of cleanliness desired, an unofficial tradition was practised by some captains which meant, in brief, roping in a large number of men for extra work in their free time. The captain simply passed the word to his commander who… gave instructions that conditions be created to rope the needed numbers in. Everything was done verbally and nowhere was there written proof, but every man on the ship was aware what was happening. The regulating staff under the command of the master-at-arms moved into action. Not one little infringement was passed up, and if no infringements existed they were invented. Consequently, every day, at commander's defaulters, there was a large crowd of men, mostly seamen of course, waiting to be punished.[10]

Whether this was resorted to or not, the duties themselves were unchanging:

…Scattered round different parts of the ship, some with emery paper, scrubbing away at the dockyard-painted steel deck to make it look like a mirror; some with wash-cloths and buckets of 'suji-muji', a liquid concoction of five parts water and five parts any kind of powerful cleanser guaranteed to remove unwanted marks more effectively than flames; and of course a large body with the inevitable 'holy stone', called by the men 'the sailor's bible'.[11]

To this desultory work the British sailor gave a fair proportion of his existence until time or higher rating exempted him from it. Boy Fred Coombs:

Below: 'Hands scrub aft.' A party of barefooted sailors scrubs the quarterdeck with heavy brushes while a petty officer supplies them with seawater from a deck hose, c.1935.
HMS Hood Association/Willis Collection

Below right: A reminder that the Marines also took a hand in cleaning the ship. This party, perhaps the crew of one of the 4in high-angle guns, are enjoying a breather and a smoke on the boat deck during a 'Stand Easy'. Men were responsible for cleaning their 'part of ship' and some of the implements of their daily work are arranged in front of them.
HMS Hood Association/Higginson Collection

…It was no surprise that our lives were to be spent not in being sailors but in endless, meaningless jobs such as chipping paintwork, washing it, and any time-consuming job that could be easily monitored. Of the jobs that we fancied, such as smacking paint about with a brush, the nearest thing we got to painting was to go round on our hands and knees scraping up after the painting party; their time was more important than ours.[12]

At such moments the imprecations came thick and fast: 'Join the Navy and see the world' and especially 'Roll on me fuckin' dozen', a reference to the twelve years of a man's first term of service. By the 1920s a new generation of naval officer was beginning to recognise the senselessness of requiring a man to devote the better part of his time to work of this sort as the Navy began to fall astern in technology and fighting efficiency. But tradition dies hard in the Royal Navy. Admiral Sir Frank Twiss, eventually Second Sea Lord, admitted as much in his memoirs:

The number of officers and men in ships was dictated by the number required to fight ships in action. […] This meant that when you weren't at war there were far more people living on board than were actually needed to keep the ship afloat, clean and working. It was, of course, accepted as gospel that men must be kept busy. People who weren't occupied became troublemakers; there was nothing else for them to do. So the routine in the Navy, particularly in big ships, was strictly designed to keep men working and keen. Looking back on it now, it was an astonishing performance. For example, a battleship in the Atlantic Fleet before the Second World War, might have nine hundred to a thousand men on board, of which only a proportion could regularly polish all the brass-work, clean all the paintwork, pick up the oil in the engine room or whatever it was, quite easily, in the first couple of hours. So what did they do for most of the day?[13]

The answer is that, in the *Hood* particularly, they continued to polish and clean until the coming war required their skills to be applied elsewhere. Still, there was no denying the pride of seeing an expanse of stained teak decking brought to a lustrous manila finish. A fortnight before his death at 98 in June 2003, CPO Harry Cutler, who went to sea in the *Hood* in 1922, recalled these lines for the author:

A few drops of water,
A few grains of sand,
A sailor with a holystone
Makes a deck look grand.[14]

The 'holystone', a sandstone block, was supplied by the Admiralty, but the silver sand favoured for scrubbing decks and woodwork had to be obtained in the traditional manner. Among the Coombs twins' first tasks on being selected to crew one of the ship's cutters early in 1936 was to sail her from Portsmouth Harbour to Hayling Island to collect a boatload. The expedition resulted not only in them missing the tide as they returned up the Solent but in their being eaten alive by sand-fleas shovelled up in the cargo as they did so. 'There was always something to learn at sea.'[15]

At 06.50, just as the men were drying down the upper deck, a bugle call summoned the Cooks of the Mess to the galley lifts bearing breakfast for the crew. Ten minutes later a mass piping by Call-boys with their Bosun's whistles had the men gratefully heading for the messdecks to tuck into the offerings of the galley. Then a chance to wash and change into the 'rig of the day' before the order was passed for 'Quarters Clean Guns' at 07.55. At the same moment a party of signalmen was gathering round the ensign staff on the quarterdeck for the first of the Navy's great rituals, morning Colours. On the stroke of 08.00 (09.00 in winter) the signal was given to a Marine corporal to ring the ship's bell eight times. At the same moment a dozen buglers on 'X' turret sounded 'Attention' as the band of the Royal Marines struck up 'God Save the King'. Men stiffened, officers saluted and all faced aft as the ensign was slowly hoisted up its staff, reaching the gold crown just as the final bars crashed out. Meanwhile, a similar ceremony was being performed with the Union Flag and seaman buglers on the forecastle. The tolling of eight bells indicated not eight o'clock but the start of the Forenoon watch, one of the six four-hourly segments into which the naval day was divided. At noon came the Afternoon watch and then at 16.00 the two dog

[12] IWM, 91/7/1, p. 42.
[13] Twiss, *Social Change in the Royal Navy*, p. 23. The Second Sea Lord is entrusted with naval personnel and manning.
[14] Conversation in Devonport, 23 May 2003.
[15] IWM, 91/7/1, p. 51.

Below: The youngest member of *Hood*'s company and a corporal of Marines pose beside *Hood*'s bell on 31 December 1928. The former will ring it sixteen times at a minute to midnight to herald the new year.
Illustrated London News

THE SHIP'S BELL

If the spirit of the *Hood* resided anywhere it was in her bell. On it the naval day was intoned in unbroken sequence while her life or the life of her commission lasted. The *Hood*'s bell seems to have been presented to the ship by Lady Hood in memory of her husband Rear-Admiral the Rt Hon Sir Horace Hood, killed at Jutland in 1916. About 18 inches high, it was cast in brass and mounted in an impressive wooden stand topped by a crown; the whole structure, kept immaculately polished, stood about 10 feet high. Attached to the tongue of the bell was a decorative lanyard done in fancy ropework. In harbour, and except in foul weather, the bell was placed on the quarterdeck; otherwise it was kept in one of the lobbies outside the captain's quarters. Until the early twentieth century a single bell had sufficed for each vessel, but the din of machinery and the increasing size of ships eventually required a second to be placed in the forward section of the ship so that the men could follow the progress of each watch. This arrangement was followed in the *Hood* until the mid-1930s when the introduction of the tannoy allowed the main bell to be broadcast throughout the ship.

The ship's bell was largely in the care of the Royal Marines. Only a corporal of Marines could move it and it was a Marine sentry who struck the bell every half hour in accordance with the clock on his beat. It was also used to summon the men to morning prayers and Church on Sunday, and clattered out noisily to announce fire or collision drill. However, the most important moment came on 31 December when the bell was used to ring in the new year. Placed on the quarterdeck, it was struck sixteen times at a minute to midnight, eight for the old year and eight for the new. This ceremony was traditionally performed by the youngest member of the crew but on 31 December 1940 it was a junior midshipman who rang in the new year, no doubt on the same bell found lying among the debris of his ship in 2001.

16 RBS, p. 94.
17 Ibid., p. 97.
18 Williams, Gone A Long Journey, p. 117.
19 SWWEC, 2001/1376, B.A. Carlisle, p. 6.

watches whose purpose is described lower down. These were followed by the First watch at 20.00, the Middle watch at midnight and finally the Morning watch at 04.00 with which the cycle was completed. Since few men carried timepieces, most relied on the ship's bell to tell them what time it was, which it did by tolling off the half-hours incrementally through each watch. So it was that a man going on duty in the Morning watch might well ask a mate to 'shake me at seven bells' of the Middle one (3.30 a.m.) so that he could have half an hour to rouse himself for work. The dog watches were divided in order to permit a daily change of watch for a ship working a two-watch routine. This routine, which the Hood observed throughout her career, was called 'watch and watch', and under it most of the ship's company was divided into two identical watches, known as Port and Starboard; the Engineering Department, however, had three watches: Red, White and Blue. These alternated duties so that every essential function was being attended to by a full complement of men at any given moment. In most cases this provided an individual with an eight-hour day of work, rising to twelve hours at sea and probably sixteen or 20 in war as need or circumstance dictated. Since a ship on war patrol required her entire crew to go to action stations at dawn and dusk each day regardless of other duties it will be understood what the impact of sleep deprivation was on their morale and efficiency. But this was exceptional and in the ordinary run of things 'watch and watch' represented a perfectly tolerable lifestyle. Thus, if the divisional system formed the basis of the ship's organisation then the watch system provided the rhythm of her routine.

Colours over, work continued about the ship. For many this meant more cleaning and polishing, a dose of compulsory 'physical jerks' under a PT instructor or, for the more expert seaman, the splicing of wire and rope, maintenance of blocks and tackles and forming of grommets and heaving lines which kept his vessel seaworthy. But for others it signalled the resumption of that other labour which filled the hours of Britain's bluejackets: care of the ship's paintwork. This was not so much the adding of fresh layers as the scraping, chipping, polishing and scrubbing which provided the perfect surface for paint to be applied. The actual application was left only to the most skilled practitioners. Cdr Rory O'Conor, doyen of Hood painters:

The correct way of applying paint is with horizontal strokes, finishing off with upward strokes. All strokes must be firm and the brush not overloaded. Painting is an art acquired with practice, and it is waste of paint to put a brush in inexperienced hands.[16]

However, the ultimate touch lay not in paint but in enamel:

If a ship has some very special lobby or surface which it is decided to enamel, with a finish so perfect as to take away the cat's breath when he sees his whiskers, then the work must be done by the most expert painter.[17]

Nor did it end there. Fine paintwork had to be protected not only from the assaults of the elements but also those of brutality. This translated into punishments for those who wantonly ill-treated paintwork and, more commonly, in the necessity for exterior surfaces to be washed down with fresh water if splashed while scrubbing decks or following rain or periods at sea. The other enemy was rust, which required the surface to be scraped down to the metal and the offending patch treated with oil. About four times a year ordinary wear and tear, a special occasion or a change of assignment would require the entire ship to be painted. This evolution, which usually took a day for the sides, masts and yards, required the ship to go 'out of routine' and as such was a welcome change for the crew. Such a moment came in September 1936 when the ship recommissioned for service in the Mediterranean Fleet. AB Len Williams:

Our first job, soon after commissioning, was to change the colour of Hood's paintwork. Almost from the time she was built, her colour had been dark Home Fleet grey, and I think we all enjoyed slapping on the Mediterranean light grey, and when completed, the old lady looked more like a ballerina. I have never seen a ship look so different![18]

'Hands paint ship' was not without its hazards. OD B.A. Carlisle, a Hostilities-Only rating aboard in the autumn and winter of 1940–1, describes an incident while painting the aft screens:

I have never showed any ability as a handyman and not surprisingly did not shine in sailors' tasks as an Ordinary Seaman. In harbour, whilst painting some of the ship's structure above the quarterdeck on a stage with a fellow seaman, I had some difficulty in easing the rope round a stanchion above us to lower the stage so I foolishly gave the rope a jerk; the stage upturned, my companion managed to hold on and I fell down unceremoniously in front of the Officer of the Watch.[19]

Of course, this zeal for cleanliness and paintwork often went well beyond the immediate needs of hygiene, maintenance and appearance. The many coats of paint slapped on in peacetime not only added to the ship's weight but represented a severe fire hazard in battle. Endless polishing could also have unexpected consequences. Vice-Admiral Sir Louis Le Bailly recalls the confusion after the Hood was bombed in the North Sea by a Ju 88 in September 1939:

...More serious was the loss of electrical power to the port

Painting ship, in this case in AP507C (Mediterranean Fleet light grey) for service 'up the Straits', c.1936–8. The men are sitting on adjustable stages doing a 'fleet' or strip down the side before moving aft to do another. Balsa rafts were provided to assist with this task though none are in evidence here. Advice and encouragement are proffered from above.
HMS Hood Association/Higginson Collection

eight-barrelled pom-pom. A circuit breaker had been knocked off by the shock. The electrical repair parties were defeated by the *Hood*'s past: brass information plates on the junction boxes detached for polishing had been muddled when replaced. Efforts to run emergency power leads to the pom-pom succeeded only in bringing some warmth to the petty officers' hot locker, not materially adding to our fighting potential.[20]

In the 1930s it apparently took £135 and four tons of paint to cover the exterior of the ship. The issuing of paint was in the hands of the Commissioned Shipwright and his men, but its supply was the responsibility of the Paymaster Commander who presided over that other great edifice of shipboard organisation, the Central Storekeeping System. On commissioning the *Hood* was provided by the Admiralty with a six-month supply of 10,000 items weighing in at over 400 tons. These items, ranging from bedding to rape seed oil, were stowed in any of 40 stores and compartments throughout the nether regions of the vessel, including the Paint Store on the lower deck forward. It was the duty of the Supply Department to keep a permanent tally of the quantity and location of these, the majority of which would eventually be issued from the Central Store on the main deck. The only items not on the Paymaster's ledger were ordnance and engineering spares and equipment, which were looked after by the Gunnery and Engineering departments respectively. The ship's stores were divided into four broad categories: Permanent Stores (such as hoses, piping and fittings for which replacement was occasionally necessary), Consumable Stores (including cleaning gear, cordage, canvas and paint), Victuals or foodstuffs of one kind or another, and finally Clothing (or 'slops') and tobacco. Clothing was purchased from the Issue Room (known as the 'slop room') on the upper deck, the men's daily Kit Upkeep Allowance of 3d. evaporating in the replacement of worn-out rig, largely as a consequence of the Navy's inability to decide on a practical working outfit for its men. The ship could store up to four months' supply of food, but meat, fish and fresh produce would be purchased from contractors ashore as the opportunity arose. There were, in addition, fourteen days' rations of 'hard tack'—biscuit and corned beef—for dire emergency. Menus for the ratings were drawn up for the approval of the Paymaster Commander by the Warrant Supply Officer and then prepared in the various galleys by over 30 cooks. Immediate responsibility for victualling rested with a pair of Chief Petty Officers supported by a number of Supply Assistants and a General Mess Party of seamen given the task of 'storing ship'. The *Hood*'s last crew produced a couple of memorable characters in this particular fief of the Supply Department. First the 'Jack Dusty' himself, CPO Supply Geoff Pope, who befriended the actor Jon Pertwee over illicit tots in a Victualling Office reeking of neat rum, and then a formidable three-badge 'tanky' in the shape of AB W.E.S. 'Darby' Allen, Captain of the Hold, two men who at the time of their death in May 1941 had given a total of eighteen years' service to the ship. The victualling party reminds us of the small groups of men who in their work and society made up the wider community of HMS *Hood*. Throughout her thousand spaces, decks and compartments dozens of such parties performed their duties with varying degrees of competence and enthusiasm, from the glamour of the admiral's barge to the

THE PAYMASTER AND HIS ORGANISATION

Until the Great War responsibility for a ship's stores and accounts had rested with a trio of warrant officers: the gunner, the boatswain and the carpenter. Without any formal training in accountancy and no clerical staff to assist them, these three had somehow managed to maintain their books and accounts in whatever spare time their technical duties allowed. With the outbreak of that conflict, however, it became obvious that the functioning of a modern capital ship required her domestic organisation to be put on a professional footing, and in 1917 responsibility was transferred to a suitably overhauled Accountant Branch. By 1922 a new Supply Branch was introducing Central Storekeeping into the Royal Navy, a system which, like General Messing in 1920, saw its first trials in the newly-commissioned *Hood*. Henceforth the paymaster's work fell into three main areas. First came the responsibility to which he owed his name, that for the men's pay and allowances, the records of which were maintained in ledgers kept by the dozen writers embarked before being forwarded to the Admiralty. Then there were the myriad stores, victuals and clothing supplies described elsewhere for whose acquisition, accounting, stowage and preparation the *Hood* relied on the services of several officers and around 50 ratings from Chief Petty Officer (Supply) to the cooks in the ship's galley. Finally, for the ablest officer there was the traditional post of captain's or admiral's secretary. In *Hood* this great organisation rested under the authority of the

Paymaster Commander who usually held the post of Squadron Accountant Officer in addition. Assisting him were a lieutenant-commander, several lieutenants, sub-lieutenants and midshipmen and the 60 specialist ratings listed. The captain and admiral were each attended by a further pay officer. In *Hood* the appointment of Captain's Secretary was held by a Paymaster Lieutenant whose duties included dealing with all mail addressed to the C.O. and keeping the service records of all officers and ratings. It was a demanding role requiring expertise in naval law, coding and ciphering as well as the timeless virtues of tact and diplomacy. The post of Admiral's Secretary, similar in nature, was taken up largely with Admiralty matters and the organisation of the Battle Cruiser Squadron. As a paymaster cadet in *Hood* from 1938–9, Keith Evans' duties thus reflected the full seagoing remit of the Accountant Branch:

I was of course still under training and spent time in the Ship's Office (getting my Ledger Certificate), Naval Stores, Victualling Office, the Galley (making bread and rolls) and the Captain's Office (for Captain's Requestmen, Defaulters, etc.).[21]

It was in *Hood*, too, that Ronald Brockman, one of the great Paymaster Vice-Admirals of the twentieth century, cut his teeth as a midshipman in 1927–8 before giving 27 years' unbroken service as secretary to Admirals Backhouse, Pound and Mountbatten between 1938 and 1965.

filthy drudgery of the Double Bottom Party. Through their labour and character the ship acquired that distinctive quality which made her what she was, set her apart from all others, caused her men to remember her for the rest of their lives.

To return to the ship's peacetime harbour routine, at 09.05 (10.05 in winter) the Bosun's call sounded 'Divisions', the second daily muster of her company. Fallen in on the quarterdeck and in the batteries, the men were inspected by their officers and reported as present and correct—or not as the case might be—before being led in prayer by the chaplain. It was traditional for the men to line the side two ranks deep and face inboard but Cdr O'Conor, ever mindful of his ship's *éclat*, had different ideas:

Hands should always fall in facing outboard at Divisions and Evening quarters. Staring at paintwork is a deadly dull occupation, and viewed from outboard the appearance of

[20] Le Bailly, *The Man Around the Engine*, p. 53.
[21] HMS *Hood* Association archives.

GROG

At 11.00 the call 'Up spirits' announced a treasured moment in the naval day, the rum issue. In 1655 the capture of Jamaica from the Spaniards for the first time brought a copious supply of rum to the English palate and within a few decades it had replaced beer as the tipple of choice in the Royal Navy. The initial tot consisted of an inebriating half pint of neat rum, a ration Admiral Sir Edward Vernon saw fit to dilute with four parts of water in 1740. Vernon's men called him 'Old Grogram' after the coat of that fabric he habitually wore and from this came their name for the frothy concoction he inflicted on them: grog. The relative proportions of spirit to water were a matter of some debate in the Navy which finally settled on an eighth of a pint of rum mixed with two parts (occasionally three parts) of water for each man aged eighteen and over. Chief and petty officers, however, continued to enjoy the privilege of taking their ration neat. The rum itself, 95.5° proof and 54.5 per cent alcohol by volume, was accurately recalled by Lt-Cdr Joseph H. Wellings U.S.N. as 'dark and tasted like [the] high-grade Jamaica rum that I drank in Kingston'.[22] In the Spirit Room on the platform deck aft the Paymaster kept a three-month supply of 1,000 gallons double-locked and under permanent Marine sentry. Each day at 11.00 a party of men including the Master-at-Arms and 'Jimmy Bungs', the ship's Cooper, headed below to tap the day's ration from the oak barrels stored there:

> As the room is below the water-line it strikes cool, but the pungent fumes of the spirit assail the nostrils of the party. So strong is the smell that sometimes, with newcomers, it has the effect of making them slightly intoxicated, much to the amusement of the old hands.[23]

The spirit was drawn off into a small oak barrico which was eventually hoisted up to the forecastle along with the rum tub itself, a large lidded affair with the inscription 'The King God Bless Him' done on the side in gleaming brass letters. At 11.50 the bugle call 'Grog' brought

Rum issue on the forecastle by Port No. 1 5.5in gun, c.1935. It is noon and the leading hands of each messdeck are ready to receive the grog in their 'fannies'. Just visible behind the barrel is the elongated barrico containing neat rum. A pair of Marines have been entrusted with the issue while a Supply rating (with ledger) and regulating petty officer look on.
HMS Hood Association/Willis Collection

the leading hands of each mess onto the forecastle where they lined up before the barrel in mess order. Here, supervised by the Warrant Officer of the Day and a regulating petty officer, the Cooper doled out the exact issue for each mess using the set of seven copper measures provided for this purpose while a Supply rating ticked off the ration in his ledger. Once the issue was complete the warrant officer passed the order to 'See it down the scuppers', the few pints of residue being deposited into the sea by Admiralty command. A related tradition was 'Splice the Main-Brace', the issue of an extra tot

of rum by the sovereign or an admiral after arduous duty or a great celebration.

Though proportions returned to earlier levels with the outbreak of war, relatively few took up their rum ration during the lean 1930s, most choosing to devote the 3d. allowance to wives and families. In 1934 only 14.8 per cent of the *Hood*'s Executive Branch took grog, while the figure for miscellaneous ratings (OAs, ERAs, Artisans, Cooks and SBAs) stood at 29.5 per cent and for the better-paid and sorely tried Engineering Department 40.4 per cent; the rum ration for officers had been abolished in 1881 and for warrant officers in 1918.[24] For those who did take their ration, however, the tot was a valuable form of currency on the lower deck. As Jon Pertwee recalled, the framework of hospitality was 'where three sippers equal one gulp and three gulps equal one tot'.[25] Under these circumstances an eighth of pint of grog could go a long way, particularly with the older rating:

> After two weeks… I had found an amenable 'Stripey' who for 'sippers' would relieve me of all future mess duties. […] During my time on the lower deck, for two sippers daily, my hammock was unlashed, hung in prime position, lashed up next morning and put away in the hammock nettings by a kindly three-badge disciple of Bacchus. For a further daily gulp another old rumpot would do all my dhobi-ing (washing). […] Two more sippers relieved me of many mess-deck chores, like washing-up, drawing stores, and food preparing. So you can see why I called anyone a fool who took threepence a day in lieu.[26]

[22] NWC, Wellings, *Reminiscences*, p. 79.
[23] Campbell, *Customs and Traditions*, pp. 66–7.
[24] See Appendix III.
[25] Pertwee, *Moon Boots and Dinner Suits*, p. 147.
[26] Ibid., pp. 146 & 147.

[27] RBS, p. 128.

the ship is enhanced by seeing the faces, rather than the backs, of those fallen in. […] When the Commander brings the Divisions from the stand-easy position to properly at ease by calling the ship's name, every man should brace up and grow a couple of inches.[27]

The conclusion of Divisions was usually the signal for a spell of competitive drill between the two watches, perhaps the lowering of all boats or the rigging of the ship's awnings. This ended with the 10.30 Stand Easy, a ten-minute break during which the men could enjoy a smoke and a breather before resuming their duties until the call for 'Up spirits' at 11.15 (traditionally 11.00) heralded the end of the Forenoon watch. By 11.40, just as the rum 'tanky' and his men were bringing the grog up to the forecastle, the decks were being tidied and secured before the men proceeded to dinner. 11.50 would find

men from each mess lined up to receive the rum ration while the Cooks of the Mess were in the Cooks' lobby collecting dinner from the galley lift. Fifteen minutes later dinner and grog were being served on the messdecks. Smoking was permitted outside and on fine days the Marine band might well play a medley of popular airs on the boat deck after dinner, the hands sitting about in the sunshine. One day a week—usually Thursday—a 'make and mend' half-holiday spared the men any further work until 15.40. Otherwise at 13.10, while the Cooks hurried to clear away the last of the dinner things, the order 'Out Pipes'—extinguish cigarettes—was passed and within five minutes the men were again forming up to be assigned work for the rest of the Afternoon watch. Work continued, interrupted by a ten-minute 'Stand Easy' at 14.20, until the order for 'Secure' was piped at 15.45. Throughout the ship cleaning gear was being stowed in deck lockers, magazines and storerooms locked and lathes silenced for the night. Then at 16.00 came the bugle for Evening Quarters.

Until the installation of a broadcasting system ('the tannoy') in about 1939, all general orders in the *Hood* were passed either by Bosun's call or bugle. The Bosun's call was used for the majority of routine orders—'Divisions', 'Secure' and 'Dinner', to name but a few—these being piped through the ship by a pair of Bosun's Mates and four Call-boys, who trilled their way across decks and along passages. The whistle was also employed on the quarterdeck in the traditional ceremony of Piping the Side whenever an officer came aboard. In *Running a Big Ship*, the manual for executive officers he published in 1937, Cdr O'Conor ruefully noted that 'Very slovenly drill is often seen at the head of the gangway when receiving officers and in piping the side'.[31] His emphasis on the subject no doubt owed much to the appalling incident at Gibraltar one evening in March 1934 when Admiral Sir William Fisher, Commander-in-Chief, Mediterranean Fleet, arriving unannounced at the gangway, found none to receive him save a solitary Marine Bugler. When Fisher emerged an hour later with 'the quarter-deck elite' in tow, the side was of course fully manned, pipes, Marine Guard and all. The bugler in question, T. McCarthy, then only fifteen, takes up the story:

> Our visitor was piped over the side and all seemed to end nicely. But no; on reaching the jetty he stopped, turned and faced us all. Then he said 'Thank you, bugler, for welcoming me aboard and doing your job properly. I salute you!' And he did just that.[32]

Apart from its ceremonial function, especially at 'Colours' and 'Sunset', the bugle joined the Bosun's call in marking off the *Hood*'s daily routine from 'Hands fall in' at 06.00 to the 'Last Post' at 21.00. The bugle was also used to pass specific orders with calls such as 'Cable Party', 'Libertymen' or 'Saluting Guns' Crew', the number of 'G's added indicating which watch was being addressed. In war, however, its intended function was to transmit vital orders ('Close all Watertight Doors', 'Darken Ship') or alert the crew to imminent danger ('Repel Aircraft', 'Gas Alarm'), for which its range and urgency were better suited than the Bosun's whistle. In the event, the introduction of the tannoy sounded the death knell of the pipe and bugle in the Royal Navy though both continued in use until after the Second World War. Writing around 1930, Rear-Admiral Arnold-Forster describes the new equipment being fitted into the major units of the Navy with a distaste shared by many officers of his generation:

> In these ships many of the orders that would have been piped on deck in stentorian tones by the boatswains' mates and repeated round the mess decks below by 'call boys' are spoken quietly into the transmitter on deck, and reproduced all over the ship in the loud raucous voice of the loud speakers.[33]

His view encapsulates the reaction of an influential group of officers to the introduction of any technology regarded as undermining the skills that had made the Navy what it was. The debate provoked by this outlook was carried into virtually every sphere of naval life, not least the *Hood* where the use

TOBACCO

Among the privileges of service in the Royal Navy was the provision of duty-free tobacco, a pound of which could be had each month for 1s. 10d. By the 1930s a majority of ratings were drawing their 'baccy' in half-pound tins which they would then roll into cigarettes, but the older men preferred to receive theirs in leaf form and make up 'pricks' in the time-honoured manner. Bill Stone of South Devon, a stoker in *Hood* from 1921–5, explains the procedure:

> The first stage of the preparation process involved cutting out the black stems of the leaves—from which snuff could be made. Having done that, you then had to damp the leaves and roll them tightly into an elliptical shape which was fat in the middle and tapered to two pointed ends. Canvas was wrapped around followed by spun yarn—all wound tightly all around. The leaves could be stored in this form and remain fresh. The men would cut tobacco off to use for roll-ups as they needed.[28]

Other recipes called for the addition of rum and the resulting plug of tobacco was also carved up for pipe smoking and chewing. But, like fancy ropework, the business of preserving leaf tobacco was a dying art in the Navy and much to the disgust of his elders the younger man tended to cigarettes rolled from the lighter tinned tobacco known as 'Tickler's'. Cigarette rolling being a rather tiresome operation, 'tickler firms' sprang up on the lower deck selling roll-ups for ha'penny a time to make a little extra on the side. Ticklers were fine for a smoke aboard but when a sailor went ashore he wanted something better and for this he turned to the 'posh' cigarettes sold in the ship's canteen. Tobacco was increasingly rationed in wartime Britain but the services continued to enjoy duty-free cigarettes, Sub-Lt John Iago reporting prices of 6d. for 20 on joining the *Hood* in September 1939.[29] But, cheap as it was, and despite being at last permitted to smoke, few midshipmen or boys could afford to take advantage.

For reasons of safety, health and productivity the Navy placed restrictions on smoking aboard, which was for the most part confined to designated areas on the open deck and limited to mealtimes, the ten-minute 'Stand easy', and off-duty periods until 21.55. Smoking below decks was permitted only in the heads, the ship's offices, the recreation space on the shelter deck and in the chief and petty officers' messes—though never in working hours. In addition, officers were allowed to light up in the wardroom after the various toasts at dinner each evening. These were the rules, but with such a high proportion of nicotine addicts of all ranks they were unlikely to be observed and smoking went on throughout the ship—even in 'B' turret where OA Bert Pitman and Commissioned OA 'Sam' Sulley puffed their way through each day on pipes.[30] For the legal smoker a total of 27 basin-shaped spitkids were placed on deck when meals and 'Stand easy' were piped, being as swiftly removed once they were over. Spittle, it should be added, was no longer an acceptable addition to the contents of the spitkid.

[28] HMS *Hood* Association archives.
[29] Iago, *Letters* (Loch Ewe, 3–5 October 1939).
[30] IWM/SA, no. 22147, reel 3 (1939–41). Commissioned OA John C. Sulley was lost with the ship in 1941.

of the ship's broadcasting system was a matter of disagreement between Capt. Francis Pridham and his executive officer, Rory O'Conor, in 1936. When entering or leaving harbour it was O'Conor's view that

> The Commander needs to have the upper deck under his instantaneous control… for a really smart effect to be obtained, and the loud-speaker equipment… is invaluable in giving him this command.[34]

But Pridham would have absolutely none of this:

> I was expected to use a telephone for giving orders to the

[31] *RBS*, p. 128.
[32] Cited in Wells, *The Royal Navy*, p. 158.
[33] Arnold-Forster, *The Ways of the Navy*, p. 27.
[34] *RBS*, p. 131.

fo'castle. This I refused to do: I had a powerful voice and except in a gale of wind when I could use a megaphone I needed no electrical aids.[35]

For all that, Pridham and his successors made frequent use of the tannoy to broadcast information on forthcoming movements and international developments over the messdecks. The pipe and bugle therefore survived in the *Hood*, though firmly harnessed to the tannoy. In the handbook for naval chaplains he published in 1944, the Rev. Beardmore, chaplain of the *Hood* between 1939 and 1941, gives a flavour of their use in war:

When you turn in at night have your clothes ready to slip on should the alarm rattlers be sounded. In day time the bugle sounds 'alarm to arms' for enemy aircraft, and 'action stations' for enemy surface craft. At night the alarm rattlers are sounded from the bridge, followed by 'action stations' on the bugle through the broadcaster.[36]

But night in peacetime held few such terrors, and after Evening Quarters was sounded at 16.00 the men either went ashore or shifted out of the rig of the day and into more comfortable gear before settling down to tea. For most their day's work was done. At dusk the quarterdeck played host to the third and most cherished ceremony of the naval day, 'Sunset', when the White Ensign was hauled down for the night. Sunset was reserved for peacetime in harbour because at sea as in war the Ensign flew until it was blown or shot away. Here is V.C. Scott O'Connor's description of it off Victoria, British Columbia one day in June 1924:

At sunset the customary ceremony of hauling down the Flag was more beautiful than usual. The Olympic Mountains that had looked down upon us from their silver solitudes up in the heavens, creatures remote and aloof in their far-off beauty, became flushed with a rosy pink; small gold clouds hung over the tops of the Canadian fir trees; and as the sun neared the horizon, the trumpeters who herald his departure, the drums that beat at the close of day, assembled for the ceremony of his passing. There they stood stiffly at attention, waiting for the word of command. At each of the flags, the Jack at the fore, the White Ensign aft, on each ship, two seamen stood waiting for the signal to haul down the Flag. Along the quarter-deck to port and starboard stood other seamen, holding in their hands the lateral cords. An Officer of the Royal Marines stood at attention, a telescope under his arm. All waited in silence for the signal. And then of a sudden it was given, and the whole line of flags came fluttering down to the surface of the quarter-deck; the bugles sounded the Last Post, the White Ensign slowly descended, as if the proud Flag were reluctant to give way to the shadows of night. Far up at the top of each tall mast, a seaman retreated step by step down the hundred rungs of a ladder, making his departure with the same calm and unhurried deliberation. At last it was over. The snows of the Olympics withdrew into their invisible monotones in a grey sky; the band struck up, its drum-beats throbbing in the clear Canadian air, and one more day closed in the life of the Empire…[37]

The men passed the hours until supper at 19.00 writing letters, playing games, mending clothes, painting, reading or studying for higher rating as the mood took them. There might be rehearsals for the S.O.D.S. Opera or training for one of the *Hood*'s many sports teams. This was also the opportunity for the trades or 'firms' to set up business in lobbies and messdecks as the tannoy broadcast the latest dance and musical hits over the ship. At 20.30 the 'Cooks' completed their day's work by clearing up the messdecks in readiness for Commander's Rounds at 21.00, a brief inspection heralded by the 'Last Post'. It took the Commander or Duty Officer about 20 minutes to thread his way through the *Hood*'s messdecks and before he had finished the men were retrieving their hammocks and slinging them for the night. By the time the Bosun's Mate called 'Pipe Down' at 22.00 a good number of his shipmates were either in the arms of Morpheus or counting the rivets in the deckhead.

Eventually the day came when HMS *Hood* put to sea. Four hours before she sailed the Engineering Department had begun to raise steam, flashing up boilers and opening the sectional valves on the steam mains to admit power to the turbines. As the moment of departure approached curls of oily smoke started to rise from funnels rumbling like thunder as they expanded in the heat of the boilers. The last boats were brought up to their davits and the cable party gathered on the forecastle for the ship to slip her moorings. Admiral Sir Frank Twiss describes the spectacle:

A battleship, especially a Flagship, leaving Portsmouth was a major event. All harbour traffic was stopped, tugs lay in readiness, special flags were flown and the great ship, with her crew fallen in on deck, the cable officer standing in the bows, the blacksmith ready to knock off the slip on a huge anchor in case of need, the Admiral on the bridge and the Royal Marine Guard and Band in white helmets paraded on the quarterdeck, awaited the moment of departure. Stationed on the quarterdeck were an Officer and a Midshipman ready to see that all was in proper ceremonial order, each wearing a frock coat or bumfreezer according to rank and equipped with a telescope. […] Immediately prior to the wire hawsers being slipped or the tugs secured there is feverish activity on the quarterdeck. The Admiral on his way to the bridge is possibly conferring with some Staff Officer, last-minute messages arrive, people leave the ship, salutes are rendered according to status, the Commander prowls around satisfying himself that all is properly prepared, the gangway or brow is ready for the crane to hoist it away and the Captain is on the bridge reassured by the report that the ship is ready for sea.[38]

The off-duty men formed up by divisions. The band struck up *A Life on the Ocean Wave*. Crowds cheered their goodbyes as the ship sheared herself from the jetty. But for the Coombs twins, Boy Seamen sailing in *Hood* for the first time in May 1935, the event was a huge disappointment:

The pride we took in our first appearance as part of the crew of the 'Mighty *Hood*' as she slid quietly and quite close to the fortifications guarding the entrance to Portsmouth

[35] Pridham, *Memoirs*, II, p. 167.
[36] Beardmore, *The Waters of Uncertainty*, p. 59.
[37] O'Connor, *The Empire Cruise*, pp. 244–5.
[38] Twiss, *Social Change in the Royal Navy*, pp. 15–16.

harbour with cheering crowds waving their farewells was soon put into [perspective] with the remark that some of the crowd were glad to see us go and the order to clean ship on leaving the land. Instead of getting a close and interesting view of the Warner Light Ship and Nab Fort with the Isle of Wight in the distance, all we had to remember that first adventure by was a close look at our decks as, on hands and knees, we rubbed the grime of Portsmouth away to reveal the near white wood that we had thought white.[39]

Once the ship was under way the Officer of the Watch shifted the log from the quarterdeck to the bridge where his duties assumed a far more critical dimension. Entrusted already with the minutiae of her routine, discipline and functioning, to him now fell the awesome responsibility of ensuring the safety of the ship and all embarked in her. Perched on the bridge—the first such structure to be enclosed in a British capital ship—it was his task to keep the *Hood* on her pre-determined course and at the stipulated speed while maintaining the closest watch for hazards both of shipping and geography.[40] His chief reference was the Captain's Standing Orders, a set of instructions based on a complete evaluation of the ship's capabilities and manoeuvrability by which she was expected to be navigated. Even with the benefit of these and up to eight bridge lookouts with high-powered binoculars, steering the ship presented a significant problem in foul weather or poor visibility, particularly if she was sailing inshore or with other vessels in company. In such cases the OOW would have recourse to the Battenberg station-keeping instrument, a pelorus for establishing relative bearings and a small rangefinder for measuring distances from nearby vessels.

But it took more than instruments to make a seaman. As Capt. Francis Pridham put it, the challenge of seamanship lay in the ability 'to foresee *all* that might happen. It is required of a true seaman that he shall be proof against such failure'.[41] No circumstance tested this ability more than heavy fog:

…In ordinary experience thick fog means a time of strain and anxiety for those on the bridge of any ship. In the vicinity of shoals, especially in tidal waters, constant care and concentration are necessary to ensure safety under way, and the risk of collision with other vessels is always present. At no other time are the faculties of sight and hearing kept so taut and alert.[42]

The onset of fog or a significant alteration of course immediately required the Captain and the Navigator to be roused from their cabins if they were not already on the bridge. The first duty of the Navigator, or 'Pilot' as he was known, was to establish the exact position of the ship. For this he relied on three instruments above all: the sextant, with which he ascertained the altitude of the sun and known stars; the chronometers, stowed in a cabinet beneath 'X' turret, which gave him the mean time at Greenwich; and the ship's compasses by which he could steer and take bearings of objects. On the bridge stood the magnetic compass binnacle and forward of it one of the gyro repeats of the master gyro compass on the lower deck. By dint of these he could establish latitude and longitude and at length lay off a course for the ship in the chart house behind the compass platform. If time or weather prevented sights being taken then he would have recourse to the echo sounder

[39] IWM, 91/7/1, pp. 42–3.
[40] It should be added that an air defence platform was fitted atop the existing structure in 1936, with which she served out the rest of her career.
[41] Pridham, *Memoirs*, II, p. 152.
[42] Arnold-Forster, *The Ways of the Navy*, pp. 57–8.

Hood sailing from Portsmouth in the autumn of 1931. Though frequently away for months at a time, her crews and their families were spared the extended foreign service routinely performed by much of the British Fleet. Other than the war, *Hood*'s longest absence from her home port was the nineteen months she spent in the Mediterranean between June 1937 and January 1939.
Bibliothek für Zeitgeschichte, Stuttgart

Her mainmast flagpole struck, *Hood* passes beneath the Forth Bridge after a spell at Rosyth on 15 July 1934. By the 1930s advances in wireless telegraphy had obviated the need for lofty 'flat roof' aerials so *Hood* was among the last ships in the Royal Navy required to perform this evolution.
HMS Hood Association/Mason Collection

43 Warden, 'Memories of the Battle Cruiser H.M.S. "Hood"', p. 83.
44 Ibid., pp. 83–4.

Below: The pain of separation. *Hood* leaves Portsmouth for the Caribbean on 6 January 1932.
Mrs Sheila Smith

which informed him what depth the ship was in, the results obtained being compared to the chart for her supposed position. Another new device fitted in *Hood* by the late 1920s was the radio direction finder with which bearings could be taken from beacons set up along the British coast. An increasing number of these also issued a sonic pulse which, when picked up on the ship's hydrophones, permitted the range to be calculated as well, though the radius of these devices limited their use to coastal waters. The results of these calculations were laid out for the benefit of the flag officer and his staff on an electronic plotting table installed on the Admiral's bridge. Mid. Ross Warden (1940–1) explains its operation:

At sea my station was in the plot room which was on the Admiral's deck below the main bridge. It was a small compartment roughly 8 ft. x 6 ft. The plotting table was approximately 3 ft. x 2½ ft. The requisite chart was set above the glass top, while underneath the glass was a circular light about the size of a sixpence within which was a cross, the centre of the cross representing the ship's position. The mechanism which drove the position indicator was far beyond my comprehension, and maintenance was the responsibility of the electrical branch. The whole purpose of the table was to keep an accurate picture of enemy dispositions relative to our own position. The Admiral [Somerville] was a regular visitor to the plot room.[43]

Sometimes, however, the plot malfunctioned:

The schoolmaster commander and I took alternate night watches which were from 10 p.m. until 6 a.m. One was allowed to relax but not sleep soundly on the small leather couch. This particular night on our return from the convoy there were few reports of enemy activity and I relaxed too well. Around 3 a.m. I was suddenly aware I had company with an alarming amount of gold lace—no less than Sir James himself. He glanced at the plot, said 'Good grief, boy! We are in the Navy, not the Army. Look at this.' To my horror the ship was proceeding at 24 knots across the French Sahara. That mechanical error was very quickly rectified.[44]

Once the ship's position had been determined and her course laid off, appropriate orders were passed via voicepipe to the steering position in the upper conning tower and to the engine room control platforms via telegraph if a change of speed was necessary. Keeping the *Hood* on a steady course was no easy task, especially in heavy seas, and no one spent longer than a 'trick'—two hours—at the wheel. A good helmsman, it was said, was born and not made and it took much skill to anticipate the effect of wind and water sufficiently to prevent the ship from yawing her way across the ocean. Mid. Robin Board R.N.V.R. spent an hour and a half conning the *Hood* off Northumberland one night in March 1934:

It was part way through the middle watch. In the wheelhouse, a surprisingly small, dimly lit cell two-thirds of the way up the great steel citadel that formed her forward superstructure, an RNVR midshipman was at the wheel. The wheel wasn't very big, and it stood on a scrubbed beech grating. In front of him was a slit in the

impressive operation—the firing of a shell with line attached across the after portion of the *Hood*. In fact, the shell landed in the middle of the Marine Band which was standing by ready to play to the men who would have to haul in the ropes and cable. [...] It is not until one is told what the exercise is to be, understands the calculation in time and distances that have to be made, that one can fully appreciate the enormous responsibility of dealing with the great masses.[72]

This subject was another on which Cdr O'Conor had very definite ideas:

It is generally agreed that an 'ocean' tow, which includes towing disabled ships out of action, as when *Indomitable* brought *Lion* home from the Dogger Bank, should and would be made with a single tow-line. 'Tow Forward' in the Service is frequently complicated as a drill, by adherence to the idea that it is desirable to provide, and to use simultaneously, two sets of hawsers, presumably with the intention of occupying all hands. There is as little room for two sets of hawsers on the average forecastle as there is for two projectiles in one gun.[73]

Another favoured exercise recreated that nightmare scenario for any capital ship at anchor: a night attack by destroyers or motor torpedo boats. In such instances the *Hood* relied for her defence chiefly on the eight (later six) searchlights controlled from the Night defence station aft. Rear-Admiral Arnold-Forster:

As darkness sets in every searchlight is kept manned. An

extra dynamo is warmed up below and kept jogging round, a leading stoker standing by to open up its steam valve instantly. A sharp look-out is kept from bridges and control positions for dim outlines of attacking destroyers. Flaming funnels may give them away, or the smell of burning oil fuel if they attack from up wind. Should the destroyers coming down from ahead succeed in locating the ship, her one object is to beat them off before they get close enough to make good shots with their torpedoes. Directly they are sighted, the captain from the bridge orders 'Switch on searchlights!' One of the foremost lights picks up the foam of a destroyer's bow wave, which always shows up first. The trainer keeps hold of that destroyer

[72] Godfrey, *Naval Memoirs*, IV, pp. 51–2.
[73] *RBS*, p. 112. Despite O'Conor's comments it is clear that *Indomitable* towed *Lion* with two hawsers, one of which broke repeatedly.

Below: Hood preparing to take *Repulse* in tow in the Mediterranean in 1937. One of *Repulse's* hawsers lies ready on her forecastle.
HMS Hood Association/Higginson Collection

Bottom: Hood oiling the destroyer *Escapade* off Spain in 1937.
HMS Hood Association/Higginson Collection

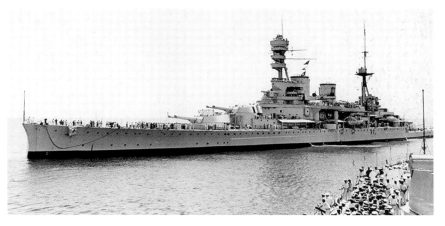

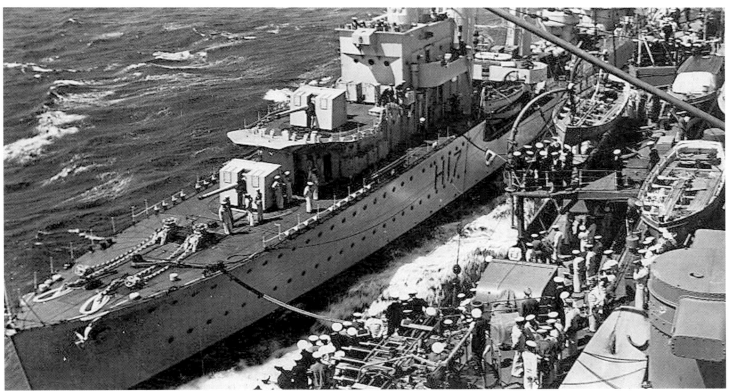

[74] Arnold-Forster, *The Ways of the Navy*, pp. 167–8.
[75] Le Bailly, *The Man Around the Engine*, p. 23. A single searchlight produced 25,000 candlepower of illumination.
[76] Arnold-Forster, *The Ways of the Navy*, p. 161.
[77] Ibid., p. 49.

with his beam as she draws rapidly aft through his appointed arc of training. He makes sure the next light has picked her up, then flicks his beam forward again to search for another bow wave. Until one of the beams settles on him, the ship's searchlights actually help the destroyer captain to make his attack. Then the effect of the steady glaring eye of the searchlight becomes dazzling and confusing, and makes it extremely difficult for those in the destroyer to judge the distance and course of the ship and to get off a good shot with their torpedoes.[74]

Needless to say, these exercises were not without danger. Louis Le Bailly recalls the effect of a quarter of a million candlepower of light directed onto his picket boat off the Spanish coast in January 1933:

> …With the whole fleet anchored in Vigo Bay, there was a night attack exercise by the fleet picket boats simulating motor torpedo boats. My picket boat led a feint attack and was soon spotted and held by a dozen searchlights as the real attack came in successfully from the other side. The result was an appalling attack of 'searchlight eye' which sent me into the sickbay.[75]

Next came paravane drill. The paravane was a torpedo-shaped minesweeping device which was streamed at the end of a lengthy cable attached to the stem of the ship. The expectation was that a mine, having fouled the cable, would be drawn onto a serrated cutter fitted to the head of the paravane where its moorings would be promptly severed. Once surfaced the mine could be dealt with by small-arms fire or otherwise detonated. Effective as they were, the real challenge of using paravanes lay in getting them in and out of the water, an evolution that required the Boatswain and his men to set up derricks on either side of 'B' turret. Rear-Admiral Arnold-Forster explains the trials of dealing with these 'uncouth monsters', which in *Hood* were stowed on the screens abaft the conning tower or in lockers behind the forward breakwater:

When the signal 'Out paravanes' is made, there is a rush to the forecastle to prepare all the gear, and a pair of paravanes is lugged along on trolleys and triced up on small davits on either side ready for dropping. When dropped into the water, they quickly disappear beneath the surface and sidle off well away from the ship. Sometimes a paravane, not approving the way it is dropped, or feeling its inside to be slightly out of adjustment, instead of diving away, turns sprawling on its back and comes flopping along the surface. It then has to be recovered and hoisted in again. Or when being got in, it may take it into its head to dive under the ship's bottom and refuse to come out when the ship is stopped for it. However, when their tricks become known paravanes give little trouble.[76]

Cruising off Spain during the Civil War Capt. Pridham always took the precaution of streaming paravanes as his ship approached any harbour suspected of having been mined by either of the warring parties. But in wartime the *Hood* routinely ran paravanes for an entire patrol, recovering them only on entering harbour.

In such drills and exercises resided much of the spirit of the interwar Navy. Beleaguered by treaty restrictions, government parsimony and loss of prestige, the Navy remained firm in the conviction that success in battle depended above all on seamanship, brawn, stamina and resource; on speed of action and obedience to orders; on efficiency honed through endless repetition and healthy competition. There can be little doubt that this ethos served the Royal Navy well during the Second World War, but it also enshrined a reticence towards technical advance and a rigid adherence to received doctrine and practice which was to cost her dear in ships and men once that conflict started.

Eventually the need to refuel or refit would bring the *Hood* back to port. Well-known and well-charted though the approaches to a harbour might be, the order was always passed for a leadsman to take his place in one of the 'chains' of the ship, the small overhanging platforms which in *Hood* were fitted on the forecastle abreast the conning tower. Rear-Admiral Arnold-Forster lovingly describes this timeless facet of the seaman's art just as it was beginning to pass into history:

> Heaving the lead is an art that can only be acquired by practice. The leadsman plants his feet firmly on his grating, leans his body well out against a stout canvas apron that is secured to the stanchions, lowers the 14 lb. lead till it hangs about twelve feet below his hand, and starts swinging it to and fro. A few strong swings brings it to the horizontal, then by a sharp jerk and good timing he takes it right round over his head, once—twice—let go! The lead shoots like a rocket into the water far ahead, whizzing the line out with it. Hand over hand the leadsman quickly hauls in the slack so as to get the line 'up and down' as the ship passes over the spot, and he judges the depth of water in fathoms by the marks on the line. […] On getting a good cast the leadsman calls out in a sing-song voice, loud enough to reach the bridge, 'By the ma-a-ark—five!' 'D-e-e-ep,—six!' and so on.[77]

Getting in the port paravane using one of the collapsible derricks in the spring of 1933. The trolley on which it will be trundled back to its housing abaft the forward breakwater can be seen lying near the derrick.
Author's Collection

Meanwhile, bugles were summoning the off-duty watch to fall in by divisions for entering harbour while the band of the Royal Marines struck up *Rule Britannia* on the quarterdeck. But this was not spectacle enough for Cdr O'Conor:

> A great ship should pass on her way, in and out of harbour, with a certain pomp and splendour and with a flourish of trumpets. For this purpose, a row of a dozen buglers against the skyline on the turrets at each end of the ship, seamen on 'B' Turret and Royal Marines on 'X' Turret, electrically controlled as one unit, and each group with their bugle major, calls the very decided attention of other ships and onlookers.[78]

And, indeed, the *Hood* never failed to impress. Here is Tim Foster's memory of her gliding into the Grand Harbour at Malta in September 1937:

> We were still securing when the Admiral Commanding Battle Cruiser Squadron's flag and the *Hood*'s spotting top arose above the silhouette of Fort Ricasoli. She seemed to be moving at great speed as she passed along the mole. From *Repulse*'s decks and with the recent experience of doing the same manoeuvre ourselves, we could enjoy and appreciate *Hood*'s movements. She is a lovely ship and looked magnificent as she slowed, came to rest, slewed and came astern, heeling as she moved in a swirl of white and green water.[79]

The ability to bring a great ship safely into harbour was an infallible test of seamanship. Between the wars no captain handled his ship with more panache and dexterity than Francis Pridham did the *Hood* during her Mediterranean interlude between 1936 and 1938. Service 'up the Straits' contained two notorious challenges for those who aspired to mastery in ship handling: coming alongside at Gibraltar and mooring at Malta, in each case without the assistance of tugs. Each presented its own special challenges. At Gibraltar the ship's passage to her moorings was complicated by the powerful wind and currents entering the harbour from the Straits, which tended to push her off course at the very moment when lack of speed on the propellers made accurate steering impossible. At Malta, meanwhile, the confines of the Grand Harbour required boldness and judgement against a very low factor of safety. Moreover, an entry was performed under the eyes of the entire port and often in a silence and stillness that permitted onlookers to hear every order passed to the forecastle. One and a half miles from the harbour the *Hood* would reduce speed from 12 or 13 knots to 6.[80] At a distance of 700 yards from the breakwater the order was passed to stop engines, the ship gliding in on her own momentum while the Engineering Department stood by to give Pridham 50,000 horsepower on the propellers once he started manoeuvring her. The *Hood*'s berth was in Bighi Bay just inside the harbour entrance and the following description by Pridham gives some idea of the consummate feat of seamanship required to place her 860 feet there:

> On arrival on the Station our entry into Malta's Grand Harbour gave me an opportunity to depart from common practice, which was to carry the ship straight up her berth

Above: Heaving the lead from the starboard chains, *c.*1927. The canvas apron keeps the leadsman's legs from getting wet. One of the tapes indicating the depth of the water in fathoms can be seen just beneath his hand.
HMS Hood Association/Reinold Collection

Above left: Lord Kelvin's Sounding Machine, which began to replace the leadsman in the chains before the First World War. This is one of the later motor-driven variants, of which the *Hood* carried one on each side of the flag deck. It offered a continuous measurement of depth by paying out or heaving in a sinker attached to a wire slung from the end of a wooden spar projecting from the side of the ship.
HMS Hood Association/Willis Collection

and then swing her 'Bows out'. The *Hood* was the largest ship ever to have entered that harbour. After experimenting with a scale model of the ship on the large-scale chart of the Grand Harbour, I decided that the safest and quickest way was to stop and swing the ship when just inside the breakwaters and then make a bold 'Sternboard' to our berth in Bighi Bay, where the ship was to secure to a large mooring buoy at each end. I then cleared the fairway quickly and so allowed other ships to enter without delay. […] As time passed and I got more experience, and with the help of noting certain landmarks which came into 'transit' thus giving me accurate positions on the chart, and an idea of her speed through the water, I became expert in this manoeuvre and got much pleasure when I succeeded in cutting off a few seconds from former times taken to be fully secured…[81]

Readers might forgive Pridham his conceit for it was in this very anchorage that Admiral Fisher had in 1901 ordered Sir Charles Beresford to 'proceed to sea and come in again in a seamanlike manner' after his ship had botched a similar manoeuvre, the beginning of a savage feud in the Navy.[82] That said, the vivid terms in which Pridham characterised the handling qualities of his ship would hardly find favour today:

> Like many good-looking ladies she is inclined to be wilful, and likes surprising you. Watch her always and very closely. If the moment she gets up to mischief you give her a good hard thump with the engines and helm she will immediately behave like a perfect lady—like her sex in

[78] *RBS*, p. 128.
[79] Godfrey, *Naval Memoirs*, IV, p. 242.
[80] Pridham, *Notes on Handling the Hood*, p. 4.
[81] Id., *Memoirs*, II, pp. 155–6.
[82] The incident is related in Chatfield, *The Navy and Defence*, pp. 41–2.

Top: The *Hood* entering Malta in the autumn of 1937. The off-duty watch is formed up by divisions on the quarterdeck and forecastle.
Bibliothek für Zeitgeschichte, Stuttgart

Above: Capt. Pridham brings *Hood* into the Grand Harbour at Malta without tugs. The paravanes have been recovered abreast 'B' turret and the cable party is fallen in ready to moor the ship c.1937–8.
HMS Hood Association/Higginson Collection

[83] Pridham, *Notes on Handling the Hood*, p. 12.
[84] Arnold-Forster, *The Ways of the Navy*, pp. 78–80

human form, she responds to a heavy hand when she knows she has deserved it![83]

Then came the complicated task of securing to the mooring buoy. Admiral Arnold-Forster describes the procedure in words which capture the minutiae of life and work afloat in the Royal Navy, the passage of a few minutes, the tradition of centuries:

As the big ship passes in through the narrow entrance between the forts at good speed, one of her cutters is manned at the davits, and with her midshipman and a crew of fourteen men, and the blacksmith with his bag of tools, is lowered near the water. The officer of the forecastle and the boatswain give orders and preparations are made for securing to the buoy. One of her huge cables is unshackled from its anchor, and its end hangs idly down from the hawsepipe. The end of the 'picking up wire,' with its spring hook like the snap at the end of a watch chain, is led from the forecastle and placed in the half lowered boat, ready to

slip over the ring of the buoy. This wire is to hold on to the buoy whilst the blacksmith shackles on the cable. The ship's engines are stopped, but she still has plenty of steerage way. When nearing the buoy the boat is slipped from the falls, drops into the water with a crash, and is whisked ahead by a vigorous rush of men on the forecastle, who haul on a boat-rope leading through a block in the eyes of the ship to the stem of the boat. A few strokes of the oars should bring the boat to the buoy, […] the two bowmen… jump on it with the picking up wire, snap it onto the ring, and the other end is carefully hove in by the capstan. The ship should then be secure enough for the blacksmith to get on with his part of the job; and he gets on the buoy with his tool bag. The end link of the ponderous cable has to be coaxed and sniggled into exact position near the ring of the buoy, then a heavy steel pin has to be inserted into tight-fitting holes in the bow-shaped shackle. To do this whilst standing on a slippery twirling buoy without dropping pin or shackle overboard is by no means easy. Small lines manned on the forecastle are passed down to the blacksmith to take the weight for him, and the boatswain on the rail watches his struggles anxiously, and gives him advice. Once the pin is entered a few blows with the maul drive it home, a small steel locking pin is driven in, and in turn secured by hammering a pellet of soft lead into its undercut hole… and nobody but the blacksmith with his special tools can get it out again. The officer of the forecastle at once sings out, 'Shackled on, sir!' to the captain of the bridge. The officer of the watch telephones down to the engine-room, 'Finished with the engines.' At the same moment, the two lower booms that boats make fast to swing out together, the main derrick is topped to hoist out the steam boat, small boats are lowered from their davits and accommodation ladders dropped. The forecastle-men haul the blacksmith up in a bowline.[84]

With this the evolution of bringing the greatest warship in the world into the Grand Harbour was over. Years later Louis Le Bailly's reminiscence summarises the impact this spectacle made on all who witnessed it:

> One of the great sights of the pre-war era in Malta was surely that of Captain A.F. Pridham bringing H.M.S. *Hood* through the breakwater, turning her on her axis (twenty-four boilers—full revs ahead starboard, full revs astern port) and securing her to her buoys fore and aft in (I seem to recall) fifteen minutes flat.[85]

For Pridham, meanwhile, the highest praise lay in the approbation of Vice-Admiral Andrew Cunningham, a renowned ship handler and the sternest of taskmasters. No wonder his midshipmen all got firsts in Seamanship in their Sub-Lieutenants' exams.[86]

Of course, even in Pridham's hands the occasional mishap was to be expected. At best this might mean a gangway smashed or a few stanchions carried away. But in a ship the size of the *Hood* the penalty of equipment failure, misfortune or misjudgement could be very heavy. Len Williams recalls the accident while coming alongside at Gibraltar on 6 March 1937 which claimed the lives of OD D.D. Smith and Corporal W.J. Hayward, R.M.:

> As we were warping our stern into the jetty by means of a wire around the after capstan, a sudden gust of wind caught the stern and tautened the wire, which became jammed on the capstan. The wire started to 'sing' and everybody jumped clear as the wire hawser snapped like a piece of thread, but one unfortunate seaman did not move fast enough, and the wire whipped back viciously and amputated both of his legs. He died the same day in hospital. One always had to be careful when using wires in conjunction with moving the ship. You had to be ready to immediately ease the wire when the strain became too great.[87]

Just as frequently the *Hood* would moor not in a harbour but in open water. Though less fraught than securing to a harbour buoy or coming alongside a jetty, the evolution of dropping anchor was not without its trials and dangers, particularly when performed with other ships in company.[88] The ship's anchors, cables, ropes and hawsers were the special responsibility of the Boatswain, and no evolution tested his skill and preparedness more. On either side of the *Hood*'s forecastle lay the two Wasteney-Smith bower anchors, each weighing over ten tons, upon which she relied for most of her anchoring and mooring. Until it was removed in 1940 a sheet anchor of similar bulk was carried through a third hawsepipe on the starboard side for use in emergencies. In a large anchorage or roadstead the *Hood* might come to with just a single bower anchor, an arrangement which allowed the ship to pivot freely on wind, tide and current. In more confined waters, however, it was necessary to drop both bowers and shackle them together by means of a mooring swivel in order to inhibit the ship's movement. Each anchor was connected to over 3,000 feet of studded cable constructed from links of steel nearly three and a half inches in diameter. These cables, stored in lockers beneath the forecastle, were released by the blacksmith administering a blow to the slip holding the anchor in

place, this promptly disappearing with a mighty splash. Out clattered the cable in clouds of rust and dirt until, at the First Lieutenant's signal, a petty officer started to check its progress at the brake of the cableholder. If the evolution had a perilous moment then this was it. Louis Le Bailly, then a cadet, recalls a close shave at Spithead in November 1932:

> At the end of the autumn cruise when *Hood* dropped anchor at Spithead with the wind and tide astern the cable holder brake failed to operate effectively. The huge cable could run out and part. The first lieutenant (a gunnery officer) used all his magnificent vocal powers to clear the fx'le. Then we retreated to the eyes of the ship where, he comfortingly told me, we should *probably* be safe. Fortunately the cable holder brake began to hold with less than half a cable of chain left in the locker.[89]

Assuming the brake held, the second anchor was released and the procedure repeated until the requisite number of shackles of cable had paid out. The next task was to equalise the length of the two cables, accomplished by working the capstans until both were taut. Now the cable party came into its own, completing the evolution with the delicate and heavy task of attaching the mooring swivel to the cables. With this the ship could be considered moored. And with this, too, the men had made harbour, with all that that implied.

In peacetime the sounding of Evening Quarters at 16.00 heralded the end of the working day for most of the crew and, for a proportion of them, an evening's run ashore with perhaps night leave until morning. By 16.45 the 'libertymen' had changed into their No. 1 suit with gold badges and 'tiddley' accoutrements and were fallen in for inspection on deck. A reading of the pertinent sections of the King's Regulations and

Libertymen in tropical rig crowd into the *Hood*'s 45-foot motor launch for a run ashore in the late 1930s.
HMS Hood Association/Sait Collection

[85] Correspondence in *Naval Review*, 64 (1976), p. 85.
[86] IWM/SA, Mid. John Robert Lang (1936–*c*.1937), no. 12503, reel 1.
[87] Williams, *Gone A Long Journey*, p. 117. For the aftermath of this incident, see ch. 7, p. 175.
[88] Arnold-Forster, *The Ways of the Navy*, pp. 89–94.
[89] Le Bailly, *The Man Around the Engine*, p. 23. The gunnery officer in question was probably Lt-Cdr Eric Longley-Cook.

90 *RBS*, p. 6.
91 Williams, *Gone A Long Journey*, p. 123.
92 Le Bailly, *The Man Around the Engine*, p. 46.
93 Williams, *Gone A Long Journey*, pp. 122–3.
94 IWM, 90/38/1, vol. III, Anecdote 3, p. 6.
95 IWM/SA, no. 11951, reel 4. Midshipman (1935).
96 HMS *Hood* Association archives.
97 Carew, *The Lower Deck*, p. 144.

Admiralty Instructions and they were boarding the ship's boats or drifter for shore. It was said that 'England's best ambassador' was 'a British Blue-Jacket walking ashore in a foreign port' and this was certainly borne out during the great cruises of the 1920s when 'Jack's' behaviour was invariably found to be exemplary.[90] But it was often a different story in home ports or at Gibraltar and Malta. Particularly Malta; AB Len Williams:

Malta provided some pretty hilarious nights which will long live in my memory and, no doubt, in the memories of hundreds of thousands of sailors the world over. We owe a lot to the patience and kindness of 'Joe', the average Maltese lodging house and bar keeper, who on numerous occasions would help the worse-for-wear matloes to bed.[91]

For the officers a typical run ashore might consist of a blow-out at the Rock Hotel at Gibraltar or an evening in the Union Club in Valletta. Louis Le Bailly:

Usually the senior engineer, Lancelot Fogg-Elliot, too busy on board to be anything but a bachelor, would dine with us weekly at Valletta's Union Club. This had a men-only entrance, but through a peep-hole one could jealously watch the poodle-fakers as they disported themselves with their damsels in the presence of some rather forbidding mothers. From frustrated voyeurism it was but a step to the long bar and a gimlet (still the in-drink) and so to the magnificent room, where the knights of Malta had once dined, and an excellent but economic meal.[92]

Though officers occasionally partook, the *Hood*'s ratings were often in search of more prurient entertainment. Len Williams:

In our runs ashore, Doug and I always included a visit to the 'Forty Three' club in Floriana. We usually started here before proceeding along the Strada Reale to the Gut. This club was run by a man of about 40, known to all the fleet as 'Charlie'. He was a female impersonator, who, when dressed up resembled Mae West and took that famous lady off to a T. [...] Sometimes we would take a bus or taxi over to

Sliema and visit one or two of the bars. These were mainly patronised by the destroyer men, since Sliema Creek was the destroyer anchorage. One bar in particular, the 'Empire', staged a female boxing contest as their cabaret show, and we sailors would be treated to an orgy of boxing contests. The contenders, dressed in one-piece swim suits, wore a coloured sash across their chests indicating a 'Miss England' or a 'Miss Austria', or some other nationality. Although to watch two buxom wenches knocking each other about seemed pretty revolting to us, most of us cheered them on as we sipped our iced beer, but the atmosphere was so clouded with tobacco smoke that it was sometimes difficult to see the contenders at all![93]

As in British society generally, attitudes towards sex in the Royal Navy were, for officers at least, a curious mixture of awareness and denial. To this outlook the lower deck often lent its tacit support. Capt. George Blundell, then a midshipman, recalls the efforts of his Westcountry coxswain, PO A.W. Jeffrey, to preserve his moral integrity during the *Hood*'s second Scandinavian cruise in the summer of 1923:

On another occasion I was driving my picket boat along what was then called 'Christiania Fjord' [now Oslofjorden] in Norway. On one side of our route was a ladies' bathing pool. It was summer and all the ladies were bathing in the nude. Each time we passed, my dear Jeff directed my attention to some feature on the opposite side of the fjord. Obviously he considered it improper for his young officer to gaze on a naked female form.[94]

In its own way, PO Jeffrey's discomfiture reflects that of the Admiralty itself which failed to include sex education in the curriculum of its officer cadets and midshipmen. A few might be taken aside for a fatherly chat by an officer or chaplain, but as Rear-Admiral Edmund Poland recalled, 'a majority of young midshipmen had their first sexual experience in a brothel'.[95] And not just their first. Paymaster Cdr Keith Evans has this reminiscence of a bordello in Malta in 1938:

Strada Stretta commonly known as 'The Gut'. Wrexford's 'Aunty' a bit of a hag I think from Northern England. Bella and Tessa may have been Maltese but I think more oriental, comfortable numbers. As Gunroom officers, most of us aged 18 or 19 (not quite under age), I think our leave expired at 19.00 (later on occasions), so we had to make way for our 'elders' from the Wardroom and Warrant Officers' Mess.[96]

As a result, incidence of venereal disease—or 'Wardroom lumbago' as it was euphemistically known on the lower deck—was a concealed but not unknown reality among the officer corps. At least one of the *Hood*'s officers 'caught a dose' during the 1936–9 commission. Confined to his cabin, he was dispatched home at the earliest opportunity.

Attitudes were rather less inhibited on the lower deck where VD remained common despite the fact that improved hygiene and education reduced incidence by more than half between 1912 and 1932.[97] Common enough, indeed, for Chief Ordnance Artificer 'Brigham' Young to give OA Bert Pitman a word to the wise on his first visit to Gibraltar in the summer of 1940:

One of the *Hood*'s steam picket boats at Navarin, Greece in July 1938.
HMS Hood Association/Souter Collection

When we went to our first foreign port, Gibraltar, he sent for myself and another youngster and he said 'I want you two to go over the border to La Línea tonight and I want you to go to a brothel, one that also has a bar. Now go into that brothel, pick the girl you'd most like to go to bed with, but don't. Get yourself a drink, in fact, have several drinks and just sit and watch her.' Well, I picked on a beautiful-looking girl, but having seen her go up and down the stairs with a couple of matloes I lost any desire to get off with her.[98]

But the temptation was always there. Walking along 'The Gut', the red-light district of Malta, sailors were wont to have their black 'silk' scarves torn off by girls eager to entice them into a brothel. Even a stroll though the Alameda Gardens at Gibraltar might lead to an unexpected liaison with a lady 'hawking her pearly' in the bushes. Equally, there was great pressure from old-timers for young sailors to prove their manhood through sexual initiation in a brothel. In the handbook for naval chaplains he published in 1944, the Rev. Harold Beardmore, *Hood*'s chaplain from 1939–41, dilated on the situation his readers might encounter:

One finds a number of men who are not hardened to loose living. Sometimes the lapse took place after a party where the man had too much to drink, and his resistance to strong temptation was weakened awhile: frequently one comes across a comparative boy who has it pressed upon him by some old-timer that he could never call himself a sailor until he had been with a woman. Thus it was in the form of an adventure that he went wrong, probably with some girl who, for want of a better term, might be called an 'amateur,' and who in the eyes of the young man was probably safe as far as disease was concerned. The important thing is to get hold of the patient before the hardened sinner endeavours to comfort him by saying, 'That's all right, mate; we all get our unlucky runs; no need to take it to heart.' This is first-class propaganda on the part of the devil.[99]

And so yarns were spun of the buxom harlots of Trinidad and St Lucia, of the 'White House on the Hill' at Arosa with its long queues of white-uniformed sailors, of the Oriental beauties of Singapore and Honolulu and of course the varied delights of Southsea and Union Street in Plymouth. But occasionally an encounter with a prostitute in foreign climes might end badly. In September 1937 an official visit to Yugoslavia to celebrate the birthday of King Peter afforded the *Hood*'s crew a week in the port of Split and its hinterland. A first run ashore found the Coombs twins and their pals in one of the harbourside cafés:

It was all very pleasant. We sat there sipping and trying to get used to their local wine or whatever it was and being served by two young and good-looking, clean and smart girls. The next thing, one of our party was seen slipping through the small door following one of the girls. The remainder could only guess what was happening but were alarmed when, a bit later, some Police and Gardia of some kind burst in the little door and could be heard storming up the stairs. Wondering what to do, we could only go outside and wait for developments and soon, after a lot of shouting and commotion, the Police bundled the girl

downstairs, knocking hell out of her just as the window went up and the fourth member of the chums came to the window, looked out and dropped his shoes out before starting to climb down a drainpipe that came down near the window. […] Quite a few people were passing and all the rest of the lads could do was to pick his shoes up for him and help him back across the lane into the café… He told us he had just finished 'emptying his kitbag' when the commotion on the stairs had started and had just got out of bed to put his trousers on when the door burst open. This gang entered and grabbed the girl and started shouting at her and giving her a good hiding. He was petrified and when they had gone looked for the best way out which was the window… After he had recovered [we] decided that the best thing was to get the hell out of it…[100]

Evidently, the pair had fallen foul of King Peter's draconian laws against prostitution.

Return to home port invariably brought pleasures of a different ilk, perhaps a reunion with wife and family or, in the case of the Coombs twins, a visit from their girlfriends after an lengthy train journey from Sheffield. It was Navy Week 1936 and, amidst a carnival atmosphere, the *Hood* lay awash with visitors in dry dock at Portsmouth. For Fred and Frank there were certain naval traditions to be lived up to if possible:

After… a good look round the ship, both above and below decks, except for not daring to offer to show the girls the Golden Rivet, which was reputed to be riveted into every R.N. ship, normally in some secluded part, well out of the way of prying eyes, we [spent the evening] passing the time away and smooching on Southsea Common and promenade, which was later to be converted into a vast, grass-covered bed. The popular tune at the time was 'Chapel in the Moonlight', but Southsea became renowned for the number of girls' knees, bent not in prayer but only earning their railway fare, and the words 'Bobbing Arseholes in the Moonlight'.[101]

As in every other sphere, the onset of war brought with it a

[98] IWM/SA, no. 22147, reel 3.
[99] Beardmore, *The Waters of Uncertainty*, p. 66.
[100] IWM, 91/7/1, p. 71.
[101] Ibid., p. 52.

Some of 'England's best ambassadors' sampling local beverages at a bar in Corfu, July 1938.
HMS Hood Association/Souter Collection

quickening of amorous life. While the *Hood* was refitting at Portsmouth in the last summer of peace, Jim Taylor and his companions on the Boys' Messdeck were given strict instructions to avoid the café at No. 12 Great Southsea Street, the petty officers' brothel.[102] Condoms were issued free and in quantity but 'Rose Cottage', the ship's VD ward with the legend 'Only those who have been purified can be pure' posted on its door, continued to have its patients, despite the red-ink entry on a man's medical history and damage to his prospects that followed.[103] In the quarterly report he submitted on the medical condition of the ship in April 1940, Surgeon-Cdr K.A. Ingleby-Mackenzie, the Squadron Medical Officer, listed four cases of gonorrhoea and one of syphilis, though two of the former were to the same man.[104] Though diagnosed and discharged to hospital, the syphilitic not untypically denied all exposure to infection, whereas the others admitted contracting theirs during the ship's brief stays at Greenock. In his report for the next quarter, which the *Hood* spent largely at Plymouth and Liverpool, Ingleby-Mackenzie recorded nine fresh cases of gonorrhoea and the installation, complete with framed instructions, of an ablution cabinet in the urinals near the port battery in which the men could discreetly take prophylactic measures after an encounter ashore.[105] Still, this shows a decided improvement on 1932, when the ship recorded a total of 75 cases of VD, many contracted during a spring cruise in the Caribbean.[106]

Needless to say, such liaisons occasionally brought consequences other than disease. With due allowance for post-war embroidering, the following aside by OD Jon Pertwee is worth citing:

Lieutenant Davies also had the well nigh impossible task of running to earth those lusty lads who had given *noms de plume* and aliases to various female conquests in port. Among the favourite names to be assumed was Able Seaman Derek Topping. When the arm of a derrick or crane is about to reach the perpendicular, the operator would shout 'Derrick Topping' meaning the crane arm had almost reached its limit. This pseudonym was frequently given after a night of love and passion, to minimise chances of identification should the sound of tiny mistakes be heard pattering up the companionway. Another much-used name was Able Seaman B.M. Lever. The initials B.M. standing for breech mechanism, and lever referring to the lever on a gun that opens and closes the breech. So pathetic letters of remarkable similarity would arrive with envelopes marked S.W.A.L.K. (sealed with a loving kiss), possibly reading:

Dear Derek,
You said you was going to rite but you never. I am now three months gone. I am disparate has I am beginning to show—wot are you going to do about it? Rite soon.
I.T.A.L.Y. Doris.
P.S. H.O.L.L.A.N.D.

These impassioned pleas were posted on the ship's notice board and brought forth little response other than cruel laughter. Derek Topping and Basil M. Lever should've felt very ashamed of themselves.[107]

The remainder, with wives or partners a world away and perhaps little inclination for adventure, had to find contentment in the privacy of their cabin, hammock or caboose and await a reunion all the sweeter for the length of its parting.

Of course, there were activities ashore beyond mixing with the opposite sex. Proverbially, there was unrestrained consumption of 'the Demon Drink', however much the Navy might try to discourage it. Jon Pertwee has this wartime reminiscence:

When at anchor in Scapa Flow, off duty liberty men used to go ashore to taste the pleasures of Lyness night-life. This, for the majority of the men, meant going to one of the enormous NAAFI canteens and, armed with Naval issue coupons, imbibing their allotted two or three pints of beer. Clever barterers, however, always managed to collect a pocket full of additional coupons, which allowed them the long-looked-for opportunity of going on a monumental 'piss-up'. After several such outings I sold my beer coupons and opted for other joys of the flesh.[108]

Getting them back on board was no mean feat. The Coombs twins had the misfortune of crewing one of the boats sent to bring the men off after a night's carousing on the Côte d'Azur in May 1938:

A lot, as drunk as newts, were stood on the wooden jetty with their girlfriends and others and would not climb aboard us. We struggled to carry some of them aboard the launch, only to see some of them crawl on their hands and knees to the other end and out again so eventually we went back to the ship with whoever would stay and went back with six big marines to get the others aboard. It went on a long time and it ended up with the cells on the ship that full of drunks that they had to release the more sober to find room for the more drunk.[109]

One of the drunks was Stoker Harry Holderness:

No one was interested in returning until a stoker petty officer, who had drunk his fill, said he was going aboard—and soon we were all following him. When the boats arrived at the *Hood*, which was three miles out, the officers were furious because the ship had not sailed. Most of us were singing and waving long French loaves. Commander Orr-Ewing called for us to be quiet and ordered the coxswains to take the boats round the ship until we were silent. But that set us singing 'Side, Side, Jolly Ship's Side'. Once round, however, we all quietened and filed aboard. The stoker petty officer, who had drunk too much, got a recommend for getting us all aboard.[110]

No wonder the task of returning a boatload of drunken sailors was among the sternest tests a midshipman could face in his time aboard. There were severe punishments for the drunk and disorderly, but with the outbreak of war came recognition of the importance of allowing the crew to let off steam and thus a more tolerant attitude towards inebriated libertymen. AB Len Williams remembers the *Hood* at Greenock in early 1940:

There was a considerable difference in height between

[102] Conversation between the author and Jim Taylor (1939–40) in Portsmouth, 6 February 2003.
[103] IWM, 91/7/1, p. 62.
[104] PRO, ADM 101/565, Medical Officers' Journal, 1 January–31 March 1940, vol. 28, ships H–I, ff. 37r–43r.
[105] PRO, ADM 101/565, Medical Officers' Journal, 1 April–30 June 1940, vol. 28, ships H–I, ff. 43v–44r & 40v.
[106] PRO, ADM 101/536, Medical Officers' Journal, 1932.
[107] Pertwee, *Moon Boots and Dinner Suits*, p. 154. I.T.A.L.Y. stands for 'I trust and love you' and H.O.L.L.A.N.D. 'Hope our love lives and never dies'. Other *noms de plume* were 'Montagu Whaler' (an allusion to the rig of one of the Navy's boats) and 'A. Vent'. Lt Horace Davies R.M. was lost on 24 May 1941.
[108] Ibid., p. 155.
[109] IWM, 91/7/1, p. 69.
[110] Cited in Coles & Briggs, *Flagship Hood*, pp. 123–4.

high and low tide in the Clyde area, and when the lads began to come back from leave, some of them the worse for wear and singing their heads off, it proved quite an evolution to get them safely down the steep ladders and into the boat. Captain Glennie, being a wise gentleman, and knowing the ways of sailors, had told the ship's company that he did not mind how his lads got back on board, provided that they DID get back. 'I do not wish to go to sea in an emergency with any of my crew missing' he warned us. Consequently, many and varied were the conditions the sailors were in when we finally got them on board. On one occasion we lowered a steel provisioning net into the liberty boat, and loading the helpless ones carefully into it, hoisted them inboard with the main derrick. However, I cannot remember us ever letting the skipper down. We always sailed with a full crew.[111]

Apparently there was no more cherished desire among certain matelots than to fetch up with a wealthy widow ashore, and in this endeavour not a few went adrift on foreign service. During the 1936–9 commission none pursued this goal more ardently than 'Tiny' Fowler, one of the ship's divers. Here is Fred Coombs' version of events. The date seems to be January 1938 and the place Marseilles:

One of the best yarns was started on that visit when Tiny Fowler, our huge… diver went adrift. Whether or when he had met his friends before could only be guessed at, but he clearly knew where to meet them because he went ashore the first night at anchor and that was the last we saw of him 'til just before we sailed, when a smart, medium-sized motor yacht came alongside. They must have known what they were doing as they came to our forward gangway… where a glamorous grandma came on the bottom platform with Tiny Fowler to do a bit of snogging before the Regulating Crushers came running down to Tiny to run him back up into custody.[112]

Three months later at Golfe-Juan Fowler was at it again:

Lofty Fowler was not allowed ashore this time but had worked them a flanker by hiding in the forepeak of the picket boat that had been used by the officers to go ashore. He went by nipping out when the officers had gone and before the crew could stop him was off. The crew swore blind that they did not know that he was aboard… but that was the last we saw of Tiny 'til the day we sailed. […] The next day when we went in to fetch the few stragglers… one of our first customers was Tiny Fowler, drunk too, but with what looked like a dowager duchess on one arm, a bunch of flowers and a basket full of eggs, some of which had got broken and were running down his trousers, on the other. If his lady friend had intended the eggs to restore his vitality she was unlucky as Tiny returned peacefully.[113]

Fowler had ample time to savour the memory in the army detention quarters at Corradino, Malta.

Then there was desertion. At no time in the *Hood*'s career did more men desert than during the World Cruise of 1923–4. Evidently, the chance of a life in the sun for a man who was

otherwise committed to another eight or ten years in the 'Andrew' was well worth the remote possibility of recapture, and by the time the Special Service Squadron sailed for Hawaii six months into the cruise 151 had deserted from her seven ships, all but ten in Australia.[114]

Needless to say, the Navy lived and worked to a harsh code of discipline, one that came down heavily on those who infringed it. Mindful of Invergordon, Capt. Rory O'Conor made no bones about the constitutional framework under which every man served:

…Those in authority can afford to act calmly, seeing that they are backed by the authority of the whole Service and the Naval Discipline Act, with the Lords Spiritual and Temporal and all the Commons in support.[115]

The point was not lost on the majority of men. As CPO Harry Cutler put it, 'We knew what to expect. Those who got into trouble were those who kicked over the traces and refused to submit to discipline.'[116] The structure of this discipline mirrored the organisation of the ship herself. LS (later Cdr) Joe Rockey of Plymouth:

The routines were quite strict and well laid down and if you did not carry them out you expected to be penalised, and if you disobeyed of course it meant that you were passed further along the chain of command, dependent on the error you'd made or what offence you'd committed.[117]

Enforcement of the King's Regulations and Admiralty Instructions by which the Navy was governed was entrusted to the Master-at-Arms and the ship's three regulating petty officers or 'crushers'. The Master-at-Arms, or 'Jaunty' as he was known, was a man to respect. An experienced petty officer selected for toughness and intelligence, the lower deck held few secrets from him. As the senior Chief Petty Officer in the ship he was the only rating afforded a private cabin and thus the privilege of sleeping in a bunk. His influence on the lower deck was enormous:

The Master-at-Arms in a ship is a man whose co-operation and friendship one should cultivate. He is as a rule most helpful when he sees you are all out to encourage him in keeping the ship free from such things as leave-breaking, theft and immorality. A good Master-at-Arms can probably do more than any other member of the lower deck towards making a ship's company happy and contented.[118]

But if the Master-at-Arms chose to wield his considerable power with a heavy hand then life for many on the lower deck could be made intolerable, as indeed it would be for any unwise enough to 'get athwart his hawse'. Occasionally the need for men to be detailed for disagreeable duty required the crushers to trawl the lower deck for volunteers and for such occasions it behoved one to be on the right side of the Jaunty and his men. But their main duty was in keeping discipline and enforcing observance of naval and shipboard regulations both ashore and afloat. This meant patrolling the messdecks for illicit drinking or proscribed games like Crown and Anchor, or against the bullying, violence and intimidation that occasionally reared its head. It might also mean landing with a shore patrol to moni-

[111] Williams, *Gone A Long Journey*, p. 140.
[112] IWM, 91/7/1, p. 63.
[113] Ibid., p. 69.
[114] O'Connor, *The Empire Cruise*, p. 228.
[115] *RBS*, p. 84.
[116] Conversation with the author in Devonport, 23 May 2003.
[117] IWM/SA, no. 12422, reel 1.
[118] Beardmore, *The Waters of Uncertainty*, pp. 53–4.

tor the behaviour of libertymen and counting them back on their return to the ship. In his capacity as head of the ship's police, the Master-at-Arms was always in attendance at Commander's defaulters, the miscreants and their crimes enumerated in a large book carried under his arm. During the regime of Cdr Rory O'Conor (1933–6), Commander's defaulters took place at 08.20 each morning save Sunday. It was a duty to which he gave the utmost importance:

The Commander needs to be in a consistently judicial frame of mind for his magisterial duties… Appearances are often misleading, and when they are unfavourable to the accused one may be misled into an injustice. Remember the old Chinese proverb: 'A man may be a teetotaller, but if his nose is red, no one will believe it.'[119]

Some 3,000 defaulters having passed through his hands during the 1933–6 commission, O'Conor was able to offer readers his accumulated wisdom on the dispensing of justice:

The majority of small offences are committed by thoughtlessness or mischance and not by intention, and after one solemn warning most men are careful not to reappear as defaulters. […] In dealing with defaulters a Commander comes face to face with an endless variety of motives and mischances which bring men to his table, cap in hand. It is a central truth of human nature that men's faults are the corollary of their virtues, and that without our faults we should be different men for good, as well as for ill. Justice is most just when tempered with mercy.[120]

Where punishment was concerned, the following measures were recommended for leave-breakers:

First offence:	If reasonable explanation—Caution
	If no reasonable explanation—Scale
Second offence:	Scale
Third offence:	Captain's Report[121]

'Scale' here meant stoppage of leave, though stoppage of pay was an additional consequence of going adrift. Other infractions would receive one of the many punishments in the naval inventory, from No. 16, an hour's extra work, to No. 10a, two hours' rifle and bayonet drill after tea. Of course, if one had an identical twin aboard it was possible to mitigate the worst effects of a punishment through artful substitution. Two sailors in this ambiguous situation were Fred and Frank Coombs, boy seamen with a knack for getting into trouble:

We had become well accustomed to doing plenty of jankers, but Gib added a further dimension as in the Med awnings were generally left rigged, which gave us the advantage of not being seen by the higher decks or the bridge. We soon came up with the idea of sharing the punishment by changing places at some place in our hour-long trot around 'A' and 'B' turrets. From our time at St Vincent we had always shared our loads in punishment by taking turns to do the mustering and the evening drill. The fact that we now had two huge turrets to screen [us] from the Instructor and four convenient hatches leading to a

lower deck to choose from made things much easier for us. No matter at which point our keeper stood to keep an eye on us, there was always one hatch not in his vision where we could change over… The other boys under punishment, who we had thought might object to our swapping over, made no secret of the fact that they were as keen as us to see our tormentors taken out for a trot. Though a lot were aware when one of us was on punishment and poor old [PO] John Bunney tried to catch us at it by nearly doing as much running as us… we were never caught doing our vanishing act as one ran up [onto] the upper deck and one went down to the lower…[122]

In the event of a serious or repeated misdemeanour the offender would be sent before the captain for jurisdiction under the Naval Discipline Act. Captain's defaulters usually took place around 11.00, the Master-at-Arms once again in attendance. The captain was the only officer aboard who could punish a man by warrant, that is either by confining him to the ship's cells for a maximum of fourteen days or by stripping him of his rate, his good conduct badges or his Good Conduct Medal if he had more than fifteen years' service. In the case of boys or midshipmen this extended to authorising a caning, administered by the Master-at-Arms to the former and the Sub-Lieutenant of the Gunroom to the latter. Officers were tried by court martial, a tribunal composed of their fellow officers acting under naval law but over whose judgements the Admiralty reserved plenary power. Really serious cases, men whose crimes fell beyond the punitive jurisdiction of the captain, were discharged to the detention quarters ashore for periods up to 90 days. Others, like Hood's mutineers in 1931, would find themselves ejected from the Navy 'Services No Longer Required' or subject to criminal prosecution.

Eventually, after two or three years, the day came for the Hood to sail for home and pay off so that another crew might recommission her. It was a solemn moment. With the off-duty watch mustered by divisions on deck, the band of the Royal Marines struck up Rolling Home and an enormous paying-off pendant unfurled from the main topgallant as she got under way, a bunch of golden bladders secured to the fly to prevent it trailing in the water. The length of the pendant traditionally reflected the duration of the commission or the number of men embarked. The same procedure, to Rule Britannia, was followed on entering harbour, crowds lining the shore while families waited on the jetty to be reunited after months, sometimes years, of separation. Within hours the ship had paid off, many of her people scattered to the four winds never to meet again.

Boats, Floats and Drifters

'There is no truer saying than the old one that "A SHIP IS KNOWN BY HER BOATS".'[123] The manning, sailing and maintenance of a capital ship's boats represents a world unto itself, rich in lore and tradition. The Hood's flotilla, constantly changing as a result of damage, exchange and the introduction of new types, usually numbered sixteen or eighteen vessels from 16-foot skiffs to the 50-foot steam pinnaces.[124] These fall into three distinct categories: sailing boats, steam boats and the motor boats which by the 1930s were on the verge of mak-

119 RBS, pp. 79 & 80.
120 Ibid., pp. 79 & 83.
121 Ibid., p. 80.
122 IWM, 91/7/1, pp. 48–9. HMS St Vincent was the boys' training establishment at Gosport.
123 RBS, p. 191.
124 See Northcott, HMS Hood, p. 59, and Roberts, The Battlecruiser Hood, pp. 18–19 for tables of the ship's complement of boats.

ing the first two extinct.

The largest of the sailing boats were the 42-foot launches, of which *Hood* always carried at least one. However, much the most important were the 27-foot whalers, 32-foot cutters and 30-foot gigs, the first two clinker-built and the last of carvel construction. These were standard equipment in the Navy, their provenance denoted by brass badges with the device of each ship affixed to their bows; those belonging to flagships mostly bore a representation of the admiral's flag. For most of her career the *Hood* carried between eight and ten sailing boats and in them she competed in the pulling regattas each summer. Gigs were stowed on the boat deck but the two whalers and two of the four cutters shipped until 1940 were kept on davits for use as seaboats, two on each side. The launching of the ship's seaboat, essential for emergencies, was one of the evolutions which punctuated the naval day. Capt. Pridham's account of the lacklustre drill he found on assuming command in February 1936 gives an idea of the procedure:

> On reaching open water, as first priority I exercised the seaboats (the lifeboats). A life-saving 'evolution' I had been brought up to regard as requiring absolute efficiency and utmost speed. I was shocked to see evidence of ignorance of the elementary details of lowering and hoisting boats at sea. The Commander expected me to stop the ship's way before he gave the order to 'slip'. I had never dreamt of such slovenliness. Hooking on and hoisting were equally lacking in any vestige of smart work. The little tricks of manipulating the boat's falls and lifelines when hooking on, which I had learned as a midshipman, were apparently unknown to my Commander or to the boats' crews. The boats were hoisted lazily at a slow walk. On seeing this I made my disapproval known to all hands by ordering the Commander to lower the boats again and have them hoisted at the run. It was a risk, but it worked.[125]

However, the workhorses of the *Hood*'s flotilla were the two 50-foot steam pinnaces or picket boats and the 45-foot barge provided for the use of the admiral and his staff. Completely decked in and capable of making 11 knots in calm water, on these magnificent vessels fell most of the ship's daily errands. Paymaster Lt-Cdr E.C. Talbot-Booth R.N.R.:

> Every day each ship of any size appoints a D.S.B. (Duty Steam Boat) which is responsible for performing most of the ordinary routine in harbour, such as fetching off postmen in the morning, running officers ashore, probably towing some heavily laden boats with liberty men going ashore in the evening and a thousand and one odd jobs. She lies at the bottom of the rope ladder attached to the boom projecting from the side of the ship until such time as she is called to the gangway to undertake some duty.[126]

Boy Jim Taylor was Bow Boy in Rear-Admiral William Whitworth's barge in the spring of 1940:

> The Admiral's Barge was a splendid craft having a crew of about six or seven: a Coxswain, a Chief Petty Officer, a Petty Officer, a Stoker and Boys on Bow and Stern. As Bow Boy I had to ensure that the boat came alongside smoothly

and had a boat hook to ensure that this was done. I was, however, not entirely free in the use of the boat hook as there was a series of defined movements to adhere to.[127]

On these steam boats a generation of sailors and midshipmen would lavish their care and attention both aboard and afloat. Boy Fred Coombs:

> One of the rewards… was to be… given the jobs as 1st and 2nd Picket Boats' crews as Fender Boys. We took a great deal of pride in polishing the black, highly polished boat's side with wax polish when lifted inboard. That black boat's side and the near white wooden decks were our responsibility and we spent hours of diligently applied hard work in polishing the… side when possible and daily scrubbing of the decks to near white with a piece of shark's skin, sand and salt water that the sun could bleach and show the regular black pitched joints up to perfection.[128]

The gleaming brass funnel of *Hood*'s 1st Picket Boat had come from the battlecruiser *Lion* in 1922 and on it Mid. Le Bailly and his companions devoted not only their time and energy but also the remains of their daily pay in Brasso. The crew beautified the

Left: 'Away seaboat!' One of the *Hood*'s 32-foot cutters being lowered fully manned from its davits in the late 1930s. The fall at the bow is about to be slipped and the men on the starboard side are just getting their oars ready. The device on the bows denotes the boat as belonging to a vice-admiral's flagship.
HMS Hood Association/Mason Collection

Left: One of the *Hood*'s cutters at sea, in this case for the melancholy task of recovering the body of a pilot officer killed in a crash off St Catherine's Point, Isle of Wight on 5 March 1935.
HMS Hood Association/Willis Collection

---

125 Pridham, *Memoirs*, II, p. 147.
126 Talbot-Booth, *All the World's Fighting Fleets*, 3rd edn, pp. 127–8.
127 HMS *Hood* Association archives.
128 IWM, 91/7/1, pp. 53–4.

One of the steam picket boats secured to the boom in a heavy swell. The midshipman in command holds the jacob's ladder for one of his men. The coxswain is at the wheel in a sou'wester. The boom was planed flat on top to allow the men to run along it. Crewmen usually boarded by sliding down the 'lizard' ropes, one of which can be seen on the right. The brass funnel tops for the *Hood*'s steam boats came from the battlecruiser *Lion*. Note the boat badge on the bow.
HMS Hood Association/Clark Collection

interior with tasselled curtains and cushion covers of duck and blue jean while those skilled in the art of fancy ropework produced turk's heads for the boat hooks and elaborate fenders for the sides. The result was a vision of gleaming paint, scrubbed wood and polished brass, the pride and joy of the two crews responsible for her. However, in Cdr Rory O'Conor's view, boat crews had not only to act the part, they had to look it also:

A clean boat is sometimes spoilt by men of indifferent appearance. Picked men, both as workers and on account of good physique, are the men to represent the ship in her boats.[129]

And so O'Conor always selected bronzed matelots of formidable aspect to crew his boats. But the ultimate touch was a distinctive outfit and very occasionally an admiral or captain was wealthy enough to dress his boat's crew in specially-tailored uniforms.

If the Navy gave great importance to the appearance of its boats then it also prided itself on their handling and operation, entrusting each to a midshipman under the fatherly eye of a coxswain. The responsibility gave him not only his first taste of command afloat but also his first prolonged contact with the men at close quarters. As O'Conor put it,

The finest training as a seaman and for command that he can possibly have is in a boat if he is given complete charge. Should the boat have two crews, there should be a midshipman for each, working only with his own crew, and hoisted in and out with them in the boat. [...] The Midshipman of a boat must share all the vicissitudes of wind and weather with his crew, and it is not right for him to accept an invitation to go below in another ship while his boat lies off, with the crew exposed to the elements.[130]

The boats' crews therefore enjoyed a spirit of teamwork and endeavour excelled by no other section of the ship's company. Mid. George Blundell was in command of the *Hood*'s 1st Picket Boat during the World Cruise of 1923–4:

Both *Hood*'s picket boats were oil-fired 50 footers. Each had a double crew of one midshipman, one Petty Officer Coxswain, two Able Seamen Bowmen, one Able Seaman

Sternsheetsman, one Stoker Petty Officer for the engine room, and one Stoker for the boiler room. At the time one did not give it a thought, but, looking back, their competence—and loyalty—were incredible. Not once during the whole of my time did my boat run out of fuel, fail to have steam immediately after being hoisted out, fail to carry out the whole trip ordered on leaving the boom, or not be manned speedily by the proper crew. On the World Cruise, when in harbour, the two picket boats ran almost continuously the whole day, the early boat mooring up at midnight and the late boat at 2 a.m. or later. [...] How marvellously all the crew backed one up: they provided all the thrill of a close-knit, trusting team. When one heard the pipe 'Away First Picket Boat' it was a point of honour to try to man the boat before one's crew. I used to hare up from the gunroom, race along the shelter deck, charge along the lower boom, and dive head first down the lizard. Once I lost my dirk doing that! On the World Cruise picket boat midshipmen always wore their dirks whether in monkey jackets or bum freezers, and, at least in *Hood*, manned and left their boats at the boom, never at the gangway.[131]

From an engineering standpoint the operation of the picket boat was like a miniature version of the ship itself. Blundell:

The engine was a twin cylinder compound reciprocator complete with condenser, air pump, circulating pump and lubricating pump. The boilers were of the small-tube 'Yarrow' type, fed by feed and fuel pumps. Forced draught could be applied by closing the boiler room hatch and running the fan. Communication between the Stoker P.O. and the Stoker was usually done by hitting the bulkhead with a ring spanner! The large propeller was right handed, and because stern power was equal to ahead power, stopping power was enormous, so that when going astern on coming alongside the stern could 'kick' quite viciously to port. A good stoker petty officer, head sticking out of the engine room hatch, one hand on the throttle valve and the other on the reversing link, was a great help in going alongside and in stopping in the right place! [...] The midshipman controlled the engines by means of a pull-up handle which rang a gong in the engine room: one gong for stop, two for ahead, three for astern, and four for ease up or slow.[132]

Whereas the smaller boats could be hoisted in and out by the 40-foot derricks and the seaboats brought up to their davits by their falls, the barge and pinnaces, each of which weighed sixteen tons, required the services of the main derrick. Rear-Admiral Arnold-Forster describes the procedure:

Silently the great steel derrick is topped up and swung out over the ship's side, the ponderous hook of its lower purchase block swaying in the air as the ship gently rolls and pitches. By means of boat ropes the picket boat, with fenders out, is slowly hauled alongside; in their plunging boat the crew, who have been preparing their stiff wire three-legged slings, lift up shoulder high the heavy ring joining the legs, and watch for a chance of slipping it over the hook of the derrick purchase. Though the motion of the ship at anchor is only slight, the 16-ton steamboat, if

[129] *RBS*, p. 131.
[130] Ibid., p. 27.
[131] IWM, 90/38/1, vol. III, Anecdote 3, pp. 1–2.
[132] Ibid.

allowed to start swinging like a huge pendulum, would do untold damage. So before the men come up out of their boat, stout 'rolling tackles' for steadying her are passed down for them to hook on. As the boat's crew swarms up the ship's side, boat ropes, derrick guys, and rolling tackles are hauled taught. All eyes are then turned towards the derrick officer who, in oilskin and sou'wester, and holding up a pair of hand flags, is silhouetted in the glare of a light high up on the after bridge. He is watching the boat rising and falling in the sea. Just before she sinks into a trough he signals 'Up purchase, full speed!' then—as the slings tauten—'Up topping lift!' The powerful electric boat-hoist motors hum round; everyone holds his breath. If well done, there is a hefty jar as the weight comes on. If not—a terrible jerk that shakes the mast, makes the whole ship quiver, and brings a tremendous strain on all the gear. As the long, dripping boat comes up out of the water, more steadying tackles are hooked on to her. A slight mistake now may stave in her planking. Firmly held, she is swung in by the derrick guys, and carefully lowered over the boat deck, where her crew and a few shipwrights wait to receive her. The warrant shipwright jumps about in the glare of the light, making frantic signals with his hand for plumbing the boat exactly over her gaping steel crutches. Pushed about and coaxed by many hands, she settles down in her close-fitting bed with a creak. The derrick head is quickly lowered and secured, and ropes coiled down.[133]

The recognised expertise of the Royal Navy in seamanship owed much to the emphasis it placed on boat handling in the training of its officers. Lt-Cdr Joseph H. Wellings, official observer of the U.S. Navy, discovered as much while staying in the ship during the winter of 1940–1:

My visit with the midshipmen developed into a sentimental journey in small boat sailing (my favorite hobby and sport). I listened to their small boat sailing expert describe the various types of sailboats and sailing races. I was certain after watching their young commissioned officers and midshipmen sail boats, that as a group they were much better small boat sailors than our younger commissioned officers and midshipmen.[134]

However, accidents were not uncommon. George Blundell:

One of my early picket boat memories lies in taking some officers from the *Hood*, alongside the detached mole at Gib., to land at Flag Staff Steps. The more junior officers, including the snotties' nurse, were sitting on the gratings on the casing, whilst the engineer, paymaster and surgeon commanders were in the stern sheets. I misjudged the alongside badly and ran the bow firmly on the submerged bottom stone platform of the steps. Being the senior officers in the boat, the three commanders, looking somewhat shaken, made to land over the bow. In ringing tones I sang out 'Nobody is to leave the boat'. I then ordered my passengers, including the three commanders, to stand on the stern sheet gratings. As the officers of commanders' rank appeared somewhat hesitant at carrying out my order to stand on the stern, perhaps I was

over-peremptory with them. However, the stern went down and the bow rose up and the crew were able to right the boat's precarious attitude. Much relieved, I sang out 'Carry on ashore'. I can see the faces of my three commanders now: the engineer looked very angry, the paymaster nonplussed, but the P.M.O. (Dudding) was beaming. In due course I was reported for insolence, my leave was stopped and I received a dozen from the sub.[135]

Nor were they the preserve of midshipmen. Louis Le Bailly recalls an incident at Malta on the morning Vice-Admiral Andrew Cunningham hoisted his flag in *Hood*, 15 July 1937:

With everybody's nerves as taut as bowstrings, it was not long before the beautiful steam barge was called away to take Cunningham to pay his respects to the Commander-in-Chief, Admiral Sir Dudley Pound. What possessed the admiral's coxswain, a rather grand chief petty officer who conversed normally only with the admiral's staff, I shall never know but just as he was about to leave the starboard quarterboom he saw the admiral descending to the quarterdeck. Quickly he rang down for Full Ahead and, turning hard-a-starboard in full view of the quarterdeck élite, placed the barge fair and square in the path of a picket boat. The barge was stove in just for'd of her boiler room and it at first seemed both boats might sink. It took 80 men on four guy ropes to work the *Hood*'s main derrick and never before had they been assembled with such speed. The admiral, by now also steaming slightly, was dispatched in the captain's small motor boat to keep his appointment with the commander-in-chief.[136]

Like much else in the Navy, the business of boat handling was distinguished by an elaborate etiquette, centuries in the making. Rear-Admiral Arnold-Forster provides a flavour of it:

…Every boat approaching an anchored warship after dark is challenged by the hail 'Boat ahoy!' sung out sharply from the bridge forward or from the quarter deck aft… It is the coxswain's business to answer the hail instantly. The correct answer depends on who is in the boat. If officers of lieutenant's rank and above are in the boat the answer is 'Aye, aye!'; for anyone below that rank 'No, no!' If the captain of the ship is in the boat, the reply given is the ship's name; for an admiral the answer is 'Flag!' A boat not coming alongside simply answers 'Passing!' […] Besides these old sea hails, the recognised salutes given by boats have been handed down by generations of seamen—except those for steam and motor boats, which are naturally more modern. The larger pulling boats—double-banked boats they are called—pull two oars from each thwart, and their salute of tossing all oars vertically in the air is an impressive one. Another salute lower in the scale for double-banked boats, and the only one for single-banked gigs, small skiffs and dinghies is to 'lay on the oars'—that is, to rest the oars for a few seconds in the rowlocks or crutches in a horizontal position in line with the gunwale. Boats under sail salute by letting fly the sheets, and the sudden flapping of the sail makes the act quite distinctive. A steam or motor boat's salute, however, is rather a poor affair. She either

'*Hood* was always a wet ship.' Sub-Lt (E) Louis Le Bailly and gunroom companions in the process of winning a bet against the wardroom that they could not sail a cutter from Tangier to Gibraltar between dawn and sunset one day in the autumn of 1938.
Vice-Admiral Sir Louis Le Bailly

[133] Arnold-Forster, *The Ways of the Navy*, pp. 108–9.
[134] NWC, Wellings, *Reminiscences*, pp. 79–80.
[135] IWM, 90/38/1, vol. III, Anecdote 3, pp. 2–3. The officers were Engineer Cdr Frank R. Goodwin, Paymaster Cdr Edgar B. Swan and Surgeon Cdr John S. Dudding.
[136] Le Bailly, *The Man Around the Engine*, pp. 40–1.

stops or eases her engines and the bow wave gradually disappears—not very impressive but all she can do.[137]

As Arnold-Forster evidently realised, the death knell of many of these traditions was sounded—quite literally—by the arrival of the motor boat with its internal combustion engine during the First World War. The *Hood*'s original outfit consisted of a 35-foot fast motor boat capable of 18 knots along with a 42-foot launch which included an auxiliary motor good for 7 knots. A second 35-footer was added in time for the World Cruise in 1923 but these two gave endless trouble on the voyage, to the great embarrassment of Temp. Lt Albert Robinson R.N.V.R., the Thornycroft salesman who joined *Hood* to promote his company's wares. Lt (E) Geoffrey Wells had the misfortune to be charged with their maintenance. His diary for Tuesday 15 January 1924 rather summarises his lot:

Motorboats would not behave as motorboats should; in fact they behaved as motorboats do. Trouble with a big T.[138]

Nor, it seems, had things changed much by 1937. After an absence of four years Sub-Lt (E) Louis Le Bailly rejoined the *Hood* at the Coronation Review at Spithead that year:

I was sad to find that the magnificent steam barge I had known as a midshipman was soon to be replaced by a three-engined speedboat designed by Vospers. The story was that the soon-to-be Vice Admiral Sir Geoffrey Blake had insisted that after the review the new barge should take him to the royal yacht to receive his accolade. This left no time for Peter du Cane, once a [lieutenant-]commander (E), now a famous boatbuilder and director of Vospers, to carry out trials. From the boat deck I watched the new barge come alongside and heard the awful mechanical crunch when the coxswain went astern. With two engines only now serviceable the odds favoured the admiral getting to the royal yacht on time but alas it was not to be. The coxswain, anxious to show off the boat's speed, opened up both throttles to the maximum whereupon the engines died. Happily for the admiral, if not for Vospers, a yellow speed boat belonging to a rival firm spotted the disaster and delivered him to the royal yacht with only minutes to spare. Poor Peter du Cane and his splendid firm were damned forever in the admiral's eyes but the beautiful old steam barge returned to the ship![139]

Mechanical unreliability staved off the inevitable during the inter-war years and the spectacle of motor boats having to be towed in by a steam picket boat was no doubt a source of gratification to officers of the old school. However, reliability and performance had in fact greatly improved by the 1930s and with it the inherent advantages of the motor boat became apparent, principally in reduced weight and manning and increased speed and flexibility. Writing in 1937, Peter du Cane summarises some of the advantages of *Hood*'s complement of five motor boats:

These modern boats ride over the waves when they are fully planing, as opposed to their predecessors' ploughing through the seas, and their seaworthiness and general riding comfort

have to be experienced to be believed, even under the worst possible conditions of sea, and in the smallest type of planing boat. [...] The hoisting weight of the modern 45-foot high-speed picket boat [i.e. motor launch] is about one-third of the weight of the steam picket boat that it replaces... and the main derrick, with its cumbersome and elaborate rigging and its heavy demand on man's time, can be dispensed with.[140]

It took 80 men to hoist out a picket boat or barge and an hour or more for steam to be got up before the midshipman could take the big brass wheel. But though in many ways easier to operate than its steam predecessor, the motor boat left rather more to the delicacy of the coxswain than had earlier been the case:

In the case of the modern high-speed boat, coxswain-control will nearly always be adopted. The coxswain stands or sits at the wheel in the ordinary way, but, instead of ringing gongs to the engine room or working an engine-room telegraph, he will move the reverse lever forwards or backwards as the case may be. The throttle, which controls the engine revolutions, will always be to his hand, but in manoeuvring, the throttle should, as far as possible, be set to predetermined low revolutions of the engine, and left there except in case of emergency. The necessary operations to control the boat will then be confined simply to the use of a steering wheel and reverse lever, which would present no more difficulty than would be the case if there were a wheel and engine-room telegraph. [...] In getting under way, it is essential to use the throttle gently in accelerating. The engines in these fast boats are of relatively high power, and damage can be done by rough use of the throttle. This precaution should also apply to throttling down the engines as well as to opening out. It is a bad practice, and almost equally damaging to an engine, to throttle down very rapidly, though this is not often realised. All movements of the throttle should be smooth and sympathetic to the engines...[141]

The last steam boat was not removed until the refit of spring 1941 but they had had one last laugh at the expense of their motorised counterparts. The ditching of the petrol tanks under air attack on 26 September 1939 meant that they alone of *Hood*'s boat flotilla were of any use when the ship made Scapa Flow the following day.[142] Her final complement included six sailing boats of the old Navy and eight motorised types of the new.

In two world wars the Royal Navy lost 21 battleships and battlecruisers and in no more than one or two cases was it possible to effect anything approaching an orderly evacuation in boats. During the 1920s the *Hood*'s boats were calculated as being able to accommodate 759 of her peacetime complement of over 1,100 men.[143] The rest would have to make do with carley floats and lifebuoys of which there were eight and eleven respectively by 1936.[144] The carley float was a canvas-covered cork ring fitted with life-lines round the edge and a wooden platform in the centre to support its occupants. In October 1939 Sub-Lt John Iago R.N.V.R. informed his family that

I find myself in charge of a carley float with six ratings; I shall expect to be piped aboard! A float is better than a boat because it can be launched by hand without a winch and will float—a boat probably won't![145]

[137] Arnold-Forster, *The Ways of the Navy*, pp. 98–9.
[138] Extracts from Diary of World Cruise, 1923–4, p. 22.
[139] Le Bailly, *The Man Around the Engine*, pp. 39–40.
[140] Writing in *RBS*, p. 120.
[141] Ibid., pp. 120–1.
[142] Vice-Admiral Sir Louis Le Bailly in *Naval Review*, 90 (2002), p. 187.
[143] *H.M.S. Hood: Notes for Visitors* (c.1925), p. 2.
[144] *RBS*, pp. 173 & 204.
[145] Iago, *Letters* (Loch Ewe, 23 October 1939).

Iago would be proved right though he could not avail himself of his carley on the morning of 24 May 1941. In the event, it was only thanks to the three-foot square biscuit floats with which she had been amply provided during her final refit that the *Hood*'s survivors were able to endure until the moment of rescue.

Though far too large to be shipped, the final unit in the *Hood*'s flotilla was her drifter, a vessel of around 200 tons, 90 feet or so in length and with a speed of about eight knots. During the Great War hundreds of trawlers and drifters from the fishing fleet had been requisitioned along with their civilian crews for patrol and minesweeping duty in support of the Navy. Most resumed their peacetime service after the Armistice but a number were retained by the Admiralty for use as tenders for capital ships, cruiser squadrons and destroyer flotillas in home waters. The aim was to reduce the burden on ships' boats by passing on to the drifter the tasks of keeping a major unit supplied and her men ferried to and from their ship. During the 1920s *Hood* was served by the *Halo* which in 1920 accompanied her mistress to Scandinavia and back. On emerging from her 1929–31 refit she was allotted the *Horizon*, to which Mid. Louis Le Bailly was assigned in the summer of 1933:

> Coal-fired, her boilers served steam reciprocating engines driving a single large propeller. [...] A couple of hundred libertymen, several tons of potatoes or cabbages, firebricks, drums of lubricating oil, everything large in numbers or dirty came our way. But there was (to me) a very grand bridge, all of eight by six feet, the wheelhouse directly below, and a crew of 12. The wardroom, constructed in the fishhold, could conveniently accommodate four for meals and three for sleep: one body on each bench beside the table and a third on it. The ship's company lived in even greater discomfort. [...] Stormy nights in the Firth of Forth, Cromarty or Scapa, with gusting winds and sometimes a strong tide, called for judgement and sea sense with little margin for error. Many were the trials and tribulations of the coxswain and engine room crew as a 17-year-old learned the tricks. Happily summer nights were short in the north and drifters, like warships, were strongly built. Somehow we survived.[146]

Inside the fishhold the *Horizon* could accommodate up to 350 libertymen in fair weather by day; by night in foul weather her capacity was limited to 206.[147] However, when sent on ahead of the *Hood* her complement was limited to twelve, all of them entitled to 'hard lying' money as compensation for their discomfort. Louis Le Bailly recalls a trip at sea:

> Either as a mark of favour or because I looked as though I needed fresh air, I learned I was to sail that evening for Portsmouth as *Horizon*'s navigator and one of the two watchkeepers under a young lieutenant, a trip of challenge. Although we midshipmen had run *Horizon* in harbour neither of us had watchkeeping certificates and had never kept watch alone in open waters. There was more to it than that. In theory *Horizon* carried enough coal for the voyage but some years before a similar fleet drifter, the *Blue Sky*, on precisely the same trip had been lost with all hands in circumstances never explained. For this reason we were instructed to close certain shore wireless stations down the east coast and report our position by morse radio. We reached Portsmouth with, literally, only a few shovelfuls of coal left in our bunkers.[148]

The *Horizon* seems to have passed to the battleship *Royal Oak* on *Hood*'s departure for the Mediterranean in 1936, though another was assigned to her on the outbreak of war. Both were to be orphaned before the last shot had been fired.

Torpedoes and Torpedomen

The *Hood*'s torpedo armament has been the subject of controversy since the time of her design and construction.[149] The final design legend of August 1917 stipulated a total of ten torpedo tubes, two submerged forward of 'A' turret and eight on the upper deck amidships. While not satisfactory, the placing of tubes above the main belt was forced on the designers by the shortage of space in a hull filled with machinery and ordnance. In September 1918 the Director of Naval Construction, Sir Eustace Tennyson d'Eyncourt, expressed concern that a detonation of these was liable to break the ship's back given their position over the main strength girders running the length of the vessel. However, the view of the Navy was that tactical considerations made torpedoes indispensable and orders were passed for the *Hood* to be completed to the approved design while the arrangements for her sisters were placed under review.[150] There the matter rested until July 1919 when the continuing demand for horizontal protection which characterises the genesis of HMS *Hood* prompted the removal not only of four of the upper-deck tubes but also the armoured box protecting the remaining two pairs of torpedoes. The understanding was that these would be retained for experimental purposes only and could under no circumstances be considered war fittings. In the event, this stipulation was ignored and the *Hood* was to serve out her time with four torpedo tubes on the upper deck. The original 5-inch protection was however restored during the 1929–31 refit. The submerged tubes were removed together with the after torpedo control tower at Malta in November and December 1937.

The torpedo owed its inception to the ingenuity of a Capt. Luppis of the Austro-Hungarian Navy and to the technical expertise of Robert Whitehead, the English manager of an engineering firm in Fiume. Whitehead produced his first prototype in 1866 but it was not until the early years of the twentieth century that a truly effective weapon appeared. The key development was the production of an enhanced system of propulsion in the form of the Hardcastle heater in 1908–9. By heating the compressed air used to power the torpedo engine the Hardcastle device doubled its speed and range to 30 knots and 6,000 yards. To this innovation was added the angled gyroscope in 1910 which permitted the torpedo to assume a course different from that on which it was launched, thus greatly enhancing the flexibility of the entire system. The *Hood* fired 21-inch Mk IV and Mk IV* torpedoes measuring nearly 22 feet in length and weighing a ton and a half. Though superseded by the Mk IX* in the 1930s, the Mk IV remained a highly sophisticated weapon containing over 6,000 parts. It was powered by a radial engine driven by super-heated steam produced by the passage of pressurised water through a combustion chamber. Kept at a constant depth by a hydrostatic valve and on a steady course by gyroscopic rudder control, the Mk IV was capable of carrying 515 pounds of TNT to ranges of 5,000 yards at 40 knots or 13,500 yards at 25 knots.[151]

[146] Le Bailly, *The Man Around the Engine*, p. 25.
[147] *RBS*, p. 192.
[148] Le Bailly, *The Man Around the Engine*, p. 27.
[149] Northcott, *HMS Hood*, pp. 10–13.
[150] See NMM, HMS *Hood*, ship's cover, II.

The forward tube of the starboard Torpedo adjusting space on the upper deck in July 1932. The reload is suspended above the tube, its warhead projecting into the armoured box. To the left another torpedo has been dismantled for servicing, the body on the right and the tail on the left.
Wright & Logan

easy recovery and then the warhead itself with its pistol, primer and detonator to explode the charge against the hull of the enemy. In wartime the sinking valve in the buoyancy chamber of the torpedo was set to activate at the end of its run to prevent it falling into the wrong hands. But at £2,000 apiece the Mk IV was among the most expensive projectiles in the Navy and losing one in peacetime could be the cause of a Board of Enquiry.[153] Even when located on the surface issuing its white plume of smoke a torpedo might yet give its recovery party a few surprises. Rear-Admiral Arnold-Forster:

A torpedo out for trouble will sometimes play tricks with the picking-up boat's crew. It stops and comes gently to the surface near the target looking mild as milk, and allows them to put securing lines on its nose and tail; then, whilst they are further attending its wants, it rushes off at full speed like a harpooned whale, towing the boat with it and threatening to swamp it. Near the end of its run a sportive torpedo sometimes has a way of trying to put the wind up amongst the boat's crew by wallowing and snorting like a porpoise.[154]

But for the two Boards of Enquiry investigating the loss of the *Hood* in 1941 her torpedoes represented a far more sinister danger to the crew. Both were concerned to explore the possibility that a detonation of the upper-deck torpedoes had caused or contributed to the loss of the ship.[155] Witnesses to the disaster and those who had recently served in her were asked whether the armoured mantlets covering the torpedo tubes were likely to have been open or closed as she went into battle. Captain William Davis, Executive Officer until September 1940, confirmed that they would have been shut.[156] An explosives expert, Capt. John Carslake, indicated that it would require not a near miss but a shell actually detonating on the warhead to cause the explosion of a torpedo.[157] Although members of the Royal Corps of Naval Constructors dissented from its findings, the second board concluded like the first that there was little evidence of a torpedo detonation and attributed the loss of the ship to a magazine explosion. Among the dissenters was a member of the second board, D.E.J. Offord, head of the Director of Naval Construction's damage section through the 1930s, and the DNC himself, Sir Stanley Goodall.[158] Though the theory of a torpedo detonation still has its adherents, subsequent analysis has tended to endorse the judgements of the two boards.[159]

The hundred men who formed the *Hood*'s Torpedo Division were as close-knit a group as any in the ship. In the mid-1930s the 'tinfishmen' produced a stylised version of the ship's badge which replaced the anchor with a torpedo. Len Williams was one of their number between 1936 and 1941:

Hood's torpedo division were a happy-go-lucky lot; we were about 90 to 100 strong and by age and service were the oldest division in the ship. Over 50% of us were three-badge men, which meant that they had at least 13 years service to their credit. At this period, most torpedomen were fairly senior men due to the great competition to get into the branch to begin with.[160]

However, the Torpedo Division's duties extended well beyond tinfish and the shale oil used to lubricate them. Until 1929 the Torpedo Branch was also responsible for the distribution of all

The tubes were loaded and traversed by hydraulic power, a torpedo kept permanently in each tube with a reload slung on rails directly above it. There were two Torpedo magazines, both just forward of 'A' turret shellroom in the hold and with a joint capacity of 32 warheads. Directly above them were the submerged tubes set *en echelon* on the platform deck. The principal working space was the Torpedo body room on the main deck which was served by a pair of elongated lifts descending to the Submerged torpedo room two decks below. Embarkation of torpedo bodies and warheads was performed through a hatch on the forecastle by the forward breakwater, the hardware being lowered through the upper deck and down to the working space below. Supplying the submerged tubes was therefore a straightforward matter but torpedoes for the above-water tubes had evidently to be trundled along the upper deck and assembled *in situ*.

How were the torpedoes aimed and fired?[152] The process was considerably easier than for guns since no elevation data was required. Target bearing and deflection data was provided by a total of eight torpedo deflection sights mounted on the fore bridge, in the conning tower and in the after torpedo control tower on the boat deck. Range was calculated on three 15-foot rangefinders, one atop the after control tower (removed in 1937) and two abreast the Midships searchlight platform between the funnels (both removed in 1940; 12-foot 5.5in rangefinders on the signal platform used thereafter). Until 1929 the resulting information was fed into the Torpedo transmitting room on the lower deck abaft 'B' turret. Here a Dreyer Table generated a setting for the torpedo gyroscopes; after 1931 this calculation was performed in the Torpedo control position on the bridge. Once set, an electric circuit was closed and the 'tinfish' fired remotely from the Torpedo control tower or the after control tower. Whereas submerged torpedoes were discharged with compressed air, the upper-deck ones were launched by a cordite charge. As the torpedo left the tube a lever controlling its supply of compressed air was tripped, the paraffin feeding the heater ignited, the oil jet triggered and the engine started with a whirl of counter-rotating propellers.

Torpedoes were provided with two detachable heads, first a practice one containing teak ballast and a calcium flare for

151 Roberts, *The Battlecruiser* Hood, pp. 17–18.
152 Ibid., p. 18.
153 At 1940 prices; the cost in 1924 was £1,200.
154 Arnold-Forster, *The Ways of the Navy*, pp. 132–3.
155 Jurens, 'The Loss of H.M.S. *Hood*', p. 152.
156 PRO, ADM 116/4351, p. 368.
157 Ibid., p. 383.
158 Brown, Nelson *to* Vanguard, pp. 162–3.
159 Eric Grove, '*Hood*'s Achilles' Heel?' in *Naval History*, 7 (1993), Summer, pp. 43–6.
160 Williams, *Gone A Long Journey*, p. 116.

electrical power on board. This, so said the ship's guide book, included 200 miles of electrical cable and 3,874 light fittings. The increasing sophistication of electrical systems of course warranted the formation of a separate branch but this had been strangled at birth by an Admiralty convinced that technical specialisation was a threat to the fighting spirit of the Navy. In lieu of this the Admiralty decided in 1929 to transfer all high-power distribution—that relating to propulsion, damage control and habitability—to the Engineer Branch while leaving the Torpedo Branch in charge of low-power electrical supply—gun firing, fire-control, emergency, searchlight and telephone circuits.[161] The *Hood's* electricity was generated by eight 200kW dynamos which supplied current at 220 volts DC into a common ring main controlled from the main switchboard on the lower deck beneath 'B' turret. Low-power supply, which depended on numerous motor generators, was controlled from a second switchboard nearby. The outbreak of war for the first time brought a university-trained electrical engineer to the *Hood* in the shape of Sub-Lt (later Electrical Lt) John Iago R.N.V.R. Within two weeks of his arrival Iago had had a new system of emergency lighting for the ship approved by Capt. Glennie.[162] Among those charged with its maintenance was LS Len Williams:

> I had recently been promoted to Leading Seaman and was put in charge of all the electrical emergency circuits, which included [automatic electric batten] lanterns, temporary circuits, sick bay operating lamps etc. I had an assistant, and it was a full-time job for we had some seven hundred of these auto lanterns alone to check over and maintain. They had to be kept charged up and periodically tested to see that the relays did not stick. In view of what happened later it was heartbreaking to know that no opportunity was given to the ship's company to make use of these safety arrangements when trouble did come.[163]

Modifications were still being made in the spring of 1941:

> During the refit I thoroughly overhauled our emergency electrical system, and with the aid of some old motor-car headlamps was able to produce some fairly efficient emergency operating lamps for our action medical teams.[164]

Nor did the Torpedomen's responsibilities end there. Along with the Engineering Department, the Torpedo Division was entrusted with the ship's ventilation which supplied or extracted air from her internal spaces along miles of trunking. The fans for the living and working spaces were powered by electric motors working on the ship's low-power supply. In order to avoid piercing the armoured bulkheads each major section of the ship was served by fans and motors on a unit system. These it was Len Williams' job to inspect:

> I changed my job onboard from Torpedo maintenance to ventilating fan maintenance which was a watchkeeping job, necessitating a visit to every running fan in the ship during one's period of duty. These large fan motors provided the forced ventilation between decks, some being supply fans and others exhaust. It was essential that the lubrication and the electrics of each fan be checked during each watch. As there were hundreds of these fans of all shapes and sizes,

Left: A Mk IV torpedo leaves one of the port upper-deck tubes on the detonation of a cordite charge. Crewmen watch beside Port No. 6 5.5in gun; late 1930s.
HMS Hood Association/Percival Collection

Below: Still issuing smoke, a practice torpedo is hoisted aboard after being recovered by one of the ship's whalers in the late 1930s. The trolley that will return it to the Torpedo body room can be seen in the upper part of the photo.
HMS Hood Association/Mason Collection

and in various awkward positions, it took one the whole of one's four-hour watch to get around them all.[165]

Although the *Hood's* ventilation system was a considerable advance on earlier designs it was found to be inadequate in extremes of heat and failed to prevent the incidence of tuberculosis aboard. Moreover, in relying on natural supplies of air drawn in through ventilation fittings out on deck it made flooding unavoidable in heavy seas, especially on the messdecks forward. At the best of times the crew lived in an environment of 'canned air' with foul smells periodically wafted through the trunking. As Surgeon-Cdr K.A. Ingleby-Mackenzie related in April 1940, not even the Sick Bay was spared:

> The atmosphere in the Sick Bay has at times become very heavy at sea: and this has been cleared by turning on an internal circulation of air in the forward end of the ship, though as the heads are involved in this circulation, the air ventilated is not always of as salubrious an aroma as one would wish. Accordingly another method has now been adopted for the Sick Bay, namely the exhausting of air from the Sick Bay by a special fan placed near the main door down into the CO_2 room: and this has had a decidedly beneficial effect: and has been regularly used of late.[166]

Unfortunate as it was, this along with the constant whirring of the fans was part of the reality of life afloat, the backdrop against which all served and from which no one was spared.

[161] Roberts, *The Battlecruiser* Hood, p. 14.
[162] Iago, *Letters* (at sea, 9 October 1939).
[163] Williams, *Gone A Long Journey*, p. 142.
[164] Ibid., p. 151.
[165] Ibid., pp. 121–2.
[166] PRO, ADM 101/565, Medical Officers' Journal, 1 January–31 March 1940, vol. 28, ships H–I, f. 37r.

5 Life Aboard

On what wings dare he aspire?
What the hand dare seize the fire?

ONE OF THE DISTINCTIVE FEATURES of life and war at sea is that a ship, however large or small she may be, is at once the home, work and weapon of all who sail in her. More than that, she is their only succour and defence against the remorseless power of wind and water which is the common enemy of all seafarers. For this reason, as for the large number of those embarked in her, the life and functioning of a warship has more of the quality of a community than perhaps any other military unit. Whereas a soldier may expect to serve out his time in the same regiment, it is the fate of a ship's company to be scattered by recommissioning or war after no more than a few years. But no matter how short her lease there is always time enough for her distinctive personality to impress itself for good or ill on all her people, and for these in their turn to leave their mark as indelibly on her. In this way the cycle is renewed in the experience of other crews and men until either the violence of the enemy or the breaker's torch fulfils her destiny. Welded in discipline, tradition and war, and yet capable of annihilation in a matter of seconds, it is the transient yet lasting quality of naval life afloat that affords it much of its fascination: short in time yet rich in memory. This is true of no ship more than it is of HMS *Hood*.

For Cadet Le Bailly, joining his first ship in 1932, his arrival aboard was a solemn and exhilarating moment.

> Thus it was that Dick Litchfield, I and two others foregathered at the Keppel's Head, Portsmouth, one evening in early August 1932. From our modest attic bedrooms we could see the quarterdeck of the great ship which was to be our home. Next morning, clad in our number one uniforms, we duly repaired on board. […] From the moment we reported to the officer of the watch, the whole rhythm of life was a boy's dream come true. They were all there, as Taffrail and Bartimeus had told us they would be: Guns and Torps, the Springer and the Pilot, the Schoolie and the Chief and the Senior, the Chippie, the Bo'sun, the PMO and of course our lord and master the Sub.[1]

Some, indeed, could say no more of the *Hood* than that her beauty was echoed in the friendly atmosphere they encountered aboard her, unusually so for a ship of her size. The Rev. Edgar Rea, joining as the ship's chaplain in September 1936, was relieved to discover several familiar faces from earlier commissions, while Paymaster Cadet Keith Evans found himself playing deck hockey within half an hour of stepping aboard. However, for most their arrival was more modest, though no less impressive for that. Hammock and kit-bag over his shoulder and ditty box in his hand, a rating would traipse up a gangway amidships to be received without fuss or cere-

mony into his new home. Ted Briggs:

> Then we were marched up the long gangway to be swallowed by this whirring monster. Everything seemed twice as big as normal. The mess decks were colossal; a series of scrubbed wooden mess-tables reached out at me like massive conjuror's fingers; mess-kids gleamed in imitation of sterling silver; even the overhead hammock bars glinted, while the faint whiff of fuel oil and the constant humming of the air vents engulfed me. This sense of space and clean-cut lines did not diminish in the boys' mess deck, where we were deposited to make ourselves at home.[2]

How different had been the reaction of Boy Fred Coombs, reaching the same messdeck four years earlier. For him and those, including his twin brother Frank, who accompanied him, the reality of life afloat evidently came as a dreadful shock:

> On joining the *Hood* in Portsmouth Dockyard on 31 March 1935, struggling up the long steep gangway with, first, our bags and, after scathing remarks about our slackness, a run back down to fetch our hammocks, we felt like flies on top of a dung heap. After a guided wander down steel ladders, on identical-looking corridors, through huge steel doors, we ended up somewhere in the bowels of what seemed like an inhuman, airless and windowless white-painted mass of long passageways and boxes, in what was, in reality, a barracks. We felt more like the maggots underneath the dung than the flies on top. […] After being led through some deserted messdecks and enclosed compartments, we found all our bags and hammocks heaped at the bottom of a steel ladder after being thrown, a deck at a time, through three decks to the lower level, which led to our mess deck. That rough handling of our hammocks was to be the first indication that life was rough at sea and on ships.[3]

The seamen's messdecks in which Briggs and Coombs were to make their home for the next few years differed little from those in other capital ships of the Royal Navy. Ranged on the upper and lower decks were fifteen enclosed messes for senior ratings and eleven open ones known as 'broadside messes' for the bulk of the ship's company—over 1,100 men in peacetime.[4] In a typical open mess, such as that of the Torpedomen and the Quarterdeckmen on the port side of the upper deck amidships, accommodation was provided for about 200 men in a space up to 70 feet long and 30 across. The main feature of each was a row of long wooden tables lying athwart the ship and supported either on folding legs or else suspended from the deckhead by means of a series of highly-polished steel bars. On either side wooden forms provided seating for up to 20

---

[1] Le Bailly, *The Man Around the Engine*, p. 20. 'Taffrail' and 'Bartimeus' were the pseudonyms of two naval writers of stature, Captain Taprell Dorling and Pay Captain Sir Lewis Ritchie.
[2] Coles & Briggs, *Flagship* Hood, p. 132.
[3] IWM, 91/7/1, p. 38.
[4] The detail in this section owes much to Mr George Donnelly (Stoker, 1936–8), to whom I express my gratitude.

very little interest, were thought to be good food to feed on. Even the maggots would have had better taste but it suited them and that was all that mattered. We went to build the mound of their ambitions.[67]

The opinions of Fred Coombs are unusual in their vehemence, particularly in the *Hood* which is remembered as a happy ship throughout most of the 1930s. But they encapsulate much of the resentment and frustration that at one time or another burned in the hearts of all ratings who went down to the sea in ships in the inter-war period. To be sure, the Coombs twins were, on their own admission, hardly whiter than white; in fact, they were notorious for always being in trouble. But their sentiments, expressed in vivid sailor's language, would have been shared by many in their more desperate moments. As Coombs recalled,

> It was explained to us by the odd older members of the crew—a lot of whom were survivors of the wartime fleets, now drastically reduced—[that they] only put up with the poor conditions and pay to avoid the mass unemployment that awaited them if they did not achieve Pension Age.[68]

Where officers and morale were concerned the view of Telegraphist Dick Jackman (1937–9) was perhaps more typical of the younger rating:

> I cannot comment on life in the wardroom, except that it was of a very high standard and very much resented by the lower deck for whom very little was done to make life enjoyable. Petty restrictions such as making the wearing of uniform compulsory at all times, ashore and afloat, with the exception of banyan parties when sports wear was worn, could have been relaxed. One needed to be a contortionist to get out of, and back into a sailor's uniform…[69]

Cdr O'Conor, that most reform-minded of officers, gauged the issue of morale in rather simpler terms. Seen from the opposite end of the spectrum, the whole problem boiled down to nagging by officers and superiors:

> The tendency to nag arises from human fretfulness, and there is nothing to surpass it for making an intelligent man feel insubordinate. Injustice is far easier to put up with than any form of bully-ragging. The Commander has to make it clear early in the commission to all those set in authority under him that, no matter what is done or left undone, he will not have things aggravated by nagging. […] If a man is sulking, the chances are that someone has been nagging him.[70]

Equally, it was as well for someone in authority to avoid any sort of confrontation with the men. The Rev. Harold Beardmore, chaplain aboard between 1939–41:

> When visiting the messdecks see that you don't get involved in an argument: *(a)* when a rating takes an opportunity of getting at you or your job, or *(b)* when he gets 'hot under the collar' about some social or service matter. It is best to send for the man at some convenient time, and discuss the

matter thoroughly over a cigarette in your cabin. One finds that when the man is by himself he is much more reasonable than when surrounded by his messmates, before whom he may like to pose as a bit of a sea-lawyer.[71]

Coombs, for his part, eventually reached the conclusion that 'the uneducated, too-thick-to-think lower end were not at a disadvantage by being uneducated if they made up their deficiency by using their common sense'.[72] Time would amply vindicate this view. As he lived to discover, the coming war altered the sailor's lot beyond all recognition. Though Coombs and his companions could not know it, they and their ship were living in the twilight years of the old Navy.

Where opinions on the men were expressed at all these were usually full of respect, affection and admiration. That of Vice-Admiral Le Bailly is typical:

> Above all we learned about sailors: from our hammock boys, who lashed up or unlashed our hammocks each morning and evening, the only people on board younger and financially poorer than we were (despite the small subvention we gave them); from our boats' crews, from the lordly chief and petty officers, from the cooper, still plying his trade, from that now unhappily extinct dinosaur, the Royal Marine gunner and from his fellow warrant officers; from them all more than any formal lecture or book could teach us.[73]

Even so, such views were often underpinned by a strong measure of suspicion. In the handbook for naval chaplains he dedicated to the *Hood*'s company in 1944, the Rev. Beardmore warned his readers against the age-old subterfuges of which sailors were capable.

> I once had to 'vet' the case of a certain rating who requested to change from C. of E. to Methodist. As the Methodist Church Party had to walk two miles to their church, and the walk included a steep hill, my suspicions were aroused. After a chat in my cabin, I realised that this

[67] IWM, 91/7/1, p. 42.
[68] Ibid.
[69] E-mail to the author, 8 January 2004.
[70] *RBS*, p. 84.
[71] Beardmore, *The Waters of Uncertainty*, p. 54.
[72] IWM, 91/7/1, p. 45.
[73] Le Bailly, *The Man Around the Engine*, p. 22. In 1932 a cadet's pay was 3/6d. and that of a midshipman 5 shillings *per diem*, which compared favourably with that received by Boys, ODs, ABs and Stokers 2nd Class and, in the case of midshipmen, Stokers 1st Class. See ch. 5, p. 140.

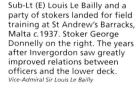

Sub-Lt (E) Louis Le Bailly and a party of stokers landed for field training at St Andrew's Barracks, Malta *c*.1937. Stoker George Donnelly on the right. The years after Invergordon saw greatly improved relations between officers and the lower deck.
Vice-Admiral Sir Louis Le Bailly

rating had a particular longing to quench his thirst on a Sunday morning about 10.00 when the sun was really hot. In the walk to church the party had to pass the Recreation Room where good beer was obtainable. The trick was to get in the last section of fours, and as they passed this welcome spot, just slip out and slip back again by mingling with the congregation outside the church later when the party fell in to return to the ship. The captain smiled when this was explained to him, and the request was not granted. We should be men without guile, but see that you are not 'sold a pup' by the old-timer who may think that because you are new to the Service he may be able to 'work a swindle' as the saying is on the lower deck.[74]

There is, of course, more than a hint of condescension in Beardmore's comment that 'They think these things out very carefully'. This attitude did not pass unnoticed. Len Wincott, Invergordon mutineer and *Hood* veteran of 1926:

If a sailor tried to explain the cause of a minor misdemeanour, the officer's foregone conclusion was always that the man was lying. Equally, it was accepted without evidence or question that the men were dull-witted.[75]

Yet, as Wincott continued,

It is greatly to the credit of the officer corps of the RN that a considerable number of them discarded this attitude, developing instead an approach based on a simple, humane principle: firm but polite.

This attitude owed much to the enhanced concern for the plight of their men that the Invergordon Mutiny brought to the upper echelons of the Navy. Even so, 1938 still found Capt. Francis Pridham having to exhort his officers to

Learn all you can about how your men live in their ship. Details of the serving of his food, where he writes his letters, the true extent of the facilities (or lack of them) for washing, shaving, keeping his kit tidy etc. Study life on the Mess Deck. Discover their recreations.[76]

And above all,

Keep in mind the very narrow financial margin within which many men and their families have to live.[77]

Concerned interest there may have been, but there were still ratings, 20-year veterans of the Navy, for whom cynicism was the ultimate lesson of their experience. Fred Coombs:

Of the others, survivors of the previous generation, most were tough old nuts with nothing to lose, their Good Conduct badges having gone with the wind many a time, and toughened up by periods of detention. [Together, this] made for a tough old navy that required tight control.[78]

Needless to say, few officers were under any illusions as to the type of man they were dealing with here. Capt. Pridham made no bones about it:

There are of course various kinds of 'black sheep'. The chap who is 'grey black' through his own foolishness, gets drunk on shore and makes himself a noisy nuisance, is no great anxiety. The really 'black' ones, the Bolshies, the coarse, the lecherous and the surly gaol bird are the dangerous ones. I have no compunction in saying that the risk we run in carrying this type justifies us hounding him down, and out, when we find him out. The Navy is not a reformatory.[79]

But there were other considerations. For most officers, iron-hard discipline served not only to restrain the unruliness and aggression that made the British sailor the formidable man he was, but also to harden him against the day when the sea or the enemy might mete out more than irksome labour or petty discipline. Fred Coombs admitted as much in recounting the following incident on the Detached Mole at Gibraltar in the autumn of 1935:

Though not very pleasant places to hang around, the toilets ashore were much sought after by some as a place to skive or perhaps read the newspaper, which at busy times in the mornings meant that queues were formed at some of the blocks. Some anxious person, crossing his legs and stamping his feet, had the idea and was given the opportunity to crumple a sheet of newspaper up, wait for the flush to run, light the paper and drop it on the outflow. The resulting yells as posteriors were singed soon meant that at the first yell everybody stood up and watched for the party piece to float past before sitting down again. This harmless form of amusement went on for weeks, perhaps months, and caused many a laugh. But there is always someone to go too far, as happened when someone used petrol to catch the lot and not the first to shout. Letting the petrol be poured slowly till it had reached the other end, he threw in his match, resulting in a huge flash which engulfed the culprit as he was the only one singed round the face and head, all others being scorched at the other end. We heard the thudding explosion from aboard and saw a line of matelots staggering to the Sick Bay in various forms of undress, mostly walking like cowboys, to have their scorch marks soothed. It was to be the last time that amusement was to be found in that form, though some wit sealed it off by putting on the notice board a notice that a delicatessen meal would be served that evening in the Sick Bay, the menu being Roast Beast Cheek, Grilled Swinging Steak and Curried Dusters. The culprit was found to be a stoker in the motor boat where the petrol had come from. It was a foolhardy trick, but if the Navy wanted crews with plenty of fire in their bellies who played hard, backing their King's Regulations and Admiralty Instructions by rigid discipline, they had to expect small explosions as devilment fired up.[80]

The challenge of harnessing this energy as war beckoned was Capt. Pridham's special concern in 1938:

[The] endeavour to bring out the fighting qualities of our men should be our constant consideration. As their leaders it is our business to inspire enthusiasm and confidence. A 'clean shoot' should be regarded as a step towards emptying the shell bays into the guts of the enemy. It is no

---

[74] Beardmore, *The Waters of Uncertainty*, p. 59.
[75] Wincott, *Invergordon Mutineer*, p. 70.
[76] Pridham, *Notes for Newly Joined Officers* (January 1938), p. 4.
[77] Ibid., p. 5.
[78] IWM, 91/7/1, p. 42.
[79] Pridham, *Lectures on Mutiny*, Part I: *Prevention*, p. 8.
[80] IWM, 91/7/1, pp. 49–50.

easy matter to bring into proper significance in peace time the importance of our fitness for fighting—our sole purpose and great responsibility. Yet few of us remember it as such for long at a time. We are inclined to forget that even in these highly mechanised days superiority in battle is far more a matter of fighting qualities in ourselves and our men than of calibre of guns and thickness of armour.[81]

To the majority of men, the *Hood*'s officers seemed, in Ted Briggs' words, to be 'like God Almighty'.[82] AB Bob Tilburn describes the attitude of most:

> In those days you were not necessarily frightened of those officers, you were in awe of them. Because they were so far above you, not only in the mental scale but in the social scale as well. It was still very feudal.[83]

Typically, Fred Coombs took a rather more jaundiced view, though it was one shared by many:

> The way of the R.N. [was] that when we went to sea on exercises we, the lower end, were too thick to understand why we did what, for [which reason we] were never informed. Steaming round the ocean was for the officers' benefit; if we were involved, the only information was that which we read on the notice board and not why […] There was still a lot at the top end who still thought that education and breeding were the be-all and end-all of Service life.[84]

Despite Coombs' remarks, considerable efforts were made after Invergordon to keep crewmen informed of the ship's movements and the diplomatic context of her activities. William James, who flew his flag in *Hood* between 1932–4, was surely the first admiral to clear lower deck to explain forthcoming exercises to the men.[85] In the 'Notes for Newly Joined Officers' he prepared during his tenure, Capt. Francis Pridham (1936–8) made it quite plain where the advantage of doing so lay:

> It is not difficult to give your men some idea of the duty the ship is being employed upon. The purpose of the exercises about to be carried out, why the ship is about to visit Arzeu or Barcelona, why the paravanes are being got out early in the morning watch, etc. etc. The more you can interest the Ship's Company in what is going on the better. Moreover, you will thereby short-circuit the disgruntled man who spreads the yarn that they are being bully-ragged and driven unnecessarily.[86]

But though the Invergordon Mutiny ushered in a significant change in officer attitudes, there can be no doubt that arrogance and thoughtlessness lay at the root of much disgruntlement and disaffection on the lower deck. O'Conor tacitly admitted as much:

> All men, young and old, are sensitive and it does not do to speak roughly, or someone will be burning with indignation from a neglect of courtesy, of which you may remain profoundly unconscious.[87]

A party of *Hood*'s officers landed for field training at St Andrew's Barracks, Malta *c.*1937. The major hurdle in officer promotion was that from lieutenant-commander to commander; fewer than half made the cut in peacetime.
Front row:
Sub-Lt (E) L.E.S.H. Le Bailly, unknown commissioned warrant officer,
Lt-Cdr C.H. Hutchinson,
Lt-Cdr M.E. Wevell,
Lt J.F.A. Ashcroft,
Sub-Lt J.S.L. Crabb.
Rear row:
Mid. D.C.S. Currey,
Mid. C.M. Bent,
Mid. T.S. Sampson,
Paymaster Sub-Lt A.B. Webb,
Mid. G.H.G. Crane,
Mid. B.C. Longbottom,
Mid. H.W. Wilkinson.
Vice-Admiral Sir Louis Le Bailly

In most instances the men could draw on a subtle and evolved language to express their disgust or disappointment at those given command over them. A tone of voice, a nuance of body language, a show of reticence, all spoke volumes to those on the receiving end. There were moments, however, when extreme aggravation called for more direct means of communication. Shoddy or listless work, mass leave-breaking and desultory performances in fleet sporting events were a sure sign of poor morale and failing leadership. The tenure of Rear-Admiral Sir Walter Cowan and Captain Geoffrey Mackworth in 1921–3 rivals the Invergordon Mutiny as the most unhappy period in the *Hood*'s long career. Both fell victim to pranks by their subordinates.[88] One fine day somebody pushed Bill the ship's goat mascot through the skylight of Cowan's sleeping cabin and into his bed. On another occasion Mackworth, who was fond of asking for working parties of six Marines, received a box of toy soldiers in the mail along with an impudent note which resulted in the entire detachment being subjected to a handwriting test. Neither culprit was ever discovered. But there were gentler ways of letting off steam. The pukka accent in which much of the wardroom spoke was the subject of ridicule on the lower deck and many was the officer who acquired a nickname. Len Wincott:

> The nicknames that men give to their officers are more informative than many people think. If an officer is given a number of nicknames, and more and more are conjured up, it is a sure sign that he is far from popular. If on the other hand he gets one which sticks to him, one can be certain that he is respected.[89]

Equally, the officer whose men called him a 'gent' was being paid their very highest compliment. But most were glad to keep their distance and generally had as little contact with officers as possible. The following remark made *en passant* by CPO Bill Lowe discloses the prevailing approach:

> …However, there wasn't a lot of games played in those days, except by the officers who used to play quite a bit, but we never used to worry about them.[90]

[81] Pridham, *Notes for Newly Joined Officers*, p. 6.
[82] Taverner, *Hood's Legacy*, p. 73.
[83] Arthur (ed), *The Navy: 1939 to the Present Day*, p. 89.
[84] IWM, 91/7/1, p. 45.
[85] Vice-Admiral Sir Louis Le Bailly, letter to the author, 22 February 2003.
[86] *Op. cit.*, p. 5.
[87] *RBS*, p. 84.
[88] HMS *Hood* Association archives; Gunner 'Windy' Breeze, R.M.A.
[89] Wincott, *Invergordon Mutineer*, p. 136.
[90] Arthur (ed), *The Navy: 1939 to the Present Day*, p. 86.

91 IWM, 90/38/1, vol. III, Anecdote 3, p. 6. The coxswain in question was PO A.W. Jeffrey (*sic*).
92 Vice-Admiral Sir Louis Le Bailly, letter to the author, 24 December 2002.
93 Le Bailly, *The Man Around the Engine*, p. 37.
94 Ibid., pp. 37–8.

Nowhere is this attitude more exquisitely captured than in the following exchange between Mid. George Blundell, then in command of the *Hood*'s first picket boat, and his Westcountry coxswain. The year is 1924.

> I have often reflected on what a lot the petty officers tactfully taught me on how to behave. One day we landed a number of officers just after lunch: the ship's company was still at work. On return I asked the coxswain (Jeffreys was his name; he was a darling man) 'What do the men think of the officers going ashore in working hours?' Jeff looked at me with that 'three badge' twinkle in his eye. 'Lor' bless you, Sir,' he replied, 'We likes to see them out of the way.' I have never forgotten that wise remark.[91]

The *Hood*'s wardroom numbered around 45 officers out of a peacetime complement of about 1,150 men. As was the case throughout the Navy, the ship's officers were divided into two branches, Executive and Civilian. The distinction is important because it was not until after the Second World War that officers of the so-called Civilian Branch could aspire to their own seagoing commands. Among the Executive Branch were the specialists in Gunnery, Torpedoes, Navigation and Signals together with the 'salthorse' officers who were content to make their careers without specialised training in any discipline. This branch was, of necessity, completed by the Captain and his principal executive officer, the Commander. Officers of the Civilian Branch wore the same uniform as their executive colleagues, though their particular specialisations were distinguished by coloured cloth between the gold stripes on their cuffs. In the case of Engineer officers this was purple. Paymasters wore white, Instructors blue, Shipwrights and Constructors silver-grey, Surgeons red and Dentists orange. Unusually for a capital ship, the *Hood*'s officer complement was

remembered as a friendly and homogenous body throughout much of her career, 'probably as happy as a big ship could ever be'.[92] However, this cannot disguise the tensions and snobbery that occasionally surfaced in the wardroom, particularly between executive officers and the Engineer Branch which was stripped of its executive status by the Admiralty in 1925. Executive officers derided engineers as 'plumbers', 'dustmen' and 'dirty fingernail types', to which the latter responded with 'dabtoes', 'crab wallahs' and 'fish heads'. In 1937 Sub-Lt (E) Louis Le Bailly, fresh from the Royal Naval Engineering College at Keyham, found himself greeted on the quarterdeck by Cdr David Orr-Ewing, a gunnery specialist, with the words 'Are you another of these pacifist subs from Keyham?'.[93] The notion that the technical disciplines were at odds with the spirit of a fighting service and their practicants ill-suited to seagoing command remained deeply ingrained. Evidently, there were many in the Navy who had as yet failed to grasp the technological realities that the coming war would so ruthlessly assert on it.

The gunroom to which, as a sub-lieutenant, a chastened Le Bailly repaired on arrival was the domain of the midshipmen, the Royal Navy's officers in waiting. Until 1932 it was part of his training as an officer that every cadet emerging from the Royal Naval College at Dartmouth should serve up to two years aboard a capital ship, and the *Hood*'s gunroom complement was never less than 25. Thereafter cadets spent a year in the training cruiser *Frobisher* before being promoted midshipmen and let loose on the fleet, a development which caused the *Hood*'s gunroom complement to drop to around fifteen with a turnover of half a dozen or so every four months. The gunroom was a large and austere compartment on the port side of the upper deck served by an adjoining pantry. Sub-Lt Le Bailly, returning after a four-year absence, was relieved to find things much as they had been during his earlier occupation:

> With some trepidation I entered the gunroom door at the armchair end reserved for sub-lieutenants. The brass stove, which I had assiduously polished, was still there and to my delight I was welcomed by a near-contemporary as the co-ruler of his little kingdom. I soon discovered that the gunroom was still a place where laughter mostly prevailed and the food as bad as ever with the same grinning, but now even more pear-shaped, messman peering through the serving hatch; where the same tin lockers in which I had kept my journal and sight book were still used by the midshipmen; where the only daylight came from the skylight. The same leather-coated cushions on the benches at the ship's side were even more worn as were the two leather armchairs of which I could now claim one.[94]

The gunroom was mostly taken up by a large polished mahogany table at which the 'young gentlemen', suitably attired, were waited on at dinner by a pair of mess stewards. During the 1930s at least, catering for the *Hood*'s gunroom was, by choice, left in the hands of a civilian messman. Louis Le Bailly:

> Dinner, as with our other meals, was dispensed by the same wily Maltese messman and his acolytes who took a shilling a day from our pay. Our wine bill was limited to 10 shillings a month as cadets and 15 shillings as midshipmen. On this we could treat ourselves to a sherry,

Members of the gunroom sharing a joke on the quarterdeck with Commissioned Boatswain J.McK. Kirkcaldy D.S.M., *c*.1932–3. Most recalled their time in the gunroom as one of learning, laughter and friendship.
Paymaster Mid. J. Charles (lost in the *Barham*, 25 November 1941), Cadet L.E.S.H. Le Bailly, Kirkcaldy, Cadet G.W. Vavasour, Mid. G.R.A. Don
Vice-Admiral Sir Louis Le Bailly

a glass of beer on guest nights and an occasional glass of Marsala when we returned, cold and shivering, with our boat cloaks and uniforms wet through from a rough boat trip. Spirits, had we been allowed them, were almost unknown to us and few could afford or wished to smoke.[95]

Though the bullying made notorious by the novels of Frederick Marryat and Charles Morgan was largely a thing of the past, the gunroom remained a spirited community which, like its public-school equivalents, deferred to authority yet frequently took pleasure in the misery of its inmates. Equally, it was often a forcing ground for lifelong friendships between officers. Ragging, especially on gala nights, was a popular and often violent diversion to which senior officers traditionally turned a blind eye, though in 1938 the gunroom created something of a stir by including inflated condoms among its Christmas decorations.[96] Rear-Admiral Peter La Niece (1940) recalls some capers off Scotland early in the war:

It was a high spirited gunroom and one evening we went ashore to Helensburgh, on the northern side of the Clyde, to see a film; on leaving the cinema we 'borrowed' a framed picture of the film star Loretta Young; this was borne back on board, signed by all concerned, and hung in the gunroom as a trophy. Later on it was captured by a raiding gunroom from another ship; in due course it was recaptured. It was then replaced by a Barber's Pole also acquired from Helensburgh. Suffice to say the Barber's Pole went from ship to ship until after the end of the war when I rediscovered it. […] I still have the picture of Loretta Young…[97]

The prevailing atmosphere is captured by Paymaster Lt-Cdr E.C. Talbot-Booth, R.N.R.:

Although discipline is probably stricter than in any other force in the world, there are times when the bounds are loosed to an extent which cannot be understood by foreigners. There are occasions when the junior members of the Ward-room Mess will make a swoop or raid on the Gun-room, or midshipman's mess and a tremendous scrap will ensue. The compliment may be returned and a fierce combat ensue on the floor of the senior mess to the detriment of boiled shirts and winged collars. Five minutes later perhaps the junior midshipman is knocking at your cabin door his hand raised to the salute while he gravely informs you that your boat is alongside.[98]

The Sub-Lieutenant of the Gunroom could be delegated the authority to administer up to a dozen cuts with a cane or dirk scabbard for minor offences, though this form of punishment was forbidden by O'Conor during his tenure as Commander in 1933–6. As he later wrote, 'The old argument, that a Snottie preferred half a dozen to having his leave stopped, is disposed of when it is realised that neither treatment is suitable for an officer'.[99] O'Conor also stamped out both early-morning gym and the degrading rites of 'creeping for Jesus' and 'fork in the beam', the gunroom punishments that sub-lieutenants had inflicted on their juniors since the days of the sailing navy.[100] The time was ripe for change:

Punishments that are suitable for schoolboys are not suitable for adolescents of the ages of 18 to 21 whom it is intended to regard as officers. We must have it one way or the other. Either treat them as schoolboys—messengers, truants—or else make up our minds that they are officers and that we are going to treat them as such.[101]

With O'Conor the midshipman of the Royal Navy finally came of age.

In most cases life as a midshipman afloat gave an officer his only taste of sleep in a hammock. With no designated sleeping compartment, midshipmen usually slung their hammocks in one of the flats on the main deck aft, sub-lieutenants enjoying the comparative luxury of a shared cabin. The large white chests with which generations of midshipmen had gone to sea were stowed in the chest flat on the port side of the main deck aft. Nearby was the Subordinate officers' dressing place and an adjoining bathroom, the former fitted with stowage for clothing and equipment and the latter with a steam main that provided just enough hot water for the sub-lieutenants' baths and no more; their juniors maintained the acquaintance with cold-water bathing struck up at Dartmouth. Touring the ship in January 1926 the journalist George Aston, who had first gone to sea before the Great War, was mightily impressed at the improved conditions for midshipmen since his day:

In my time he had only a chest (for which he paid) to wash in and to keep all his clothes in. Then he was given a 'bathroom', so called, with flat tin baths. Still only the chest flat to dress in. Now he has a chest, provided by the Government, a chest of drawers and part of another one, a bathroom as on shore, with hot and cold water, and a dressing place with lots of room to keep his gear—in *Hood* long lines of hooks and spreaders for coats etc. etc. Nowadays he has his sextant supplied, instead of paying for it.[102]

On the basis of a fortnight spent aboard while the ship was refitting at Portsmouth in June 1939, Mid. H.G. Knowles would certainly not have agreed.

The gun-room's only ventilation is a solitary skylight, while the chest flat and sleeping flat lack even that. The chest flat, recently a thieves' paradise, has always to be kept locked, while nine of us try to keep our clothes in our trunks, no chests having been supplied, most of the hanging room already taken up by the coats of other midshipmen in a space far too small, where everything disappears unaccountably amongst a maze of trunks and boxes.[103]

Austere as it was, life as a midshipman in *Hood* was taken with stoicism and humour, a common sentiment of difficulties shared and challenges surmounted in the formative phase of one's career. Louis Le Bailly:

I and my group (1932) lived quite happily in the Flat around the X turret barbette as there was no room in the chest flat. Much clothing was common and one of my messmates had a large stamp made which inscribed his handkerchiefs with 'Stolen From…'.[104]

95 Ibid., p. 23.
96 HMS *Hood* Association archives, Paymaster Cadet Keith Evans.
97 La Niece, *Not a Nine to Five Job*, p. 29.
98 Talbot-Booth, *All the World's Fighting Fleets*, 3rd edn, p. 223.
99 *RBS*, p. 28.
100 IWM/SA, Rear-Admiral Edmund Poland, no. 11951, reel 4.
101 *RBS*, p. 28.
102 KCL, LHCMA, Aston 1/10, pp. 52–3.
103 IWM, 92/4/1, 9 June 1939.
104 Vice-Admiral Sir Louis Le Bailly, letter to the author, 22 February 2003.

105 Moran, *The Anatomy of Courage*, pp. 92–3.
106 *RBS*, p. 27.
107 Warden, 'Memories of the Battle Cruiser H.M.S. "Hood"', p. 84.
108 IWM, 90/38/1, vol. III, Anecdote 3, p. 4.
109 IWM/SA no. 11951, reel 5.
110 *RBS*, p. 27.
111 IWM, 92/4/1.
112 Jenson, *Tin Hats, Oilskins & Seaboots*, pp. 90 & 96–7.

Above all there was pride. Lord Moran captured it perfectly in *The Anatomy of Courage*:

> That a boy has set his heart on this tough service goes for something. He has initiative; he is a cut above the ordinary. Long before the Hitler Youth was thought of, the Navy caught him young and soaked him in the pride and joy of a great tradition.[105]

The midshipmen's education, welfare and leave arrangements were entrusted to a lieutenant-commander known colloquially as 'Snotties' Nurse'. The incumbent was often a sympathetic figure who had assumed this duty by choice, but, as O'Conor lamented, his brother officers tended to regard midshipmen either as messengers or, in the worst cases, 'as schoolboys and their natural prey'.[106] Ross Warden, who served aboard as a midshipman R.N.V.R. in 1940–1, puts it in perspective:

> The rank of midshipman is very precarious and one learns to treat certain ranks with suspicion, especially that of Lieutenant-Commander. Commanders and above (the majority) seem to mellow with seniority: it may be the start of a second childhood, but when they hand out justice you can almost sense them thinking: 'Well, I was once a midshipman myself.' By and large we were exceptionally fortunate with our Lieutenant-Commanders: there was just one snake in the woodpile, who apparently enjoyed making our lives miserable.[107]

Warden and his companions were able to take their revenge on Lt-Cdr Snake with a packet of Ex-Lax on the *Hood*'s return from the Mediterranean in August 1940, but such *schadenfreude* was not always possible. More often than not the snotty, or 'wart' as he was often known, had to accept his lot with only the lower deck to console him. Looking back on the early 1920s, Capt. George Blundell recalled how 'ships' companies of those days seemed nearly always kind and sympathetic to the "middies". Perhaps they saw in them a kindred "depressed class"'.[108]

They did to a degree, and often went to great lengths to cover up for young officers in trouble, though not always for the reasons Blundell thought. All the same, as Rear-Admiral Edmund Poland recalled of his three-man motor-boat crew in 1935, 'they owned me, wouldn't let anybody be beastly to me'.[109] While it was never entirely reciprocated, the lasting respect engendered for ratings by those who were later to command them remained one of the greatest strengths of the Royal Navy.

As future officers, midshipmen were assigned important duties afloat, chief of which was that of Midshipman of the Watch. As deputy to the Officer of the Watch he was expected to assume control of the ship's routine, discharging his duties on the quarterdeck in harbour and from the bridge at sea. This involved taking sun and star sights and assisting him in keeping the deck log as well as running errands of one sort or another. The most coveted responsibility, however, was command of one of the ship's boats, a skill upon which the Navy placed the greatest emphasis. The business of boat handling not only gave a midshipman a feel for command and seamanship but allowed him to make his mistakes in a relatively controlled environment; as O'Conor put it, 'a picket boat smashed may one day mean a battleship saved'.[110] Most mornings began with physical training followed by morse, flag-hoisting or semaphore exercises before breakfast, after which he might be told off for duties by his divisional officer. But mercifully a midshipman's life was not always so demanding. Often as not it provided an essential primer in the minutiae and routine of naval life. Here is Mid. Knowles' journal entry for Saturday 16 June 1939 as the ship lay at Portsmouth:

> Substituting duty midshipman for Hill who has gone home on weekend leave, I turned out early to run and heat the bath-room water, and call the remainder of the midshipmen at 06.30. A new set of hammock-boys having arrived, after I had finished the first half of relieve-decks I made out labels for our hammocks so that we should in future sleep in the same one every night. The forenoon I spent titivating my journal, going ashore to play tennis at the United Services' Club after lunch. A two-hour dogwatch passed uneventfully.[111]

Beyond his ordinary duties, a midshipman's week was filled with classes and study for the Sub-Lieutenants' exam. In the Midshipmen's Study on the main deck right aft and in turrets, engine spaces and elsewhere around the ship, an Instructor officer and a range of warrant and petty officers gave theoretical and practical classes in gunnery, torpedoes, wireless, navigation and engineering. The Sub-Lieutenants' exam consisted of a number of written papers, exercises and evaluations culminating in 'the Board', a *viva voce* grilling on seamanship by a panel of senior officers. The concluding part of a midshipman's qualification rested in his journal, which he was required to keep daily and illustrate with maps, pictures and technical drawings of naval interest. Infinite care and attention was lavished on these, which remain a valuable source of information on the daily life of the ship. For Latham Jenson of Calgary who joined *Hood* as a midshipman R.C.N. in December 1940, his journal was nothing less than a hobby.[112] During the Sub-Lieutenants' exam held aboard in April 1941 it got the only perfect score in the Home Fleet and Jenson went on to become a

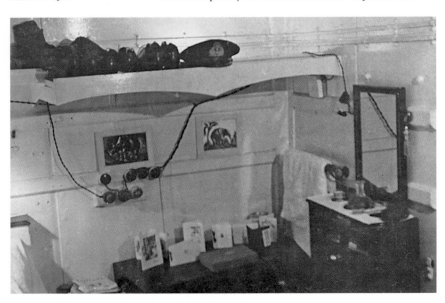

The cabin of Sub-Lieutenant John Iago R.N.V.R. on the main deck near 'X' turret. These cabins were designed for two officers and had no scuttles. It is Christmas 1940 and a number of cards are arranged on the table. Above it are scraper board drawings from his girlfriend Aline. To the right is a mirror stand and towel rail with stowage for cap and shoes above. Iago was an electrical engineer and wired a sophisticated lighting system for his cabin.
Mrs Bee Kenchington

distinguished illustrator after a career in the Royal Canadian Navy. The completion of the four-day exam was greeted with jubilation by the successful candidates. Ted Briggs, then a Boy Signalman, recalls the celebrations of Jenson's group, the very last to achieve promotion from the *Hood*:

> I remember this particular session because after it was over there was a riotous party in the midshipmen's gunroom, of which the ship's company got to hear. After the gin, beer and 'el torpedo' and 'depth charge' cocktails had flowed, bottles began to fly—and trousers, too. One lieutenant was cut by a piece of shattered glass, before all the popular officers were debagged by the 'mids'.[113]

For a time boys and midshipmen might share duties and instruction, but on promotion the enormous social gap asserted itself and their ways parted forever. As on the lower deck, an officer's status was denoted by his accommodation, which ranged from a shared cabin on the main deck aft to the palatial apartments for the admiral and captain described elsewhere. Officers' cabins had always been a case of 'multum in parvo'—much in little—but, as on the messdecks, the first impression seems to have been of airy spaciousness in comparison with other ships. A typical cabin, fifteen feet long, ten wide and twelve high, was entered through a door fitted with louvre windows which slid behind a rifle rack facing the lobby. Lit by a scuttle and a lamp at the deckhead, its furniture consisted of a bunk bed set on a unit of drawers laid fore and aft along the ship's side, an upright wardrobe for uniforms, further drawers, a foot locker for shoes, and a desk and chair. A pair of shelves, a mirror and a small stand attached to the painted bulkheads completed the fittings. The only semblance of permanent decoration lay in the two laths of teak that ran along each bulkhead and to which pictures could be secured with screws. Because the officers' cabins aft were prone to flooding, the corticene flooring was rarely mitigated by any carpeting while a set of rails on each bunk bore witness to the occasional need to wedge oneself into bed in heavy weather. Even so, efforts were made to beautify the surroundings with chintz curtains and lampshades and the usual selection of family or *risqué* pictures as the taste and attachments of the incumbent dictated. In larger cabins the décor extended to framed pictures, ornaments and perhaps a ship model under glass for the mantelpiece. Sub-Lt John Iago, who joined the ship from civilian life in September 1939, brought his skills as an electrical engineer to bear in the decoration of his cabin:

> I've had the same cabin all the time. It looked very bare to begin with but now I have improved it. I have made the spare bunk into a sort of sideboard and have framed and put up pictures, mainly from magazines. This evening I have been fixing up a system of indirect lighting, which is very fine. All lights are concealed and shine up on to the deck head and I have a bed light and a dressing table light. It all looks very pleasing and I am thinking of having some yellow or red bulbs in a few of the holders. Altogether there are 12 small bulbs now. Also there is a special shaving light, which comes on with my razor![114]

After lights out Iago no doubt drifted off to sleep to the same chorus that had lulled generations of officers at sea:

> On one's first night in a warship there are many strange sounds to wonder at, for in addition to the customary creakings and groanings of an ordinary ship, the rifles in their racks add their clatter to the din of the steering gear; a battleship wallows with a long slow roll and the rhythmic rattle of the small arms which accompanies each change becomes a pleasing tattoo which lulls one to sleep.[115]

What distinguished the Royal Navy from many of its foreign counterparts was the degree of personal service an officer could expect on board. All from the rank of lieutenant onwards were assigned a Marine servant to rouse him in the morning, fill his tub in the officers' bathroom, see to his clothing and laundry and keep the cabin and its contents clean and tidy. The same service was expected with rather less justification during wartime. On 6 July 1940, three days after the attack on Oran, one officer felt moved to issue the following complaint in a letter home:

> Have been having a bit of domestic trouble! My new man is always too busy to clean shoes, or to make my bed before teatime—I may change him for one of my torpedo men.

The Marine in question presumably had his hands full as the *Hood* beat back to Gibraltar after covering the *coup de grâce* on the battlecruiser *Dunkerque* at Mers-el-Kebir. Despite the many black and Filipino stewards engaged by his own navy, this state of affairs appears to have come as something of an eye-opener to Lt-Cdr Joseph H. Wellings U.S.N.:

> My servant calls me at 08.00, brushes my clothes, shines my shoes and lays out the rest of my clothes. Right this moment my *bed* is turned down, pajamas laid out evenly, slippers under the bed. I take my bath before dinner in order not to go out afterwards and possibly catch cold— (yes, the tub is drawn—or rather the water is drawn and just at the correct temperature).[116]

[113] Coles & Briggs, *Flagship* Hood, p. 195.
[114] Iago, *Letters* (Scapa Flow, 27 August 1940).
[115] Talbot-Booth, *All the World's Fighting Fleets*, 3rd edn, p. 190.
[116] Wellings, *On His Majesty's Service*, p. 82.

The officer's wardroom looking forward and to starboard in the 1920s. On the mahogany tables are some of the trophies won by and presented to the ship throughout her career and travels. A pair of skylights, low-slung lamps and naked bulbs illuminate an unexpectedly austere space. On the far side, under portraits of King George V and Queen Mary, are two serving hatches from the wardroom pantry. *Sellicks*

H.M.S. "HOOD". The Ward Room.

Personal attention of this sort more than made up for the comparatively primitive washing facilities aboard. All cabins were fitted with hot and cold running water but the wash basins drained into copper receptacles which had to be emptied by hand. In the largest cabins and compartments the ultimate touch before they were replaced with electric stoves was a coal fire kept regularly stoked by a Marine servant. If the *Hood* was remembered as a comfortable ship it was to the senior officers' quarters that she owed this reputation.

The heart of the officers' world was the large suite on the forecastle deck amidships known as the wardroom. First came the anteroom, lit by a large skylight on the boat deck and furnished with a pair of leather-upholstered settees and a club fender round the stove. Here, under a large bookcase holding the wardroom library, officers gathered for drinks before lunch and dinner. A doorway, later converted to an arched opening guarded by a curtain, led into the wardroom proper, a lofty space lit by further skylights and a row of scuttles overlooking the port battery. The wardroom was dominated by the four large mahogany tables at which the officers ate their meals waited on by Royal Marine attendants. Unlike *Iron Duke*, *London* and *Sheffield*, the *Hood* had never been presented with a great silver service, but in cabinets about the room, on its walls and tables were the mementoes and trophies of her voyages across the world: the silver-mounted elephant's tusk given at Freetown in December 1923 and the trophy heads of lion, tiger, bison and moose presented thereafter along with countless cups, salvers and centrepieces in silver and gold. All were landed in August 1939 to be destroyed in the Portsmouth Blitz. A third settee filled one corner while a kneehole desk opposite allowed officers to compose letters on the ship's crested stationery. The furnishings of what was by earlier standards a somewhat austere space were completed with a piano—much used on guest nights—a pair of stoves under mirrored mantelpieces, sundry cupboards and a large buffet from which attendants served food passed through a hatch in the wardroom pantry.

As in the other officers' messes, wardroom catering lay at the discretion of its members.[117] Throughout much of her career the *Hood*'s wardroom appears to have left the matter in the hands of a messman who provided three meals a day plus tea against a monthly deduction from officers' pay. Generous as it was, no opportunity was lost for adding to wardroom fare. On Sunday 18 May 1941 a last fishing trip on the shores of Scapa Flow brought Lt-Cdr Roger Batley a 2-lb. sea trout and the wardroom a catch of 50 fresh lobsters which he relieved from an old fisherman for two shillings apiece. Breakfast was served between 07.30 and 09.00, lunch between midday and 13.00, tea at 15.30 and finally a formal dinner at 20.00 sharp. At sea, and especially in wartime, a more relaxed routine prevailed, with meals being largely on a self-service basis. The food prepared in the wardroom galley was expected to be of an extremely high standard and even in wartime was the equivalent of a fine restaurant. Indeed, Sub-Lt John Iago R.N.V.R. is unlikely to have been the first wartime officer to question whether such lavishness was appropriate in view of the dearth on the Home Front:

I don't think it would hurt us to have a great deal less, especially in view of shortages elsewhere. Breakfast: Porridge or cereals followed by grilled herrings or some other fish. Next course, eggs and bacon, then toast and marmalade or

honey to finish. We have a three- or four-course lunch, small tea (just tea and cakes) then we round off the day with a four-course dinner at sea and six courses in harbour.[118]

Even Lt-Cdr Wellings of the U.S. Navy, a service known for its generous fare, was taken aback at the range of foods on offer, though he was perhaps not the first American to be stunned at the sight of a monumental English breakfast:

The food is much better than at the main office. Grapefruit every morning so far, cereal or rolled oats, ham or bacon and eggs, toast, marmalade or butter (or both) and coffee. How is that for a breakfast? I have given up afternoon tea as I don't want to gain on this job which is much easier than my last one.[119]

For his part, John Iago found his expanding waistline a matter of some embarrassment while his relatives in suburban London subsisted on wartime rations:

Have gained 1 st. 4 lbs. since joining the Navy, which explains why my reefer jacket would not meet and has had to go back to Gieves for adjustment![120]

However, wardroom catering was not without its mishaps. Some consternation was caused in 1935 when it was discovered that PO Cook Sultana, a Maltese, had been using his armpit to shape the beef rissoles that were a wardroom favourite.[121]

In the 1920s at least, the atmosphere in the wardroom, particularly where meals were concerned, had something of the character of an English country house or a gentleman's club ashore, with all their quirks and mannerisms. Sailing in *Hood* during the world cruise of 1923–4, the writer V.C. Scott O'Connor noted 'a little fad in the Navy… that no one is very fit to talk to at breakfast', though Aston and later Wellings found their messmates cheerful enough.[122] The fact that O'Connor was on record as saying that all naval officers were 'born idiots' cannot have endeared him to the wardroom.[123] It was supposedly taboo to discuss women, religion and politics, though the drift to war presumably meant that at least one of these topics was frequently broached. Clinking glasses was regarded as a portent of death, the threat usually warded off by fining the culprit a bottle of port. It was common for officers to carry an engraved napkin ring from wardroom to wardroom, the names of their ships being added to it with each passing commission. Drinks were served before and during lunch and dinner in harbour, but the restrictions on alcohol at sea were strictly adhered to. There was no ban on drinking at sea, and indeed non-watchkeepers were entitled to three tots of alcohol a day, but it was 'not done' for any watchkeeper to partake. It was a different matter in harbour, but even there consumption was regulated with monthly 'wine bill' allowances of 10 shillings for cadets, 15 for midshipmen and £5 for officers, each drink being entered in the wardroom wine book and subject to regular scrutiny by the captain. Even at official parties the amount drunk was recorded and tabulated against the 'monthly mess share'.

As the admiral and the captain usually dined alone there was no special seating at table except for the Mess President and Vice-President who held office for a week at a time. Officers dressed for dinner, which consisted of mess jackets,

117 This section owes much to the memories of Vice-Admiral Sir Louis Le Bailly.
118 Iago, *Letters* (Loch Ewe, 3 October 1939).
119 Wellings, *On His Majesty's Service*, p. 81.
120 Iago, *Letters* (Greenock, 22 December 1939). Gieves was the principal Navy tailor.
121 IWM/SA, Rear-Admiral Edmund Poland, no. 11951, reel 5.
122 O'Connor, *The Empire Cruise*, p. 81.
123 Lt (E) Geoffrey Wells, *Diary of World Cruise*, p. 4.

winged collars and bow ties in peacetime but no more than reefers in war, though a stiff collar would be added in harbour. Officers of the Royal Marines wore the tight breeches that were traditional in the Corps, some like Lt A.H.R. Buckley of the 1923–6 commission exercising their right to don the blue mess dress of the defunct Royal Marine Artillery. Grace would be said if the chaplain were present, all standing until the Mess President had taken his seat. Then course after course would be served by a phalanx of attendants in white mess tunics, twice weekly to the accompaniment of a Royal Marine orchestra in the anteroom. As Wellings, unaccustomed to this luxury, put it, 'music at dinner does aid one's digestion', though his contentment no doubt owed something to the alcohol which was never served in his own navy.[124] In keeping with the tradition of the Royal Navy, the Sovereign was toasted while officers remained seated, followed by a toast to the relevant potentate if foreign guests were aboard. So it was that the *Hood*'s wardroom found itself drinking the health of Chancellor Hitler when officers of the *Deutschland* came aboard at Gibraltar in June 1937. At Scapa three years later it was the turn of the President of the United States to have his health drunk, Lt-Cdr Wellings observing protocol with a toast to King George VI.

Little has survived to record the mood of the *Hood*'s wardrooms in either peace or war, though one thing was quite clear: it didn't do to be a teetotaller in such society. The following advice given by the Rev. Beardmore to aspiring naval chaplains speaks volumes.

> A teetotaller certainly starts scratch in any mess, and finds life rather difficult, especially on a foreign station, where there is a lot of entertaining to be done, and where each officer has to do his bit. I think the average Naval officer considers a padre to be a good messmate if he has learnt how to drink sensibly; they look upon him as a normal person, and looking back, I can remember getting inside the shell of many a 'reserved' or difficult messmate over a glass of wine, and making a valuable contact.[125]

As in the gunroom, there were times when alcohol and high spirits turned the normally august surroundings of the wardroom into something of a mêlée, particularly Thursday evenings in harbour—Guest Night. Beardmore, who had no doubt sat through all too many during his two years as the *Hood*'s chaplain, felt moved to issue this warning:

> The Chaplain who thinks it is a popular thing to be broadminded, and accepts everything that is said and done in a Wardroom Mess, doesn't *really* command respect. Officers expect the Chaplain to be different from them, and if at rather a late party he joins in, or condones, the more vulgar songs that are sung from time to time, he lets the side down in their eyes, to say the least of it.[126]

Officers who stayed up drinking were often only a step away from out-and-out rowdyism. In what was perhaps the last letter he ever wrote, the ship's First Lieutenant, Lt-Cdr John Machin, confessed with ill-concealed pride that he had cracked a rib during a recent guest-night caper.[127] But there were times when matters got really out of hand. One night off the Yugoslav port of Split in September 1937 Lt Gresham

Grenfell, creeping on all fours under the wardroom tables, stalked the row of trophy heads on the forward bulkhead with a loaded shotgun. Selecting the moose as his target, he calmly emptied both barrels into it, blasting off an antler to the consternation of those present.[128] Unfortunately, some of his shot passed through a scuttle and lodged in the hammock of a sailor sleeping in the passage outside. The antler was glued back on and the sailor fobbed off with beer, but, as Fred Coombs said, 'if the Navy wanted crews with plenty of fire in their bellies who played hard… they had to expect small explosions as devilment fired up'.[129] Evidently, this was as true of the *Hood*'s officers as it was of her men.

The *Hood* was the finest ship in the Navy and it can come as no surprise that her wardroom should have included several whose accomplishments past, present and future place them among the élite of a great service. To describe the wardroom of 1936–9, the *Hood*'s last peacetime commission, is therefore to give a flavour not only of its character over the previous 20 years but of the calibre of men who made up the officer corps of the British Navy.[130] The Executive Officer for most of the commission was Cdr David Orr-Ewing, later captain of the fast minelayer *Abdiel* when she was mined and sunk at Brindisi in September 1943, and eventually Commander-in-Chief Home Fleet after the war. Among his many accomplishments was the ability to drink beer standing on his head.[131] Lt-Cdrs H.A.L. Marsham and C.H. Hutchinson had distinguished careers in the Submarine Service during the coming war, the former as C.O. of HMS/M *Rover* and the latter in command of HMS/M *Truant*. Hutchinson ended the war as Chief of Staff to Admiral Sir Bernard Rawlings in the British Pacific Fleet and became captain of the Royal Naval College at Dartmouth. Lt Roger Hill, who hated big-ship life, went on to win a D.S.O. assisting the crippled tanker *Ohio* into Malta while in command of the destroyer escort *Ledbury* in August 1942. His *Hood* messmates, however, would remember him chiefly for his devastatingly beautiful Swedish wife and her equally entrancing friends. Among the Engineer Branch were Cdr (E) Peter Berthon, already Dean of the Royal Naval Engineering College at Keyham and the moving spirit behind the foundation of its great successor at Manadon. His future son-in-law,

Another view of the wardroom, this time looking aft in July 1932; the angle of view is in the opposite direction to the previous photograph. The doorway on the right leads to the anteroom. Note the pictures screwed into laths of teak running along each bulkhead. To the left is an oil fire. The chairs are standard Navy wardroom issue.
Wright & Logan

[124] Wellings, *On His Majesty's Service*, p. 81.
[125] Beardmore, *The Waters of Uncertainty*, pp. 16–17.
[126] Ibid., p. 16.
[127] Geary, *H.M.S. Hood*, p. 38. Letter dated 16 May 1941.
[128] Rea, *A Curate's Egg*, pp. 142–3, corrected by Vice-Admiral Sir Louis Le Bailly, letter to the author, 13 November 2002.
[129] IWM, 91/7/1, p. 50.
[130] These details owe much to the memories of Vice-Admiral Sir Louis Le Bailly.
[131] IWM/SA, Mid. John R. Lang, no. 12503, reel 1.

Lt (E) Louis Le Bailly, survived the sinking of the cruiser *Naiad* off Sidi Barrani in March 1942 and went on to become naval attaché in Washington D.C. and finally, as Vice-Admiral, Director General of Intelligence. A distinguished Marine officer was Lt 'Black Jack' Macafee who, as Provost Marshal in Alexandria during the war, closed all the principal male brothels and managed with a single Marine company to maintain order when troops of the Australian 9th Division arrived on leave from the desert. Then there were the characters. Cdr (N) D.H.S. Craven, a keen jockey who managed to persuade the wardroom to buy a horse at Malta in 1938, a decision it would regret once it became obvious the animal would never win a race. In one of the most extraordinary capers to take place between the wars, Lt Guy Horsey, then based at RAF Gosport, had in June 1936 managed to crash his Blackburn Baffin onto the bows of the liner *Normandie*.[132] Horsey was reprimanded and dismissed the FAA after the French Line sent the Admiralty an enormous claim for compensation. A few months later he joined the *Hood* along with another high-spirited lieutenant, Gresham Grenfell. His wardroom antics apart, Grenfell was probably the finest Divisional Officer of the 1930s. At a time when young stokers were joining the *Hood* as never before, Grenfell, then Boys' Divisional Officer, made a lasting impact on morale by encouraging comradeship between boy seamen and their peers in the Engineering Department. The following memoir of a boys' party ashore in 1938 is a mark of the man:

> As an illustration of how much he was respected and even loved I recall going ashore with him and a mass of boys including their football team in Marseilles. The French team never turned up. So Grenfell doled out francs to each boy and told them they were to catch the 18.00 boat back to the ship. With Marseilles the hotbed of brothels and other exciting pursuits I doubted if even one boy would show up. They ALL did even if one or two were a bit tipsy.[133]

It was, thought the Rev. Beardmore, a truly exceptional officer who could get on in the Navy as a teetotaller and a non-smoker. One such was Constructor Cdr W.J.A. Davies, capped 22 times for England in rugby and remembered as one of the greatest half-backs in the history of the game. Davies' international career was interrupted by service in *Iron Duke* during the First World War but he went on to lead England to two famous Grand Slams in 1921 and 1923. The steadying influence of a distinguished paternal figure of Davies' stature was a priceless asset in the young and boisterous wardrooms of the inter-war years. A messmate, the Rev. Edgar Rea, was to remember him thus:

> Although old enough to be father to many of us, he was humble, approachable and quite unaffected by the great name he had made. Even the most junior officers were permitted to tease him and no one enjoyed it more than Davies. The number of parties and receptions which he attended during his great rugger days must have been legion and yet I think I am right in saying that he remained throughout, both a teetotaller and a non-smoker. Unlike so many people on social occasions, he never looked uncomfortable without a glass in his hand.

He could sit or stand in any circle, he alone without a drink, and join in the conversation and laughter without appearing ill at ease. In every respect he was a fine example to the young, with whom he was so very much at home.[134]

The gunroom of the time also contained a number who would distinguish themselves in later years, including Mid. D.C. 'Bull' Wells, eventually Vice-Admiral Commanding, Royal Australian Navy. But if the *Hood*'s wardroom was one of accomplishment it would prove also to be one of sacrifice, and there were many, destined no doubt for high rank, who were not to survive the Second World War. Lt-Cdr (later Cdr) E.O. Unwin, Squadron W/T officer first on Cunningham's and then Layton's staff, suffered a harrowing death in the Atlantic after the light cruiser *Dunedin* fell victim to *U-124* in November 1941. Lt-Cdr (E) Lancelot Fogg-Elliot, then a commander, perished together with his entire engineering staff when the cruiser *Galatea* was torpedoed and sunk by *U-557* off Alexandria in December 1941. Mid. O.S.V. Waterlow, a holder of the D.S.C., was listed as missing, presumed killed after the submarine *Talisman* failed to return from a patrol off Italy in September 1942. Of the five Australian midshipmen shipped in 1938 only one survived the 1940s. Two of them, T.E. Davis and I.T.R. Treloar, were serving in the cruiser HMAS *Sydney* when she was lost with all hands following a punishing engagement with the German raider *Kormoran* off Australia in November 1941. Another, Mid. B.M. McFarlane, perished when the midget submarine *X22* collided with HMS/M *Syrtis* in the Pentland Firth in February 1944. A fourth, K.A. Seddon R.A.N.R., died in the destroyer HMAS *Nestor* in January 1947. For the *Hood*'s officer complement as for the ship herself, the price of admiralty was to be exacted in full.

Naturally, the *Hood*'s wardroom was not without its share of timeservers, failures and non-entities, those who, in O'Conor words, lacked 'the spark of leadership,... the ability to organise, and the will to carry things through'.[135] Nor could its society very well be described as a 'band of brothers'. The 'community of sentiment' preached by Admiral Lord Fisher prior to the First World War would not be realised until the Navy finally embraced the technical realities of its calling in the 1950s. But, as on the lower deck, the *Hood*'s wardroom was imbued with a certain spirit which her officers would carry with them in the trials to come—of pride, confidence and satisfaction in hard-earned victory; above all, of what it meant to love one's ship.

For a community like the *Hood*, organised entertainment served not only to relieve the drudgery and routine of life at sea but also to provide an outlet for the talents of those who perhaps yearned for a different career than that which fate had allotted them. Its other virtue lay in the opportunity it afforded men to vent the frustrations that attended a sailor's life while at the same time strengthening the communal bonds that made a ship's company what it was. For all its greatness, the Navy of *Hood*'s peacetime career was fraught with tension, bitterness and insecurity. In war her men had to come to terms with fear, depression and uncertainty. Under these circumstances it was only natural that interested officers and men did all they could to foster the camaraderie and unity of purpose which was reckoned to be the essence of a successful ship. For others, mean-

[132] Rea, *A Curate's Egg*, p. 141, corrected by Sturtivant & Cronin, *Fleet Air Arm Aircraft, Units and Ships 1920 to 1939*, p. 141.
[133] Vice-Admiral Sir Louis Le Bailly, letter to the author, 13 November 2002.
[134] Rea, *A Curate's Egg*, p. 144.
[135] *RBS*, p. 149.

while, their interest rested purely in the diversion and escapism represented by it, the fleeting opportunity to express themselves unhindered by the call of work and discipline.

As in almost every aspect of her life, many of the *Hood's* shipboard celebrations and entertainments were rooted in naval tradition. On Christmas morning, with an evergreen garland secured to the masthead, the Captain visited each mess to greet his men and acknowledge the efforts they had made to embellish their space with seasonal decorations. On New Year's Eve there was the ceremonial ringing of the ship's bell followed by toasts and dancing in the wardroom, the admiral, captain, wardroom, gunroom and warrant officers all in attendance. Then there was the elaborate 'Crossing the Line' ceremony described elsewhere, together with the legion customs and traditions that punctuated the commission of every ship in the Navy. An affable admiral might set the tone by putting on an entertainment of his own, though these were invariably officer-only affairs. One such was given by Rear-Admiral Sir William James in his quarters at Gibraltar in February 1933:

> My cabins were lit with dim red lamps, there were musicians in native dress tapping drums and blowing into reed instruments, there were some fine-looking Arabs with cutlasses at the doorways and for refreshments there were boar sandwiches and other African tit-bits. The officers of the *Hood*, who filled the native roles, were always ready to enter into the spirit of this kind of entertainment.[136]

But the most pungent and momentous entertainment was that provided by the Ship's Own Dramatic Society in its S.O.D.S. operas. For an evening or more a mixed cast of officers and men had something approaching *carte blanche* to comment on the life and personnel of the ship and the triumphs, mishaps and adventures of her commission. Rigged on the quarterdeck, a variety programme of off-colour songs, sketches and performances interspersed with acts of genuine talent were held together by the Bandmaster and his musicians. The earliest group for which details survive is 'The Frolics' which performed throughout 1921. At Gibraltar in February 1934 the ship put on a 'musical fantasy' entitled *Pirates* which included the wives of two officers among the cast. The entertainment, which was reviewed in London by *The Tatler*, made a wry comment on the incident at Cromarty the previous October when a harmless drill devised by Rear-Admiral James using matelots in pirate garb resulted in banner headlines of unrest and violence in the *Hood*.[137] But earlier, as the ship steamed away from Invergordon on 17 September 1931, a S.O.D.S. opera had provided the first step in the long road to recovery from a real mutiny.

The crew produced several musical ensembles including a male voice choir, a seamen's dance band—the 'Bandits Dance Orchestra' of the mid-1930s—and most notably the '*Hood's* Harmony Boys', a 30-strong accordion and mouth organ band formed in 1937 which continues to evoke fond memories among its surviving players and *aficionados*. The Harmony Boys were unique in drawing their original complement from the ship's stokers under the direction of Chief Stoker Cathmoir. Thanks to funds from the Canteen Committee, they were kitted out in splendid cream silk outfits adorned with green piping—the ship's colours. The value of a successful group like the Harmony Boys lay in its ability to enhance the reputation of the

ship both ashore and throughout the fleet. Stoker Ken Clark, a member between 1938–40, recalls a night in Malta:

> When we were in port we would often find a bar and put on some entertainment for the sailor and locals alike. I remember one occasion in particular when we were in Malta. We played through one or two numbers then one of the locals said 'I have a complaint about the band'. 'Oh, dear', we thought. But fortunately the chap only wanted to complain that we had been providing the entertainment but had not been supplied with drinks by the bar manager. We had some great times in the harmonica band and I often wondered how they were getting on after I left the ship.[138]

The Harmony Boys were good enough to broadcast a live performance on Maltese radio in 1938 and continued to thrive into the war years under new leadership, though their practising, usually done in the Schoolroom or the Reading Room, was by then restricted to time in harbour.

Other shipboard associations were dedicated to mutual assistance and improvement. During the 1933–6 commission a Mutual Aid Society was established aboard which maintained a membership of over 800 men.[139] Against a monthly deduction of a shilling from his pay a member was guaranteed a grant of up to £5 for travelling expenses incurred while on compassionate leave, £5 should he be invalided out of the Service and £10 to his nominee in the event of his death. When the ship paid off in June 1936 more than 80 per cent of the money subscribed was returned to the members. As Cdr O'Conor, a keen sportsman, noted, not only were men able to receive compensation in the event of some personal calamity, but the Ship's Fund upon which they traditionally relied could devote a greater part of its resources to recreational and sporting activities. In the early days the *Hood* presumably hosted a chapter of the Royal Naval Temperance Society (Templars) but if so there are few memories of it. The one fraternal organisation for which details are available is the Royal Antediluvian Order of Buffaloes, which had a lodge aboard until 1931.[140] In October of that year allegations that the lodge in the battleship *Valiant* had been used as cover for illegal gatherings before the

136 James, *The Sky Was Always Blue*, p. 168.
137 Ibid., pp. 172–4, and Coles & Briggs, *Flagship* Hood, pp. 78–9.
138 HMS *Hood* Association archives.
139 *RBS*, pp. 155–6.
140 Carew, *The Lower Deck*, pp. 166 & 250–1.

The *Hood's* Harmony Boys seen on the boat deck beside Port No. 2 5.5in gun, *c.*1938. The two officers are Lt-Cdr (E) Lancelot Fogg-Elliot (lost in the *Galatea*, 15 December 1941) and Lt (E) Louis Le Bailly. Between them is the leading light of the Harmony Boys, Chief Stoker Cathmoir. They often played in other ships and were known for a particularly fine rendition of *Hearts of Oak*.
HMS Hood Association/Sait Collection

141 Le Bailly, *The Man Around the Engine*, p. 23.
142 Cunningham, *A Sailor's Odyssey*, pp. 184 & 189–90.
143 Le Bailly, *The Man Around the Engine*, pp. 46–7.
144 Coles & Briggs, *Flagship* Hood, p. 93.
145 IWM/SA, no. 22147, reel 4.
146 *The Chough*, April 1936, p. 27.

Invergordon Mutiny resulted in the Admiralty withdrawing the Order's right to meet on board HM ships. The allegations were never proved and no evidence was presented against the *Hood*'s lodge but the die was cast and little was heard of her Buffaloes thereafter. The *Hood* no doubt also played host to branches of the large number of lower-deck societies that followed the rise of naval trade unionism prior to the Great War, but, again, these are poorly documented. Only the Engine Room Artificers' Society is known to have been represented aboard in the late 1930s though its activities had clearly been in abeyance for some time.

In line with the Navy's idea of suitable activities for its men, a majority of off-duty recreations were sporting in nature. At sea and weather permitting, deck hockey on the quarterdeck after tea was a perennial favourite for officers, 'an exhausting and often bloody game with a rope grommet puck, bent walking sticks and no rules'.[141] Officers also indulged in the traditional pursuits of hunting, shooting and fishing, for which the *Hood*'s frequent stays in Scottish waters provided ample opportunity. Rear-Admiral James participated in a boar shoot not far from Algiers in February 1933 and officers rode to hounds with the Calpe Hunt in Spain when the ship docked at Gibraltar each winter, but the weekly shooting parties that were a distinctive feature of life in the Mediterranean Fleet were only rarely savoured by the *Hood*. Vice-Admiral Andrew Cunningham, then in command of the Battle Cruiser Squadron, was able to indulge his passion for trout fishing in the hills above Split and, with less success, in Corsica when the *Hood* called there in 1937 and 1938.[142] Polo and squash at the Marsa Club in Malta and tennis with officers of the French navy were prominent in the Mediterranean between 1936 and 1939. For the keen cyclist there was the Wheeler's Club while the summer and autumn cruises to Scotland offered plenty of golf on the seaside links, the *Hood*'s players being divided by handicap into two leagues. Swimming and sunbathing were among the main attractions of the Mediterranean for both officers and men, including the novel recreation of water ski-

ing behind the *Hood*'s 30-foot motor boat for the former. Louis Le Bailly, then a Sub-Lieutenant, describes a typical Sunday ashore at Malta in 1937 or '38:

> Sunday divisions and church were obligatory but, unless there was a sailors' picnic, the bachelor's routine was invariable: change into old clothes, pack bathing gear and take a dghaisa to the Sliema Club… There on Monkey Island we could laze, sustained by cheap gin, a blistering curry, followed by blessed sleep on the warm rocks, a bathe and lustful discussions on the poodle-fakers and their companions' physical attributes 30 yards across the channel of water. Then iced almond cake for tea and a slow dghaisa back to the wardroom cinema.[143]

At Gibraltar the nearby beach at Rosia Bay was traditionally reserved for officers and nurses of the garrison, but the six months *Hood* spent alongside between the autumn of 1935 and the summer of 1936 demanded special arrangements for the men. The ever-resourceful O'Conor responded by turning the catamarans between ship and mole into a lido complete with coconut matting and lounge chairs.[144] Swimming races and rowing were encouraged. Fishing was allowed off the decks after tea was piped or on make-and-mend afternoons, but at no time was it permitted out of scuttles and ports. At Scapa Flow in 1940–1 OA Bert Pitman spent many an off-duty hour fishing for mackerel over the ship's side, often having to share his catch with marauding 'shitehawks', the epithet sailors gave to seagulls in the firm conviction that they were the spirits of thieving dockyard maties.[145] Never a ship to pass up the chance of a contest, one evening towards the end of March 1936 over 60 of the *Hood*'s men took part in an angling competition on the Detached Mole at Gibraltar.[146] Not much was caught but Ginger, one of the ship's cats, had a field day with the bait. O'Conor's other innovation was in converting the South Mole coalshed into a cinema, stage and boxing ring with shovels, hoses and whitewash. The first shipboard cinematograph was

A relaxing afternoon during the dog watches on the forecastle off Palma in 1938. Note the hawser reel and ventilation trunking against 'B' turret and the large mushroom vents on the right. A paravane has been stowed on the starboard forward screen.
HMS Hood Association/Clark Collection

installed in the battlecruiser *Queen Mary* before the Great War, but in promoting cinema as a suitable diversion both ashore and afloat O'Conor anticipated the work of the Naval Film Service, then still in its infancy. Films were an expensive commodity but by sharing them with other ships and charging an admission of 2d. per man and 1d. per boy the burden on the Ship's Fund was significantly lessened.[147] By 1938 movies were being shown on two or three evenings a week between decks or in the Starboard Battery. There were also screenings in the wardroom to which the gunroom officers were always invited.

The introduction of regular film screenings presumably had an adverse impact on the popularity of traditional off-watch recreations but these continued to be enjoyed by the men. Darts and 'uckers—a type of ludo—were played on messdecks and in recreation spaces, as were bridge, whist, cribbage and mahjong, but all forms of gambling for money stakes were prohibited, including betting and bookmaking. Naturally, this did not stop proscribed games such as brag and Crown and Anchor being played, and many was the man who lost his pay for a few hours' illicit entertainment. For others there was much amusement to be had in setting up a 'solo school' for ha'penny or 'tickler' (cigarette) stakes. Bridge, whist and, in wartime, poker for money stakes, were played in the wardroom and billiards was a favourite after-dinner activity for officers in the 1920s. Dancing seems to have diminished in popularity after the First World War, but music grew in importance and many played instruments either privately or in one of the ship's ensembles. Sub-Lt John Iago relates the following in a letter home in December 1939:

> I have played a good deal of bridge when off watch and my piccolo has come in to favour again which I play in my cabin. Pillinger has moved out and a chap with an accordion has arrived in his place. I think worse noises come out of our cabin than out of any other in the ship![148]

During the 1930s broadcast music and radio programmes became a significant part of shipboard life thanks to a number of technical innovations, including the installation of a broadcasting system ('the tannoy') in about 1935 and acquisition of a radiogram and gramophones. Once again, O'Conor was in the vanguard of these reforms:

> Broadcast programmes, backed up by gramophone records, play a big part in life on board ship. Men are keenly interested in the affairs of the day, and crucial pronouncements by statesmen unfailingly attract attentive crowds to the loud-speakers. The time of pipe-down has frequently to be deferred in response to a request to keep the wireless going, and the cause is as likely to be an important speech from London or Geneva as a 'big fight'.[149]

However, as the Rev. Beardmore relates, no doubt from bitter experience, widespread interest and the sailor's natural curiosity meant that such novelties had to be carefully guarded:

> You will find that there are a large number of ratings in these days who appreciate other music than 'swing' and 'jazz' and welcome a concert of really first-class music. Try to obtain a radiogram for the use of the ship's company

Marines play a game of 'uckers in the starboard battery, c.1935. The pile of 5.5in cordite cartridge cases behind indicates that the gun may shortly be in action.
HMS Hood Association/Willis Collection

and have it fixed in some convenient place where you can use it for concerts. See that it is always kept locked until required for a concert, otherwise its life will be short, ruined by the rating with an inquiring mind, who has 'never really understood how one of these 'ere things works.' The answer is, it works no more.[150]

Handicraft competitions in leather, usually under the chaplain's auspices, were another popular diversion on the lower deck, as was tapestry among the older men. Although it was already a dying art in the Navy, fancy ropework continued to be formed in the fo'c'sle messdecks and in private cabooses on the boat deck. Wherever long-service able seamen had responsibility for a part of the ship no opportunity was missed to enliven it with superb workmanship. Heads of gangways, man ropes and hammock lashings all received the fruits of their labour, but the finest work was reserved for the ship's boats. Tiller handles, boat hooks and other accoutrements were lovingly embellished with turk's heads and elaborate coach whipping and fenders laboriously crafted out of 50 yards of hemp rope. For a few shillings an officer could have his telescope ornamented with intricate rope grommets.

Trades, or 'firms' as they were known, represented an important source of income for many ratings, particularly in the depressed 1930s. Closely regulated by the Navy, only a limited number of men were permitted to do business aboard in each of the recognised trades. By the late 1930s the *Hood*'s allowance was for six tailors, nine cobblers or 'snobs', six barbers and a pair of photographers.[151] Prices were controlled, with boot repairs running from 7d. for a simple rubber fitting to 4s. 6d. for a

[147] *RBS*, p. 151.
[148] Iago, *Letters* (at sea, 7 December 1939). Temp. Lt (E) E.W. Pillinger (1939–c.1940).
[149] *RBS*, p. 152.
[150] Beardmore, *The Waters of Uncertainty*, p. 43.
[151] *RBS*, pp. 218–19.

A space rarely photographed: the Barber's shop on the upper deck where Stoker Bill Stone plied his trade between 1921 and 1925; seen here in 1940 or 1941.
HMS Hood Association/Ian Watts

complete sewn heel and sole job. Haircuts were 4d. for officers and men but free for boys at certain hours. Lots were drawn among the six barbers embarked in 1937 for the privilege of plying their trade in the ship's barber shop for six-month spells. Stoker Bill Stone (1921–5) was one of the lucky ones:

The 'Barbers' Shop' in *Hood* was on the port side of the upper deck—one deck down. I remember that it certainly was a lovely room with a 6-foot wide mirror, water geyser and all the equipment that a budding barber needed. The other thing that struck me about the room was that it was a rather odd shape. This was due to the fact that one of the walls was curved. The wall was formed by the massive vertical steel cylinder or 'barbette' which ran down through the ship and on top of which sat 'B' turret.[152]

At 4d. per cut it was possible for a man to double his naval income by devoting the better part of his spare time to his second career, though, as Stone discovered, this was only feasible if the integrity of one's colleague could be counted on:

Unfortunately, a while later I found out that the Marine Bandsman with whom I shared the shop was 'playing dirty' with me. We each charged 4d for a cut and the money was supposed to go into a kitty to be shared out at the end of the week. Being the new boy I had accepted this arrangement in good faith. However, I started to think that my share seemed low for the number of cuts that I was doing and eventually realised what was happening. The Bandsman was often being given a sixpence by his customers which he would put in his top pocket. He would then give them the 2d change out of the shared kitty which I was filling with my own takings! This meant, of course, that of the 4d that I put in only 2d remained there for the payout at the end of the week. When that arrived and the money was halved between us I was ending up with only a penny a cut! One night when he went out I took the opportunity to confirm my suspicions and found several sixpence pieces in his top pocket. When he came back I confronted him and said that one or other of us had to go. I didn't tell him that I had found the evidence in his top pocket—his conscience would

tell him that. It didn't come to either of us having to leave but the takings were a lot higher from then on although I never really trusted him again afterwards.

Tailoring was another important trade, much patronised by the men for natty shore-going uniforms. 'Jewing firms' as they were known might consist of three men, one with the machine, another making buttonholes and a third sewing them on. In 1937 a sailor's No. 1 suit cost 15s. 6d. if the tailor supplied the material and 7 shillings if it was provided by his client. During the world cruise of 1923–4 AB William Collier made over 300 uniforms at 7 shillings a time, a significant income for the period.[153] Indeed, after the pay cuts of 1931 a married man might well rely on the extra income to keep his family above the bread line, and competition for the few official berths was fierce. For others there were a few shillings to be made taking in laundry, lashing hammocks or setting themselves up as 'tickler' firms rolling cigarettes out of duty-free tobacco. There were other avenues as well. Skilled men could bolster their income in the ship's workshops by turning out 'rabbits', items for personal use made from Navy materials in Navy time. Then there were those who earnt a lucrative but highly illegal income lending money to their shipmates at rates of 25 shillings to the pound or higher. Evidently, though the Navy might regulate the transaction of business aboard there were no end of ways by which men could make a little on the side.

On joining the ship around 1930 a boy seaman—rated Boy 1st Class—would receive a weekly pay of just 8s. 9d., rising to 14 shillings on being rated Ordinary Seaman by the age of eighteen. Promotion to Able Seaman at nineteen brought 21 shillings a week, with an additional 3d. per day for each of the three Good Conduct badges he could be awarded after three, eight and then thirteen years of service. Leading Seamen earned 30s. 4d. a week. Qualifying for a specialist rate earned up to 3d. a day with a further 3d. for those who abstained from taking up their grog ration—a pertinent comment on the Navy's priorities before the Second World War. In view of the arduous nature of their work Stokers 2nd Class got 17 shillings per week, advancing to 25 shillings once they were rated 1st Class. Petty Officers, meanwhile, received 42 shillings a week and Chief Petty Officers the princely sum of 52s. 6d. To these figures marriage and child allowances were added for men aged 25 and older. In HMS *Hood* the men were paid every other Friday.[154] In good weather Pay Tables were set up in the port and starboard lobbies off the quarterdeck, the men filing past in Ship's Book number order to receive their pay. Once at the Pay Table a writer called out names from a ledger and the amount each was due, the men holding out their caps to receive the contents of an envelope tipped onto it by the Paymaster.

While many were, in O'Conor's words, happy to toddle complacently towards their pension, for others their time aboard represented another rung on the ladder of promotion and advancement. For a Boy Seaman the passage of a year or two would finally bring him 'man's rating' and promotion to Ordinary Seaman, with a marked improvement in status and conditions. Fred Coombs:

Come the 31st March 1937 we were rated up to Ordinary Seaman, a milestone for us as it meant that we at last got away from the hated Boys' Division, were left more to our

The *Hood* in Colour

THE IMAGES ON THESE PAGES are stills from two colour films shot by the *Hood*'s Chief Engineer, Cdr (E) R.T. Grogan, who joined the ship on 5th May 1939 and perished with her two years later. The footage, which was shot with a 16-mm cine-camera, dates from the summer of 1939 to the autumn of 1940 and reveals the ship from the time of her full-power trials in June or July 1939, through the early months of the war and finally to the period following her Mediterranean interlude in the summer of 1940. The intended result, a film titled *The War from the Hood* with soundtrack, has yet to come to light but the surviving footage provides a remarkable visual record of the ship as she entered the concluding phase in her life. Robert Terence Grogan was born in Kent in *c*.1901 and presumably entered Dartmouth around the outbreak of the First World War. A brilliant engineer with a reputation for breakneck driving at Brooklands, Grogan was appointed to *Hood* having been Senior Engineer in the new cruiser *Sheffield*. But Grogan's main shipboard hobby was film-making and sound recording. The latter not only allowed him to record the King's radio broadcast while the rest of the wardroom slept off Christmas lunch in December 1940, but also to install a device beneath the log of the forward control platform to catch engine-room gossip from Lt (E) Louis Le Bailly.[1]

The first showing of Grogan's uncut work appears to have been to a wardroom audience in October 1939. This material seems mainly to have been of the ship running full-power trials that summer (nos. 5–12) but no doubt included footage of the *Spearfish* episode the previous month (see p. 190) when Grogan is recorded as having been on deck with his camera. The shots of the flag deck (nos. 15–17) probably also date from this period. Grogan was in action again in mid December when *Hood* escorted the first Canadian troop convoy of the war into Greenock with *Resolution*, *Repulse* and *Warspite* in company (no. 21). The appearance of either *Georges Leygues* or *Montcalm* in one of the sequences suggests he was also filming during the patrol conducted with the French navy at the end of November. By early 1940 Grogan's work had been given sanction by the Admiralty and was being broadcast by British Gaumont News, though usually in black and white. Years later, Rear-Admiral Peter La Niece, a midshipman aboard in the first months of 1940, recalled standing beside Grogan as he shot some of the footage that has become the stock of countless war documentaries:

The Engineer Commander was a movie camera buff and his reputation was such that he had been issued with an official camera by the Admiralty. I was standing right beside him when he took the very sequence which found its way into the archives and which still reappears time and again in documentaries on television; whenever I see this clip of capital ships ploughing through heavy seas I am always reminded of these patrols.[2]

Grogan's camera appears again during the *Hood*'s Mediterranean interlude, first at Gibraltar (no. 22) and then apparently during one of her sorties into the western basin. The last identifiable footage is of the ship at Rosyth in the autumn of 1940 (no. 23). Reports of further wardroom screenings in October 1940 indicate that Grogan had shot footage of *Hood* and *Ark Royal* under Italian aerial bombardment in July or August but this ordeal is not among the frames captured here.[3] Perhaps in some forgotten loft or packing case lies a canister of film and its synchronized radiogram entitled *The War from the Hood* waiting to add a further dash of colour to her last years. Let us hope so.

---

[1] Iago, *Letters* (Greenock, 25 December 1940), and Vice-Admiral Sir Louis Le Bailly, letter to the author, 1 February 2004.
[2] La Niece, *Not a Nine to Five Job*, p. 29.
[3] Iago, *Letters* (Scapa Flow, 10 October & 1 November 1940).

1 *Hood* glides past the camera on her way out of Portsmouth to run trials off the Isle of Wight in the summer of 1939. Men are fallen in by divisions on the forecastle, boat deck, quarterdeck and atop both 'B' and 'X' turret. Note the bluish-grey hue of AP507A (Home Fleet dark grey) in which she has just been painted.

2 The *Hood*'s Marine detachment fallen in beside 'X' turret as the ship warps away from the jetty at Portsmouth in the summer of 1939. The band marches on the quarterdeck. *Repulse* lies astern.

3 An Admiralty tug helps the *Hood* out of Portsmouth in the summer of 1939. Starboard No. 3 5.5in gun is visible on the right.

4 *Hood* seen from her port quarter in a still from the same sequence as the first image. The Marine detachment is still fallen in on the quarterdeck.

5 *Hood*'s forecastle wreathed in spray as she reaches her best speed in the summer of 1939. This sequence was filmed from the starboard side of the Compass platform overlooking the 30ft rangefinder atop the main director.

6 The same view seen from the Admiral's bridge. The conning tower rises on the left while 'Squeak', the starboard 0.5-inch machine-gun mounting, sits under a tarpaulin on the right.

7 & 8 The funnels seen from the port side of the Admiral's bridge during the *Hood*'s full-power trial in June 1939. In the second image excess steam can be seen roaring out of the safety valves. Note the struts supporting the funnels and the 44in searchlight on the right.

9 The after funnel and the spotting top seen during full-power trials in June 1939. Note the white base of the fore topmast abaft the aloft director.

10 Waves begin to lap onto the quarterdeck during the *Hood*'s full-power trial in June 1939. An awning stanchion and an electric winch lie between 'X' and 'Y' turrets.

11 The quarterdeck during the *Hood*'s full-power trial in June 1939. An awning stanchion has been struck in the foreground while the base of an ammunitioning davit lies beyond.

12 Water boils under *Hood*'s stern during a full-power trial in June 1939. This foreshortened view of the quarterdeck seems have been taken from the port side of 'X' turret.

13 Parties of men being told off for work on the forecastle in the summer of 1939. Most have gas masks slung over their shoulders in canvas bags. This view was shot from the starboard side of the flag deck.

14 Men clamber into one of the *Hood*'s 25ft fast motor boats in a heavy swell, *c*.1939. Though shaded by the ship's side, the red corticene decking is just discernible on the left of the image.

15–18 Boy signalmen at work on the starboard side of the flag deck, *c*.1939. Flags are being selected from the lockers and bent to the halyards before hoisting. The refit of February–June 1939 extended both flag decks and enclosed their after ends with new lockers, seen in nos. 15–17. Another addition of the February–June refit is visible in no. 17 in the shape of Starboard No.1 twin 4in mounting. The boys are carrying gas masks.

19 'X' turret trained to starboard, *c*.1939–40. The muzzles are protected from the weather by canvas covers.

20 The port side of the quarterdeck with 'X' and 'Y' turrets trained to starboard. A man can be seen emerging from the access hatch behind the rangefinder of 'Y' turret.

21 *Hood*'s quarterdeck awash in enormous seas during the escorting of the first Canadian troop convoy into Greenock, December 1939. *Resolution* astern. A still from this sequence was produced aboard for sale as a postcard.

22 The *Hood* seen at Gibraltar in the summer of 1940. Men can be seen lining the Commander's lobby in their tropical rig. The lighter shade of paint discernible in this image suggests that the *Hood* may have received her final shade of AP507B (Home Fleet medium grey) earlier than previously thought. Note the wooden ladders on the aft screen and the grey floats and boats.

23 Dawn at Rosyth in the autumn of 1940. The view is from the quarterdeck looking forward. Port and Starboard No. 3 twin 4in mountings can be made out on either side of 'Y' turret. The Forth Bridge is in the background.

24 Sunset as the Atlantic breaks over *Hood*'s decks during the winter of 1939–40.

HMS *Hood*, May 1941

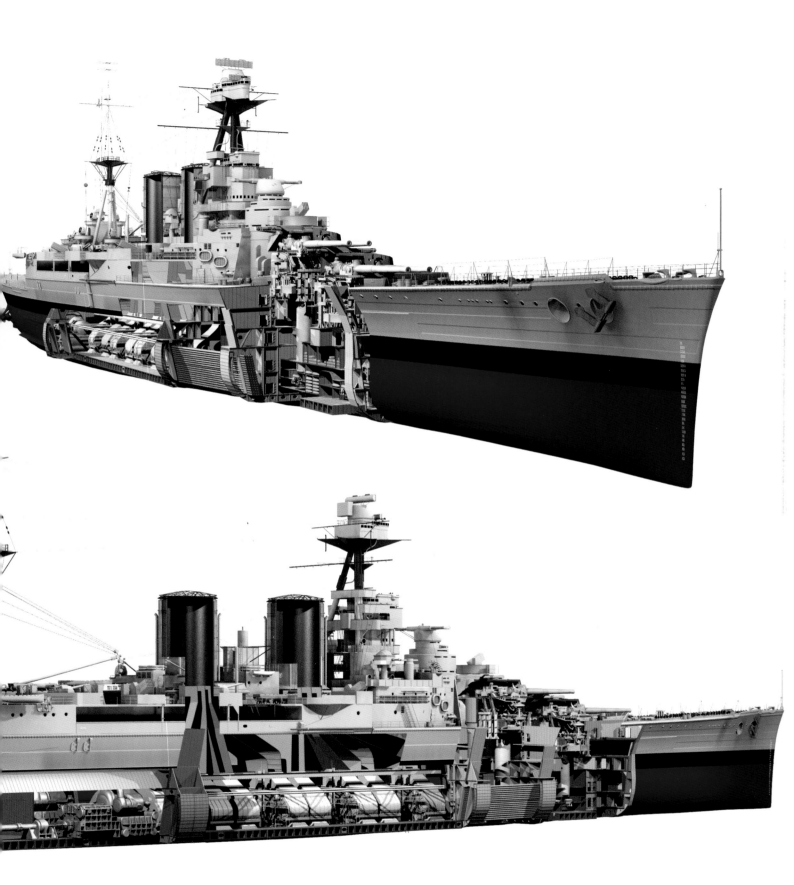

The 15-inch Mk II turret and its loading system

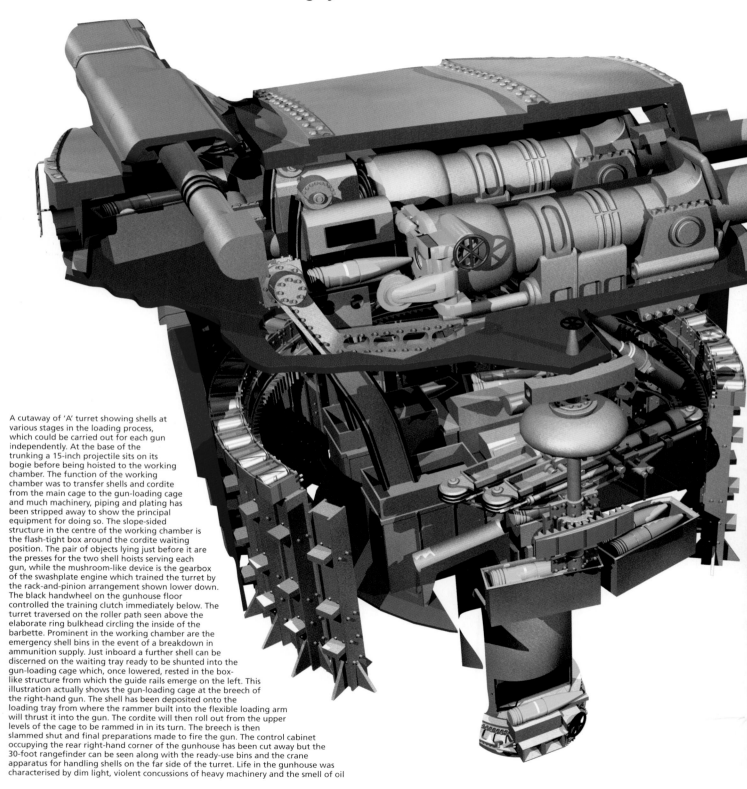

A cutaway of 'A' turret showing shells at various stages in the loading process, which could be carried out for each gun independently. At the base of the trunking a 15-inch projectile sits on its bogie before being hoisted to the working chamber. The function of the working chamber was to transfer shells and cordite from the main cage to the gun-loading cage and much machinery, piping and plating has been stripped away to show the principal equipment for doing so. The slope-sided structure in the centre of the working chamber is the flash-tight box around the cordite waiting position. The pair of objects lying just before it are the presses for the two shell hoists serving each gun, while the mushroom-like device is the gearbox of the swashplate engine which trained the turret by the rack-and-pinion arrangement shown lower down. The black handwheel on the gunhouse floor controlled the training clutch immediately below. The turret traversed on the roller path seen above the elaborate ring bulkhead circling the inside of the barbette. Prominent in the working chamber are the emergency shell bins in the event of a breakdown in ammunition supply. Just inboard a further shell can be discerned on the waiting tray ready to be shunted into the gun-loading cage which, once lowered, rested in the box-like structure from which the guide rails emerge on the left. This illustration actually shows the gun-loading cage at the breech of the right-hand gun. The shell has been deposited onto the loading tray from where the rammer built into the flexible loading arm will thrust it into the gun. The cordite will then roll out from the upper levels of the cage to be rammed in in its turn. The breech is then slammed shut and final preparations made to fire the gun. The control cabinet occupying the rear right-hand corner of the gunhouse has been cut away but the 30-foot rangefinder can be seen along with the ready-use bins and the crane apparatus for handling shells on the far side of the turret. Life in the gunhouse was characterised by dim light, violent concussions of heavy machinery and the smell of oil

A cutaway of the hull abreast 'A' and 'B' turrets. The view shows the box construction of the double bottom, the shell bins and shellrooms in the hold, and the magazines on the platform deck, the latter protected by a layer of 2-inch plate with a further three inches of armour on the main deck above. To the left is a section of the elaborate underwater protection scheme together with the belts of 12- and 7-inch armour and the round-down of 2-inch plating which constituted the *Hood*'s main defence against shellfire. Dominating the image are the revolving structures of 'A' and 'B' turret, weighing approximately 890 tons each from the gunhouse to the base of the trunking in the hold. In each case a shell can be seen on its bogie on the lower platform, waiting to be clamped to the inside of the trunking for hoisting to the working chamber. Just below the working chambers the trunking has been cut away to show the cylinders of compressed air used to clear the guns after each firing. The structures projecting into the gun well are the lateral guides for the barrels and, forward of them, the cylinders by which each was elevated and depressed.

The boiler rooms and their operation

Three views of 'Y' Boiler Room, looking in each case from the starboard to the port side of the ship. The first view shows the general arrangement of the space from the so-called stokehold on the lower platform deck. The six boilers faced each other in rows of three, each tended by a stoker under the control of a Chief Stoker and his PO Stoker assistant. The apparatus against the column in the centre of the picture is a bilge and fire pump in the event of flooding or a conflagration. The second view, taken from almost the same position, shows one of the boilers in greater detail. The eight rectangular structures in the lower and middle section contain the air boxes for draught and, in the centre, the oil sprayers which fed the brick-lined furnace burning inside. Lying diagonally on each side are the boiler casings themselves with their mass of tubes. The furnace heated the water in these tubes, converting it into steam which gathered in a drum seen at the top of the boiler behind the gantry. This level, known as the upper stokehold, was in the care of a Leading Stoker water tender charged with monitoring the automatic feed water regulators of each row of boilers. The failure of these regulators required an immediate changeover to hand operation in order to prevent a major boiler explosion. The handwheels ranged at the end of rods on the left were for checking and regulating the feed water, while the lengthy one on the right operated the safety-valve easing gear, employed when there was a surfeit of steam in the boiler. The final view is taken from the level of the fan compartment, though much detail, including the fan flat itself, has been stripped away to provide this vista. Emerging from each boiler are the uptakes which vented smoke and gas into the after funnel. Running on either side are the boiler pipes supplying the steam mains leading to the turbines in the Forward Engine Room. The atmosphere of 'Y' Boiler Room with all six boilers lit must be imagined as one of oppressive heat against the shriek of sound and gale of wind produced by the high-pressure fans.

PETS AND MASCOTS

Sailors are traditionally fond of animals and virtually every ship had a pet as its mascot. *Hood* was, of course, no exception, and few ships can have had more than she during her long career. Her first mascot was Bill, the goat presented to the ship by Rear-Admiral Cowan (1921–3) and which on one occasion paid an unexpected visit to his sleeping cabin.[187] Bill seems not to have outlasted Cowan's tenure but the World Cruise of 1923–4 was to turn the *Hood* into a veritable menagerie. At least one cobra appeared with its snakecharmer at Trincomalee but once *Hood* reached Australia animals started coming aboard to stay. There was Joey the wallaby at Fremantle, Thomas the kangaroo at Adelaide and a variety of other local fauna including a ring-tailed possum, a pair of cockatoos and numerous parrots. To these a kiwi—Miss Apteryx Australis—was added in New Zealand, though no substitute was found for her insectivorous diet and she did not survive the voyage. A journey to Calgary yielded at least one beaver, and a marmoset and flying-squirrel had joined the throng by the time *Hood* reached Devonport in September 1924. Most were offloaded to zoos but Joey remained until patience finally ran out in 1926, prompting Lady Hood to present the ship with Angus, a pedigree bulldog. A number of men kept their own pets aboard, mainly in the form of songbirds since larger animals required the permission of the Commander. In May 1936 a visit to the Canaries brought numerous birds onto the lower deck though, as Boy Fred

A cheery party on 'A' turret and the forward breakwater at Scapa Flow in the autumn of 1940. With them is Bill, the Rev. Harold Beardmore's bull terrier. Also there is Fishcakes, held by the second man from the right. The forward UP launcher can be seen on 'B' turret.

Coombs explains, appearances were deceiving:

…With abject poverty everywhere even the boys could afford the nick-nacks and canaries in wicker cages though, as in Madeira, most of them turned out to be brownish mute canaries when the yellow powder came off. Soon after we came home again but this time only to be recommissioned and return as part of the

Mediterranean Fleet. There was very few canaries surviving by then, though occasionally the sight could be seen of some sad-faced matelot whispering in some secluded corner of the upper deck and pleading 'Sing, you bastard, sing' to his mute canary which, more than likely, would be laying on its back with its legs in the air when we reached the colder northern climes.[188]

The first ship's mascot of the 1930s seems to have been Judy, the West Highland terrier Cdr Rory O'Conor brought with him in 1933. However, it was during this commission that *Hood* received two of her best-loved pets, Ginger, a large red mackerel tabby and white cat, and Fishcakes, a tuxedo. This duo became an inseparable part of shipboard life during *Hood*'s last three commissions, a status quo that no doubt suffered a severe upset with the arrival of the Rev. Harold Beardmore's bull terrier Bill in June 1939. Though friendly enough to people, Bill had a violent streak and was known to have done away with more than one sheep.[189] However, Bill nearly met his maker when the ship was being depermed at Rosyth in early 1941, being unfortunate enough to cock his leg on a length of electric cabling and receive in return what Jon Pertwee later described as 'a severe whack in the winky'.[190] Bill left with Beardmore in February 1941, being spared the fate that apparently claimed Ginger and Fishcakes. R.I.P.

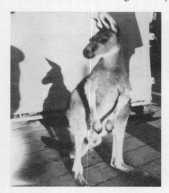

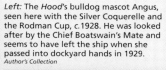

Above: Joey the wallaby who joined in February 1924 and stayed until passing to a zoo in 1926. Remembered for his boxing and an insatiable appetite for tobacco.
Mrs Margaret Berry

Right: 'Ever the best of friends.' Ginger and Fishcakes in the late 1930s. Sadly, the evidence is that they both perished with the ship.
HMS Hood Association/Mason Collection

Top centre: Ginger and an unidentified terrier on one of the pom-pom mountings, c.1935. Ginger was not to have his tail much longer; it had to be amputated after being trapped by the lid of a wash-deck locker.
HMS Hood Association

Centre: Ginger in his salad days, c.1933.
HMS Hood Association/Higginson Collection

Right: Fishcakes in the port battery, c.1935.
HMS Hood Association/Willis Collection

Left: The *Hood*'s bulldog mascot Angus, seen here with the Silver Coquerelle and the Rodman Cup, c.1928. He was looked after by the Chief Boatswain's Mate and seems to have left the ship when she passed into dockyard hands in 1929.
Author's Collection

6 Disaster and Recovery, 1931–1936

And what shoulder and what art
Could twist the sinews of thy heart?

IN THE SPRING OF 1931 the *Hood* finally emerged from her lengthy refit and resumed her exalted status as flagship of the Battle Cruiser Squadron, Atlantic Fleet. In May she completed to full complement and a month later sailed from Portsmouth for the usual summer spell at Portland. However, it was quite obvious that matters had changed greatly since she had paid off and passed into dockyard control at Portsmouth two years earlier. For one thing she was now a Pompey ship, having exchanged the outspoken Westcountrymen of her first four commissions with the more stolid crews of the Portsmouth Division. But above all, the world to which she returned seemed very much less stable than it had in the summer of 1929. In October of that year the Wall Street Crash precipitated an economic depression that by the autumn of 1931 had put over 2.5 million men out of work and brought the National Government of Ramsay MacDonald to power in Britain. With the economy in crisis, on 31 June of that year the Committee on National Expenditure chaired by Sir George May recommended sweeping wage cuts for civil servants including the armed forces, declaring that 'No officer or man serving His Majesty has any legal claim to a particular rate of pay'.[1] For those sailors who kept abreast of political events, who read *The Fleet* and participated in messdeck discussions about welfare, pay and representation, here was the first inkling of trouble ahead.

Despite these developments, the first few months of the *Hood*'s commission passed off uneventfully as the crew laboured to slough away the dirt and disorder of a prolonged period in dockyard hands. Sea trials off Portland were followed in July by a visit to Torbay where the flag of Rear-Admiral Wilfred Tomkinson was hoisted for the first time. Though it had little bearing on subsequent events, his arrival on board was at best inauspicious. Vice-Admiral Eric Longley-Cook, then the ship's First Lieutenant and Gunnery Officer, has left this account of Tomkinson's opening gambit:

> We sailed early one fine morning to take station astern of the Battle Cruiser Squadron. I was on the bridge and wondered what the Admiral's signal would be. 'Glad to see you back'? 'Welcome back to the BCS'? No. A flag signal 'Manoeuvre badly executed'; from tails up to tails nearly down. Next morning, Sunday 08.00 in Torbay, we hoisted the flag of ACQ. At 09.00 he arrived on board, walked round divisions, then 'clear lower deck, everyone aft'. From the after capstan the Admiral addressed us. Summarily he said 'I was the first Captain of this ship and until you reach something like the standard in which I left her, I shall not be satisfied'. Now, we had worked very hard indeed to get her from dockyard condition to fleet condition, so tails went down even lower. So on we went, not entirely happy.[2]

The crew no doubt recognised this as a particularly *gauche* example of the ploy often resorted to to goad men into action, but Tomkinson remained highly unpopular in this his first and last seagoing command as an admiral. However, this state of affairs was greatly mitigated by Cdr C.R. McCrum, an exceptional executive officer and much admired by his men. Years later LS Sam Wheat recalled him thus:

> I'll always say we had the most excellent Commander you could ever have. He's the best admired Commander I've ever known or ever served with, and that was Cdr McCrum. And he was a diplomatic chap.[3]

The months to come would require all of McCrum's powers of diplomacy. Meanwhile there was a lengthy refitting at Portsmouth during which *Hood* was once more the main attraction at Navy Week. Summer leave was taken by watches. Morale was good and the atmosphere calm. It was against this backdrop that the *Hood* sailed from Portsmouth on 8 September to participate in the autumn gunnery cruise of the Atlantic Fleet off Scotland. Though few of her men suspected it, even as she headed north the seeds of disaster were in the wind. The mass disobedience that the Navy had been spared since 1797 was about to return. 'Mutiny' was at hand.

Though not known for dissidence, the *Hood* had had her share of lower-deck unrest during the militant years following the First World War. In March 1921 the ship fell under the thrall of Rear-Admiral Sir Walter Cowan and his Flag Captain, Geoffrey Mackworth. Cowan, an aggressive blood-and-guts officer of the old school, had already weathered three mutinies, one as captain of the pre-dreadnought *Zealandia* in 1914 and latterly as Senior Naval Officer, Baltic, where in 1919 there were serious cases of insubordination aboard the gunboat *Cicala* and in his own flagship, the cruiser *Delhi*. The *Delhi* incident had been provoked largely by the tactlessness of her captain, Mackworth, who Cowan unwisely brought with him to the *Hood*. It was to prove an unfortunate pairing, exacerbated by events. Within a month of their arrival the *Hood* was at Rosyth where three battalions of sailors and Marines were landed to help maintain essential services during the rail, bus and coal strikes. With lower-deck unionism at its height it was not long before elements of the *Hood*'s company began to express their solidarity with the strikers ashore. One day during Commander's Rounds the Executive Officer Richard Lane-Poole entered one of the seamen's messes to find it festooned with red bunting.[4] Service against the Bolsheviks in the Baltic had made Cowan particularly sensitive to the spread of Communist ideas in the Navy and he immediately ordered two able seamen to be court-martialled for mutinous practice. When they were acquitted for

[1] Carew, *The Lower Deck*, pp. 154–5.
[2] HMS *Hood* Association archives, Address to the Association, 24 May 1980, in 1980 newsletter, p. 2. ACQ was the traditional pendant code for Admiral Commanding, Battle Cruiser Squadron.
[3] IWM/SA, no. 5807.
[4] Carew, *The Lower Deck*, pp. 128 & 213.

want of evidence an incensed Cowan responded by court-martialling Master-at-Arms William Batten for 'concealing a mutinous practice' and Stoker John Hall for inciting the same. The case against Batten was also dismissed but Hall was sentenced to three years' hard labour. Meanwhile, Cowan was warning the Admiralty that discipline in the Battle Cruiser Squadron 'hangs by a very slender thread, chiefly by reason of the mass of mischievous and revolutionary literature, which floods the country'.[5] It seems that Cowan greatly exaggerated the significance of the incident, but nonetheless the rest of the commission was characterised by a remorseless emphasis on discipline and efficiency that made for an extremely unhappy ship. Matters were not helped by Mackworth's increasingly irrational outbursts and the demise of his relations with Cowan himself. Sporadic disturbances and pranks continued, culminating in the spring of 1923 in the refusal of the ship's company to enter the Combined Fleet Regatta, a traditional means of expressing resentment. As one officer recalled, even in 1926—three years after the end of the commission—'the Cowan-Mackworth combination was still an evil legend in the Atlantic Fleet'.[6] By contrast, the next major outbreak of industrial unrest, the General Strike of May 1926, apparently had little effect on the *Hood*, which was rushed to the Clyde and spent nearly two months lying quietly at Greenock. Among those drafted aboard while a majority of the crew were ashore guarding mines, dockyards, depots and factories was one AB Len Wincott. Wincott's memory of the episode is typical of his jaundiced style:

> Then a whole battalion of seamen from the depot were despatched on an aircraft carrier to the Clyde for the purpose of guarding 'important objectives'—that is, the mines and factories belonging to private individuals where the workers were on strike. We were dumped on the *Hood* which was anchored off Clydebank and there for six weeks we stood guard over holy-stones and wash deck gear until again somebody remembered our existence and brought us back in comfortable railway carriages. It was at that time that reducing the sailor's 'over-generous pay' was

being considered—no doubt to make up for the vast cost of our useless round-trip to Scotland.[7]

Despite the fears of Cowan and a generation of senior figures in the Royal Navy, it was not political ideology but the policy and attitudes of the Admiralty itself that constituted the chief source of discontent on the lower deck.[8] The Admiralty not only failed to recognise the extent to which the First World War had altered the British social order, it also took an inordinately long time to accept that the Navy was drawing into its ranks men with aspirations and a level of education unknown in the pre-war fleets. Against the backdrop of social and political change at home and abroad these developments coincided with the growth of the lower-deck societies. In the years before the Great War the lower deck had for the first time found representation by means of a range of semi-unionised societies, most of which confined their membership to a branch or trade such as the Engine Room Artificers' Society.[9] During the war these societies together with *The Fleet*, the influential newspaper edited by Lionel Yexley, successfully lobbied for the improvement in lower-deck pay that culminated in the 1919 settlement which at last provided the British sailor with an adequate compensation for his services. Though it had yielded on this matter the Admiralty was concerned at the increasingly politicised nature of the societies' activities and in 1920 issued a fleet order which effectively destroyed their capacity for organised representation. Their function as a mouthpiece for lower-deck grievances and welfare issues was taken by a system of conferences set up under the auspices of the Admiralty, the first of which met in May 1922. Predictably enough, the conference system proved ineffectual in the role for which it had been established and by the late 1920s the lower deck was aware that its voice had been stifled. Already in 1925 economic considerations had obliged the Admiralty to introduce a lower pay scale for all new entrants to the Service, though assurances were given that the earlier rates would be honoured for all currently in receipt of them. The 1925 pay scales were to have serious consequences for the Navy. The two-tier structure was not only resented by those who

[5] Ibid., p. 130.
[6] Bennett, *Cowan's War*, p. 68.
[7] Wincott, *Invergordon Mutineer*, p. 38. The pay cuts had in fact been made in 1925. The aircraft carrier was probably HMS *Furious*.
[8] Carew, *The Lower Deck*, ch. 6–8.
[9] Ibid., *passim*.

A rather grubby *Hood* sails from Portsmouth in June 1931 after two years in dockyard hands. Rear-Admiral Tomkinson did not like what he saw when she reached Torbay in July. Note the new seaplane arrangements on the quarterdeck.
U.S. Naval Historical Center, Washington

'Pay-out day' by Jack Kettle. The inroads made into lower-deck pay illustrated on a postcard sold in *Hood* at the time of Invergordon. Note the smugness with which the officers have been portrayed.
Mrs Sheila Smith

[10] Pensions were to be reduced to the March 1930 levels, a reduction of 2½d. per day to 8d.
[11] See Roskill, *Naval Policy*, II, pp. 93–4. Whether or not Tomkinson saw this cipher before 13 September is a matter of some debate; whatever the case, he gives no indication of having absorbed its contents before the arrival of the Admiralty Fleet Order detailing the same on the 12th.

The *Hood* lies peacefully at Invergordon, probably in May 1932, just eight months after the Mutiny.
Royal Naval Museum, Portsmouth

found themselves receiving less pay for equal work, but did nothing to alleviate the blockage in promotion caused by the mass of men who had achieved higher rating during the Great War. Under these circumstances the failure of the welfare conferences and the closing of official channels of representation hastened the decline of the lower-deck societies and drove men to a more radical expression of their grievances. When in September 1931 the Admiralty tamely acceded to a government proposal that the pay of the entire Navy be reduced to the 1925 levels the stage was therefore set for the Invergordon Mutiny.[10]

The circumstances under which the 1931 pay cuts were decided upon and the catalogue of error, oversight and incom-

petence that attended their promulgation to the Atlantic Fleet as it gathered in the Cromarty Firth lie beyond the scope of this volume. Suffice to say that confusion following the sudden hospitalisation of Admiral Sir Michael Hodges (Commander-in-Chief, Atlantic Fleet) on Monday 7 September apparently prevented the ranking officer, Rear-Admiral Tomkinson in the *Hood*, from learning of the extent of the cuts until events were already well in train. An Admiralty cipher prepared for this purpose on 3 September (AM. 1738) Tomkinson either never saw or failed to take in.[11] On Thursday 10 September, with the fleet still on exercises in the North Sea, the Chancellor of the Exchequer, Philip Snowden, delivered an emergency budget speech to Parliament in which the pruning of government expenditure was finally made public. Despite indications from the BBC later that day, it was not until the day's papers came aboard once the fleet had dropped anchor at Invergordon on Friday 11th that those on the 1919 scale—over 70 per cent of the Navy—learnt that their basic pay was to be reduced by up to 25 per cent. But this was not all. Not only had the Admiralty betrayed its solemn guarantee of 1925, but in sanctioning the government package it had effectively permitted the cuts to be made in inverse relation to rank and seniority. Whereas the basic pay of many able seamen would be cut from four to three shillings a day (25 per cent), that of an admiral of the fleet suffered only by a matter of 17 per cent. Though the proportional cut was in fact rather lower when the allowances earnt by

most were included, the inequitable division of the reductions, the manner in which they became known, the speed with which they were to be implemented and the likely impact on the men's families and prospects provided the basis for the Invergordon Mutiny.

The unfolding of the 'breeze' at Invergordon has been treated elsewhere and the account which follows will confine itself largely to the *Hood*'s involvement.[12] Although the mutiny owed its impetus to a spontaneous reaction by the fleet at large, it is clear that the seat of the movement, insofar as there was one, lay in ships of the Devonport Division, notably the battleship *Rodney*, the cruiser *Norfolk* and the minelayer *Adventure*, together with the battleship *Valiant* of Chatham. Feelings had been running high in Devonport since January when bad leadership in the submarine depot ship *Lucia* resulted in 31 members of her crew barricading themselves below deck, an incident which led to four men being court-martialled and another ejected from the Navy.[13] But above all the mutiny owed its support to the 'staid hands', those leading seamen, able seamen, stokers and Marines on the 1919 pay scales who represented the group worst affected by the cuts. However, the practical difficulties of fomenting a mutiny in a dozen or more ships largely prevented the operation of any central organisation and the degree of participation of individual vessels rested mainly on the morale, convictions and mood of their crews as events unfolded. So it was with the *Hood*, in which the impending cuts were apparently discussed at several illegal meetings before the ship reached Invergordon on Friday 11 September. With Admiral Tomkinson and his staff still oblivious to the unrest on the messdecks, the *Hood* passed quietly into harbour routine, most of those off watch spending the afternoon of Saturday 12th at the Invergordon Highland Games where the ship's Marine band formed one of the attractions. That night, just as a bundle containing the sixteen-page Admiralty Fleet Order 2339/31 detailing the cuts reached the *Hood*, the naval canteen ashore was alive with men anxiously discussing the measures, details of which had been broadcast in the BBC's evening bulletin. At this meeting it was apparently agreed that a larger gathering should be held the following day and canvassing for action to be taken over the cuts proceeded both in and between ships thereafter.

Early the following day came the first indication that trouble was in store. During Divine Service that Sunday morning the AFO was posted on the *Hood*'s notice boards, so confirming the worst fears of the lower deck. Even before the Rev. Turner had issued his benediction, the congregation in the Starboard Battery could hear threatening voices being raised against the cuts: 'It's the lot!…. And they've bloody well had it!'[14] Shortly before midday Lt-Cdr Harry Pursey, one of the handful of officers to have won promotion from the lower deck and later a distinguished Labour MP, was approached by a trusted member of the lower deck. Shown a copy of one of the Sunday papers with banner headlines of the cuts, he was told 'The lads won't stand for this'.[15] Within a few minutes Pursey had passed the paper to Cdr McCrum, to whom he offered the following prescient warning:

If these cuts are not reduced there will be trouble …. If there is trouble, it will be on Tuesday—at eight o'clock…. Four capital ships due to sail. … It's tailor-made for the job.

The capital ships in question were *Valiant*, *Nelson*, *Hood* and *Rodney*, due to sail on the morning of Tuesday 15th for gunnery exercises in the North Sea. McCrum dismissed the suggestion, assuring Pursey that 'We shall be all right on this ship'.[16] Events were to prove otherwise.

Meanwhile, leaders were emerging from the 12,000 men gathered in the Cromarty Firth. Out of the blue fug that filled every flat, caboose and messdeck came the germ of plans that could only be implemented in concert with a significant part of the fleet. These meetings were largely the preserve of stokers and seamen of at least six years' seniority yet below the rating of petty officer. 'Petty officers made themselves scarce, and the younger ratings were kept out of it, some accused of letting the others down by enlisting on lower pay.'[17] OD Roland Purvis of the battleship *Malaya* lost count of the number of times he was told 'Push off, sonny, this is nothing to do with you.'[18] One of the leaders, AB Len Wincott of the *Norfolk*, had already taken advantage of the Catholic mass celebrated in the *Malaya* that Sunday morning to gauge opinion in the fleet and pass word of the canteen meeting that night. At midday Capt. J.F.C. Patterson of the *Hood* received intelligence of this gathering from his counterpart in the *Warspite*, though Tomkinson was apparently not informed and no pre-emptive action was taken. Quite the contrary, leave was given at 13.00 as usual and men began to pour ashore. Even in view of the football final being held that afternoon, the number of libertymen heading for Invergordon was unprecedented. Although Patterson and McCrum found nothing untoward during a visit ashore, the men knew different and by late afternoon many were drifting away from the football pitches and into the large canteen overlooking the anchorage. The *Hood*'s contingent, whose team had defeated *Norfolk* 2–nil, no doubt had something to quell their anger but it could only be a temporary palliative. The men were angry at the cuts and at the breach of faith implied by them; angry above all that the government and the Admiralty thought them stupid enough to take it lying down. LS Sam Wheat:

Austen Chamberlain [First Lord of the Admiralty] was the bloke—they'd've crucified him if they could've bloody got him, believe you me. […] Because he thought that none of the Navy had any intelligence at all. […] To take a shilling a day from each one was, to put it mildly, bloody silly. […] I mean, they thought that the chaps were unintelligent and this is really what caused it. I think they'd've got away with it if they'd said 'Well, we're going to reduce your pay by 5per cent' or whatever it is… But to do that made them look like nincompoops, as though they didn't know anything at all.[19]

Besides, there was the very real issue of whether the men's families could subsist on the new rates. As one of the *Hood*'s leaders put it in a letter to *The Daily Herald* a few days later,

We are fighting for our wives and children. The cuts cannot hit us on board ship. We have not to keep ourselves except in a few essentials, some clothing, soap, shoeblacking and so on. We have cut out the luxuries long ago. We cannot do it on less than 5s. a week. Our wives, after the rent is paid, have no more than a pound. How can they stand a cut of 7s. 6d.?[20]

Rear-Admiral Wilfred Tomkinson, whose career was broken by the Invergordon Mutiny.

Capt. Julian Patterson: powerless to influence events.

[12] For the background see Carew, *The Lower Deck*, and especially id., 'The Invergordon Mutiny'. For the mutiny itself, see Edwards, *The Mutiny at Invergordon*, Owen, *Mutiny in the Royal Navy* (the Staff history), Divine, *Mutiny at Invergordon*, and Roskill, *Naval Policy*, II, pp. 89–133. Wincott, *Invergordon Mutineer* is a highly suspect account; see the critique of it by Cdr Harry Pursey in NMM, Elkins/11. The essential chronology is provided by Pursey, 'Invergordon: First Hand—Last Word?'. However, the only comprehensive coverage is Pursey's unfinished history of the mutiny, a draft of which survives in NMM, Pursey/14. For the *Hood*'s involvement, see Ereira, *The Invergordon Mutiny* and Coles, *Invergordon Scapegoat*, pp. 113–31.
[13] Carew, *The Lower Deck*, pp. 140–1.
[14] Pursey, 'Invergordon: First Hand—Last Word?', p. 159.
[15] Ibid., p. 160.
[16] NMM, Pursey/11.
[17] Carew, *The Lower Deck*, p. 160. The 'lower pay' in question refers to the 1925 scales.
[18] Ibid., p. 249.
[19] IWM/SA, LS Samuel George Wheat, no. 5807.
[20] *The Daily Herald*, 17 September 1931, p. 2.

What began as a sombre occasion gathered steam as the evening wore on and the depth of feeling began to make itself felt. Many, including LS Charles Spinks of the *Hood*, clambered onto tables to deliver speeches and opinions that often owed more to alcohol than common sense. But among them was Wincott, a born orator, who, taking up a theme already mooted, urged the men to remain in their ships and implement a campaign of passive resistance when the order came to put to sea. His words had an electrifying effect on the crowd, now over 600 strong. One who heard them was Rear-Admiral E.A. Astley-Rushton, commanding the 2nd Cruiser Squadron, who found himself outside the canteen as Wincott was in full flow. Astley-Rushton immediately informed the shore patrol, manned that night by men of the *Warspite*, which promptly called for reinforcements from the *Hood*. By the time these appeared an increasingly rowdy gathering had dispersed and the men were heading back to their ships, many singing *The Frothblower's Anthem*—'The more we are together the merrier we will be...'—though some in the *Hood*'s drifter felt the need to shout 'We're not yellowbellies!' to taunts from others.[21] As they did so the *Nelson*, Hodges' flagship, finally steamed into Invergordon carrying the Admiralty cipher warning of the cuts that had supposedly been in Tomkinson's hands a week earlier, along with AL. CW. 8284/31 of 10 September, a letter to all flag and commanding officers justifying the measures. Astley-Rushton came aboard *Hood* to discuss the events ashore with Tomkinson, but these were dismissed as being of no consequence and the Admiralty was signalled to this effect the following morning.

Despite the taunts, the *Hood*'s libertymen returned to a ship in which, as LS Sam Wheat put it, the overwhelming sentiment was 'No, we ain't 'avin' this'.[22] Nonetheless, the men settled down for the night and the ship's routine began normally the following morning though Cdr McCrum, sensing the volatile atmosphere, limited work to 'a little General Drill' which was performed in a somewhat perfunctory manner.[23] Shortly after 10.00 Tomkinson signalled his captains ordering them to explain the contents of AL. CW. 8284/31 to the men. He was no doubt astonished to learn that it had been received in only five of the twelve ships in harbour, and it is no surprise that subsequent efforts to interpret the cuts tended to poison the atmosphere still further. So it was in the *Hood*, where the mood of the men was being stoked by copies of the *Daily Worker* which had come aboard that morning. The order to clear lower deck was passed at 11.45, but according to Pursey Capt. Patterson's recommendation that the men bring hardship cases to the attention of their divisional officers was greeted with angry calls of 'We're all hardship cases!'[24] His suggestion that they refrain from illegal action and channel their grievances through him can't have cut much ice either. However, daily routine continued and shore leave was granted at 16.30, this despite every indication in the *Hood* and elsewhere that a further meeting was planned for the canteen that evening.

Among the many hundreds going ashore that Monday evening was Lt Robert Elkins, in command of the *Valiant*'s shore patrol and charged with arresting anyone suspected of subversive activity. As on the previous night, at least 600 men gathered in the canteen to hear speeches and settle on the action to be taken. The speeches were mostly of an inflammatory nature and it was while AB 'Ginger' Bond of the *Rodney* was delivering one of these that Elkins reached the canteen at

18.15. Gaining entry, he met a hostile reception, being struck by a beer glass and eventually bundled out into the cold, the doors locked behind him. However, he succeeded in being readmitted to the meeting, which broke up to reassemble on a nearby recreation ground. Having called for the *Hood*'s reinforcing patrol Elkins followed the crowd to a spot where men were speaking from the roof of a wooden hut. Among them was a Marine, apparently from the *Hood*, whose medals denoted him as a veteran of the Great War:

> He talked a good deal about pay and War Service, and again demanded 'What are we going to do about it?' This time the crowd called out 'Pack up!', and he said 'Tonight or tomorrow?' There was a good deal of laughing and someone said 'After breakfast—when we've had it!'[25]

At 19.30 the meeting adjourned back to the canteen, though many took the opportunity to get off to their ships. By this time the *Hood*'s patrol had made its appearance under Lt-Cdr L.G.E. Robinson who marched into the canteen with the intention of closing it for the night. Robinson got up on the bar but was hard put to it to make himself heard over the noise:

> For some minutes I was shouted down, but the majority of the men were shouting 'Give him a fair hearing'—'Let's hear what he's got to say', and eventually I had silence. I told the men they were going the wrong way about things and would only bring discredit on themselves and the Navy. That they should bring up any complaints in the Service manner and that I would permit of no more speeches.[26]

Robinson's speech impressed Wincott and ended the meeting but it swayed only a minority, who were violently overborne by the rest. As the men headed for the jetty to return to their ships they did so in the certain knowledge that an irrevocable decision had been taken: the Atlantic Fleet would not be sailing on the morrow.

Down on the jetty the libertymen embarked for their ships in what Tomkinson later described as 'a very disorderly manner'. Shouts of 'Don't forget—six o'clock tomorrow' were drifting across the anchorage as searchlights began to play over the pier. Those in the *Hood*'s drifter, the *Horizon*, were belting out stanzas of *The Red Flag*, a court-martial offence. The din interrupted a dinner party being given by Tomkinson for the fleet commanders, the Officer of the Watch, Lt J.S. Gabbett, ordering the *Horizon* to lay off until the men were silent. However, the singing was a clear indication to the *Hood*'s lower deck that something had been settled ashore. By the time Elkins got away from the pier to report to Tomkinson at around 21.00 a crowd of over 100 cheering men had gathered in the eyes of the ship where a rating was inciting them to refuse work in the morning. Boy Harold Prestage R.N.V.R. recorded the scene:

> A stoker spoke, very emotional about keeping wife and two kids on three shillings a day. He said he owed ten pounds, how was he to pay? Several others spoke. They say we on the *Hood* are blacklegs and cowards, our people did not seem to support the crowd on shore much. At last after much haggling they decide to down tools at eight o'clock tomorrow morning.[27]

[21] Ereira, *The Invergordon Mutiny*, p. 60, and Coles & Briggs, *Flagship Hood*, p. 54.
[22] IWM/SA, no. 5807.
[23] Cited in Ereira, *The Invergordon Mutiny*, p. 65.
[24] Pursey, 'Invergordon: First Hand—Last Word?', p. 160.
[25] NMM, Elkins/2, Report, p. 3.
[26] NMM, Pursey/15.
[27] Cited in Ereira, *The Invergordon Mutiny*, pp. 80–1.

Once again, the lack of enthusiasm for action noted among the *Hood*'s contingent ashore is significant in the light of subsequent events. Certainly, as a newly commissioned ship with a high level of morale her men were unlikely to share the militant tendency which characterised *Valiant* and *Rodney*. Whatever the case, her officers were under no illusion as to the gravity of the situation. Gabbett greeted Elkins on the quarterdeck with the information that there had been trouble aboard.[28] On his way to the wardroom he met Lt-Cdr Longley-Cook who invited him to dinner aboard the following week 'if there were still a Navy'. Already at least one messdeck had sent a representative to its divisional officer.[29] Not the least informed was Tomkinson who, as Elkins put it, gave the impression of knowing 'a good deal about it already', though clearly did not think it 'so bad as it sounded'. With this view a majority of the senior commanders were in agreement. How wrong they were.

McCrum had the forecastle cleared by the Master-at-Arms and one of the regulating petty officers, but a number of men were detailed by the ship's committee to spend the night on deck and send down a warning if any attempt were made to weigh anchor.[30] The size and composition of this committee, how it came into being and the means by which it influenced events in the *Hood* and liaised with those in other ships remains shrouded in mystery. Indeed, virtually nothing of the internal structure and organisation of the *Hood*'s mutiny has survived for posterity. Neither, at 70 years' remove, can the atmosphere prevailing on the *Hood*'s decks and messes, in her

passageways and spaces public and private during those six fateful days be reconstructed in any but the vaguest terms. Both then and later the crew closed ranks to protect the identity of the 'spokesmen' who organised the mutiny and those who succoured and lent it their support, often at the cost of their careers in the Navy. But, for the committee as for the ship herself, the moment of truth was drawing near.

That night, in an incident no doubt repeated countless times on the lower deck, R.A. Feltham was roused by a leading hand and told to lash up and stow in the morning but obey no orders thereafter.[31] On Tuesday 15 September the crew duly turned to at 06.00 but all eyes were on *Valiant* and *Rodney* upon whose action the success or failure of the mutiny depended. Full muster in the *Hood* encouraged her officers to believe that their ship would remain unaffected by what all now sensed was coming, but in this they were soon to be disabused. Making his way down to the boiler rooms, Stoker Walter Hargreaves found his progress barred by a big stoker who told him to 'get back' and left him in no doubt of the result if he didn't.[32] When by 07.00 it was obvious that neither *Valiant* nor *Rodney* was being prepared for sea, the forecastles of the eight major vessels left in the anchorage began to fill with crowds of cheering men. Stoker Charles Wild shut down the hydraulic pumping engine on which he worked, downed tools and headed forward.[33] At around 07.45 Cdr McCrum went forward, climbed onto one of the ship's capstans and implored the men gathered among the shackles to return to work. The request was politely declined

A gathering on the *Hood*'s forecastle during the Invergordon Mutiny, probably Wednesday 16 September 1931. *Illustrated London News*

[28] NMM, Elkins/2, Diary, p. 1.
[29] NMM, Pursey/15. R.A. Feltham to Cdr Harry Pursey, Gosport, 22 October 1961.
[30] IWM/SA, Stoker 2nd Class Charles Edward Wild, no. 5835.
[31] NMM, Pursey/15.
[32] IWM/SA, no. 5831. Stoker 2nd Class (1931).
[33] IWM/SA, no. 5835.

and his place taken by a sailor intent on stopping the ship weighing anchor. Four decks below a party of men led by a chief stoker refused to allow the Engineer watchkeeper to run the capstan engine.[34] In the cable-locker flat a similar effort to unshackle the bridles by the Torpedo Officer, Lt-Cdr J.F.W. Mudford, provides a cameo of the quiet resistance encountered by officers of the Atlantic Fleet that morning:

> With petty officers and a few available hands from the cable party I went on to the forecastle to unshackle the first bridle. No marines were present in the cable-locker flat so that both the naval pipes and cable lockers had to be uncovered by my small party. The demonstrators were standing over both bridles and the hawsepipe cover, which was still in place. I went amongst them to view the cables and was immediately hemmed about by the crowd who stood a yard or two away from me. One man shouted 'What's the use of trying to take the ship to sea like this?' I said 'What about it! If I give order to heave in, are you going to stop me?' They replied 'Yes, Sir, we shall have to'. I felt it would be unwise to use force without instructions to do so from higher authority, and the futility of giving a direct order to so large a number of men, when I knew I could not possibly enforce that order, was too obvious.[35]

Indeed, the strategy couldn't have been simpler. R.A. Feltham:

> It was made quite clear that we were to keep everything clean and ship-shape, and that the object was to keep the Fleet from going to sea until something was done about our pay.[36]

'Colours' was carried out with due ceremony on the quarter-deck at 08.00, but no sooner had they been hoisted than cheering erupted across the anchorage. Only 30 per cent of the *Hood*'s crew fell in for work at 08.30 and the howls of derision directed at them from the *Rodney* settled the matter. The Invergordon Mutiny had broken out.

The sequence of events in the *Hood* over the hour or so that followed remains unclear. There are unsubstantiated reports that Lt-Cdr Pursey volunteered to go forward and clear the forecastle with his revolver.[37] If true, the offer was wisely declined by McCrum who had already informed Capt. Patterson that 'no good purpose was likely to be served by my also addressing them'.[38] However, it does seem that a large meeting then took place in the fore topmen's mess on the upper deck amidships at which an unnamed AB made it perfectly clear to all and sundry that 'We're not going to let this bloody ship sail'.[39] It was also made plain that this was not a mutiny but a strike, and that there was to be no violence. When it was over parties of men returned to the forecastle where a heavy wire hawse was rove through the cables and round the capstan to prevent the anchor being slipped.[40] Shortly after 09.00 Tomkinson cancelled the planned exercise and informed the Admiralty of the situation. Much to the officers' surprise, once it became obvious to the crew that the *Hood* would not be putting to sea the ship slipped quietly back into harbour routine. Normal work and divisional drill continued against the background of sporadic cheering between ships, not all of it cordial: it is quite obvious that the *Hood*'s return to work provoked considerable resentment in

the *Rodney*. Nonetheless, parties of men kept a permanent watch on the forecastle, from where any developments were communicated to the messdecks below. As AB Fred Copeman of the *Norfolk* later explained, the choice of the forecastle was an obvious one:

> If you're on the forecastle no one else can get there. The hatches from the seamen's mess deck lead directly to the forecastle. If the marines are with you no one can do anything about it. Every ship did the same.[41]

But it wasn't all toil and angst. Many took the opportunity of 'having a good time' in the benign autumn weather. The ship's deck hockey tournament was advanced and rehearsals began for a concert party.[42] On the *Rodney* one of the messdeck pianos was hoisted onto a turret for a stoker to keep the men entertained with the latest music-hall hits. He was flung out of the Navy for his pains.

Communication with neighbouring ships—*Rodney*, *Dorsetshire* and *Warspite* in *Hood*'s case—was carried out in the first instance by means of flags and then by the use of caps, short-arm semaphore and aldis lights. Wireless was used briefly until cut off in mid-morning. Quite frequently the messages transmitted were no more than 'sticking out okay', for which regular crossing of forearms, lowering of the Union Flag at the jackstaff or hourly cheering sufficed. In this the mutineers made use of the subtle body language with which sailors always communicated. Len Wincott:

> …If the crew of a passing motorboat from another striking ship showed crossed forearms, it conveyed to us that the men of that ship were still solid in their strike. This was not a planned signal. The crossed forearms were one of many unofficial signals that had entered Navy life years and years before and actually meant 'Tie up' or 'Finish'. In our particular circumstances at Invergordon it was automatically adopted to mean something more.[43]

The ship's boats were active throughout, used by both mutineers and officers, though manned by petty officers in the latter case. Discipline in the *Valiant* collapsed to such a degree that the *Hood* was obliged to provide a boat for the use of her captain. Officers had difficulty communicating from ship to ship but Tomkinson was saved by the loyalty of the *Hood*'s telegraphists thanks to whom he maintained steady contact with London.

Needless to say, the officers of the Atlantic Fleet found themselves in an exceedingly difficult position. Not only had they received no more warning of the cuts than the men, but the erosion of discipline was profoundly disturbing for those accustomed to orders being obeyed without question. Many would have preferred Tomkinson to have taken a firmer line but others, perhaps for the first time in their careers, were completely at a loss as to what to do. The frustration that caused Lt-Cdr R.H.S. Rodger of the *Norfolk* to ask 'What do you want?' of Wincott and his companions therefore went hand in hand with a growing anger at the Admiralty that had landed them in this ghastly situation.[44] As one of the *Hood*'s lieutenant-commanders told LS Sam Wheat, 'This is the worst bastard thing the Admiralty has ever done to us'.[45] It fell to Tomkinson to bring an initially belligerent Admiralty to a full

[34] IWM/SA, Stoker 1st Class Nicholas Smiles Carr (1930–*c*.1933), no. 5809.
[35] Cited in PRO, ADM 178/110, Capt. Patterson's Report of Proceedings, 21 September 1931, p. 4.
[36] NMM, box 15.
[37] IWM/SA, no. 5809.
[38] PRO, ADM 178/110, Patterson's Report of Proceedings, p. 3.
[39] IWM/SA, LS Samuel George Wheat, no. 5807.
[40] IWM/SA, no. 5807 & 5835.
[41] Cited in Carew, 'The Invergordon Mutiny', p. 182.
[42] Coles & Briggs, *Flagship* Hood, p. 62.
[43] Wincott, *Invergordon Mutineer*, pp. 121–2.
[44] Ibid., p. 123.
[45] IWM/SA, no. 5807.

realization of the issue facing the Navy. Orders were passed for the investigation of hardship cases to begin and at midday Tomkinson let it be known that he was sending the Chief of Staff, Rear-Admiral Reginald Colvin, to London by air to confer with Their Lordships. These measures evidently had their desired effect and the atmosphere in the *Hood* eased as the men decided to await the response of the Admiralty. For many, indeed, it was their first opportunity to reflect on the day's events and the possible consequences. As Stoker Charles Wild put it, 'Everybody was really kind of stunned with what they were doing… I think everybody was apprehensive of what was going to happen'.[46] That evening the ship's cinema was rigged and the men settled down for a tense night.

The first indication of a response came with the morning papers on Wednesday 16th, in which the Admiralty's optimistic characterisation of the mutiny as 'unrest among a proportion of the lower ratings' provoked considerable anger. During the 10.30 Stand Easy Lt-Cdr Pursey was again approached by a rating brandishing a newspaper:

'It's all up again, sir', 'Why?', 'Admiralty statement "unrest"'. … 'What do they want us to do? Chuck the bloody guns overboard?'[47]

The news caught the *Hood* at a particularly delicate moment. Not for the first time the resumption of work after Stand Easy was received with some disgust in the nearby *Rodney*, herself largely at a standstill. Opinions were hardened by the rumours circulating during 'Up Spirits' at 11.15 that the ship was to be interned at Scapa Flow or placed under close arrest at Portsmouth. For a few hours the *Hood* teetered on the brink of open mutiny and only resolute action by McCrum prevented her joining the most militant ships in the fleet. Capt. Patterson:

The normal work of the ship proceeded throughout the forenoon, though the atmosphere was somewhat strained. It unfortunately happened that the turn of the tide coincided with 'Stand Easy' in the forenoon, with the result that the two ships [*Hood* and *Rodney*] were swung parallel with one another. A mutual demonstration of cheering between the men assembled on *Rodney*'s forecastle and the men who had gone forward for a smoke during 'Stand Easy' in *Hood* took place. These men returned to their work after 'Stand Easy' but there is little doubt that some signals and signs were exchanged to the effect that *Hood*'s ship's company were not supporting the cause with sufficient enthusiasm. During the dinner hour one or two leading seamen reported to the commander that the feeling on the mess decks was growing strongly in favour of stopping work, and that the life of those against it was being made difficult. It became evident from various sources that the men would probably not 'Turn To' after dinner, and just before the routine time for falling in the hands the Senior Engineer reported to the Commander that the stokers appeared to be not coming down below. In order to avoid an open demonstration, the hands were piped to 'Make and Mend Clothes'. This took them somewhat by surprise and resulted in their proceeding down below to sleep instead of cheering on the forecastle.[48]

For the *Hood* at least this was the high point of the mutiny. However, there was not much longer to wait. Tomkinson had finally succeeded in bringing home to the Admiralty the dire consequences that might ensue from its refusal to make the necessary concession. At 15.10 the following signal was received from London:

The Board of Admiralty is fully alive to the fact that amongst certain classes of ratings special hardship will result from the reduction of pay ordered by H.M. Government. It is therefore directed that ships of the Atlantic Fleet are to proceed to their home ports forthwith to enable personal investigation by C.-in-C.s and representatives of Admiralty with view to necessary alleviation being made. Any further refusals of individuals to carry out orders will be dealt with under the Naval Discipline Act. This signal is to be promulgated to the Fleet forthwith.[49]

Tomkinson allowed the gist of the signal to reach the men in the form of a 'buzz', the eternal currency of the lower deck. The news was received with relief by some but many regarded it with deep suspicion. The directive was interpreted, rightly, as an attempt to end the mutiny and winnow the ringleaders out from the rest. The signal immediately caused a rupture between those for whom a return to home ports meant another spell of leave and those, usually from Scotland and the North of England, who tended to regard it as a potential trap. It was in this atmosphere that Capt. Patterson cleared lower deck at 16.45 and addressed the ship's company from 'A' turret while Tomkinson looked on from the bridge:

…I informed the ship's company of the decision. At the same time I informed them that I could guarantee that any rumours as to this being a ruse to divide the Fleet were entirely unfounded and that any further refusal on their part would do still further harm to their cause. The information was received in silence, and the men then dispersed.[50]

The speech was certainly not received in silence. In fact, it was punctuated by a stream of ribald comment from his audience: 'All me eye and Betty Martin' … 'Scapa Flow' … 'Spithead' … 'We stay here…'.[51] Worse, during his address Patterson made the mistake of mentioning that 'Of course, we haven't had the Royal Marines up here', a comment that was taken as a veiled threat. For a crew suspicious that the ship might be boarded by Marines at Spithead it met with a predictable response: 'You get the bastards up here!', a reaction which, among other things, shows how difficult had been the position of the *Hood*'s Marine detachment.[52]

As was no doubt the intention, the Admiralty signal provoked considerable debate in the fleet and prompted choruses of shouting and cheering across the anchorage. AB Alex Paterson, later a commander and one of the few willing to show his opposition to the mutiny, recalls the aftermath of the captain's speech in the *Hood*:

Within five minutes a two-badge able seaman convinced nearly everyone the signal to sail was a trick to get the ships to sea and to separate them so they lost mutual support, which would lead to the arrest of the leaders. He claimed

46 IWM/SA, no. 5835.
47 Pursey, 'Invergordon: First Hand—Last Word?', p. 162.
48 PRO, ADM 178/110, Patterson's Report of Proceedings, pp. 4–5. The suggestion that a 'Make and Mend Clothes' be piped was apparently made by Pursey himself; Pursey, 'Invergordon: First Hand—Last Word?', p. 163. The Senior Engineer was Lt-Cdr (E) B.W.G. Clutterbuck.
49 Reproduced in Divine, *Mutiny at Invergordon*, p. 171.
50 PRO, ADM 178/110, Patterson's Report of Proceedings, p. 5.
51 Pursey, 'Invergordon: First Hand—Last Word?', p. 163.
52 IWM/SA, LS Samuel George Wheat, no. 5807.

the cuts would be made and money never restored. He then called for a vote, with a show of hands. Those in favour of not putting to sea were overwhelming. Only four hands were raised in favour of weighing anchor.[53]

But debate continued and the concerns of the crew eventually boiled down to whether the ship would indeed return to Portsmouth, and what their reputation would be if they allowed her to do so. On the other hand, no ship wished to face the wrath of the Admiralty alone at Invergordon. Lt-Cdr Pursey captures the dilemma of a majority of the crew:

Master-at-Arms reported to Commander: 'Stoker X wishes to see you, sir.' Stoker: 'We've had a meeting on the fo'c'sle and we've decided: if other ships don't go…we won't go. If other ships go…we will go…. We won't stay here alone…. Can you please tell us whether the other ships will go?' Commander: 'Quite honestly…I don't know. When I do I will let you know.'[54]

The first sign that a decision had been reached came at 17.00 when the full engine-room watch turned to for lighting up the boilers. However, cheering and shouting continued from the forecastle where the cable party was prevented from doing its work. AB Paterson:

As we came through the forward screen of the forecastle, we were greeted by loud cheers and laughter from what seemed to be most of the ship's company. Several sailors, who were sitting on the lashed cables, eyed us suspiciously. One glance by us was enough to decide that the anchor couldn't possibly be weighed without a full party. [Lt-Cdr] Longley-Cook was politely informed they had no intention of moving without the use of force. Longley-Cook did not argue and withdrew to report to the captain.[55]

Nonetheless, by 20.00 the men were preparing for sea and the dire agreement made between Patterson and Capt. J.B. Watson of the *Nelson* that the cables be parted if necessary had never to be implemented.[56] Parties of men began taking their stations, the bridles were unshackled and the hawse rove through the cables the previous morning was removed without difficulty. However, Tomkinson was by no means certain that the rest of his command would follow suit. Indeed, at 19.45 he signalled the Admiralty that 'I am not sure that all ships will leave as ordered but some will go'. In the event, a change of orders allowing ships to proceed independently rather than by squadron extinguished the last embers of resistance. By 23.30 the fleet had cleared Invergordon.

No sooner had the last ship passed through the Sutors guarding the entrance to the Cromarty Firth than the aftermath of the Invergordon Mutiny began. On the evening of Thursday 17th the *Hood*'s officers were invited to a S.O.D.S. opera performed by the ship's company which, as Pursey recalled, 'treated [the] whole affair as one big lark'.[57] But no one could be under any illusion as to the challenges that lay ahead. That morning married men on the 1919 scales had made it plain that they did not wish their hardship statements to be taken by

divisional officers with no experience of family affairs. Cdr McCrum obliged with the unprecedented step of himself receiving their statements in his cabin. It was the start of a new era in officer–sailor relations.

Shortly after 06.30 on Saturday 19 September the *Hood* docked at Portsmouth. Leave was given until Monday evening and the pubs of Pompey filled with blabbing sailors, Communist agitators and badly disguised secret-service agents. Hardship statements continued to be taken, but on 21 September the government announced that the pay cuts would be reduced to a maximum of 10 per cent. In the event an order passed on 1 October placed the entire Navy on the 1919 rates *less* 11 per cent. The lower deck could savour a victory of sorts but for the government and the Navy the damage was done. News of the mutiny had been followed by a run on the pound and within days it was announced that Britain had been forced off the Gold Standard. Meanwhile, the Admiralty began to set its house in order through a policy of punitive action and vigorous self-exculpation. On 6 October Admiral Sir John Kelly, a confidant of King George V and much respected on the lower deck, succeeded Hodges as Commander-in-Chief, Atlantic Fleet. It was a condition of Kelly's acceptance that he be allowed to make a clean sweep of the fleet and sweep he did. He was particularly adamant that the Invergordon ringleaders be rooted out and expelled from the Navy. Despite the amnesty promised by Chamberlain to Parliament after the fleet had left Invergordon, 120 men were confined to barracks before it sailed north in early October, ten of them from the *Hood*. No sooner had the general election of 27 October returned MacDonald's National Government than most of these were discharged, the first of nearly 400 undesirables to be ejected from the Navy over the next few months.[58]

Nor were these the only casualties. Despite favourable remarks on his conduct, in its zeal to absolve itself of blame the Board of Admiralty began gradually to lay responsibility for the mutiny at Tomkinson's door. There is certainly much in the view that Tomkinson allowed matters to develop by not preventing the meetings being held ashore, but his treatment by the Admiralty represents the final chapter in one of the most discreditable episodes in its history. After a decent amount of time had been allowed to elapse, on 2 February 1932 the Admiralty issued two letters addressed to Tomkinson, the first promoting him vice-admiral and curtailing his tenure as squadron commander by eight months, and the second censuring him for his handling of the mutiny. Of this Tomkinson received his first inkling by means of a BBC broadcast picked up in the *Hood*'s W/T office as she lay off Trinidad on 16 February. Tomkinson fought a bitter rearguard action but it was to no avail and his career in the Navy was broken.

It is a measure of how out of touch the Admiralty was that no official investigation of the causes of the Invergordon Mutiny was ever carried out, a decision which provoked much criticism in the Navy. Months after the event senior officers were still unaware whether their conduct had met with the approval of the Admiralty or if they would eventually join the list of casualties. The gulf-like gap between the views of the Board on the one hand and those of the officers who lived through it on the other is nowhere better demonstrated than in the extracts which follow. First the Admiralty's view, promulgated to the Atlantic Fleet in October:

[53] Cited in Coles & Briggs, *Flagship Hood*, p. 65.
[54] Pursey, 'Invergordon: First Hand—Last Word?', p. 163.
[55] Cited in Coles & Briggs, *Flagship Hood*, p. 66.
[56] Ereira, *The Invergordon Mutiny*, p. 137, and Coles, *Invergordon Scapegoat*, pp. 130–1.
[57] Pursey, 'Invergordon: First Hand—Last Word?', p. 163.
[58] See also Coles & Briggs, *Flagship Hood*, pp. 70–1.

The Board of Admiralty has given full consideration to the reports received on the serious refusal of duty which occurred in some of the principal ships of the Atlantic Fleet at Invergordon on the 15th–16th September last. Notwithstanding the decision that, owing to the exceptional circumstances, no disciplinary action should be taken, this insubordinate behaviour was, in Their Lordships' opinion, inexcusable.

Their Lordships note with great satisfaction that, in the whole of the rest of the Navy, the ships' companies acted, at a very critical time, in accordance with the high tradition of the Service. They desire, however, to impress on all Officers and Men that this failure in discipline by a small part of the Fleet has done grave injury to the prestige of the whole Navy and to the country.

They look with confidence to every Officer and Man to do his utmost to restore the proud position the Royal Navy has always had in the eyes of the world.[59]

Against this 'ineffable display of smugness' can be set Capt. Patterson's reasoned conclusions as to the cause of the mutiny, in which, like Tomkinson, his sympathy with the men is quite apparent:

I am of the opinion that the primary cause of the intense outburst of feeling on the part of the lower ratings was the sudden shock they received in the announcement of the reductions without any previous preparation. The feeling of unjust treatment was sufficient to unite them and make them very easily influenced to take strong and concerted action on their own lines, rather than await more patiently the orthodox methods which they were convinced would not be effective in the short time available.[60]

The gently chiding tone of Patterson's comments no doubt helped seal his fate as well, and he surrendered his command together with Tomkinson in August 1932. Within a few months, however, the Board that had presided over the Invergordon Mutiny was itself no more, and by year's end the Atlantic Fleet had become the Home Fleet.

Historians will record that the 'quiet mutiny' was in fact less a mutiny than a strike, though it was one which after the frustrations of the Great War and the trials of the 1920s came close to destroying the Navy. Luckily, a new Board of Admiralty proved equal to the task of restoring its fortunes. For the *Hood*, too, a new regime awaited, one that, for a few fleeting years, brought her to the height of her glory. For the lower deck, meanwhile, the Invergordon Mutiny was looked back on as a rubicon in its relations with authority. As LS Sam Wheat put it,

It did a bit of good. It did make them see that you had intelligent people in the Service, and that they were not going to be trampled on.[61]

How this realization affected the *Hood* is what concerns us next.

The appointment of 'Darby' Kelly brought a breath of fresh air to the Atlantic Fleet. No sooner had his appointment taken effect than he was moving from ship to ship, addressing the men in their own pungent language, admitting past wrongs and attempting to instil confidence in the future. Anxious no doubt to lay a ghost, within a month of the mutiny Kelly had brought the fleet back to Invergordon for a week of intensive drill where earlier it had lain idle. Despite Kelly's report at the end of November that the fleet was at a high level of efficiency, morale remained low, particularly in the *Hood* which Tomkinson suggested should be recommissioned with a fresh crew. To have done so would have placed her in the same category as the *Valiant* and the *Adventure*, which were ignominiously paid off before the end of the year. The Admiralty refused and Christmas leave was taken early. In the New Year Tomkinson led the *Hood* on a spring cruise to the Caribbean accompanied by *Repulse*, *Norfolk*, *Dorsetshire* and *Delhi*. Under normal circumstances this might have acted as a huge fillip for morale but the cruise was overshadowed first by enormous seas between the Lizard and the Azores and finally by the news that both Tomkinson and Patterson had fallen victim to the attrition of senior officers that followed the mutiny. It is also clear that Tomkinson's personality made for an extremely unhappy wardroom, and by the time he hauled down his flag on 15 August 1932 the Admiralty had reconsidered its earlier decision not to pay off the *Hood*.

The arrival of Rear-Admiral William James that same day heralded a new era for the *Hood*, one which was to make a lasting impression on the Navy as a whole. The collective sigh of relief is captured in a stanza by Paymaster Lt J.T. Shrimpton, a member of Tomkinson's staff, penned two days before James' arrival:

The summer days are on the wing,
The bathers' cries are echoing,
When news of a momentous thing
Through the warm air goes humming;
We hear the staff now softly sing,
'The King is dead—long live the King!'
The new régime, the new régime,
The new régime is coming.[62]

William James was born into one of those upper-middle class families from which the Navy has drawn much of its officer corps. His early years were blighted by the portrait of him as a child executed by his grandfather, the artist Sir John Millais, which, as the advertisement for Pear's soap, became one of the first icons of British marketing. From this came an enduring nickname: 'Bubbles'. Despite this stigma, James entered the Navy where he was in the vanguard of officers who embraced the revolution in gunnery led by Admiral Sir Percy Scott at the turn of the twentieth century. He first came to prominence in 1909 as Gunnery Officer of the cruiser *Natal*, his crews smashing all records for speed and accuracy during the annual firing competitions of the Home Fleet. More even than his technical ability, James had the gift of drawing the best out of his men and when W.R. Hall, his last captain in the *Natal*, was appointed to the battlecruiser *Queen Mary* in 1913, James followed as executive officer.[63] Between them, Hall and James refined the divisional system and devised a revolutionary watch routine destined to be adopted by all British capital ships on the out-

[59] Reproduced in Divine, *Mutiny at Invergordon*, pp. 208–9.
[60] PRO, ADM 178/110, Patterson's Report of Proceedings, p. 6; Tomkinson's conclusions in his Report of Proceedings, 22 September 1931, p. 13, are remarkably similar.
[61] IWM/SA, no. 5807.
[62] [Shrimpton], *Verses*, p. 3.
[63] James, *The Sky Was Always Blue*, pp. 77–82.

Vice-Admiral William James inspecting the port side of the boat deck abreast the forward funnel in 1933 or 1934. Inboard, covered in a grille, is one of the vents for 'A' and 'B' boiler rooms. Third from right is Lt-Cdr J.H. Ruck-Keene; fifth from right is Capt. F.T.B. Tower and next to him is Cdr Rory O'Conor. It was under James that the *Hood* began her lengthy recovery from the Invergordon Mutiny.
HMS Hood Association/Willis Collection

break of the Great War. This implemented, they turned to conditions aboard, and it was in this ship that cinema, a chapel, bookstall and electric washing machines made their first appearance afloat in the Royal Navy. Next they saw to improved bathing facilities for stokers and allowed petty officers to rearrange their accommodation in line with their new standing in the Service. James left the *Queen Mary* in January 1916, just months before she was destroyed at Jutland, but the ideas and procedures pioneered in her were enshrined in *New Battleship Organisations*, the influential manual on ship husbandry he completed early that same year.[64]

The *Hood* therefore provided fertile ground for James' particular talents, and rarely can a ship have needed them more. As he later wrote,

> I never met a more unhappy party than when I relieved Tomkinson. He and his Flag Captain Patterson were at daggers drawn, and the Commander, McCrum, had lost all interest through being hunted by Tomkinson whose habit it was to find fault with everything.[65]

As so often, James brought with him as Flag Captain a companion from earlier days, in this case Thomas Binney, his executive officer in the cruiser *Hawkins*. It was to prove an inspired choice. Judging that the *Hood* had 'a first-rate lot of officers and a fine ship's company', within weeks these two had persuaded the Admiralty to drop its decision to pay her off, judging this 'a confession that it was beyond the powers of naval officers to dispel the gloomy atmosphere and restore vitality and happiness'.[66] But restore them they did. James' overture to the crew on his arrival set the tone for the rest of her peacetime career. Admiral Longley-Cook remembers the occasion:

> We sailed to Southend and again on a Sunday forenoon 'clear lower deck, everyone aft'. He addressed us. How differently! 'I am proud to have joined you' and for the

first time in my eighteen years at sea I was told what the peacetime job of the Royal Navy was. To train for war in order to keep the peace. To 'show the flag'. In home waters to show the British public what they were paying for and abroad to be good ambassadors for Great Britain. From then on it was 'tails up'.[67]

True to his word, James' tenure began with week-long visits to Southend and then Hartlepool, one of the towns worst affected by the Depression. Children's parties were held aboard and entertainments arranged for the men ashore. At Hartlepool the ship played the town at water polo and hundreds of jobless miners were invited aboard to have tea with the men. As a display of the Admiralty's new sensitivity it could hardly have been bettered. Apart from eliciting some dreadful stanzas of poetry from James, the *Hood*'s visit to Hartlepool left a lasting impact on one small boy who had to content himself with admiring her from afar: Ted Briggs. Thereafter the ship went from strength to strength. Kelly's campaign to restore confidence and morale after Invergordon turned on a relentless programme of drill, exercises, training, discipline, housekeeping and sport, and James did not disappoint. Within the space of a year the *Hood*, showing unusual proficiency in gunnery, had demolished a battle practice target, won the fleet anti-aircraft gunnery competition and become 'Cock of the Fleet' at the Home Fleet Regatta in May 1933. In October of that year a landing party near Invergordon was performed with such enthusiasm that James had to rebut claims, splashed in banner headlines around the world, that the *Hood* was in the grip of another mutiny.

Apart from the leadership provided by James and Binney, the recovery of the *Hood*'s morale owes much to her executive officer, Cdr C.R. McCrum, to his right-hand man and Mate of the Upper Deck, the ex-lower deck Lt-Cdr Harry Pursey, to the First Lieutenant Lt-Cdr Eric Longley-Cook, and to Engineer Cdr A.K. Dibley. Among the *Hood*'s officers were at least two more who had benefited from the Mate Scheme, Lt (E) Ernest Mill (later a rear-admiral) and Sub-Lt T.J.G. Marchant. Pursey seems to have had a share of unpopularity as 'the Commander's nark' but the fact that three of the ship's officers had begun their careers on the lower deck cannot have been lost on the crew and such evidence as survives suggests an unprecedented *entente* between officers and men in the months and years after Invergordon. There is evidence, too, that the broader outlook of the engineer officer began to make itself felt in relations with the lower deck; men who, in Len Wincott's words, were 'not dependent for prestige on any particular show of aloofness from the mob'.[68] Like so much else in the locust years, the mechanics of this process now seems lost to posterity, but the accomplishment is real enough. Though largely overshadowed by the regime that followed it, there can be no doubt that the successes of the mid-1930s would not have been possible without the qualities of leadership shown after Invergordon. James did not strike his flag until the summer of 1934, but when he recalled his tenure as having been surrounded by 'officers and men who had responded eagerly to everything I had asked of them... in an atmosphere of happiness and high endeavour', it was to the 1931–3 commission that he was referring above all.[69] Yet it was not all happiness. Morale had improved markedly but problems remained which lay at the heart of the crisis affecting the Navy as a whole. The

[64] Cdr W.M. James, *New Battleship Organisations and Notes for Executive Officers* (Portsmouth: Gieve's, 1916).
[65] CAC, ROSK, card index.
[66] James, *The Sky Was Always Blue*, p. 163.
[67] HMS *Hood* Association archives, Address to the Association, 24 May 1980, in 1980 newsletter, p. 2.
[68] Wincott, *Invergordon Mutineer*, p. 72.
[69] James, *The Sky Was Always Blue*, p. 179.

Invergordon Mutiny exposed many failings in naval organisation, but in shipboard life it did so in three areas above all: in the widespread disillusion over prospects and promotion; in the strained relations that existed between departments; and finally in the failure of the divisional system in which the Admiralty had reposed such confidence. The restoration of the *Hood* as the greatest ship in the Navy in the years to come cannot be understood without reference to these issues.

Through the 1920s promotion to leading seaman and petty officer had been slowed by the great numbers of men who had achieved higher rating during the First World War. Although a man was entitled to take the examination for leading seaman at 21, it might be six or seven years before a vacancy allowed him to be rated accordingly. Wincott was a case in point, passing quickly for leading seaman but still an AB at the time of his discharge from the Navy several years later. This situation provoked considerable resentment on the lower deck, and it is no surprise that the *Hood*'s petty officers and chief petty officers did their best to keep out of the way during the 'breeze' at Invergordon. Their unenviable position is captured in a paragraph of Tomkinson's official report:

> The attitude of the Petty Officers from the outset appears generally to have been a passive one. They carried on with their own work, but made little attempt to get the lower ratings to work, and on Wednesday [16 September] it was reported to me that some Petty Officers were showing signs of joining up with the disaffected men. This was to be expected as time went on, since their sympathy was with the men in their grievance, if not with their method of indicating it.[70]

Nonetheless, by the late 1930s many considered that the petty officer of the Royal Navy was not the man he had been twenty years earlier. Francis Pridham, Captain of the *Hood* between 1936–8, puts it in perspective:

> One too often hears it said that our Petty Officers are a poor lot and are of a lower standard as such than they have been in past. I believe this is an exaggeration. It has never been within my experience to find a high proportion of Petty Officers individually competent to influence a ship's company. For this we have always been dependent on a few outstanding Petty Officers possessing high qualities of character and personality. These Petty Officers have not acquired these qualities through training; they are still to be found, and I believe always will be. It is unreasonable, however, to expect a high percentage.[71]

> Do not expect too much of your Petty Officers. We cannot expect that their standard shall be a very level one; large numbers are being made and many are of very limited experience. Endeavour to avoid putting one in charge of a job without first discovering whether he knows how to set about it.[72]

Certainly, a petty officer's rating was not one to which as many men of real ability now aspired. Enormous damage was done by the mutiny itself, which disillusioned younger men as to the value of a naval career at the very moment when the older were

beginning to retire into civilian life.[73] Some looked elsewhere, but the 'hungry '30s' left most with little alternative but to sign on for a second term of service. During the 1930s the Navy therefore found itself saddled with a rump of long-service ratings whose sole ambition was to reach Pension Age with the least possible sacrifice of energy. These men, the 'three-badge Barnacle Bills' of the battlefleets, not only resisted promotion but poured scorn on the ambitions of younger men, ridiculing the 'killick' anchor device which denoted a leading seaman's rating and undermining his authority on the messdecks. No wonder Capt. Rory O'Conor, late of the *Hood*, admitted of leading seamen in 1937 that many 'cannot say boo to a goose'.[74] But, as Capt. Pridham told his officers, even younger petty officers had difficulty keeping the older men in line:

> Keep your eye on the older Able Seamen. In these days the fact that an Able Seaman is wearing three badges, or ought to be, is in many cases proof of his unsuitability. Their influence with the younger men is considerable and frequently bad. [...] Bear in mind that the young Petty Officers and Leading Seamen have a difficult job. They find themselves in charge of men older than themselves (to whom the young seamen defer) and some of these will endeavour to trip them up. If you spot any sign of insolence or disobedience do not wait for the Petty Officer to complain or run him in.[75]

However, as Pridham recognised, resistance to promotion and the responsibilities that went with it ran deep on the lower deck. The system introduced by the Navy to accelerate the promotion of suitable characters, the so-called 'Red-ink recommend', enjoyed only limited acceptance among the men:

> It is also our business to instruct and educate our men with a view to inducing ambition to better their positions in the Service, as distinct from their rates of pay. It is well known that few men on the Lower Deck regard special promotion with any enthusiasm. Trade Unionism and an innate fidelity to their own kind limit their aim to one of general security, i.e. equal opportunity to rise steadily on a pay scale. The principle underlying the 'Red recommend' is foreign to their upbringing and environment and is regarded with suspicion. The Service aspect does not enter their heads. [...] Few men volunteer readily to move outside the ordinary run.[76]

The result by the mid-1930s was that the Navy had insufficient men of calibre for higher rating, a state of affairs that was not reversed until improved wages, expansion and the approach of war altered the views and prospects of the lower deck. Despite his plans, it was often Barnacle Bill's fate to see his term of service extended through the war years, though, as Wincott recalled, he and his like 'were to prove their worth a hundred-fold at Dunkirk' and in a thousand battles after.[77]

Nor did the tensions end there. Friction among seaman ratings over the issue of promotion was matched by that between the various departments into which the lower deck was divided: seamen, artisans and artificers, stokers and Marines. These not only served very different functions but inhabited separate messes and barely fraternised with one another. Ron Paterson,

[70] PRO, ADM 178/110, Report of Proceedings, p. 12.
[71] Pridham, 'Lectures on Mutiny', Part I: 'Prevention', pp. 5–6.
[72] Pridham, 'Notes for Newly Joined Officers' (January 1938), p. 5.
[73] Carew, *The Lower Deck*, pp. 176–7.
[74] *RBS*, p. 107.
[75] Pridham, 'Notes', pp. 2 & 6.
[76] Ibid., p. 5.
[77] Wincott, *Invergordon Mutineer*, p. 177.

[78] Cited in Rogers, 'H.M.S. *Hood*', p. 40.
[79] IWM/SA, no. 749, p. 19.
[80] *RBS*, p. 64.
[81] [Browne], 'A Low Tech Naval Landing Party', p. 263.

Boy Seaman and OD in *Hood* between 1933–6, describes the situation:

> Of course, you didn't meet anyone outside your own department, so the only time you'd meet the engineering lot and the Marines would be on shore, when there was a sports day.[78]

Divisions of this sort were of course in the nature of any large and sophisticated community, but they were greatly exacerbated by conditions in the Navy as the 1920s wore on. The Artisan Branch, which comprised no more than 5 per cent of the crew, consisted of tradesmen—coopers, shipwrights, smiths, joiners, painters and plumbers—recruited from civilian life to perform essential maintenance of the ship and her fittings. While a majority of the crew observed a four-hour watch system, artisans, who were designated as 'daymen', generally worked regular daytime hours and turned in at night like civilians. Equally, whereas the hands were roused at 05.30 to clean ship, artisans enjoyed what was known as 'Guard and Steerage', the right to stay in their hammocks until 06.00 or 06.30. This, together with their higher pay and petty officer's rank and uniform, was the cause of much resentment on the lower deck, to which their unfortunate official designation as 'Idlers' lent some credence. Plumber 4th Class Ernest Taylor, a veteran of *c*.1926–8, recalls the atmosphere:

> The only compliment we used to get was that we were the idle rich… and that summed us up in a way of speaking to the lower deck…. They didn't seem to appreciate the work we did, and of course the fact that we… weren't raised from our hammocks until six or six-thirty… I think generally speaking—just generally speaking—the lower deck was a little bit jealous of that, that we had this extra hour, and of course we were, well, the nobodies if you like, except in the trousers.[79]

Though subject to the same norms of service and advancement as artisans, the critical role performed by artificers in maintaining the ship's engineering, electrical and gunnery systems spared them the same degree of opprobrium. Even so, Cdr O'Conor did well to ensure that

> Every hammock in the ship should be lashed up and stowed by 06.45 on every morning of the commission, including Sunday and not excluding anyone…[80]

But such tensions were trivial compared to those which often prevailed between seamen and the Royal Marines.

The ancestors of the Royal Marines had first gone to sea in the 1660s, but the role of the Navy's sea soldiers and the discipline for which the Corps was known had maintained a clear distinction between them and their seaman shipmates. The 'leathernecks' as sailors called them were not only 'sworn men' but preserved a martial bearing which was anathema to most seamen. While the Marine regarded his seaman counterpart with 'tolerance bordering on condescension' in military matters, the latter viewed him as generally somewhat lacking in imagination in everything else.[81] Neither view had much to recommend it. The skill and calibre of the Marines was widely respected and the ship's band was one of the great assets of life afloat. But at Invergordon it was the sailor's traditional suspicion of the Marines as the officers' first line of defence against mutiny that had reared its ugly head. Though it flared briefly in the *Hood* this sentiment developed no further because cooler heads kept her Marine detachment in its barracks on the upper deck. By contrast, relations between stokers and Marines were generally good, even if the only point of agreement was a mutual dislike of seamen.

The engineering revolution of the late nineteenth century brought large numbers of stokers into the Royal Navy, men whose arrival had a profound impact on the tenor of life afloat. If sailors deplored the stoker's lack of training in seamanship and pitied him his existence in the bowels of the ship, then the latter, who enjoyed better pay, considered theirs a less monotonous and regulated way of life. The differences did not end there. Whereas boy seamen joined the Navy at sixteen, the stoker was often recruited in his twenties from the industrial and mining centres of Britain and consequently possessed a very different outlook and mentality. Indeed, with neither the attachment to naval tradition of the seaman nor his connection to the age-old forcing grounds of the Service, stokers added a breadth to the Navy which contributed greatly to its character if not its harmony. The discordance was perpetuated by the Admiralty which, in failing to acknowledge the critical role of naval engineering, failed also to provide stokers with the necessary formation to make good that potential. This state of affairs was but one aspect of the reluctance of the inter-war Navy to embrace the technical realities of its calling, from which every branch suffered in one way or another. By no means, then, could it be said of the *Hood* that she was 'of one company'. In her, as elsewhere in the Navy, it required officers of the very highest calibre to bridge the gap between distinct worlds. That the opportunity and the men were found to do so before the onset of war is to the eternal credit of both.

By the late 1920s the mechanisms reluctantly established by the Navy to attend to lower-deck requests and grievances had

Fraternisation between seamen and Marines at Malta in the late 1930s. Rare before the 1930s but an indication of the changing character and morale of the Navy as war approached.
HMS Hood Association/Higginson Collection

quietly fallen into stagnation. With them went the lower-deck societies which, having been deprived of their capacity for representation in 1920, could offer little incentive for membership. The Admiralty, for its part, had begun to emphasise that the correct channel for welfare issues lay not in collective representation but in the relationship between an individual rating and his commanding officer: the divisional system. The divisional system of warship organisation was refined by Capt. Hall and Cdr James in the battlecruiser *Queen Mary* shortly before the Great War. This began by separating the crew into a dozen or more groups based on their trade and the part of the ship for which they were responsible. Each division was placed under a lieutenant or lieutenant-commander who was charged with its discipline, training, clothing and organisation. It was also the divisional officer's responsibility to familiarise himself with the personal circumstances of each man and provide him not only with counsel and assistance in domestic and service matters, but also with an avenue for voicing grievances if necessary. But it was in this, the most critical area of its organisation, that the divisional system had proved unequal to the demands placed on it in the years leading up to the Invergordon Mutiny. For one thing it was neither accessible nor equitable enough to function effectively. Any sailor wishing to speak to his officer was required to make out a written request and hand it to the divisional petty officer who would then submit it to the officer in question. The interview itself might be witnessed by the divisional petty officer with perhaps even a 'crusher' in attendance. Moreover, the statutory punishments for those bringing charges or voicing complaints that were subsequently judged to be unfounded naturally dissuaded many from taking their problems to officers in the first place. Even if the complainant were vindicated, the liability of being a 'marked man' thereafter was often viewed as being too great to warrant the risk. When a man did approach his officer it was often to meet with a frosty reception. On the eve of the Invergordon Mutiny an attempt by a chief petty officer in the *Hood* to warn his divisional officer of the plans that were afoot received the order to 'Get below or you're in the Commander's report for prosecution in the morning'.[82] Neither the modifications made to the King's Regulations and Admiralty Instructions in this respect in 1929 nor those added after Invergordon could dispel the overriding impression on the lower deck that

> …you had nobody to represent you in the Navy in those days…. I don't think [the officers] would stand up for you, not the lower-deck man, not at that time.[83]

Evidently, the success or failure of the divisional system depended on the degree of interest shown by the officer concerned. To some extent this interest depended on morale, and the morale of the officer corps of the Royal Navy had been destroyed by the Geddes Axe of 1921 which beached a third of its number. But where the Admiralty proved itself incapable of effective leadership in this matter one officer set himself to influence his peers with a tested paradigm. That officer was Rory O'Conor. The paradigm was HMS *Hood*.

Rory Chambers O'Conor was born into an Anglo-Irish family

in Buenos Aires in 1898.[84] In 1911 he entered the Royal Naval College at Osborne and spent much of the Great War in the gunroom of the pre-dreadnought *Prince of Wales* in which he saw action in the Dardanelles. A formidable sportsman, O'Conor represented the Navy at rugby between 1920–4, leading the United Services team during the 1921–2 season. His appointment to the Royal Yacht *Victoria and Albert* on being promoted lieutenant in 1919 was an early sign of favour but it was as a divisional officer in the battleship *Barham* between 1921–2 that he first came to prominence, Capt. Robin Dalglish noting his 'exceptionally good command of men'.[85] Specialising in gunnery, he divided most of the next ten years between HMS *Excellent*, the gunnery school in Portsmouth Harbour, and various shore and seagoing appointments including the cruiser *Emerald* and the battleships *Resolution* and *Royal Sovereign*. Promoted commander in 1931, it was while he was on the staff of *Excellent* that O'Conor learnt of his selection as the *Hood*'s executive officer, an appointment which took effect when she recommissioned at Portsmouth in August 1933.

Despite being the subject of an ample biography the reasons for O'Conor's preferment at the age of only 34 remain unclear. His zeal and talent apart, the appointment seems to have owed much to Admiral Sir John Kelly, Commander-in-Chief, Home Fleet, under whom he had served in the *Resolution* in the Mediterranean in 1924–5. Whatever the case, O'Conor was one of a generation of younger officers determined to take a hand in restoring the tarnished prestige of the Navy; for whom the surest means to a happy and successful ship lay in a genuine interest in the welfare of her men; for whom the Royal Navy was great enough to afford every man the chance of a fair hearing; for whom punishment existed chiefly to maintain discipline rather than to enforce compliance, and for whom the mere exercise of that discipline could never substitute for engaging the men as befitted their skills and responsibility. Above all, O'Conor and his like brought to their work both a heightened sensitivity to the plight of the ordinary sailor and an enhanced perception of his value as an individual. Among the first of this band was Sir Atwell 'Lou' Lake, Bt., who as executive officer of the *Nelson* had been among the few to emerge with any credit from Invergordon. Although a more formal officer than O'Conor, it was Lake's force of character, love of ship and respect for his men that had made the difference in *Nelson* in September 1931. Another was C.R. McCrum whose tact and powers of leadership delivered into O'Conor's hands a vessel ripe for the changes he would bring to her life and organisation. Far more than her flag-showing, the *Hood*'s reputation as the greatest ship in the Navy during the 1930s rests on the leading role she played in the introduction of a new dialogue between officers and men, to which first McCrum and then O'Conor made a vital contribution.

The task of executive officer in a capital ship was among the most challenging the Navy had to offer. Admiral Lord Chatfield, whose two-volume autobiography is one of the finest evocations of life in the Royal Navy ever written, provides the following descriptions of a commander's lot:

> There is no greater test of character in the world than to be the executive officer of a big ship. Many shun the responsibility and seek a less exacting duty, such as the command of a small ship; but few captains can efficiently

[82] NMM, Pursey/14, part 3 of book draft, p. 59.
[83] IWM/SA, Stoker 1st Class Nicholas Smiles Carr, no. 5809.
[84] Nixie Taverner, *A Torch Among Tapers* (Bramber, W. Sussex: Bernard Durnford, 2000).
[85] Ibid., p. 10.

86 Chatfield, *The Navy and Defence*, pp. 51 & 77.
87 Cited in Taverner, *A Torch Among Tapers*, p. 223.
88 *RBS*, p. 21.
89 Ibid., p. 10.

command a great ship's company unless they themselves have been through the mill, can realize the Commander's difficulties day by day and feel the pulse of his men.

If the executive officer of a big ship… wishes to succeed he must, as a first rule, know everything that goes on in the ship. He must be constantly visiting every part of it and be closely in touch with the ship's company's life and thought. He will thus understand his men, rectify just grievances in time and stop abuses before they can spread. His capacity will be accurately appraised by his officers and still more accurately by the ship's company, who will soon take his measure, and the evilly inclined soon know how far they can go in safety.[86]

Equally, the price of failure was very great. Remote as the captain often was from the men, the commander was unquestionably the key figure in the life of a major ship. On him depended the spirit with which his crew approached every endeavour. For him they might either do the least they could get away with or else slog their guts out.

O'Conor's arrival in the *Hood* provided an early indication of how the orchestra of shipboard life was to be tuned for the rest of the commission. Louis Le Bailly, then a midshipman, remembers the occasion in August 1933:

I suppose the greatest impact was when he tore up the voluminous Standing Orders and substituted his own 'Ten Commandments'. Their introduction to the new ship's company was dramatic. There was… a magic lantern on the quarterdeck and the ten were put on one by one as he explained their relevance. Then almost from a puff of smoke,

Admiral Sir John Kelly, so beloved by the sailor, appeared from the after hatchway and gave a stirring address.[87]

Implicit in O'Conor's 'Ten Commandments' was the notion that every man who gave of his best could expect fairness, respect and consideration from his superiors; that there were rewards for hard work, and that no one could go very far wrong so long as he kept the interests of the ship at the forefront of his mind; that no ship could be regarded as successful if she were not happy, and that all had a share in this endeavour. Never before had such a contract been laid before the lower deck of the Royal Navy, nor was such a system ever sold to her officer corps in such persuasive terms. The assessment of the 1933–6 commission which follows is based not only on the memoirs of those who lived it, but on *Running a Big Ship on 'Ten Commandments'*, the influential manual on ship organisation O'Conor published a year after leaving the *Hood*.

The linchpin of the *Hood*'s 'Ten Commandments' was O'Conor himself. What set him apart was his accessibility with respect to the entire crew, of which the outward sign was his celebrated open-door policy.

In the course of the day's work innumerable people have business to do with the Commander of a big ship, and his ready accessibility is a matter of importance. Even with a properly decentralised organisation, it is inevitable that the Commander should be constantly sought after for consultation, advice, approval, permission, information, and a hundred and one other reasons. […] The Commander wants to feel free to wander about the ship at will, seeing the hands at work and getting to know them. But there is a time for everything, and there should be at least one hour, both in the forenoon and afternoon, when the whole ship knows that there is *one* place where he can almost certainly be found, and available.[88]

That place was his day cabin. Mindful of Invergordon, here O'Conor acted out the central tenet of his ethos: that it was an officer's duty to make himself a channel for the problems and grievances of those placed under him; that it was his responsibility to ensure that every man could turn to him for a fair hearing:

In a great ship's company, there must inevitably arise every variety of problem for the individuals composing it— problems of life, love, leave, illness, death, and hardship of all kinds arising from work, pay, food, sleep, to mention only a few. No request must be ignored—all must be considered and given a sympathetic hearing, and the men encouraged to come forward.[89]

The other visible sign of this interest was the length to which O'Conor went to memorise the names of the *Hood*'s 1,300 crewmen. Although he tacitly admitted being able to hold no more than 600 in his mind at one time, the general impression was and remains that he came to know the name of every man on board. Whatever the reality, the endeavour had a marked impact on the atmosphere aboard:

Until you know a man's name he has no separate identity for you. Directly you know it, a bridge is slipped across the

---

CDR RORY O'CONOR'S 'TEN COMMANDMENTS', AUGUST 1933
SHIP'S STANDING ORDERS

1   The Service The Customs of the Service are to be observed at all times.

2   The Ship The Good Appearance of the Ship is the concern of everyone in *Hood*, and all share the responsibility for this.

3   The Individual Every man is constantly required to bring credit to the Ship by his individual bearing, dress and general conduct, on board and ashore.

4   Courtesy to Officers The courtesy of making a gangway, and standing to one side to attention when an officer passes, is to be shown by every man. If an Officer passing through men during stand-easy, meal hours, etc., carries his cap under his arm, it will indicate that no attention, other than clearing a gangway, is required.

5   Execution of Orders All orders, including those passed by Bugle and Pipe, are to be obeyed at the Run.

6   Punctual Attendance at Place of Duty Every man is personally responsible, on all occasions, for his own punctual attendance at his place of duty.

7   Permission to Leave Work A man is always to ask permission before leaving his work.

8   Reporting on Completion of Work Any man on finishing the work for which he has been told off, is to report to his immediate superior. Parties of men are to be fallen in and reported.

9   Card-playing and Gambling While card-playing is allowed at mess-tables and on the upper deck, any form of gambling is strictly prohibited. Gambling includes all games of chance played for money stakes.

10   Requests Any man wishing to see the Commander is to put in a request to his Officer of Division. In urgent cases his request is to pass through the Master-at-Arms and Officer of the Watch.

Early on the morning of 10 May 1940 the German Army launched its great offensive in the West. Within two weeks the War Cabinet, its troops outmanoeuvred and its strategy in disarray, was taking the first steps towards the withdrawal of the British Expeditionary Force from the Continent. As these momentous events unfolded across the Channel the *Hood* was quietly completing her refit first at Plymouth and then at the Gladstone Dock in Liverpool where Mussolini's declaration of war was greeted with looting of businesses and boarding of Italian vessels berthed there. A boarding party from the *Hood* was detailed to take over the freighter *Erica* whose crew promptly surrendered. The party returned soon after with the Italian ensign, an autographed portrait of Mussolini for the gunroom, and generally rather the worse for drink, the British matelot's unerring nose for alcohol having taken him directly to the spirit store.[118] When the *Hood* finally emerged from Liverpool on 12 June it was to find the evacuation from Dunkirk over and the Royal Navy girding itself to lift the remnants of the Allied armies from northern and western France. On 17 June, as the *Hood* lay at Greenock with the liners of convoy US3 about her, the French government asked Germany for an armistice. Five days later the new premier, Marshal Pétain, accepted Hitler's terms, thereby bringing the Battle of France to a close. That night in one of his periodic broadcasts to the ship Capt. Glennie asked his crew to remember that, though 'we were likely to have certain dislikes for our previous allies,… we were to treat them, even now, as our friends and try to realize their terrible fate in the hands of the Nazis'.[119] There was certainly frustration but also relief that another dismal episode was over, that 'On consideration, not having to defend France may be a blessing in disguise'.[120] But, as the *Hood*'s company was shortly to discover, France's agony was not yet over.

With the entry of Italy into the war the Admiralty began taking steps to fill the void created by the collapse of French power in the western Mediterranean with a significant force of British ships. However, once the terms of the Franco-German armistice became known in London, as they had by 25 June, it was plain that this squadron must have a far more urgent remit. Under the terms of the armistice, the French fleet, still largely intact, was to be 'demobilized and disarmed under German or Italian control'. This clause did not satisfy the British government which was already moving to prevent scattered units and squadrons of the French Navy falling into the hands of the Axis. The officer chosen to enforce this policy in the western Mediterranean was Vice-Admiral Sir James Somerville who assumed command of Force H on 27 June. First constituted as a hunting group during the search for the raider *Admiral Graf Spee* in October 1939, Force H was now transformed into an independent command based on Gibraltar but directly responsible to the Admiralty in London. Over the next eighteen months Somerville's 'detached squadron' asserted a control over the western Mediterranean which would not be relinquished while the war lasted. This accomplishment, together with the many famous actions in which it was involved, gives Force H a special place in the history of the Royal Navy. It was to join this squadron as flagship that the *Hood* was ordered south from Greenock on 18 June, reaching Gibraltar five days later with the carrier *Ark Royal*.

Above: Vice-Admiral Somerville's 35ft fast motor boat slung beneath the main derrick in July 1940. The canvas-covered mounting on the left is Port No. 3 4in gun. The ready-use ammunition lockers on the right are nestled beneath the pom-pom bandstand.
Bibliothek für Zeitgeschichte, Stuttgart

Left: A photo of 'X' and 'Y' turrets supposedly taken during the bombardment of Mers-el-Kebir, 3 July 1940.
HMS Hood Association/Mason Collection

[118] See RNM, 1998/42, Journal of Mid. P.J. Buckett, R.N.V.R., 11 June 1940, and IWM/SA, Sub-Lt (E) Brian Scott-Garrett, no. 16741, reel 1.
[119] RNM, 1998/42, Journal of Mid. P.J. Buckett, at sea, 22 June 1940.
[120] Iago, *Letters* (at sea, 18 June 1940).

The first task to which Force H was committed was the neutralisation of the French Atlantic Fleet at Mers-el-Kebir near Oran in Algeria. After two days of earnest deliberation in Somerville's cabin, Force H sailed from Gibraltar on 2 July stiffened by units of Admiral Sir Dudley North's North Atlantic Command. There can be no doubt that Somerville's task was among the most unenviable ever assigned to a British commander. His brief from the War Cabinet was to lay before his French counterpart, Amiral Marcel Gensoul, the following options for the disposal of his fleet, which consisted of two modern battlecruisers, two elderly battleships, a seaplane carrier and six large destroyers: that he (a) put to sea and continue the fight against Germany; (b) sail with reduced crews to a British port; (c) do likewise to a port in the French West Indies; or (d) scuttle his ships at their berths. Should these prove unacceptable a fifth was to be offered, namely that Gensoul demilitarise his force at Mers-el-Kebir. Any measure resorted to would have to be enacted within six hours, a proviso which greatly hindered both admirals' freedom of manoeuvre. In the event of these proposals being rejected Somerville was to present Gensoul with the ultimatum of having his fleet destroyed at the hands of Force H.

Shortly after 08.00 on the morning of 3 July Force H appeared off Mers-el-Kebir. Somerville had already sent the destroyer *Foxhound* ahead with his emissary Capt. Cedric Holland, but it was not until 16.15 that the latter gained direct access to Gensoul. The protracted and ultimately fruitless negotiations between the British and Gensoul, the stirring of the French navy across the western Mediterranean and the mounting pressure from London all lie beyond the scope of this volume.[121] Suffice to say that by 17.30, some three hours after the expiry of his original ultimatum, Somerville found himself with no alternative but to open fire. Within a few minutes Boy Signalman Ted Briggs was hoisting the order for instant action to the starboard signal yard. Shortly before 18.00 it was the order to open fire that he bent on to the halyard:

> The response was immediate. Just as I turned round to watch, the guns of the *Resolution* and *Valiant* roared in murderous hair-trigger reaction. Then came the ting-ting of our firing bell. Seconds later my ears felt as if they had been sandwiched between two manhole covers. The concussion of the *Hood*'s eight fifteen-inch guns, screaming in horrendous harmony, shook the flag deck violently.[122]

Moments later the harbour at Mers-el-Kebir was being crucified by the first salvoes of British 15in ordnance. Within three minutes the battleship *Bretagne* had blown up with huge loss of life. Her sister *Provence* and the battlecruiser *Dunkerque* had to be beached after sustaining repeated hits, the latter mainly under *Hood*'s fire. The destroyer *Mogador* lost her stern to a direct hit which left her a smouldering wreck in waters turned black with oil and writhing bodies. With the harbour shrouded in a dense pall of smoke, at 18.04, nine minutes after the action had commenced, Somerville gave the order to cease fire. A few minutes later increasingly accurate salvoes from the shore battery at Fort Santon obliged the *Hood* to return a withering fire while the squadron sailed out of range under a smokescreen. This might have been the end of the affair except that at 18.18 reports began reaching *Hood* that a battlecruiser

was emerging from the harbour. Initially dismissed by Somerville and his staff, by 18.30 it was apparent that the *Strasbourg*, unscathed by the holocaust enveloping her companions, had negotiated the mine barrage laid by aircraft from *Ark Royal* and was making for Toulon with five destroyers. *Hood* turned to give chase, working up to over 28 knots at the cost of a stripped turbine while *Ark Royal* prepared to launch an air strike in the fading light. The *Hood* again came under attack as the pursuit developed, first from a salvo of torpedoes fired by the light cruiser *Rigault de Genouilly* and then by a flight of bombers from Algeria. However, bomb attacks by Swordfish aircraft failed to slow the *Strasbourg* and at 20.20 a dispirited Somerville called off the chase. A second Swordfish strike at 20.55 reported two torpedo hits but the *Strasbourg*'s speed remained unimpaired and she reached Toulon without damage the following day. Three days later an announcement by Amiral Jean-Pierre Estéva at Bizerta that 'The damage to the *Dunkerque* is minimal and the ship will soon be repaired' brought Force H back to Mers-el-Kebir where Swordfish from *Ark Royal* put paid to her operational career.

So ended one of the most regrettable episodes in the history of the Royal Navy. As Somerville put it in a letter to his wife,

> We all feel thoroughly dirty and ashamed that the first time we should have been in action was an affair like this. [...] I feel sure that I shall be blamed for bungling the job and I think I did. But to you I don't mind confessing I was half-hearted and you can't win an action that way.[123]

It was, he added, 'the biggest political blunder of modern times and I imagine will rouse the world against us'.[124] Those who expressed an opinion did so largely in the same vein. Writing to his family on 6 July, Sub-Lt Iago echoed Somerville's fears for the wider implications of the engagement:

> I think that the events in Oran were a great pity—they solved the problem of the French fleet but I hope we shall not look back on it as too much of a mistake. Lord Haw-Haw has evidently been rendered speechless with anger—or perhaps it is that we just can't pick him up on the wireless.[125]

In fact, Lord Haw-Haw, like the rest of the German propaganda machine, made enormous capital out of the incident, christening Force H 'Somerville's assassins' in one particular broadcast. There was grim amusement to be had from this but also anger; anger against the Axis for precipitating the disaster, and anger against Gensoul for not continuing the war alongside the British. Above all there was chagrin and astonishment that matters should have come to such a pass. But for all that there was no shortage of pragmatic opinion in the *Hood*. Mid. Philip Buckett's was one:

> Coming back past the harbour we could still see large columns of smoke and small fires coming from the ships and the town behind. We realised, too, how unpleasant the action had been. Nevertheless it had been our duty and we had done it successfully.[126]

There were other voices too, overheard by Somerville and related with some disgust to his wife: 'It doesn't seem to worry the

[121] See Warren Tute, *The Deadly Stroke* (London: Collins, 1973) and Brodhurst, *Churchill's Anchor*, pp. 152–66.
[122] Coles & Briggs, *Flagship* Hood, pp. 167–8.
[123] Simpson, (ed), *The Somerville Papers*, p. 109.
[124] Ibid., p. 108.
[125] Iago, *Letters* (Gibraltar, 6 July 1940).
[126] RNM, 1998/42, Journal of Mid. P.J. Buckett, 3 July 1940.

Christmas Day was spent between Iceland and the Faeroes but the men made the best of it. Boy Bill Crawford's illicit diary records it thus:

> (3.30 p.m.) Considering where we are we had a good Christmas to-day. She went to action Stations early this morning, there has been no work, smoking in the Messdecks and plenty to eat. Made up concerts down below.[2]

Plenty to drink, too. Mid. Robin Owen:

> Some of us were invited to join in the traditional 'rounds' of the messdecks where the sailors had just had their rum ration and some were doing their best to enjoy themselves with a singsong. One of my boat's crew invited me to join in with a particularly graphic song about the attributes of his 'Girl Salome'. Never having heard it before, about all I could do was to laugh and applaud loudly and move on as soon as I decently could.[3]

Hard as the circumstances were, the spirit of comradeship never faltered in *Hood*, and the remarkable coming-together of branches and ranks which characterised the Navy at war was echoed in this ship as much as any other. On Christmas morning the midshipmen hosted the sergeants of Marines together with the chiefs and petty officers to drinks in the gunroom before lunch. On New Year's Eve it was the turn of the warrant officers, the Master-at-Arms and the Marine Colour Sergeant to join every officer in the ship from Vice-Admiral Whitworth to the most junior midshipman for Hogmanay in the wardroom. Whitworth led his party in highland reels to the skirling of bagpipes though the dignity of Colour Sergeant Gough and CPO Chandler the Jaunty prevented them going this far.[4] Two short patrols later and the *Hood* found herself at Rosyth, her crew dispersed by watches on their first leave in six months.

On 16 January 1941 the *Hood* edged into Rosyth dockyard for what would be her final refit.[5] Drained of oil and emptied of ammunition, the ship was hauled by tugs through the outer lock from the Forth and over to the flooded dry dock. Hawsers were then secured to her fairleads and she was drawn by electric capstans bow-first into No. 1 dock, one of the few capable of accommodating her 860 feet. Once her bows had filled the niche at the head of the structure the caisson was closed and the water pumped out until the ship had come to rest on an arrangement of carefully-laid baulks of timber chained to the bottom of the graving dock. Over in the fitting-out basin the new battleship *Prince of Wales* was in the final stages of completion. Immediately parties of dockyard maties began coming aboard, welders, caulkers and shipwrights to replace fittings and equipment and effect repairs on her tired hull and structure. Particular attention was paid to the deck seams on the forecastle through which water poured into the ship at sea. Planking was renewed and pneumatic caulking tools put to work on the overlapping plates to staunch the leaks that were making life unbearable on the lower deck. The hull itself was inspected and scraped clean before a squad of formidable ladies with brushes on lengthy poles began applying a new layer of red lead paint. In earlier years prolonged spells in harbour and in temperate waters would have revealed a layer of marine growth encrusted on the ship's bottom. This time

The long hard winter of 1940–1. The crew of Port No. 3 4in gun stand down for a mug of tea or ky. They are rigged for Atlantic patrol duty in duffel coats together with caps and balaclavas knitted on the Home Front.
HMS Hood Association/Whitewood Collection

inspection showed it to be largely stripped of paint by the severity of her wartime service, fresh coats being applied over bare metal. Also at Rosyth was a team of engineers from John Brown & Co. led by Willie McLaughlin, eventually that company's chief engine designer.[6] The *Hood* was completed with Clyde-built Brown-Curtis geared turbines which McLaughlin and his men now spent a week dismantling and inspecting for damaged nozzles and misaligned wheels. Blades were renewed in the starboard inner turbine, stripped in the pursuit of the *Strasbourg* after the bombardment of Mers-el-Kebir.[7] However, the main work centred on the installation of radar, namely a Type 284 gunnery set on the spotting top and Type 279M air-warning equipment on the mainmast. The matter was of course shrouded in the greatest secrecy. One of the dockyard welders was Ian Green of Glenshee:

> I welded a platform below the cross-trees and the shipwright and me were told that this was a crow's nest for a look-out. Radar was not mentioned for obvious security reasons but it could well have been fitted by electricians subsequent to our work. It did not occur to me at the time that there was no direct access to this position as we had worked off bosun's chairs set up by Dockyard riggers—a hairy experience in the conditions at that time. […] Any seaman given the look-out job up there would have died of hypothermia in no time![8]

These installations also required the removal of the fore topmast and the hanging of new yards on both the mainmast and the spotting top. Green recalls a brief interruption to his work on the latter:

> My job was to weld new signal yardarms to the fore and after masts. Having completed the task of hauling heavy welding cables I tacked the arms into position but had to stop work as a young Signalman appeared to tell me that

[2] IWM, 92/27/1, diary for 1940, p. 128.
[3] Owen, *HMS Hood* (unpublished memoir), p. 2.
[4] Colour Sergeant John M. Gough and CPO Alfred J. Chandler were lost on 24 May 1941.
[5] This section owes much to the assistance of Mr Ian A. Green, welder at HM Dockyard Rosyth from 1939–42.
[6] I owe this information to the kindness of Ian Johnston of the Glasgow School of Art.
[7] Robertson, 'H.M.S. "Hood"' in *Ships Monthly*, 16 (1981), no. 4, p. 28.
[8] Letter to the author, 7 January 2004.

[9] Letter to the author, 25 November 2003.
[10] RNM, 1998/42. The turbine repair actually consisted of replacing the blades in the starboard inner unit. Both of the ship's steam picket boats were replaced by motor boats.
[11] IWM, 92/27/1, at sea, 18 March 1941. Crawford was lost with the ship in May 1941.
[12] IWM/SA, no. 16741, reel 1.
[13] Iago, *Letters* (at sea, 9 October 1939).
[14] Ibid. (Rosyth, 20 August 1940).

King George VI was coming aboard. From our high view-point we watched him piped onto the Quarter Deck to be greeted by Admiral [Whitworth] and the Captain before going below. Sleet was beginning to blow in the wind so, anxious to get down into a warm mess-deck, the Signalman asked me if he could crawl out on the yards to fix the halliards. Considering we were 80 ft. up plus another 57 ft. to the dock bottom I told him he would have to wait until the work was finished otherwise he would be going down with the ironwork.[9]

It was 6 March 1941 and by the time Mid. Philip Buckett returned from leave on the 17th the refit was well nigh complete. His journal entry summarises the changes:

The refit has been a fairly extensive one, and many improvements and long-needed repairs have been made, more especially to the gunnery section. High-Angle and Low-Angle Radio Direction Finding has been installed and vast alterations have been made in the compass platform and on the Evershed Bearing Transmitter platforms on the wings of the bridge. Many repairs have been carried out in the Engineer's Department including the replacement of the broken turbine and the renewal of many other parts and machinery. The installation of Radio Direction Finding has led to much more intricate control systems in the Air Defence Position and of course in the directors. We have had a very difficult job trying to learn the position of all the instruments and the job they perform. Other smaller items of interest completed recently include the new screens in the after ends of the batteries and the removal of the fore-top mast. The second picket boat has been replaced by a 35-foot motor-boat.[10]

There had been another change also. On 15 February Capt. Irvine Glennie, recently promoted rear-admiral, had left the ship to be replaced by Ralph Kerr, who had made his name in destroyers. Kerr's new command had still to work up after her refit but as so often these plans were disrupted by news that

German raiders had broken out into the Atlantic. On the after-noon of 18 March the *Hood* passed under the Forth Bridge for the very last time and hastened in search of the enemy. After a few blessed weeks of leave, the sight was more than Boy Bill Crawford of Edinburgh could bear:

Dearest Mum,
Well, I got back to the ship and we are now away. Gee, I wish you had said for me to stay awhile, I know it's wrong to say that, but I sure am fed up. I got aboard at 2 o'clock, and have to see the Commander for being 6 hours adrift and not two as Nunky thought. They must have thought I was in the dockyard when Nunky phoned. I don't know what I will get and I don't really care. I feel kinda sick, can't eat and my heart is in my throat. It took me all my time not to cry as we came down the river. But I'll have a good one when I manage to get turned in, Mum, and I might feel better after it.[11]

There was further disappointment for, despite hopes of an inter-ception on 20 March, Admiral Günther Lütjens, the German squadron commander, slipped through the net and reached Brest with *Scharnhorst* and *Gneisenau* on the 22nd. Low on fuel, dawn on the 23rd found the *Hood* back at Scapa Flow.

It was at this time that the name 'Bismarck' was first uttered in the *Hood*. On 14 February 1939 the first German battleship since the Great War was launched at the Blohm und Voss ship-yard in Hamburg. The *Bismarck* mounted eight 38-cm guns on a standard displacement of 41,800 tons, nearly 40 per cent of which was devoted to armour protection (as against 33.5 per cent in *Hood*). She was 823 feet long and capable of 30 knots. Commissioned in August 1940, she underwent exten-sive trials and exercises in the Baltic before being deemed ready for service in April 1941. The appearance of the *Bismarck* for the first time presented the *Hood* with an oppo-nent armed and powered to the same standard as she. Until that moment much of the *Hood*'s crew had been glad to regard her as largely invulnerable to German surface vessels. As Sub-Lt (E) Brian Scott-Garrett (1940–1) later recalled, 'There was always a feeling of superiority about the *Hood*, that she was a magnificent great ship, that nothing would ever go wrong with her'.[12] The fate of the *Courageous* and *Royal Oak* soon demon-strated U-boat attack to be a serious threat but the danger of air power seems to have had rather less impact despite the known weakness in her horizontal protection. Two weeks after *Hood* was bombed by a Ju 88 in the North Sea Sub-Lt John Iago advised his family to 'Console yourself about air attack on us; we think it would be quite impossible for aeroplanes to sink us—you should see our armour plate!'[13] Nor, by all appear-ances, did Italian high-level bombing in the Mediterranean the following year shake his confidence:

The more I have to do with it, the more faith I have in this ship. Bomb splinters only spoil the paintwork and aircraft are finding out that it is better to keep clear of us.[14]

Admittedly such opinions may owe more to a desire to calm family nerves than any firm conviction on the subject; Paymaster Lt-Cdr A.R. Jackson (1938–40) can't very well have been serious when he penned the following to his wife on 20 September 1939, three days after the loss of the *Courageous*:

King George VI received on the *Hood*'s quarterdeck during her final refit, Rosyth 6 March 1941. Ordinary Signalman Ted Briggs was surprised to note that he seemed to be wearing make-up.
Mrs Doreen Miller

I shouldn't be too worried in relation to me when you think of the *Courageous*. *Hood* is a very different kind of ship, and also is constructed quite differently, and so the chances of our being sunk, even if we are hit, can be considered negligible.[15]

But the *Bismarck* was a very different matter. AB Len Williams remembers the tenor of messdeck discussions during his last months in the ship in 1941:

As an ex-member of *Hood*'s crew I can recall numerous discussions we had in our mess about a possible meeting with either *Bismarck* or her sister *Tirpitz*. We were not at all happy about such a prospect. We knew our weakness and the risks of not having an armoured deck. We had the speed, yes, and we had the gun power; but we did not have our armour in the right place![16]

By the end of April few in the *Hood* can have had much doubt as to the vulnerability of their ship in the event of a confrontation with the *Bismarck*. On the 19th, following reports that *Bismarck* had sailed from Kiel towards the North Sea, Vice-Admiral William Whitworth issued his battle orders should contact be made. Sub-Lt R.G. Robertson R.N.V.R., who joined the ship at Devonport in May 1940, recalls Whitworth's instructions:

Next day Admiral Whitworth made known his plans if an enemy report was received; our escorts, the cruiser *Kenya* and three destroyers, would act as a searching force, and if the *Bismarck* were encountered we would close on the enemy at speed in order to bring the guns of the *Hood* within effective range. If possible, we would make the approach end-on so as to present the minimum target.[17]

For the first time, too, a fatalistic note emerges in correspondence from the *Hood*. On 1 May Lt-Cdr Roger Batley wrote this to his sister Mary:

I am sorry Uncle Roger has gone. But quite agree, suddenly—like he & Charlie—is by far the best way to go, & I hope when my time comes that I shall go that way also.[18]

Even Boy Bill Crawford sensed that something was up:

We haven't been away very long, but have had some tense hours since I left. And now that Germany has started sending her warships out there looks as if there will be <u>action</u> for the Fleet soon. Anyway, the sooner we get them the better.[19]

That day was not far off. Almost a decade earlier a walk on the shores of the Cromarty Firth in May 1932 had left Mid. Louis Le Bailly with a terrible premonition of the fate that awaited his ship:

We trained so hard that one day in the Cromarty Firth the chaplain gave us an afternoon off to play the wardroom at golf on the lovely course at Nigg (alas no longer in use). Later we were also to be the wardroom's guests in the pub (still there). Thus it was, at peace with ourselves, and pleasantly tipsy from a modest, but, for us, unusual

Hood's nemesis: the *Bismarck* seen at Kiel on 15 September 1940 shortly after commissioning. The radar and rangefinder installation on the foretop has yet to be fitted.

quantity of McEwans Scotch Ale, that we walked back to the jetty through the heather-scented twilight to the sorrowful questing note of the curlew. I remember shivering, as if drenched in ice, and putting it down to the McEwans I had imbibed. But it was late in May, possibly the 24th, the day HMS *Hood* blew up in action with the *Bismarck* and all but three of her 1500 crew lost.[20]

For Le Bailly, now Senior Engineer of the cruiser *Naiad*, there was to be one last visit:

Seventeen months [after leaving her], in April 1941, HMS *Naiad* anchored close to *Hood* in Scapa Flow. The midshipmen for whose engineering instruction I had been responsible, had just passed for sub-lieutenant and were celebrating their success and departure and requested my assistance. Hearing that I had accepted, [Lt-Cdr (E) J.G.M.] Erskine invited me to supper after the gunroom had finished with me. When leaving I found a couple of dozen or so of the ship's company, not all from the engine department, waiting to say goodbye and to wish me luck. Who arranged this, I shall never know. In less than six weeks they all were dead.[21]

Death in battle has an arbitrary quality impossible for any survivor to explain or grasp. To be spared the fate of one's comrades, to find oneself preserved when they have lost everything, is beyond the capacity of reason; for some, indeed, physical survival proved to be beyond mental endurance. The fate of the *Hood*, annihilated in a matter of seconds, affords this reality a

15 IWM, 65/45/2.
16 Williams, *Gone A Long Journey*, p. 153.
17 Robertson, 'The Mighty *Hood*' in *Ships Monthly*, 10 (1975), no. 6, p. 7.
18 HMS *Hood* Association archives. At sea, 1 May 1941.
19 IWM, 92/27/1, Scapa Flow, 23 March 1941.
20 Le Bailly, *The Man Around the Engine*, p. 26.
21 Ibid., p. 55. Lt-Cdr John Erskine was lost on 24 May 1941.

22 Jenson, *Tin Hats, Oilskins &
   Seaboots*, p. 96.
23 SWWEC, 2001/1376, p. 6. The
   May Board in fact took place
   before the loss of the ship.
24 Pertwee, *Moon Boots and Dinner
   Suits*, pp. 164–5. Pertwee states
   Capt. Glennie as his interviewer
   but this must be an error.
25 HMS *Hood* Association archives.
   There were several deserters from
   the *Hood*.
26 I am grateful to Mr Adrian
   Burdett for sharing this memory
   with me.
27 HMS *Hood* Association archives.
   Scapa Flow, 12 May 1941.
28 RNM, 1981/369 no. 148.

The boat deck seen from the spotting top in the autumn of 1940. Note the two 44-inch searchlights on the platform abaft the funnel and four more installed on the after superstructure. Starboard No. 2 UP launcher lies on the left of the photograph together with four of the seven 4in Mk XIX mountings. Numerous ready-use ammunition lockers are distributed across the boat deck. The grime of a year of war service is apparent. See the photograph on p. 35 for a peacetime comparison.
Bibliothek für Zeitgeschichte, Stuttgart

starkness which sets her loss apart from most others. Submarine crews were routinely wiped out but ships' companies much less often: the destroyer *Exmouth*, the corvette *Gladiolus* and the cruiser *Sydney* are among the few examples in the Second World War. Others suffered a slow and terrible attrition by fire and water: the cruisers *Dunedin*, *Neptune* and *Indianapolis*, the *Scharnhorst* and *Bismarck* herself. But one needs to return to the First World War to find precedent for large ships being destroyed with all but a handful of men: the vanquished of Coronel and the Falklands; above all the disasters at Jutland which prefigured that of *Hood* herself. The experience of those who survived the loss of the *Hood* will be dealt with in due course. But what of those who were spared death yet had to live the experience vicariously in the sufferings of those who replaced them, who escaped through an inscrutable turn of fate? Some like PO Len Williams, drafted on promotion in February 1941 after five years in the ship, had reached the end of a particular phase in their career. The time had come to move on. Others like OA Bert Pitman got an unexpected 'pierhead jump' to another ship, in his case the battleship *Barham* whose sinking he survived later that year. In April Latham Jenson was one of the last party of midshipmen to take their Sub-Lieutenants' exams in *Hood*. The stakes couldn't have been higher:

…Those of us facing our examinations for acting sub-lieutenant those lovely Scapa days in April had lots to reflect upon, more than we knew. Failure, and consequently remaining on board for another run, in this case would actually mean death![22]

Others survived by being selected for officer training. After a statutory three months as Ordinary Seamen on the lower deck, those who wished to receive a commission or who had otherwise been identified as being of officer material were tested and, if successful, drafted for further training ashore. One such was B.A. Carlisle:

Despite the fact that I was a clumsy Ordinary Seaman it fortunately did not stop me from being chosen to go for a Commission. About every three months the Captain of the ship (Glennie at the time) presided over a Board to decide who was potential Officer material, and my Board must have been in January 1941. Having had the privilege of public school education and having been a prefect and an officer in the school O.T.C., I fortunately did satisfy the Board that I was Officer material, although very sadly some of my friends from a similar background failed the Board, and as there was no further Board until May, went down with the ship…[23]

Another was Jon Pertwee, unwittingly passed as a CW ('Commissions and Warrants') candidate after half an hour explaining the finer points of broadcast radio to Capt. Kerr.[24] He and OD Howard Spence were part of the last draft to leave the *Hood* on or about 21 May, the eve of her sailing against the *Bismarck*. But as Spence's memoir reveals, there were other ways of escaping the *Hood*:

Some 13 of our crew, myself and Jon Pertwee included, had draft chits to go south. Another was a matelot who had hit a PO with a rifle. On route to Pompey I stopped at a pub near Victoria station in London (Waterloo had been bombed) and at the end of the bar was a stocky chap in nondescript clothes—he was a deserter from the *Hood*—neither of us spoke, but went our separate ways.[25]

Lucky as they were, there were men who enjoyed even greater good fortune. A day or two before she left Scapa for the last time Sub-Lt R.G. Robertson was taken ill with a perforated duodenal ulcer and transported across the Flow to the hospital ship *Amarapoora*. Another, Mid. Harold Carnell, given compassionate leave from the *Hood*, was recalled by telegram but failed to reach Scapa thanks to a protracted wartime rail journey.[26] Then there were those for whom Fortuna's wheel turned in the contrary direction. As Lt-Cdr Roger Batley, a member of Vice-Admiral Whitworth's staff, informed his sister on 12 May, his remaining in the ship depended on whether the new admiral, Lancelot Holland, liked the cut of his jib.[27] The admiral evidently did. Two days later another staff officer, Paymaster Lt Robert Browne, wrote telling his parents that

I am staying on here for about 5 weeks with the new Admiral until they are all settled in, then I will be relieved. As to what follows once again I cannot say.[28]

Others went to their deaths with an eagerness that haunted those who remembered them. Surgeon Lt-Cdr R. Ransome-Wallis R.N.V.R. was Principal Medical Officer of the cruiser *London*:

I also recollected sadly a very young midshipman who had spent a couple of days in *London*'s Sick Bay. He had

recently been sunk in another ship and had only survived after a bit of an ordeal. He said to me rather bravely 'But I shall be all right now sir, I am going to the *Hood*'.[29]

A similar tale is told by Mid. Ross Warden, drafted from the *Hood* in February 1941:

One day late in the month of February I was told to report to Lieutenant-Commander Pares and was informed that I had been reappointed. This was a blow but worse was to follow. 'What to, sir?' 'First Lieutenant of a patrol drifter' was the answer. There was an expression to go 'From the sublime to the Gor-Blimey'. This was it! Commander Pares was a very fine officer and one of the gunroom favourites. I protested and said it was like going from the Ritz-Carlton to a flop-house. In return I was given almost fatherly advice, that appointments were final and the sooner I learnt this the better. It was then a question of packing and saying farewell to the finest bunch of boys with whom it was possible to serve. The next stage was a depressing rail journey to Loch Ewe on the north-west coast of Scotland, where I relieved a midshipman Williams as First Lieutenant of His Majesty's Drifter *Fairweather*. The crew looked like a bunch of pirates; the armament consisted of an antiquated three-pounder gun, five rusty depth charges and a temperamental Lewis gun. It came as an almost unbelievable shock two months later when the loss of the *Hood* was announced. [. . .] I could not help but think of Williams' enthusiasm. At least he went with the most gallant of company.[30]

For those who were spared like Warden and Carnell there was no doubt enormous relief, but also a measure of guilt, guilt that they had not been there with their friends, guilt that someone had died in their place. So it is when a great ship and her company are destroyed. Short of nuclear war, only in naval combat is it possible for a unit to be annihilated in battalion or double battalion strength in the twinkling of an eye. On this awful reality rests much of its depth and fascination. For HMS *Hood* that dread moment had come.

We turn now to the most challenging aspect of the *Hood*'s career, the manner in which she met her end. Detailed as it is, this volume makes no claim to technical mastery of the *Hood*'s labyrinthine structure and systems. Its perspective is that of those who served in her in peace and war and its aim is to provide a framework of information within which this community can be understood. Though study of the history, structure and functioning of the ship inevitably permits certain ideas to be advanced regarding the conduct of her final battle and the nature of her sinking, those reading it will find no new theory on the causes and process of that disaster. The complexity of the task and the wealth of new but disparate information provided by the discovery of the wreck makes this a matter for expert analysis rather than uninformed speculation. Rather, the pages that follow attempt to describe the *Hood*'s last battle from the largely conjectural point of view of those who experienced and in almost every case died in it; and from the actual point of view of those who witnessed or otherwise lived the event by proxy, people fated to suffer its emotional consequences for the rest of their days.

The events leading up to the sinking of the *Hood* have been

Painting the ship's side in *Hood*'s final colour scheme, AP507B (Home Fleet medium grey), at Scapa Flow in October 1940. Note the splinter protection around the four installations visible along the port side of the boat deck (left to right): Port pom-pom ('Peter'), Port No. 1 4in gun, Port No. 2 UP launcher and Port No. 2 4in gun. Obscured behind No. 1 4in gun is the No. 1 UP launcher beside which AB Bob Tilburn sheltered during the last action. The battery is empty and largely plated over. On the spotting top the 15-foot rangefinder has been removed but the director and its hood remain. These alterations were all made in three successive refits between February 1939 and May 1940.

[29] Ransome-Wallis, *Two Red Stripes*, p. 34.
[30] Warden, 'Memories of the Battle Cruiser H.M.S. "Hood"', p. 85. Lt-Cdr (T) Anthony Pares and Mid. Roderick Williams R.N.V.R. were both lost with the ship.

recounted many times and need only be summarised here from the massive bibliography generated by it. By the spring of 1941 the Admiralty was girding itself for an onslaught of German commerce-raiding sorties against convoys in the Atlantic. On 14 February the heavy cruiser *Admiral Hipper* returned to Brest having sunk over 30,000 tons of merchant shipping. At the end of March the armoured cruiser *Admiral Scheer* reached Norway after a prolonged sortie during which sixteen merchantmen and the armed merchant cruiser *Jervis Bay* had been destroyed for a total of nearly 115,000 tons. All the while the battlecruisers *Scharnhorst* and *Gneisenau* were abroad in the Atlantic, making Brest on 22 March after a two-month operation during which 22 ships had been sunk or captured and the entire Atlantic convoy system disrupted. Then on 19 April came reports that the new battleship *Bismarck* had sailed from Kiel steering north-west towards the North Sea. These proved false, but apart from drawing the *Hood* into the Norwegian Sea on another wild goose chase they decided Admiral Sir John Tovey, Commander-in-Chief Home Fleet, to maintain a permanent vigil on the northern exits leading to the Atlantic. Meanwhile a concerted campaign of minelaying and above all aerial bombardment greatly reduced the options open to the German High Command. In early April it seemed as if the *Scharnhorst* and the *Gneisenau* might be unleashed with *Bismarck* and the heavy cruiser *Prinz Eugen* in a catastrophic breakout into the Atlantic. In the event, boiler repairs to the *Scharnhorst* made her unavailable before June while the *Gneisenau* was heavily damaged in repeated attacks on Brest by RAF Bomber and Coastal Command. To the north, extensive minelaying in the Denmark Strait and the Iceland–Faeroes gap narrowed the already constricted waterways through which any German force had to pass in order to reach the Atlantic shipping lanes.

By early May persistent German aerial reconnaissance between Greenland and Jan Mayen Island had made it increasingly plain to the Admiralty that the long-awaited appearance of

the *Bismarck* was nigh. Already on 28 April the *Hood* had sailed from the dismal anchorage of Hvalfjord in southern Iceland as distant cover for two eastbound convoys against surface attack. For a time it was thought that an attack on Iceland or Jan Mayen might be afoot but by 18 May Tovey and his staff had concluded that a naval breakout was the more likely outcome and on that day the heavy cruiser *Suffolk*, then on patrol in the Denmark Strait, was warned to be on her guard for the appearance of German warships. These fears were confirmed on 21 May with news that a German squadron was refuelling near Bergen in Norway. This was the *Bismarck* and the *Prinz Eugen* which had sailed under Admiral Lütjens from the Baltic port of Gdynia (Gotenhafen) on either side of midnight on the 18th. Their departure had been delayed almost a month by the mining of *Prinz Eugen* in the Fehmarn Belt off Kiel; Lütjens would have had it delayed until the *Scharnhorst* or *Tirpitz* were ready to join him but he was overruled by Grössadmiral Erich Raeder, the head of the German Navy. The aim was to enter the Atlantic on a commerce-raiding sortie via the Denmark Strait, but 'Rhine Exercise' (*Rheinübung*) as it was called was compromised from the outset. Even before it had cleared the Kattegat, the body of water separating Denmark and Sweden, the German squadron was sighted by the Swedish cruiser *Gotland* which promptly reported the matter to the naval authorities ashore. Lütjens' foreboding was to be realised for by the end of that day, 20 May, the report had reached the Admiralty in London. On the morning of the 21st the *Bismarck* reached Grimstadfjorden near Bergen and it was here that an RAF Spitfire photographed Lütjens' force from an altitude of 25,000 feet. That evening, just as *Bismarck* and *Prinz Eugen* put to sea once more, Admiral Tovey ordered the Battle Cruiser Squadron to sail from Scapa to Hvalfjord. At 23.56 *Hood* and *Prince of Wales* and six destroyers weighed anchor and exited the Flow shortly after midnight under a veil of rain and mist. By 01.00 on the 22nd they were through the Hoxa Boom and out into the Atlantic. The chase from which the *Hood* would not return had begun.

Bismarck seen from *Prinz Eugen* en route to Gdynia (Gotenhafen) in March 1941. She is wearing the Baltic camouflage pattern which was overpainted during *Rheinübung*.

Vice-Admiral William Whitworth struck his flag on 8 May, being succeeded four days later by Lancelot Holland, Vice-Admiral Battle Cruiser Squadron and Second-in-Command, Home Fleet. Relatively little is known about Holland who was born at Eydon in Oxfordshire in 1887 and specialised in gunnery before the First World War. He first comes to prominence as Assistant Chief of Naval Staff at the Admiralty in 1937–8 and then as Rear-Admiral 2nd Battle Squadron in 1938–9. In 1939 he was briefly appointed as the naval representative to the joint Air Ministry-Admiralty staff advising on enemy attacks on shipping before being given command of the 18th Cruiser Squadron the following year. In November 1940 this force took part in Operation 'Collar', one of the early defended convoys in the Mediterranean which resulted in the inconclusive Battle of Cape Spartivento off Sardinia. Just a week before he joined *Hood* Holland had led his cruiser squadron north to Jan Mayen to capture the German weather trawler *München*. On the 7th she was surprised and boarded by the destroyer *Somali* which managed to recover cipher material of great importance to the breaking of the Enigma code. 'Len' Holland, as he was known to his friends, was part of a clique of officers, eventually headed by Dudley Pound, which monopolised many of the senior posts in the Navy from the early 1930s.[31] The Battle Cruiser Squadron was to have been his last seagoing command before he returned to the Admiralty as Pound's Vice Chief of Naval Staff in succession to Rear-Admiral Sir Tom Phillips in late 1941. He had hopes of one day becoming First Sea Lord. It was not to be.

Holland had of course little opportunity to make an impression on the ship's company. A more reserved man than Whitworth, one of the very few opinions on him to have survived is that of Lt-Cdr Roger Batley to his sister on 19 May, three days before *Hood* sailed on her last voyage:

Last night I dined with the new Admiral. I like him. We had gulls' eggs, soup, lobster & pheasant.[32]

Equally, little survives to record the atmosphere in the *Hood* as she sailed to her fate. The only source of note is Ordinary Signalman Ted Briggs' memoir of the bridge and boys' mess deck, but it is possible to imagine the preparations and emotions throughout the ship as she girded her loins for the coming battle.

Initially, however, there was nothing to indicate that this sortie would not end as inconclusively as those which had preceded it. The squadron had been ordered to refuel at Hvalfjord on 22 May before joining the heavy cruisers *Norfolk* and *Suffolk* on patrol in the Denmark Strait. Routine range and inclination exercises were performed during the forenoon and then the afternoon watches of the 22nd. The crew viewed the chances of encountering the enemy on this their fifteenth war patrol since returning from Gibraltar the previous summer with some scepticism. The *Hood*, after all, had not laid eyes on an Axis man o'war since 1938. However, all this changed at around 20.30 when the Battle Cruiser Squadron was ordered to abandon its passage into Hvalfjord and make directly for its patrol line in the Denmark Strait. An RAF reconnaissance flight over Grimstadfjorden that afternoon had found the anchorage empty. Though Tovey and his staff did not know it, *Bismarck* and *Prinz Eugen* had been racing north for 24 hours. The news evidently came as something of a shock in the *Hood*:

As soon as the *Hood* had altered course in accordance with the [20.30] signal of the C-in-C, Commander Cross updated the ship's company of the situation, and for the first time the nervous feeling of an approach to battle began to build up. 'Perhaps this is it,' I wondered. 'Perhaps this is the big one.' The feeling that I was hungry, yet did not want to eat, nagged at my stomach. Looking around me, I could see my mates yawning nervously and trying to appear unconcerned. We all knew it was an act, yet we did not discuss the possibilities of action seriously.[33]

For all this, the morning of the 23rd brought a familiar sense of anti-climax. The night had passed off uneventfully; the sun rose to the usual routine of action stations and endless vigil, of frigid watches staring into the grey unity of sea and sky. AB Robert Tilburn, manning a 4in gun on the boat deck, was clad in long johns, a vest, sweater, overalls, trousers, overcoat, duffle coat, oilskins, anti-flash gear, tin helmet, gas mask and gloves.[34] Another range and inclination exercise was held in the afternoon watch as the weather began to deteriorate. Those off duty played cards, read and wrote letters destined never to be sent as Vera Lynn echoed across the mess decks, the last woman's voice many of them would ever hear.

At 19.30 that evening this reverie was abruptly and definitively broken. Ten minutes earlier the *Suffolk*, patrolling 100 miles north-west of Iceland, sighted the *Bismarck* and *Prinz Eugen* as they began the southward leg of their passage through the Denmark Strait. From the mists enveloping him Capt. R.M. Ellis signalled 'From *Suffolk*: Enemy in sight'. A few minutes later the *Norfolk*, wearing the flag of Rear-Admiral W.F. Wake-Walker, strayed too close to the edge of the fog bank shrouding her and was immediately given a taste of the *Bismarck*'s gunnery, straddled before she could regain cover. Three hundred miles due south Holland left his admiral's bridge and installed himself on the compass platform with Capt. Kerr and his staff. At 19.39 he ordered the Battle Cruiser Squadron to work up to full speed and shape an intercepting course of 295 degrees. A little after 20.00 a signal from *Suffolk*, now shadowing by radar, confirmed that it was the *Bismarck* and her consort towards which he was heading at an aggregate speed of some 50 knots. After a day of routine the revelation that battle was again a distinct possibility had a sobering effect in the *Hood*. Nothing, not even Mers-el-Kebir, had prepared them for this impending collision. Ted Briggs:

With this sudden diversion the ship's company were alive again to the realization that deadly action could be just ten hours away. The back of my neck began to prickle with excitement, and I found myself stuttering slightly, a nervous habit which until then I had managed to conquer since the age of ten.[35]

Within an hour of the alteration of course Holland's squadron was crashing into a full gale at 27 knots, wind and water forcing *Hood* and *Prince of Wales* to train their forward turrets to port. The *Hood*, battered and riven by war, was as beautiful as ever as she steamed into her last battle. The sight offered her consorts in the hours left to her cannot have differed greatly from that recalled by the Rev. Gordon Taylor from the destroyer *Arrow* off Iceland on Easter Sunday, 13 April 1941:

31 Stephen, *The Fighting Admirals*, pp. 35 & 117.
32 HMS *Hood* Association archives. Scapa Flow, 19 May 1941.
33 Coles & Briggs, *Flagship Hood*, p. 202.
34 IWM/SA, no. 11746, reel 1.
35 Coles & Briggs, *Flagship Hood*, p. 203.

Traditionally reckoned to be the last image of *Hood* as an effective unit, taken from *Prince of Wales* during the voyage to the Denmark Strait on the afternoon or evening of 23 May. The weather has required the forward turrets of both ships to be trained to port. The relative positions of the two ships are almost identical to those they assumed as battle was joined the following morning.

I took no services that Easter Day, for the sea was too rough and the closest attention had to be paid to the *Hood* as she made flag signals to her escorts—but I watched her for hours on the *Arrow*'s bridge. As she was only about two cables (or 1200 feet) abeam away from me she was truly a magnificent sight as she drove along, zig-zagging to foil U-boats, in the green and gold sea whenever the sun came out upon her. [...] I felt unbelievably privileged to be watching her and [...] had already decided the whole experience of seeing the *Hood* that morning would be completely imperishable, and so it has proved to be for 60 years.[36]

Before long the buffeting endured by the four destroyers left in the squadron had obliged them to reduce speed to avoid structural damage. At 22.00, as the destroyer screen fell astern, a broadcast by Cdr Cross informed the men that contact with the enemy was expected at 02.00 on the 24th and that they had two hours to change into clean underwear and ready themselves before the ship went to action stations. Ted Briggs:

Apprehension was heavy in the air. I think that most of my mates, like myself, were fearing not instant oblivion but the horror of being fearfully wounded or mutilated and screaming out in painful insanity. I had the depressing dread of being afraid of fear and showing it. Yet I was not feeling afraid—just wound up. I wanted the action to be hurried on, and yet at the same time I did not want it to happen. Wouldn't I wake up tomorrow in my hammock and find it was all a mistake?[37]

His sentiments are echoed by Bob Tilburn:

Everyone was prepared as far as they could be. Everyone knew that there would be casualties, but it would be someone else, not you. No one thought that the *Hood* would be sunk. No one gave it a thought. But there would

be casualties, which were to be expected.[38]

And so the last preparations were made. The last shells fused and torpedo warheads inspected, the fire and damage-control parties mustered, the galley fires extinguished and instruments laid out in the Medical Distributing Stations. Words exchanged, bladders emptied. At midnight the bugle sounded its galvanising call over the tannoy and the men hastened to the positions from which their minds had not strayed in many hours.

Shortly after midnight Holland ordered the *Hood*'s immense battle ensign hoisted, but even as it unfurled in the wind events 120 miles to the north were eroding his tactical advantage. By 00.30 it was obvious that the *Suffolk*, the only vessel in Wake-Walker's force equipped with effective search radar, had lost contact with the enemy in a blizzard. At this Holland informed his squadron that if contact were not regained by 02.10 he would alter course to the south until such time as it had been re-established. In the event, Holland decided not to wait that long and at 02.03 he hauled *Hood* and *Prince of Wales* round onto a course of 200 degrees, the last reported heading of the German squadron. Having now caught up with the heavy ships his destroyers were ordered to continue their search to the north and played no further part in the interception. The men went down to the second degree of readiness.

Until then Holland had intended to close the *Bismarck* at speed from her port bow, a tactic which would not only shorten the range between the two squadrons in quick time but minimise the number of guns that could be brought to bear against him as he did so. By the time *Suffolk* had reported regaining contact at 02.47 and the *Hood*'s relative bearing on the enemy been determined, the *Bismarck* was 35 miles distant and steering a diverging course at 28 knots. This meant that Holland had not only 'lost bearing' on the enemy, but had no prospect of regaining it either. Rather than the end-on attack for which he had planned, any approach had now to be made on the *Bismarck*'s port beam and in the teeth of her main armament. As at Trafalgar, the Battle Cruiser Squadron would have to endure a prolonged exposure to the full weight of enemy fire before being able to bring its own broadsides to bear. Aware of the *Hood*'s vulnerability to plunging fire, on 19 May Holland had endorsed the tactics laid down by Whitworth a month earlier in the event of an encounter with the *Bismarck*, and from these he seems never to have strayed.[39] Holland's adherence to this plan despite the adverse tactical situation that now presented itself has been the subject of trenchant criticism. The outcome of the Battle of the Denmark Strait leaves no doubt how disastrous it proved to be. However, like most *a posteriori* judgements of this sort, these criticisms generally fail to embrace the wider context of Holland's decision-making. For an officer who had served during the First World War, who recalled the unbearable frustration of an unwilling and elusive enemy and the chagrin of tainted victory, there could only be one tactic against the principal unit of the new German navy. Despite Jellicoe's caution and the vague caveats of the Fighting Instructions as they applied to battlecruisers, the tradition of the Royal Navy was to bring the enemy to battle no matter what the risk or tactical disadvantage implied by it.[40] On this her matchless fighting record was built. On this, too, one of her greatest ships was to be sacrificed.

At 03.40 Holland ordered revolutions for 28 knots and

36 Taylor, *Remembrance Day Sermon*, pp. 8–9.
37 Coles & Briggs, *Flagship* Hood, p. 205.
38 HMS *Hood* Association archives, taped interview.
39 Robertson, 'HMS *Hood*: Battle-Cruiser 1916–1941', p. 165.
40 PRO, ADM 239/261, *The Fighting Instructions* (1939), §300–6.0

brought *Hood* and *Prince of Wales* onto a course of 240 degrees to force the enemy to battle. By 04.30 visibility had improved and dozens of pairs of eyes were scanning the north-western horizon where, 30 miles off, *Bismarck* and *Prinz Eugen* were steaming towards their unexpected encounter. Shortly after 05.00 Holland passed the order to 'Prepare for instant action', the men rousing themselves to the first degree of readiness. On the compass platform actors took their places for the final drama. Ted Briggs:

> In the dimness of the binnacle and chart-table lights I could make out a stage-like setting. On the starboard, facing forward, stood the robust figure of Commander E.H.G. 'Tiny' Gregson, the squadron gunnery officer, and Lieutenant-Commander G.E.M. Owens, the admiral's secretary. Alongside, centre of stage, in the captain's chair was Admiral Holland, with Captain Kerr on his right. Then on the port side were [Lt-Cdr H.D.] Wyldbore-Smith, Commander S.J.P. Warrand, the squadron navigating officer, eighteen-year-old Bill Dundas, action midshipman of the watch, Chief Yeoman [George Carn], who was attending the captain, Yeoman [George] Wright, who looked after the demands of the officer of the watch at the binnacle, and myself, who was required to attend the flag lieutenant and answer voice-pipes. All the officers, except Holland and Kerr, were huddled in duffle coats, over which was anti-flash gear, topped off by steel helmets. Some had their gas-masks slung on their chests. [...] The short, slim admiral preferred to emphasize his rank by wearing his 'bum-freezer' type of greatcoat. He sat bolt upright, with his binoculars' strap around his neck, his fingers somewhat nervously tapping the glasses themselves.[41]

Then they were upon the enemy. At 05.35 lookouts in *Hood* and *Prince of Wales* sighted the German squadron at a range of approximately 38,000 yards. Ted Briggs:

> The sighting was reported by voice-pipe from the spotting-top as 'Alarm starboard green 40.' I did not have any binoculars, so I could not see the top-masts, which everyone else was focusing on, but the maximum visibility from our perch was seventeen miles at this time. Almost in a whisper Captain Kerr commanded: 'Pilot, make the enemy report.'[42]

Holland's force was sighted almost simultaneously by the German ships but its presence was already suspected. At 05.15 hydrophone operators in *Prinz Eugen* had detected the sound of high-performance turbines to the south-east and it was on this horizon that two columns of smoke were spotted in the cold light of morning. At 05.37 Holland ordered a 40-degree turn to starboard which placed Lütjens' force broadside on and fine on his starboard bow. And so the *Hood* screamed into battle at almost 29 knots. Twenty degrees off her starboard quarter lay *Prince of Wales* at a distance of four cables (800 yards). To Kapitänleutnant Burkard von Müllenheim-Rechberg, surveying the spectacle from *Bismarck*'s after gunnery control position, the squadron looked like 'an enraged bull charging without knowing what he's up against'.[43]

Waiting to be hoisted from the *Hood*'s flag deck was Flag 5,

the order to *Prince of Wales* to open fire. Shortly after leaving Scapa on the 22nd Holland signalled Capt. John Leach of the *Prince of Wales* what his gunnery tactics would be:

> If the enemy is encountered and concentration of fire required, the policy will be G.I.C. (individual ship control); if ships are spread when enemy is met they are to be prepared to flank mark as described in H.W.C.O. 26.[44]

Translated, these instructions called for *Hood* and *Prince of Wales* to concentrate their fire on *Bismarck* while the now-absent escorts positioned themselves to provide corrections for gunnery range and deflection. This decision was confirmed in a second signal at 00.30 on the 24th which also stated Holland's intention that *Norfolk* and *Suffolk* should engage *Prinz Eugen*. In the event, neither aspect of Holland's plan came to fruition. Radio silence prevented the orders being transmitted to *Norfolk* and *Suffolk*, which consequently took no part in the battle. Moreover, in requiring *Prince of Wales* to maintain such close order Holland not only denied Leach the freedom to manoeuvre his ship but made it possible for the Germans to find his range with a minimum of targeting adjustment after *Hood* was lost. The first circumstance was probably inevitable; the second rather less so.

But this lay in the future. At 05.49 Holland ordered a further turn of 20 degrees to starboard to close the range once more. A minute later he ordered concentration on the leading ship in the German squadron. This was not *Bismarck* but *Prinz Eugen*

41 Coles & Briggs, *Flagship* Hood, pp. 205–6. Dundas had joined the ship on 6 January 1941.
42 Ibid., p. 210. 'Pilot', the Navy nickname for a navigator, here refers to Cdr S.J.P. Warrand.
43 Von Müllenheim-Rechberg, *Battleship* Bismarck, 2nd edn, p. 137.
44 PRO, ADM 116/4352, p. 392, Captain J.C. Leach, 'Narrative of Operations against *Bismarck*', 29 May 1941.

Sketch map of the Battle of the Denmark Strait, 24 May 1941. Courses, times, ranges and relative positions approximate.

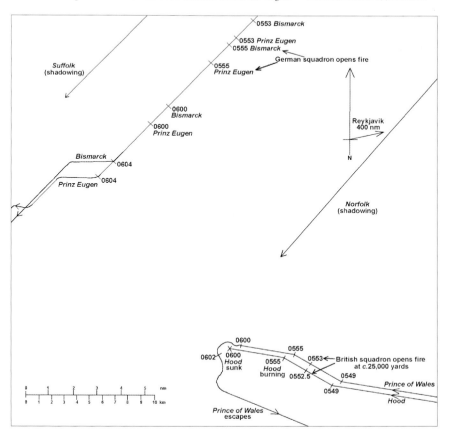

The *Hood*'s forward turrets and bridge structure seen from the forecastle in April 1941. The Type 284 gunnery radar fitted at Rosyth a month or so earlier is visible on the aloft director. Though operational it is not known to have been used in the Denmark Strait. Beneath the spotting top the Torpedo lookout platform has been dismantled. The UP launcher on 'B' turret is hidden under canvas. The two forward Mk III HACS directors can be seen on either side of 'B' turret and the two forward UP mountings (similarly wrapped in canvas) on either side of 'A' turret. The compass platform from which Briggs and Dundas escaped is the glazed structure above the armoured director. Tilburn sheltered beside Port No. 1 UP launcher and got clear of the ship from the forecastle just forward of it.

which Lütjens had ordered into the van after his flagship's radar had broken down while engaging *Norfolk* the previous evening. The error was immediately spotted in *Prince of Wales* and fire redistributed accordingly, but it was against *Prinz Eugen* that *Hood*'s forward guns now trained with an awe-inspiring rumble. None would survive from the *Hood*'s turrets but the following passage by Admiral of the Fleet Sir Henry Leach, turret officer in *Duke of York* at the Battle of North Cape, gives an impression of the atmosphere as their crews went into action:

> Then came the long-awaited order 'All positions stand to!' In an instant, tiredness, cold and seasickness were shed and all hands became poised for their individual tasks. 'Follow Director', and the huge turret swung round in line with the Director Control Tower. 'All guns load with armour-piercing and full-charge—load, load, *load*!'; the clatter of hoists as they brought the shells and cordite charges from the magazines, the rattle of rammers as they drove them into the chambers of the guns and the slam of the breeches as they closed were music to all. Then a great stillness for seemingly endless minutes, disturbed only by the squelch of hydraulics as layers and trainers followed the pointers in the receivers from the Director. 'Broadsides!', and the interceptors, connecting the firing circuits right up to the Director Layer's trigger, were closed; a glance at the range receiver whose counters were steadily, inexorably, ticking down…[45]

Then the ticking stopped. At 05.52 *Hood* fired her opening

salvo against *Prinz Eugen* at a range of 25,000 yards. *Prince of Wales* followed against *Bismarck* a few seconds later.

Elsewhere in the ship the moment of firing doubtless came as an intense, almost exquisite release of nervous tension. Years later, Ted Briggs recalled casting his mind over the ship and her crew as she went into action:

> I could visualize how the mates I knew in other departments would be preparing. Ron Bell was on the flag deck at the other end of the voice-pipe I was manning. His voice did not betray any signs of funk, as I was sure mine did. Near him would be [Frank] Tuxworth, helping to handle the halyards and still joking, no doubt. Alongside in charge of the flags I guessed that Yeoman Bill Nevett would be as outwardly calm as ever, despite the pallor of his face. On the boat deck I knew another mate, Petty Officer Stan Boardman, would be readying the crew of [Sammy], the starboard multiple pom-pom. Would he be thinking of his adored wife and his newly born baby or would he be questioning what on earth he could do with his anti-aircraft guns against the *Bismarck*'s fifteen-inchers? And what of the sick-bay, where I had spent the first few days of my life in the ship? There the 'tiffies' under Surgeon Commander [Henry] Hurst and Sick-Bay Petty Officer [George] Stannard would be sterilizing operating instruments, laying out blankets, making sure bandages were handy.[46]

In the damage-control centre the First Lieutenant Lt-Cdr John Machin awaited the first call on his organisation. Standing by to repair damaged circuitry or perhaps on duty in the high-power switchboard room for which he was responsible was the ship's electrical engineer, Lt John Iago. Not far away the Marine bandsmen chased pointers and wound wheels in the Transmitting Station as the *Hood*'s guns struggled to find the range. There was ERA Bertie Hemmings, immured perhaps in his workshop, and OD Philip X and Boy Bill Crawford in ammo supply somewhere, listening as the Rev. Patrick Stewart broadcast what Briggs remembered as a 'very calm, matter-of-fact running commentary' of events over the tannoy.[47] Further below, in spaces Stewart's voice would never penetrate, Sub-Lt (E) John Cambridge, late of the Yarrow Co., Glasgow, tended the ship's boiler rooms in an inferno of heat and hell of noise. Then there was the 'Chief' himself, Cdr (E) Terence Grogan, performing a miracle of naval engineering from the control platform of the Forward Engine Room. To this miracle the speed of his ship and the efforts of her consort to keep pace bear witness. Vice-Admiral Sir Louis Le Bailly (1932–3, 1937–9):

> I shall always hope that, just as he died, he became aware that the brand-new HMS *Prince of Wales* was having difficulty in keeping up with her twenty-year-old flagship as Grogan drove *Hood* into her last battle.[48]

Like much else during her last minutes, the number and placing of the *Hood*'s salvoes is a matter for conjecture.[49] AB Bob Tilburn recalled six salvoes from the forward turrets and Ted Briggs at least one from 'X' turret but the actual numbers may never be established. It seems likely that she did indeed redirect her fire from *Prinz Eugen* to *Bismarck* but at what stage and to what effect is not known for certain. Holland had pro-

45 Cited in Winton, *Death of the Scharnhorst*, p. 183. The only major difference between the *Duke of York* and the *Hood* in this description is broadside firing, which the Royal Navy employed in night actions; the *Hood* began with salvo firing. Admiral Leach is the son of Capt. John Leach of the *Prince of Wales*.
46 Coles & Briggs, *Flagship* Hood, p. 209.
47 IWM/SA, no. 10751, reel 2.
48 CAC, LEBY 1/2, MS of *The Man Around the Engine*, ch. 12, p. 9.
49 The chronology followed in this account is based on the frequently updated distillation of research provided in Paul Bevand & Frank Allen, 'The Pursuit of *Bismarck* and the Sinking of H.M.S. *Hood*' on www.hmshood.com, to which acknowledgement is hereby made.

hibited the use of radar during the approach to battle but it must be supposed that *Hood*'s Type 284 gunnery set was in action by the time she opened fire. What is certain is that none of her shells registered on their targets. The reasons for this are not far to seek. Not only had her firepower been reduced by half by the angle of approach, but the turret rangefinders were being drenched in spray as she thundered into a head sea at 29 knots, the speed at which vibration in the spotting top became 'excessive'.[50] Gunnery conditions that morning closely matched those recorded by Capt. Pridham in the spring of 1938 and the pneumatic cleaning apparatus attached to the rangefinder windows is unlikely to have coped with the deluge.[51] The 15-foot rangefinder in the aloft director had been removed in 1940 so accuracy must therefore have rested on the 30-foot rangefinder in the armoured director, such information as may have been provided by radar and the *Hood*'s inadequate Mk V Dreyer Table. In view of the conditions, the probable need to shift target and the high rate of change of range as *Hood* closed the enemy, her failure to land a hit is not to be wondered at.

No such difficulty faced *Bismarck* and *Prinz Eugen* and the Battle of the Denmark Strait would provide a further demonstration of the lethal accuracy of German gunnery. After a brief delay the German squadron took *Hood* under fire against the morning horizon. Soon their shells were screaming in 'like an express train going through a tunnel'.[52] *Bismarck*'s first salvo, unleashed at 05.55, fell just wide. Her second straddled, the *Hood* pressing on between towering geysers of water. But it was *Prinz Eugen* which drew first blood. A shell from her second salvo struck *Hood* on the boat deck, the Rev. Stewart calmly informing the crew that 'That sound you heard was *Hood* being hit at the base of the mainmast'. As Briggs recalled, the blast sent those on the compass platform sprawling over the deck:

> Then I was flung off my feet. My ears were ringing as if I had been in the striking-chamber of Big Ben. I picked myself up, thinking I had made a complete fool of myself, but everyone else on the compass platform was also scrambling to his feet. [Cdr (G) E.H.G.] 'Tiny' Gregson walked almost sedately out to the starboard wing of the platform to find out what had happened.[53]

When he returned it was to inform Holland that 'She has hit us on the boat deck and there is a fire in the ready-use lockers'.[54] Etched on Briggs' memory was the grin on Gregson's face as he uttered these words, the grim satisfaction of the fighting officer whose ship was at last to win her spurs. If so, the sensation was a fleeting one because *Hood*'s agony had already begun. *Prinz Eugen*'s shell had started an uncontrollable fire among dozens of ready-use lockers for 4in and UP ammunition which soon began to take a terrible toll of the boat-deck personnel. Mindful of Oran, orders had been passed for the gun crews to take cover in the lobby beneath the bridge structure when action commenced and it was here, between the Reading Room and the dental surgery, that many gathered.[55]

One of those who stayed behind was AB Bob Tilburn, a member of the crew serving Port No. 1 gun abreast the after funnel. As the ammunition began detonating PO Edward Bishop came aft and ordered Tilburn and two others to help put it out, to which they wisely told him 'When it stops exploding, we will'.[56] However, others were spotted from *Prince of Wales* making futile efforts to control the blaze with deck hoses.[57] The same wind that was dousing the *Hood*'s rangefind-

50 Northcott, *HMS* Hood, p. 14.
51 See ch. 2, p. 52.
52 IWM/SA, no. 10751, reel 2.
53 Coles & Briggs, *Flagship* Hood, p. 214.
54 PRO, ADM 116/4351, p. 364.
55 IWM/SA, no. 11746, reel 1.
56 Arthur (ed), *The Navy: 1939 to the Present Day*, p. 91.
57 PRO, ADM 116/4351, p. 251.

Bismarck silhouetted by her own gunfire during the Battle of the Denmark Strait.

The port side of the boat deck seen from the level of the after air-defence position in the autumn of 1940. All three port-side 4in mountings can be made out. It was in this cluttered space that ready-use ammunition caused an uncontrollable fire during *Hood*'s last minutes.

[58] Mr James Gordon, conversation with the author, 5 January 2004.
[59] PRO, ADM 116/4351, p. 148.
[60] Arthur (ed), *The Navy: 1939 to the Present Day*, p. 91. It should be noted that the incident related by Tilburn is corroborated in no other known source though a hit in this position was recorded by Flight Lt R.J. Vaughn in a Sunderland flying boat of 201 Squadron; PRO, AIR 15/415. I am grateful to Frank Allen for drawing this point to my attention.
[61] Coles & Briggs, *Flagship* Hood, pp. 214–5.
[62] Ibid., p. 215.
[63] PRO, ADM 116/4351, p. 198.

ers with spray fanned this fire into an enormous conflagration that swept back over the roof of 'X' turret, pulsating in a lurid pinkish flame as ammunition went off like fire crackers.[58] Rear-Admiral Wake-Walker describes the scene from *Norfolk*, 30,000 yards off:

I can describe it best as a brilliant rose colour with no yellow or white in it. [...] This was at the time the fire first appeared in the *Hood*. [...] I watched this fire and it then spread forward until its length was greater than its height and after a time it died down, particularly at the forward end. I thought that they may be able to get this fire under. Previous to this I had been so impressed by the fire that [I thought] the ship would not continue as a fighting unit.[59]

But much worse was to come. No sooner had Bishop returned to the bridge structure to report the matter to an officer than a shell landed inside making a terrible execution of the 200 men sheltering there, a massacre only Tilburn lived to relate.[60]

Up on the compass platform this carnage unfolded not in the eyes but in the ears of those present. Ted Briggs:

Then came a crazy cacophony of wild cries of 'Fire' through the voice-pipes and telephones. On the amidships boat deck a fierce blaze flared. This was punctuated by loud explosions. The torpedo officer [Lt-Cdr Anthony Pares] reported by phone: 'The four-inch ready-use ammunition is exploding.' I could hear the UP rockets going up, just as they had roared off accidentally in Gibraltar a year earlier. Fear gripped my intestines again as agonized screams of the wounded and dying emitted from the voice-pipes. The screeching turned my blood almost to ice. [...] But the bursting projectiles were making a charnel-house of positions above the upper deck. The screams of the maimed kept up a strident chorus through the voice-pipes and from the flag deck. I was certain I heard my 'oppo' Ron Bell shouting for help.[61]

Echoing the assessment of Tilburn and his companions, Holland ordered the fire on the boat deck to be left to burn until the ammunition had been expended. He had, in any case, far more pressing concerns than this. The *Hood* was being hammered and the moment when the squadron's full weight of fire was brought to bear could not be delayed much longer. At about 05.55 Holland passed the order for a 20-degree turn to port to open the 'A' arcs of 'X' and 'Y' turrets. Ted Briggs:

'Turn twenty degrees to port together,' he commanded. Chief Yeoman [Carn] passed the word on to the flag deck, where surprisingly someone still seemed to be capable of obeying orders. Two blue—flag 2, a blue pendant—went up the yard-arm. I remember musing: 'Not everyone on the flag deck is dead then.'[62]

On came the *Hood*, shells raining down as her after turrets strained against the stops to find bearing on the enemy. His approach completed, at approximately 06.00 Holland ordered another 20-degree turn to port. It was just seven or eight minutes since she had opened fire. Until now Holland and his officers had followed the progress of the battle with the steely composure of their forebears, outwardly unperturbed by the havoc being wreaked on their ship. But this detachment was not to last. Even as the *Hood* began to execute her turn a shell from *Bismarck*'s fifth salvo was hurtling in from about 16,000 yards. With it came the mortal hit. Capt. John Leach of *Prince of Wales*:

I happened to be looking at *Hood* at the moment when a salvo arrived and it appeared to be across the ship somewhere about the mainmast. In that salvo there were, I think, two shots short and one over, but it may have been the other way round. But I formed the impression at the time that something had arrived on board *Hood* in a position just before the mainmast and slightly to starboard. It was not a very definite impression that I had, but it was sufficiently definite to make me look at *Hood* for a further period. I in fact wondered what the result was going to be, and between one and two seconds after I formed that impression an explosion took place in the *Hood* which appeared to me to come from very much the same position in the ship. There was a very fierce upward rush of flame the shape of a funnel, rather a thin funnel, and almost instantaneously the ship was enveloped in smoke from one end to the other.[63]

For Ted Briggs, time, which had been passing with agonising slowness, seemed now to stop altogether:

> As the *Hood* turned, X turret roared in approval, but its Y twin stayed silent. And then a blinding flash swept around the outside of the compass platform. Again I found myself being lifted off my feet and dumped head first on the deck. This time, when I got up with the others, the scene was different. Everything was cold and unreal. The ship which had been a haven for me for the last two years was suddenly hostile.[64]

Bob Tilburn and his companions were face down in the lee of the port forward UP launcher when *Hood* received her death blow:

> The next shell came aft and the ship shook like mad. I was next to the gun shield, so I was protected from the blast, but one of my mates was killed and the other had his side cut open by a splinter. It opened him up like a butcher and all his innards were coming out.[65]

This shell or another from the same salvo seems to have passed through the spotting top because the boat deck was now showered with debris and body parts from the upper reaches of the bridge structure. Tilburn, struck on his legs by a torso, turned to vomit excruciatingly over the side.

Back on the bridge there was a fleeting air of normalcy before the enormity of what had taken place set in:

> After the initial jarring she listed slowly, almost hesitatingly, to starboard. She stopped after about ten degrees, when I heard the helmsman's voice shouting up the voice-pipe to the officer of the watch: 'Steering's gone, sir.' The reply of 'Very good' showed no signs of animation or agitation. Immediately Kerr ordered: 'Change over to emergency steering.' Although the *Hood* had angled to starboard, there was still no concern on the compass platform. Holland was back in his chair. He looked aft towards the *Prince of Wales* and then re-trained his binoculars on the *Bismarck*. Slowly the *Hood* righted herself. 'Thank heaven for that,' I murmured to myself, only to be terrorized by her sudden, horrifying cant to port. On and on she rolled, until she reached an angle of forty-five degrees.[66]

Realising the ship was finished, those on the compass platform began to file noiselessly out of the starboard door. Only Holland and Kerr remained, the admiral broken in his chair and beside him his flag captain, struggling to keep his footing as the *Hood* capsized. Neither made the slightest effort to escape. By the time Briggs emerged from the compass platform and began to move towards the Admiral's bridge the *Hood* was almost on her beam ends. Halfway down he was washed off the ladder and into the sea. For Mid. William Dundas, who had spent the battle manning phones and voice pipes on the compass platform, the pitch of the deck prevented him reaching this exit and he was forced to kick his way through a window as the platform met the water. Though these two cannot have been more than a few yards apart their subsequent experiences differed in several important respects. As Briggs recalled from their discussions later, Dundas struck out to put distance between himself and the ship but was soon dragged under by suction as the *Hood* left the surface. Almost as quickly he was caught in a burst of escaping air and shot to the surface far enough away to make good his escape. Briggs, on the other hand, had a much more prolonged ordeal:

> This was it, I realised. But I wasn't going to give in easily. I knew that the deckhead of the compass platform was above me and that I must try to swim away from it. I managed to avoid being knocked out by the steel stanchions, but I was

[64] Coles & Briggs, *Flagship* Hood, p. 215.
[65] Arthur (ed), *The Navy: 1939 to the Present Day*, p. 91.
[66] Coles & Briggs, *Flagship* Hood, pp. 215–6.

Hood explodes at 06.00 on 24 May 1941.
U.S. Naval Historical Center

not making any progress. The suction was dragging me down. The pressure on my ears was increasing each second, and panic returned in its worse intensity. I was going to die. I struggled madly to try to heave myself up to the surface. I got nowhere. Although it seemed an eternity, I was under water for barely a minute. My lungs were bursting. I knew that I just had to breathe. I opened my lips and gulped in a mouthful of water. My tongue was forced to the back of my throat. I was not going to reach the surface. I was going to die. I was going to die. As I weakened, my resolve left me. What was the use of struggling? Panic subsided. I had heard it was nice to drown. I stopped trying to swim upwards. The water was a peaceful cradle. I was being rocked off to sleep. There was nothing I could do about it—good night, mum. Now I lay me down… I was ready to meet God. My blissful acceptance of death ended in a sudden surge beneath me, which shot me to the surface like a decanted cork in a champagne bottle. I wasn't going to die. I wasn't going to die. I trod water as I panted in great gulps of air. I was alive.[67]

On the boat deck Tilburn looked up from his retching to see the bows rising out of the water. Knowing the end had come, he immediately abandoned the UP launcher whose splinter shield had served him so well and dropped down onto the forecastle abreast the compass platform from which Briggs and Dundas were making their escape. There was not a moment to lose. The first waves were lapping onto the decking as the *Hood* began to heel over. He barely had time to strip off his battle helmet and many layers of clothing before being swept into the sea. Tilburn did his best to get clear of the ship but everywhere the speed of her destruction was outpacing the efforts of the crew to separate their destiny from hers:

I had my sea boots on and a very tight belt. I paddled around in the water and took my knife and cut my belt so I could breathe properly. Then I looked around and saw the ship was rolling over on top of me. It wasn't a shadow, it was a big mast coming over on top of me. It caught me across the back of the legs and the radio aerial wrapped around the back of my legs and started pulling me down. I still had my knife in my hands so I cut my sea boots off and shot to the surface. I looked up to see the *Hood* with her bows in the air. Then she slid under.[68]

In each of these cases the time elapsed between the fatal hit and the moment of abandoning ship seems to have been little more than a minute. Tilburn was clearly the only man in the vicinity capable of getting away, testament to the attrition of her boat-deck personnel once the *Hood* came under fire. But at least three others were seen trying to escape from the compass platform, an unnamed Officer of the Watch, Cdr Gregson and Cdr John Warrand, the Squadron Navigating Officer, who graciously gestured Briggs to pass ahead of him as they made their exit. Distinct as their experiences were, there is one aspect of their ordeal that unites the three survivors: the release of air from collapsing boilers and bulkheads which propelled them to the surface. As a result Dundas, Tilburn and Briggs all emerged on what had been the port side of the ship, some distance from her towering wreck and from each other. But for this phenom-

enon the *Hood* might have been lost with all hands.

So it was that, a little after 06.00 on the morning of 24 May, the pitiful remnants of the *Hood*'s crew found themselves adrift among the sparse wreckage of their ship in a 15–20 foot swell. The battle raged on under leaden skies. Beneath them the pride of the Royal Navy and 1,415 of her company were sinking to the bottom of the Atlantic.

'If ever a ship died in action, the *Hood* did.'[69] How was the greatest ship in the British Navy transformed from an effective fighting unit to a shattered wreck in a matter of seconds? How could she disappear from the face of the water within three minutes? For over 60 years these questions have exercised an increasingly broad spectrum of writers and readers. The opinions generated have frequently owed more to imagination than research but the raw material on which the more rational conclusions have been drawn rests principally in the transactions of the two boards of enquiry conducted in 1941, together with an increasing fund of structural and operational data and personal memoirs from both sides.[70] To these sources must now be added the preliminary findings of the expedition which discovered the wreck in 2001.[71] It is on this material and the inferences that can be drawn from it that the following paragraphs are based.

None of the survivors formed any great impression of the event which destroyed the ship beyond that she had been wrecked by a major explosion aft. The main visual evidence for that explosion comes from *Prince of Wales*, steaming 800 yards off the *Hood*'s starboard quarter. As the battle unfolded most of those on her disengaged port side could do nothing but watch the flagship trading salvoes with the enemy. Their first impressions of note centre on the boat-deck fire resulting from the hit by *Prinz Eugen* in the early stages of the action. However, the dominant memory is of the cataclysmic explosion following *Bismarck*'s fifth salvo. The result of this is not in any doubt. It ignited the 112 tons of cordite stowed in the *Hood*'s after magazines. After a brief pause an immense pillar of orange flame towered 600 feet over the ship in a roiling cloud of grey smoke. A few seconds later it was seen to collapse outwards into a funnel-like shape leaving her wreathed in a shroud of smoke. The explosion was first seen in the vicinity of the mainmast, its strength venting through the engine-room exhaust housings on the boat deck and then among the after turrets themselves, which were tossed bodily into the sea. When the smoke began to clear those in *Prince of Wales* beheld a desolate sight: some 300 feet of the after section of the *Hood* had been ravaged by the explosion. The inferno raging inside permitted Lt-Cdr A.H. Terry to distinguish the frames on her starboard side as the ship capsized, the bottom plating blown out between 'X' turret and the mainmast.[72] Waves lapped against the shattered hull. The remnants of the stern stood up briefly before breaking off together with over 200 feet of wreckage. On *Prince of Wales*' bridge Boy James Gordon found himself staring into a severed section of the ship.[73] What had been whole and intact moments earlier now lay tortured and eviscerated. On both sides the sight was more than many could bear looking at.

Hood's agony was not prolonged. As Capt. Leach related, once the quarterdeck had gone the remains of the ship settled quickly by the stern:

[67] Ibid., pp. 216–7.
[68] Arthur (ed), *The Navy: 1939 to the Present Day*, p. 91.
[69] Bradford, *The Mighty* Hood, p. 184.
[70] The conclusions and transcripts (second board only) of the boards of enquiry are in PRO, ADM 116/4351 & 4352. The war diary of the *Prinz Eugen* and reports of her officers are available on www.kbismarck.com. The major technical analysis is W.J. Jurens, 'The Loss of H.M.S. *Hood*—A Re-examination' in *Warship International*, 24 (1987), no. 2, pp. 122–61.
[71] See William Jurens et al., 'A Marine Forensic Analysis of HMS *Hood* and DKM *Bismarck*' in *Transactions of the Society of Naval Architects and Marine Engineers*, 110 (2002), pp. 115–53.
[72] PRO, ADM 116/4351, p. 40
[73] Conversation with the author, 5 January 2004.

I formed the impression that the gunwale of the *Hood* was just showing outside the cloud of smoke and quite a short distance above the water, I should say about two to three feet.[74]

By the time Tilburn got away the funnels were completely awash. Having heeled seven or eight degrees to starboard with the concussion of the explosion, the *Hood* righted herself before assuming the movement to port from which she never recovered. Soon her bows began to rise in response to the flooding of the stern, the dual motion causing her to pivot round on her axis as she subsided into the depths. The final plunge brought her bows up almost perpendicular, some 250 feet of the ship standing clear of the water. Then the end came, her bows pointing heavenward, the barrels of 'B' turret slumped hard over and the waves creaming over her hull one last time. To a German observer the spectacle seemed 'like the spire of a great cathedral'.[75]

The speed with which the *Hood* sank—under three minutes—can be accounted for by the enormous damage inflicted on her hull and internal structures and the flooding of her engine spaces. The extent of this damage was revealed when the upturned midsection of the ship was found in 2001. With this discovery the full magnitude of the disaster that had befallen her became apparent. What, though, was the ultimate cause and process of that event? This the boards of enquiry which followed the loss of the *Hood* were above all concerned to establish. Not only was the matter of the gravest importance to the Navy but there were lessons to be drawn for the design and fitting out of its heavy ships; lessons, it was felt, that should have been learnt after Jutland. The sense of dismay is captured in the letter the First Sea Lord, Admiral of the Fleet Sir Dudley Pound, sent to the Controller of the Navy, Vice-Admiral Bruce Fraser, on 28th May:

> Now, after the lapse of 25 years, we have the first close action between one of our capital ships and that of the Germans since the Battle of Jutland and the *Hood* has been destroyed in what appears to the onlooker to be exactly the same manner as the *Queen Mary*, *Indefatigable* and *Invincible*, in spite of the action which was taken subsequent to Jutland to prevent further ships being destroyed as a result of 'flash'.[76]

No one who witnessed the loss of the *Hood* could have had any doubt that it was the detonation of her after magazines that destroyed her. The question, both then and now, was quite how this had occurred. The first board convened under the presidency of Vice-Admiral Sir Geoffrey Blake (who had flown his flag in *Hood* from 1936–7) on 30 May and submitted its report just three days later. It determined that one or more shells from *Bismarck* had landed in the vicinity of the main-mast and reached the *Hood*'s 4in magazines, which had been doubled in size in 1939–40. The explosion of these had in turn brought on the detonation of the 15in magazines. Though this finding was subsequently endorsed, the enquiry had taken no technical advice, left no minutes, and limited its interviews to a handful of officers; of *Hood*'s survivors only Mid. Dundas had been called. Above all, it had summarily dismissed what many influential commentators regarded as a likely cause of

the explosion: the detonation of the upper-deck torpedoes. A second board had therefore to be convened under the presidency of the *Hood*'s last peacetime captain, Rear-Admiral H.T.C. Walker. This began by taking evidence from 176 witnesses to the sinking while advice was solicited from a range of former officers and technical experts. The first interviews were held in the cruiser *Devonshire* on 12 August, continuing the following day in the *Suffolk*. The sessions were completed at Dorland House in London between 27 August and 5 September, to which both Tilburn and Briggs were summoned. Dundas was not able to attend but evidence gathered from the survivors of the *Bismarck* was taken into consideration. Throughout the proceedings the board took pains to establish whether or not the boat-deck fire and the ship's torpedo armament had any bearing on her loss. Its conclusions, submitted on 12 September 1941, were little removed from those of the first board. They read as follows:

1. That the sinking of *Hood* was due to a hit from *Bismarck*'s 15-inch shell in or adjacent to *Hood*'s 4-inch or 15-inch magazines, causing them all to explode and wreck the after part of the ship. The probability is that the 4-inch magazines exploded first.

2. There is no conclusive evidence that one or two torpedo warheads detonated or exploded simultaneously with the magazines, or at any other time, but the possibility cannot be entirely excluded. We consider that if they had done so their effect would not have been so disastrous as to cause the immediate destruction of the ship, and on the whole, we are of the opinion that they did not.

3. That the fire that was seen on *Hood*'s Boat Deck, and in which UP and/or 4-inch ammunition was certainly involved, was not the cause of her loss.[77]

Though there continue to be dissenting voices, with these conclusions a majority of expert opinion is now in essential agreement. However, although the boards established with some certainty that a shell from the *Bismarck* had brought on the detonation of the *Hood*'s after magazines, it was not possible for any determination to be made as to the trajectory of the projectile. The question, of course, turned on whether the *Hood* had been struck on the boat deck or whether penetration had occurred below the waterline. Essentially, whether it was horizontal or vertical armour that had been defeated. Both of these possibilities are consistent with the geometry of the ship, and credence was lent to the latter by the 15in shell which penetrated *Prince of Wales* below the waterline during the same action. However, in view of the highly uncertain trajectory of a shell under water this seems the less likely of the two scenarios. But, as W.J. Jurens wrote in 1987, 'The exact origin of the explosion is now, and shall probably always remain, somewhat in doubt', destined ever to remain in the limbo of conjecture.[78]

This view was borne out in the summer of 2001 when the wreck of the *Hood* was filmed by Blue Water Recoveries at a depth of approximately 9,000 feet. Lying amidst three vast debris fields were the bow and stern sections (c.165 and 125 feet respectively) and, at some remove, an upturned section of the hull some 350 feet long. Missing were approximately 225

74 PRO, ADM 116/4351, p. 198.
75 Jurens, 'The Loss of H.M.S. *Hood*', p. 137.
76 PRO, ADM 116/4351, p. 14.
77 Ibid., p. 108.
78 Jurens, 'The Loss of H.M.S. *Hood*', p. 155.

feet, corresponding to the area between 'Y' turret and the middle engine room inclusive.[79] The stern section had been seen to break away at the surface, but the real surprise of the expedition was the severed bow section, lying on its port side wrapped in anchor cable. It seems probable that the break was owed first to structural weakening when the bow rose out of the water and then to implosion damage once the ship left the surface, though arguments have been made for a major explosion in the vicinity.[80] The other revelation was the unprecedented degree of implosion damage inflicted on the hull as the *Hood* sank. This field of desolation stretching across a mile of the ocean floor yielded few reminders of the ship as a living entity. One item, however, could hardly have been more poignant: the ship's bell, on which the New Year had been tolled in on 31 December 1940.

Where the process of the explosion is concerned, one can do no better than cite the conclusion reached by Jurens in 1987. His hypothesis is based on the detonation of a 15in shell in or near the 4in magazines aft:

If this occurred, and ignition of the propellant in the magazines followed from it, then a large part of the rapidly expanding gas bubble would have taken the path of least resistance and vented into the engineering spaces immediately forward of this area. For a time the sheer inertia of *Hood*'s structure would have slowed expansion in any other direction. Once the expanding gasses had reached the engine rooms, the quickest exits to the outside would have been the series of massive exhaust vents located on the centreline immediately forward of and aft of the mainmast. These huge ducts, changing in size and shape as they rose through the ship, ended in roughly square vents 1.8 meters [each] side on the boat deck. It was as spectacular, near-vertical columns of flame from these vents near the mainmast, foreshortened to observers on surrounding ships, that the explosion first became visible. Shortly thereafter, the entire stern of the ship exploded. At the time of the blast, the Board of inquiry calculated the 'X' 15-in magazine contained about 49 tons of cordite, 'Y' magazine contained 45 tons, and the 4-in magazines contained about 18.5 tons. The uncontrolled burning of this quantity of propellant in the after magazines might have slowed briefly as the volume of the engineering spaces served as a space into which the gasses could expand, and as the vents directed much of the combustion products outboard. But although this expansion and venting could temporarily relieve the pressure, it could never be enough to prevent an explosion from eventually tearing the ship apart.[81]

But it takes a former crewman to convey the reality of this event as it engulfed his friends and smashed through passageways and messdecks long frequented and fondly remembered. Leonard Williams (1936–41):

In a tremendous flash, a split second of searing time, *Hood* was gone, rendering all our efforts null and void. After serving for four and a half years in the ship I knew every compartment, nut and bolt in her. I can almost picture the terrible scene between decks when that fatal shell struck. The gigantic sheets of golden cordite flame sweeping through the

narrow corridors and passages, incinerating everything in its path. The terrific hot blast, the bursting open of the armoured hull under the colossal pressure; and, finally, the merciful avalanche of the cold sea, cleansing the charred and riven wreck, and bringing peace to those gallant souls I knew so well. On more than one occasion I have dreamed this scene and have returned to consciousness with the thought that 'There, but for the grace of God went I.'[82]

The lack of survivors was due not only to the enormity of the explosion but the speed with which it brought on the sinking of the ship. Except for a few, sealed in compartments as yet untouched by the unfolding catastrophe, the end must have come very quickly in fire, water and displaced machinery. Only those in exposed positions had any hope of survival but the hit on the spotting top and the terrible attrition on the boat deck and in the bridge shelter had accounted for most of these when the end came. Fewer than a dozen men can have got into the water, where layers of protective clothing worn over uninflated lifejackets will not have improved their chances. Those who survived to be rescued did so by the greatest providence.

Those who see warships as pieces in an elaborate board game abstracted from the reality of combat would do well to remember the hell of destruction brought down on their crews at the hour of their death, their vessel become a storm of fire and metal, burning oil and escaping steam, of collapsing bulkheads and walls of water. As much as any ship, the *Hood* was destroyed with all the energy of her creation. One can put it no simpler.

Having reached the surface Dundas, Tilburn and Briggs each swam away from the wreck and at length selected one of the numerous three-foot square biscuit floats with which the *Hood* had been equipped during her final refit. Dundas was able to manoeuvre himself into a seated position on his but the others couldn't perform the feat of balance necessary and lay belly-down on their floats. In this way they paddled towards each other, dodging patches of oil and wreckage and looking in vain for any other survivors. Overhead a Sunderland of 201 Squadron spotted 'one large red raft and a considerable amount of wreckage amidst a huge patch of oil'.[83] Briggs and Tilburn were exhausted from their ordeal and only Dundas' encouragement prevented them succumbing to the sleep from which they might never have awoken. The first hour or so was spent singing and recounting the stories of their escape but they had drifted apart by the time *Electra*, a destroyer of Holland's escort, appeared on the scene at about 08.00. Aboard the storm-battered *Electra* the crew readied themselves for a flood of survivors which never came. Edward Taylor:

The truth slowly dawned on us as we made ready to pick up hundreds of injured and wounded men from the grey cold sea. We could not turn out our boats as they were smashed, hanging in the davits. Blankets, medical supplies, hot beverages and rum were got ready. Scrambling nets were flung over the ship's side, trailing into the water. Men were lining the side ready with hand lines, eyes straining into the greyness ahead. It was only what seemed like a matter of minutes when we broke out of a mist patch into the clear. And there it was. The place where the *Hood* had sunk.

[79] It should be noted that there is currently some doubt as to which engine room this is.
[80] The case for an explosion of the forward magazines is put in Mearns & White, Hood and Bismarck, pp. 206–7, and countered in Jurens et al., 'A Marine Forensic Analysis', p. 146.
[81] Jurens, 'The Loss of H.M.S. Hood', pp. 155–7.
[82] Williams, Gone A Long Journey, pp. 142–3.
[83] PRO, AIR 15/415.

Wreckage of all descriptions was floating on the surface. Hammocks, broken rafts, boots, clothes, caps. Of the hundreds of men we expected to see there was no sign. An awestruck moment and a shipmate next to me exclaimed 'Good Lord, she's gone with all hands.' We nosed our way slowly amongst all the pitiful remains of books, letters, photos, and other personal effects floating by and a shout went up as a man appeared clinging to a piece of flotsam a little further away. Two more were seen—one swimming, the other appeared to be on a small float. I went down the scrambling net with several other men and the water was around our knees. We hung on to the net, our arms outstretched as the first man floated alongside. Quickly we grabbed him and lifted him onto the net. Careful hands on deck reached down and hauled him up to the deck. He was wrapped in a blanket and taken forward onto the Mess deck, our ship's Doctor and sick berth attendants taking care of him. Another man had been brought in further along the ship's side and a line had been passed to the third one and he was hauled to the side and brought aboard.[84]

Ted Briggs recalls the moment of rescue:

Slowly the *Electra* approached my raft, on which I was prostrate. Then a rope sailed into the air in my direction. Although I could not feel my fingers, somehow I managed to cling on to it. A man yelled unnecessarily at me from the scrambling net: 'Don't let go of it.' I even had the heart to retort: 'You bet your bloody life I won't.' Yet I was too exhausted to haul myself in and climb the net. After nearly four hours in the sea my emotions were a mess. Tears of frustration rolled down my oil-caked cheeks again, for rescue was so close and I could not help myself. I need not have worried. Several seamen dropped into the water, and with one hand on the nets they got me alongside and manhandled me up to the bent guard-rail, which had been battered by the storm, and into the waist of the *Electra*.[85]

No bodies were to be seen. Among the few items recovered was a Marine's cap inscribed RMB/X 738, to Musician William Pike who no doubt met his death in the Transmitting Station. After a forlorn search through the wreckage the *Electra*, desperately low on fuel, turned for Reykjavik where she arrived that evening, discharging the survivors to hospital.

The destruction of the *Hood* was an awesome spectacle which caused a temporary lull in the Battle of the Denmark Strait. In the *Bismarck* astonishment turned swiftly to unbridled exultation. Kapitänleutnant von Müllenheim-Rechberg:

They just stared at one another in disbelief. Then the shock passed and the jubilation knew no bounds. Overwhelmed with joy and pride in the victory, they slapped one another on the back and shook hands. Their superiors had a hard time getting them back to work and convincing them that the battle wasn't over and that every man must continue to do his duty.[86]

In the *Prince of Wales*, by contrast, the sight was met with stunned silence. 'Not a word was said.'[87] There was, in any case, precious little opportunity for reflection. No sooner had the

Three stokers resting against one of the boat deck crutches in 1940 or 1941. Behind them is the base of the mainmast and beyond it the after superstructure with two of its 44-inch searchlights. The structure on the left is the old Secondary battery room. To the right is the port aft 0.5in machine gun and Port No. 2 4in mounting; the barrels of Port No. 3 mounting are just visible beyond.
Mrs Doreen Miller

Germans regained their composure than a storm of shellfire began to burst round *Prince of Wales* which was struck seven times in as many minutes by both *Bismarck* and *Prinz Eugen*. Among the hits was a 15in shell which passed through the compass platform killing or wounding everyone on it save Capt. Leach and the Chief Yeoman of Signals. However, the *Bismarck* was not to emerge from her moment of triumph unscathed. Despite problems with her turrets that eventually reduced her to only three operational guns, *Prince of Wales* was able to score three hits on the *Bismarck*, one putting a boiler room out of action and the other contaminating two of her oil tanks. With this the battle ended, *Prince of Wales* retiring under a smoke screen while Lütjens turned for Brest. 'Rhine Exercise' was effectively over but the Royal Navy was to have its revenge. A wrathful Admiralty summoned every unit at its disposal to prevent *Bismarck* reaching harbour. Force H was brought up from Gibraltar and convoys ruthlessly stripped of their escort. Three days after the *Hood* was sunk the *Bismarck* suffered her own calvary under the withering fire of *Rodney* and *King George V*. After a savage two-hour engagement *Bismarck* disappeared with over 2,200 of her crew.

The first indication of disaster in the Denmark Strait came in a terse signal from Rear-Admiral Wake-Walker to the Admiralty and Tovey, then at sea in *King George V*: '*Hood* blown up in position 63° 20′ N., 31° 50′ W.' This signal, made at 06.15 and classified as 'Secret' by Wake-Walker, took some time to reach its intended recipients. However, the '*Hood* sunk' signal made by *Prince of Wales* shortly after was intercepted across the Atlantic and beyond. Capt. Philip Vian was commanding the escort of convoy WS8B west of Ireland when the news reached him in the destroyer *Cossack*: 'I believe I felt no stronger emotion at any time in the war than at the moment when I read this signal.'[88] So it was throughout the Navy. In the cruiser *Hawkins* lying at Durban Paymaster Lt Keith Evans (1938–9) was one of many veterans unable to control his emotions:

84 HMS *Hood* Association archives.
85 Coles & Briggs, *Flagship* Hood, p. 221. The amount of time the survivors spent in the water seems to have been nearer two hours.
86 Von Müllenheim-Rechberg, *Battleship* Bismarck, 2nd edn, p. 144.
87 James Gordon, conversation with the author, 5 January 2004.
88 Vian, *Action this Day*, p. 56.

On that fateful day, after visiting Capetown and the Seychelles, we were coming alongside Mayden Wharf in Durban when on the tannoy of another ship (I think *Dorsetshire*) we heard the announcement 'We regret to announce that in action with the German Battleship *Bismarck* in the Denmark Strait off Greenland, H.M.S. *Hood* has been sunk, it is feared with considerable loss of life'. All hands on deck seemed to stop what they were doing for about a minute (in fact more likely several seconds). As a former shipmate I just could not comprehend that the Mighty *Hood* had gone and am not a bit ashamed to say that I began to cry.[89]

For others, grief for lost friends was tinged with a desire for revenge. Lt-Cdr George Blundell, a midshipman in the *Hood* between 1922 and 1924, was First Lieutenant of the *Nelson* off Freetown:

…The captain came on to the bridge and said 'The *Hood's* been sunk by the *Bismarck*.' I thought for a moment he was fooling. […] I felt terrible thinking of Tony (Lieut. Commander Anthony Pares…)… I can hardly believe that lovely ship is gone nor that one 15-inch shell can do such a horror. […] All I hope and pray for is that we get the *Bismarck* in revenge. It would be terrible for her to get away. Those poor fellows in *Hood*—Tony, Tiny Gregson, dear old Grogan, Tubby Crosse [*sic*]. […] It is a rotten war. What is the point of it?[90]

At the same moment the Navy was suffering terrible losses in the withdrawal from Crete. Lt-Cdr (E) Louis Le Bailly was Senior Engineer of the cruiser *Naiad*:

…When I went aft… the commander broke the near unbelievable news that *Hood* had blown up. That there was another world outside the conflict in which we were engaged was difficult enough to comprehend, that the navy should be fighting two such great sea battles, so many thousand miles apart, was almost beyond understanding; but that the ship in which I had been weaned and had come to love should have disappeared in seconds was a kick in the stomach.[91]

In the *Rodney*, escorting the troopship *Britannic* westwards across the Atlantic, news of the death of her 'chummy ship' came as a numbing blow. Her chaplain, the Rev. Kenneth Thompson, describes the atmosphere in a ship which, days hence, would exact the Navy's revenge:

We have taken some hard knocks this war, and there were others still to come, and many, for all we know, still in store. But it is doubtful if anything could equal the Captain's tragic broadcast that the *Hood* had been sunk with very few survivors, and that the *Prince of Wales* had been hit and forced to break off the engagement. It is difficult adequately to describe the gloom that existed; food went untouched in most messes, and many men, especially those who had served in the *Hood*, went about their work in a daze. For a time one of the chiefs cheered his mess with the suggestion that perhaps the signal had been misread, but that consolation was very quickly

removed. The *Hood* had indeed been lost, together with most of her ship's company.[92]

Others knew of the action before they learnt its outcome. Two hundred and fifty miles to the south-east stokers in the steamer *Zouave*, sailing in convoy SC31, picked up the reverberations of a distant battle. On the bridge Capt. William Cambridge was losing his son John in one of *Hood's* boiler rooms.[93]

In Berlin Goebbels crowed triumphantly at the news. At the Admiralty, meanwhile, it was received with a mixture of shock and stoicism. Civil Service Telegraphist Gladys Wilkin was on duty in the Admiralty Signals Department on what had been a heavy night of bombing:

The Signals Department was situated beneath Admiralty Arch; roughly beneath the left hand pillar looking down the Mall. […] On the night of 24th May 1941 there was a particularly bad air raid on London and a direct hit struck the above mentioned pillar, killing a dispatch rider standing beside his motor-cycle at that spot and damaging a portion of the Signals Department below. Now, it just so happened that at that particular time several members of the Signals staff were either at rest, supper, off sick or just not on duty. There was not terribly much 'traffic' that night and I was working two positions. On one position I received the signal that H.M.S. *Hood* had been sunk; this was marked 'MOST SECRET' and needed to be handed immediately to the Officer in Charge. I was shocked, stunned and unhappy. For another reason also. One of the telegraphists with whom I was particularly friendly at this time was a girl we all called 'Len' because her surname was Leonard. […] Her fiancé was a member of the crew of the *Hood* and when she came back from supper I was unable to tell her of the signal because of its classification. Naturally, she learned eventually when lists of the casualties began coming in.[94]

Though no less of a shock, for any aware of the *Hood's* design the news came as no particular surprise. Capt. William Davis, a Deputy Director of Operations at the Admiralty, had been *Hood's* Executive Officer until September 1940:

The loss of the *Hood* was a tremendous shock to all of us, and especially to me as her last Commander, but I certainly knew of her extreme vulnerability to 15 inch fire with only 3 inches of mild steel armour protection over her magazines. […] The *Hood's* destruction was unlucky, but to me not unexpected for she was not fit to take on modern 15 inch gunfire.[95]

Luck was one of the themes of the communiqué released by the Admiralty later that day. At nine p.m. on the 24th the country at large was made aware of the disaster in a BBC radio broadcast:

British naval forces intercepted early this morning, off the coast of Greenland, German naval forces, including the battleship *Bismarck*. The enemy were attacked, and during the ensuing action H.M.S. *Hood* (Captain R. Kerr, C.B.E., R.N.), wearing the flag of Vice-Admiral L.E. Holland, C.B., received an unlucky hit in a magazine and blew up. The

89 HMS *Hood* Association archives.
90 IWM, 90/38/1, diary entries for 24 & 25 May 1941, vol. II, p. 63. Cdr W.K.R. Cross was the *Hood's* Executive Officer.
91 Le Bailly, *The Man Around the Engine*, p. 83.
92 Thompson, *H.M.S. Rodney at War*, pp. 40–1.
93 I am grateful to Mr Peter Cambridge for drawing this circumstance to my attention.
94 Miss E.G. Wilkin, letter to the author, 6 December 2003.
95 CAC, ROSK, file 4/7 'Note by Admiral Sir William Davis', pp. 5–6.

Bismarck has received damage, and the pursuit of the enemy continues. It is feared there will be few survivors from H.M.S. *Hood*.

The news was received with utter disbelief. OD James Edwards (1933–4):

> I was in a pub and had just ordered a pint of beer when the news came over the radio and the pub went totally quiet. I looked at my pint and could no longer face it, so I walked out, leaving it untouched on the bar. I had lost friends and companions but above all I had lost the beautiful ship which gave me my first real sea-going experience and I felt shattered.[96]

OD Howard Spence, part of the last draft to leave the ship before she sailed against the *Bismarck*, got home just as the news was breaking:

> I arrived home at Portsmouth by 24th May 1941 and heard a radio announcement that HMS somethingorother had been sunk—we could not catch a name, but I had a presentiment that it was the *Hood*, and this was confirmed the next day. A telegram arrived for my parents and I took it from the telegraph boy: 'Regret your son missing, presumed killed.' A further telegram arrived dated 29th May 1941: 'Your son not on board, regret anxiety caused.'[97]

But most relatives had no such reprieve and for them life would never be the same again. Some, indeed, suffered a double tragedy. At least four pairs of brothers were lost in the *Hood*, including George and Arthur Brewer of Newfoundland. For Portsmouth, heavily blitzed since 1940, the loss of its greatest ship together with virtually her entire crew was almost beyond endurance. Sheila Harris, just five at the time, recalls the atmosphere:

> H.M.S. *Hood* and its loss became the topic of conversation that permeated everything. I can only describe the atmosphere now when I look back as that of a pall of shock and misery descending on the city and its environs. Every conversation wherever people gathered was constantly punctuated by the word '*Hood*'.[98]

Nor was Portsmouth the only city to grieve. In their undemonstrative way the people of Glasgow also mourned the loss of 'oor ship'. On 30 May, Sir Stephen Pigott, Managing Director of John Brown & Co., submitted the following in his report to the Board of Directors:

> The loss of this great Clydebank-built ship has caused genuine depression and regrets with all at Clydebank, and through the medium of the shop stewards we are endeavouring to exhort the workers to give expression to their feeling by increased effort on the work in progress… A letter expressing sympathy and regret at the loss of HMS *Hood* has been sent to the Controller of the Navy.[99]

Before the 24th was over one of the ladies entrusted with the task of maintaining the Admiralty's warship index made a final entry on the *Hood*'s card: 'At 06.35 today blew up and

sank in action in the Denmark Strait.'[100] That evening Churchill descended to the parlour at 10 Downing Street in a sombre mood. The *Hood* had been destroyed and the *Bismarck* was at large in the Atlantic:

> [Vic Oliver, his son-in-law] wrote of an evening in 1941 when Churchill came down from his study 'looking inexpressibly grim'. Scenting there had been a disaster but knowing he would not reveal it, Mrs Churchill quietly poured him a glass of port. Oliver went to the piano and, on reflection, began Beethoven's *Appassionata* sonata. Churchill rose to his feet and thundered: 'Stop! Don't play that!' 'What's the matter?' asked Oliver. 'Don't you like it?' 'Nobody plays the *Dead March* [*sic*] in my house,' said Churchill. Knowing that Churchill was notoriously unmusical, the company laughed. Oliver turned back to the piano. 'But surely, sir, you can tell the difference between this…'—and he struck a few chords of *Appassionata*— 'and…' Before he could finish Churchill thundered again: 'Stop it! Stop it! I want no dead march, I tell you.'[101]

Ted Briggs as a Yeoman of Signals in the headquarters ship *Hilary*, c.1944. He is the last surviving member of *Hood*'s final company.
Ted Briggs

The outlook, indeed, could hardly have been grimmer. As Churchill recalled,

> The House of Commons… might be in no good temper when we met on Tuesday. […] How would they like to be told… that the *Hood* was unavenged, that several of our convoys had been cut up or even massacred, and that the *Bismarck* had got home to Germany or to a French-occupied port, that Crete was lost, and evacuation without heavy casualties doubtful?[102]

On the morning of the 27th Churchill was able to announce the sinking of the *Bismarck* to Parliament but nothing could efface the destruction of the *Hood* on, of all days, Empire Day—24 May. From a material standpoint Germany's loss had been much the greater. Her only commissioned battleship had been sunk with huge loss of life including that of the Kriegsmarine's most distinguished seagoing commander. But the *Hood* had a symbolic power out of all proportion to her value as a fighting unit and her annihilation had an effect on morale exceeded only by the fall of Singapore in February 1942. Both events raised in the minds of ordinary Britons the spectre of total defeat. And both in their different ways had far-reaching consequences for the prestige of the British Empire. But that lay in the future. For now the gleaming sword of the Navy had been unmade, never to be reforged.

So to the aftermath. In Yorkshire Applegarth School transferred its affiliation to *King George V*, the battleship that had led the final attack on the *Bismarck*. From Bubulu, Uganda, a young Jeremy Woods sent Churchill his accumulated savings of two shillings towards the construction of a replacement. Lt-Cdr Wellings had a letter to his friend Warrand returned to the U.S. embassy in London as hundreds must have found their way back to families and friends struggling to cope with their loss. In March of 1942 Canon Thomas Browne of Newmarket received from the Navy the sum of £18 7s. 2d., the balance of his son Robert's pay. The final reckoning came to 1,415 men including four Polish midshipmen and four Free French ratings; representing the Empire were men from the Australian

96 Cited in Taverner, *Hood's Legacy*, p. 119.
97 HMS *Hood* Association archives.
98 Letter to the author, 2 December 2003.
99 Cited in Johnston, *Ships for a Nation*, p. 224.
100 The actual time was of course 06.00.
101 W.F. Deedes in *The Daily Telegraph*, January 2001.
102 Churchill, *The Second World War*, III, p. 312.

(four), Canadian (three), Indian and New Zealand navies (one each), and several ratings from Newfoundland.

The loss of the *Hood* was very much present as the conflict drew to a close. There are many descriptions of Sunset, the ceremony which closed the naval day, but none more moving than Louis Le Bailly's memory of evening on 2 September 1945, the day the Second World War ended. The ship was *Duke of York* and the place Tokyo Bay:

> When Admiral Fraser arrived the Quartermaster reported 'Sunset, sir'. The 'Still' sounded. The Royal Marine Guard presented arms and the band played *The day Thou gavest Lord is ended*, interspersed with the Sunset call as only Royal Marine buglers know how. For the first time in six bitter years the White Ensign came down. Many, perhaps most, had never before savoured the magic of this moment when the busy life of a warship is hushed and the evening comes. Others of us, standing at the salute, were in tears as we remembered those who would never again see 'Colours' in the morning or hear the bugles sound 'Sunset' at dusk. I thought of all those friends in *Hood* who had come to see me off and the many many others… As the White Ensign came into the hands of our Chief Yeoman and the 'Carry on' sounded, we realised that on board all the great US ships around us every activity had stopped, their sailors facing towards the British flagship and saluting us.[103]

In the years that followed Band Corporal Wally Rees R.M., he of the effervescent trumpet, could never speak of his companions in the Transmitting Station without tears welling in his eyes. In the United States Rear-Admiral Ernest M. Eller would remember how 'Her loss hurt me deeply'.[104] For his compatriot Rear-Admiral Joseph H. Wellings, who learnt the news in the *Rodney*, shock and sadness were accompanied by a sense that things had changed for ever:

> I was shocked because the *Hood* had been the symbol of British naval supremacy for over 20 years, and saddened because of the loss of so many friends.[105]

And so the *Hood* passed into history. Her epitaph? Leonard Williams:

> It was a very long time before I got over the shock of *Hood*'s loss. As a ship's company we had been together a very long time. We had shared the joys and excitement of peace. In war we had welded ourselves into true comradeship that had weathered the Arctic gales and outshone the Mediterranean sun. As long as sea history is written, *Hood* and her gallant band of men will be remembered, and theirs will be a golden page in the book of time.[106]

WAR ORGANISATION OF THE
BRITISH RED CROSS SOCIETY AND
ORDER OF ST. JOHN OF JERUSALEM
Wounded, Missing and
Relatives Department
7, Belgrave Square, London S.W.1

18th July, 1941

Dear Mrs. Foster,
We have received your letter asking for news of your husband:-
Algernon Thomas Foster, A.B., P/JX.172627,
H.M.S. *Hood*.

I am sorry that we have no news that we can send you of your husband, and in view of the sad fact that he has been officially posted as 'missing, presumed killed', I am afraid we must not encourage you to hope too much that we shall be successful in obtaining any further information about him.

We would like to assure you, however, that should any news of him be received at any time, you will be informed immediately.

May we send you the deep sympathy of this department in your sorrow.

Yours sincerely,

Margaret Ampthill
(Chairman)
[RNM, 1999/19, unnumbered.]

WAR ORGANISATION OF THE
BRITISH RED CROSS SOCIETY AND
ORDER OF ST. JOHN OF JERUSALEM
Wounded, Missing and
Relatives Department
7, Belgrave Square, London S.W.1

17th December, 1941

Dear Mrs. Foster,
We have received your letter of December 15th with reference to your husband:
Algernon Thomas Gloster Foster, P/JX.172627, H.M.S. *Hood*.

We deeply regret that we have no further news to send you of him and in view of the fact that only three survivors, whose names have been published in the press, have been heard of, we dare not encourage you to hope that we shall ever succeed in obtaining further news of him.

Had your husband been picked up by a German U-boat, he would be a prisoner of war and his name would have been sent to us long before this by the International Red Cross Committee at Geneva whose delegates visit all prison camps and who send us the name of every prisoner as soon as he has been given his registered number and the address of his prison camp is known.

We are so sorry to write you such a discouraging letter and would like to tell you how much we feel for you in your great sorrow at the loss of your husband who gave his life gallantly for his country.

Yours sincerely,

Margaret Ampthill
(Chairman)
[RNM, 1999/19, unnumbered.]

[103] Le Bailly, *The Man Around the Engine*, pp. 125–6.
[104] Eller, *Reminiscences*, II, p. 429.
[105] NWC, Wellings, *Reminiscences*, p. 167.
[106] Williams, *Gone A Long Journey*, p. 154.

Conclusion

The bridge seen at nightfall on 20 May 1937.
HMS Hood Association/Higginson Collection

THERE IS A SPECIAL QUALITY about the battlecruiser *Hood* which resists any single definition. It has to do with her beauty and her destructive power, with her gilded years of peace and then her annihilation in war, of sinuous strength and desperate fragility. Most of all, perhaps, it has to do with the association between these elements and what she represented. The *Hood* came to symbolise two things above all: the perpetuation of the British Empire and all that the Royal Navy wished for itself. Once she had gone nothing could or would ever be quite the same again and the passage of time has only sharpened that impression. In the fifteen months that separate the destruction of the *Hood* in May 1941 and Operation 'Pedestal' in August 1942 the Royal Navy lost many of her most famous ships: the *Barham* off North Africa and *Ark Royal* off Gibraltar; *Repulse* and *Prince of Wales* off Malaya; *Hermes* in the Indian Ocean and *Eagle* in the western Mediterranean; and of course *Hood* herself at the beginning of this period together with dozens of cruisers, destroyers, submarines and escorts. Though these disasters did not alter the outcome of the war they encapsulate a loss of power and prestige from which there would be no recovery. And of these blows none fell heavier than that of *Hood*, lost with virtually her entire company in a tragedy which has come to stand for the calvary of the Royal Navy as a whole during the Second World War.

Nor is this all. For many the passing of the *Hood* represents not only the closing phase in the Royal Navy's age of greatness but also a vanished era in British industrial power. One needs to look back to the age of the great cathedrals and monasteries to find a parallel for the enormous technical and financial endeavour represented by the 'Great Naval Race' of the early twentieth century. As in the High Middle Ages, the construction of the *Hood* united the zeal, skills and energy of entire communities, and as then the scale of the enterprise reflects the confidence and vaulting ambition of her creators, to build bigger and better to an end and for a purpose greater than themselves. Despite her flaws, this circumstance makes the *Hood* as much a triumph of the shipbuilder's art and organisation as she was of naval power and administration and it must be a source of profound sadness that not one of the great British capital ships of the first half of the twentieth century has survived to mark this achievement for posterity.

There is another tragedy, too, and this is that *Hood* went ill-prepared to her moment of reckoning in the Denmark Strait. This circumstance had not only to do with unsatisfactory protection, a motley assemblage of secondary armament and the inscrutable turns of Fortuna's wheel. It was also the product of economic decline and financial parsimony, diplomatic incompetence and political upheaval; of the strategic and military failure that placed her under *Bismarck*'s guns when she might otherwise have been quietly scrapped or in the throes of reconstruction. Then there is the Battle of the Denmark Strait

itself, a particularly stark example of the dichotomy between strength and power in capital-ship design. Here, after a brief engagement between two ships of comparable armament, the *Hood* blew up with virtually her entire crew before she could land a single hit on the enemy. Over the next three days the *Bismarck* was in turn hunted down and finally battered to destruction without inflicting any significant damage on her tormentors. There are lessons to be drawn from the experience of both vessels: that what makes a ship in peace is assuredly not what makes her in war; that the power of a capital ship equates to the strength which permits her to suffer a measure of the punishment she would mete out to others; and that there is a further distinction to be drawn between what keeps a ship fighting and what keeps her from sinking. For *Bismarck* that distinction was very great; for *Hood* it was barely perceptible. Two great ships, each vulnerable in her own way.

To have witnessed the collapse of the World Trade Center on 11 September 2001 is to appreciate how a great entity many years in the making can be destroyed in the passage of a few seconds. But the tragedy is not one of structure so much as of humanity. With *Hood* as with *Bismarck*, *Arizona* and *Yamato*, it was less a ship than a community that was destroyed, the community evoked here by LS Leonard Williams (1936–41):

> Here we lived together as a giant family. We knew each other's failings and weaknesses, and liked each other in spite of them. We slept in close proximity, in swaying hammocks. We even bathed together in the communal bathrooms. In fact we lived candidly with one another, accepting the rough with the smooth. This sharing and living together forged a comradeship which one can never find in civilian life. Nor was the ship herself left out of our lives, for everything we did was for her. On our smartness, the way we dressed, in fact everything we did depended our ship's efficiency rating in the fleet. She was our constant task mistress. While we could, and often did, call her all the rough names under the sun when things went wrong, heaven help those, not of our company, who tried to do the same. This is the team spirit we miss when we leave the service, for it is something very fine. Something which, through countless ages, has scaled the highest mountains, fought and won hopeless battles...[1]

It was her men who breathed life into her, made her rich in history, character and memory from the splendours of Rio to the stygian waters of the North Atlantic. In *Hood* the notion of the warship as a tool of peaceful diplomacy reached its zenith, not only in her graceful form, speed and armament but also in the qualities of her people. The *Hood* was undeniably an engine of war, but as with the greatest weapons her career was as much about preserving life as about taking it. Of her many legacies this shall perhaps prove the most enduring.

[1] Williams, *Gone A Long Journey*, p. 141.

Appendix I Admirals, Captains, Commanders and Chaplains by Commission

Commission	Flag Officer, BCS	Commanding Officer	Executive Officer	Chaplain
1. 29 March 1920	Rear-Admiral Sir Roger B. Keyes 18 May 1920	Capt. Wilfred Tomkinson 1 January 1920	Cdr Lachlan D.I. MacKinnon May 1919	Rev. William R.F. Ryan March 1920
	Rear-Admiral Sir Walter H. Cowan 31 March 1921	Capt. Geoffrey Mackworth 31 March 1921	Cdr Richard H.O. Lane-Poole 31 March 1921	Rev. Arthur D. Gilbertson 19 April 1922
2. 15 May 1923	Rear-Admiral Sir Frederick L. Field 15 May 1923	Capt. John K. Im Thurn 15 May 1923	Cdr Francis H.W. Goolden 15 May 1923	Rev. Harold Q. Lloyd 6 June 1923
3. 7 January 1926	Rear-Admiral Cyril T.M. Fuller 30 April 1925	Capt. Harold O. Reinold 30 April 1925	Cdr Arthur J. Power 27 July 1925	Rev. G. St L. Hyde Gosselin 20 July 1925
4. 28 August 1928	Rear-Admiral Frederic C. Dreyer 21 May 1927	Capt. Wilfred F. French 21 May 1927	Cdr Douglas A. Budgen 15 July 1927	Rev. Gerald P.O. Hill 1 September 1926
Under dockyard control at Portsmouth 17 May 1929–10 March 1931		Lt-Cdr (T) W.M. Phipps-Hornby 29 April 1929 Lt-Cdr (T) J.F.W. Mudford 8 December 1930		
5. 12 May 1931	Rear-Admiral Wilfred Tomkinson 12 July 1931	Capt. Julian F.C. Patterson 27 April 1931	Cdr C.R. McCrum 9 March 1931	Rev. Archer Turner 25 April 1931
	Rear-Admiral William M. James 15 August 1932	Capt. Thomas H. Binney 15 August 1932		Rev. James C. Waters 5 January 1932
6. 30 August 1933	Rear-Admiral Sidney R. Bailey 14 August 1934	Capt. F. Thomas B. Tower 30 August 1933	Cdr Rory C. O'Conor 30 August 1933	Rev. David V. Edwards 11 August 1934
7. 8 September 1936	Vice-Admiral Geoffrey Blake 22 July 1936	Capt. A. Francis Pridham 1 February 1936	Cdr David Orr-Ewing 15 July 1936	Rev. W. Edgar Rea September 1936
	[Capt. A. Francis Pridham] 25 June 1937 (acting)			
	Vice-Admiral Andrew B. Cunningham 15 July 1937	Capt. Harold T.C. Walker 20 May 1938		
	Vice-Admiral Geoffrey Layton 22 August 1938			Rev. Thomas H. Horsfield 9 November 1938
Refitting at Portsmouth 23 January–12 August 1939		[Cdr William W. Davis] 30 January 1939 (acting)	Cdr William W. Davis 30 January 1939	
8. 2 June 1939	Rear-Admiral William J. Whitworth 1 June 1939	Capt. Irvine G. Glennie 3 May 1939		Rev. Harold Beardmore 16 June 1939
	Vice-Admiral Sir James Somerville 30 June 1940			
	Vice-Admiral William J. Whitworth 10 August 1940	Capt. Ralph Kerr 15 February–24 May 1941	Cdr William K.R. Cross 8 September 1940–24 May 1941	Rev. R.J. Patrick Stewart 27 February–24 May 1941
	Vice-Admiral Lancelot E. Holland 12–24 May 1941			

Note: Dates given are mainly those of arrival in the ship as against date of appointment. Dates of departure are often earlier than those of a successor's arrival.

Hood anchored in Cawsand Bay, *c.*1922.
Author's Collection

22–24 January Carries out gunnery practice with HMS *Warspite* and 8th Destroyer Flotilla east of North Rona.
24 January–9 February At Greenock.
9 February Departed Greenock on patrol with HMS *Warspite* and eight destroyers.
9–18 February At sea.
10 February From area west of Hebrides proceeds northwards with HMS *Warspite* and eight destroyers to cover Scandinavian convoys.
12–14 February On patrol north-west of the Shetlands.
16 February Heads east with HMS *Warspite* and seven destroyers to support the boarding of the *Altmark* if necessary.
18–19 February At Greenock.
19 February Departed Greenock with HMS *Warspite* and *Rodney* to cover convoy DN14 (Kirkwall–Scandinavia).
19–24 February At sea.
20–22 February Covers convoy DN14 from position north-east of Shetlands.
21 February From Admiralty: 'Owing to congestion in home yards it will be necessary to carry out retubing of condensers of *Hood* at Malta where she can be taken in hand about 3 March. Minimum time required for this work is 45 days. *Hood* should be sailed for Malta after *Renown* has finished giving leave.' (Order later rescinded.)
23 February Makes for the Clyde with HMS *Rodney* and eight destroyers after providing distant cover for convoy HN14.
24 February–2 March At the Clyde.
2 March Departed the Clyde with HMS *Valiant* and six destroyers to cover Norwegian convoys and Northern Patrol.
2–7 March At sea.
3 March On patrol 60 miles East of the Faeroes.
5 March With HMS *Valiant* and five destroyers including HMS *Kelly* covers convoy ON17 and ON17a from Norway.
7–14 March At Scapa Flow.
8–9 March Visited by the Rt Hon. Winston Churchill, First Lord of the Admiralty.
11 March Flag of William J. Whitworth, Rear-Admiral Commanding Battle Cruiser Squadron, transferred to HMS *Renown*.
14 March Departed Scapa Flow for Greenock.
14–15 March *En route* to Greenock escorted by three destroyers.
15–30 March At Greenock.
25 March Declared unavailable for operations in Freetown–Dakar area in view of need to retube condensers.
29 March 'Owing to political situation it has been decided that retubing of condensers of *Hood* is to take place at Devonport instead of Malta. Ship can be taken in hand now.'
30 March Departed Greenock for Plymouth.
30–31 March *En route* to Plymouth escorted by three destroyers.
31 March–27 May At Plymouth.
4 April–23 May Taken in hand for refitting, retubing of condensers, etc.
13 April Landing party of 250 Marines and Seamen from *Hood* (together with ship's howitzer) depart by train for Rosyth to participate in Operation 'Primrose', the occupation of Ålesund, Norway.
15 April Party departs Rosyth in HM sloop *Black Swan*.
17–18 April Party disembarks at Åndalsnes.
30 April–1 May Main body of landing party reembarks in HMS *Galatea* at Åndalsnes.
3 May Twenty members of expeditionary force return to *Hood*.
6 May Rest of expeditionary force (except three injured men) return to *Hood*.
27 May Departed Plymouth for Liverpool escorted by HM destroyers *Witch*, *Escort* and *Wolverine*.
27–28 May *En route* to Liverpool.
28 May–12 June At Liverpool.
28 May–12 June Taken in hand for refitting and repairs in Gladstone Dock.
11 June Boarding party from *Hood* captures Italian SS *Erica*.
12 June Departed Liverpool escorted by HMC destroyers *Skeena*, *Restigouche* and *St Laurent* to cover ANZAC Troop Convoy US3 (RMS *Queen Mary*, *Empress of Britain*, *Aquitania*, *Mauretania*, *Andes* and *Empress of Canada*) from Bay of Biscay to the Clyde.
12–16 June At sea.
14–16 June Meets convoy US3 in Bay of Biscay, escorting it to the Clyde with HMS *Argus*, *Dorsetshire*, *Shropshire*, *Cumberland* and nine destroyers.
16–18 June At Greenock.
18 June Departed Greenock escorted by HM destroyers *Fraser*, *Restigouche*, *Wanderer*, *Skeena* and *St Laurent* to join HMS *Ark Royal* 250 miles west of Malin Head and proceed to Gibraltar.
18–23 June *En route* to Gibraltar.
18 June Meets HMS *Ark Royal*.
23–26 June At Gibraltar.
26 June Departed Gibraltar towards Canary Islands with Force H including HMS *Ark Royal* and five destroyers to intercept *Richelieu*, reported sailed from Dakar, and escort her if possible to Gibraltar.
26–27 June At sea.
27 June *Hood* turns for Gibraltar after *Richelieu* reported returned to Dakar after sighting HMS *Dorsetshire*.
27–28 June At Gibraltar.
28 June Departed Gibraltar towards Canary Islands with HMS *Ark Royal* against reports, later proved incorrect, that *Richelieu* had left Dakar; returned to Gibraltar immediately.
28 June–2 July At Gibraltar.
30 June Flag of Sir James Somerville, Vice-Admiral Commanding Force H, hoisted.
2 July Departed Gibraltar with Force H—HMS *Ark Royal*, *Valiant*, *Resolution*, *Arethusa*, *Enterprise* and eleven destroyers: 8th Destroyer Flotilla (*Faulknor*, *Foxhound*, *Fearless*, *Forester*, *Foresight* and *Escort*); 13th Destroyer Flotilla (*Keppel*, *Active*, *Wrestler*, *Vidette* and *Vortigern*)—to carry out Operation 'Catapult', the neutralisation of the French fleet at Mers-el-Kebir, Algeria.
2–3 July *En route* to Mers-el-Kebir.
3–4 July Off Mers-el-Kebir.
3 July 17.55–18.04: Force H shells French fleet in harbour resulting in destruction of *Bretagne* and serious damage to *Dunkerque* and *Provence*; 18.09–18.12: shore batteries engaged; escaping *Strasbourg* pursued until 20.22; *Hood* suffers splinter damage and two slight casualties.
4 July *En route* to Gibraltar.
4 July Unsuccessfully attacked by French bombers.
4–5 July At Gibraltar.
5 July Departed Gibraltar with Force H (HMS *Ark Royal*, *Valiant*, *Arethusa*, *Enterprise* and ten destroyers) to implement Operation 'Lever', air strike against *Dunkerque* beached at Mers-el-Kebir.
5–6 July *En route* to Mers-el-Kebir area.
6 July Off Mers-el-Kebir; air strike launched from HMS *Ark Royal* 90 miles north-east of Oran.
6 July *En route* to Gibraltar.
6–8 July At Gibraltar.
8 July Departed Gibraltar with Force H—HMS *Ark Royal*, *Valiant*, *Resolution*, *Arethusa*, *Enterprise*, *Delhi* and ten destroyers: 8th Destroyer Flotilla (*Faulknor*, *Foresight*, *Fearless*, *Foxhound* and *Escort*); 13th Destroyer Flotilla (*Keppel*, *Douglas*, *Vortigern*, *Wishart* and *Watchman*)—to mount diversionary attack on Italian airfield at Cagliari, Sardinia while two convoys sail from Malta to Alexandria.
8–11 July At sea.
9 July Force H suffers high-level attack from Italian S.M.79 bombers; no damage; planned air strike against Cagliari airfield abandoned; Force H turns for Gibraltar.
11–31 July At Gibraltar.
27 July UP mounting on 'B' turret accidentally fires off 20 charges over harbour; three ratings badly burnt.
31 July Departed Gibraltar with Force H (HMS *Ark Royal*, *Valiant*, *Resolution*, *Enterprise* and nine destroyers: *Faulknor*, *Foxhound*, *Forester*, *Foresight*, *Hotspur*, *Greyhound*, *Gallant*, *Escapade*, *Encounter* and *Velox*) to carry out Operation 'Hurry', diversionary attack on Cagliari airfield while *Argus* flies off aircraft for Malta.
31 July–4 August At sea.
1 August Force H suffers high-level attack from Italian S.M.79 bombers; no damage.
2 August Escorted by *Hood*, HMS *Ark Royal* launches air strike on Cagliari airfield while HMS *Argus* flies off twelve Hurricanes for Malta from a position south-west of Sardinia; Force H turns for Gibraltar.
2–4 August *En route* to Gibraltar.
4 August Departed Gibraltar with HMS *Ark Royal*, *Valiant*, *Arethusa*, *Enterprise* and nine destroyers (including *Faulknor*, *Foresight*, *Forester*, *Foxhound* and *Escapade*) for Scapa Flow.
4–10 August *En route* to Scapa Flow.
6 August In company with HMS *Arethusa* and *Foxhound*, meets HM destroyers *Tartar*, *Bedouin* and *Punjabi*.
8–10 August Escorted to Scapa Flow by HM destroyer *Escapade*.
10–16 August At Scapa Flow.
10 August Flag of Sir James Somerville, Vice-Admiral Commanding Force H, transferred to HMS *Renown*; that of William J. Whitworth, Vice-Admiral Commanding Battle Cruiser Squadron, transferred from *Renown*.
16 August Departed Scapa Flow for Rosyth escorted by HM destroyer *Vimiera*.
16–24 August At Rosyth.
17–24 August Taken in hand for replacement of 'A' turret's left 15in gun.
24 August Departed Rosyth for Scapa Flow escorted by four destroyers.
24–25 August *En route* to Scapa Flow.
25 August–13 September At Scapa Flow.
13 September Departed Scapa Flow for Rosyth with HMS *Nelson*, *Rodney*, *Bonaventure*, *Naiad*, *Cairo* and seven destroyers against possible German invasion.
13–28 September At Rosyth.
28 September Departed Rosyth with HMS *Naiad* to intercept enemy cruiser and convoy reported off Stavanger.
28–29 September At sea.
29 September–15 October At Scapa Flow.
15 October Departed Scapa Flow with HM destroyers *Somali*, *Eskimo* and *Mashona* to cover attack by Force D (HMS *Furious*, *Berwick* and *Norfolk*) on Tromsö, Norway.
15–19 October At sea.
17 October Made for Scapa Flow in view of bad weather.
19–23 October At Scapa Flow.
23 October Departed Scapa Flow with HMS *Repulse*, *Dido*, *Phoebe* and destroyers *Matabele*, *Punjabi* and *Somali* towards Obrestad to investigate reported enemy movement.
23–24 October At sea.
24 October Made for Scapa Flow.
24–28 October At Scapa Flow.
28 October Departed Scapa Flow with HMS *Repulse*, *Furious* and six destroyers (including HMS *Eskimo*) to intercept enemy raider reported by SS *Mahout* in North Atlantic.
28–31 October At sea.
31 October–5 November At Scapa Flow.
5 November Departed Scapa Flow with HMS *Repulse* and 15th Cruiser Squadron (*Dido*, *Naiad* and *Bonaventure*) and six 'Tribal' class destroyers including HMS *Eskimo*, *Mashona*, *Matabele*, *Punjabi* and *Somali* to cover approaches to Brest and Lorient against return of *Admiral Scheer* following attack on HMS *Jervis Bay* and convoy HX84.
5–11 November At sea.
9 November Abandoned patrol area west of Land's End to refuel at Scapa Flow.
9–11 November *En route* to Scapa Flow with HMS *Phoebe*, *Naiad* and three destroyers including HMS *Eskimo* and *Sikh*.
11–23 November At Scapa Flow.
23 November Departed Scapa Flow with HM destroyers *Cossack*, *Sikh*, *Eskimo* and *Electra* to cover operations by 1st Minelaying Squadron and HMS *Aurora* and destroyers *Keppel*, *Bath* and *St Albans* in the Denmark Strait.
23–29 November At sea.
24 November Joined with 1st Minelaying Squadron and HMS *Aurora*; Direction Finding hut on mainmast gutted by fire.
25 November Off Reykjanes, Iceland.
29 November–18 December At Scapa Flow
4 December Visited by new Commander-in-Chief Home Fleet, Admiral Sir John Tovey.
11 December *Hood* inspected by Admiral Tovey.
18 December Departed Scapa Flow with for tactical exercises with HMS *Nelson*, *Repulse*, *Nigeria*, *Edinburgh*, *Manchester*, *Aurora* and numerous destroyers south-west of Faeroe Islands.
18–20 December At sea.
20–24 December At Scapa Flow.
24 December Departed Scapa Flow with HMS *Edinburgh*, *Cossack*, *Echo*, *Electra* and *Escapade* to form patrol in Iceland–Faeroes gap against passage of *Admiral Hipper*.
24–29 December At sea.
29 December–2 January 1941 At Scapa Flow.

1941

2 January Departed Scapa Flow with HM destroyers *Echo*, *Sikh*, *Electra* and *Eskimo* to cover operations by 1st Minelaying Squadron north and south of the Faeroe Islands.
2–5 January At sea.
5–11 January At Scapa Flow.
11 January Departed Scapa Flow with HMS *Repulse*, *Edinburgh*, *Birmingham* and destroyers *Somali*, *Eskimo*, *Tartar*, *Bedouin*, *Escapade* and *Eclipse* to cover two large convoys against suspected German raider.
11–13 January At sea.
13 January Off Dunnet Head; *en route* to Rosyth with HM destroyers *Echo*, *Electra* and *Keppel*.
13 January–18 March At Rosyth.
16 January–17 March Taken in hand for refit and turbine repairs.
17 January Visited by the Prime Minister, the Rt Hon. Winston Churchill
15 February Captain Ralph Kerr assumes command.
17 February Fire in Warrant Officers' galley.
6 March Visited by King George VI.

18 March Departed Rosyth to search for *Scharnhorst* and *Gneisenau* 200 miles southwest of the Faeroe Islands.
18–23 March At sea.
19 March Joined HMS *Queen Elizabeth*, *Nelson*, *London* and destroyers *Eskimo*, *Electra*, *Arrow*, *Inglefield*, *Echo* and *Eclipse* off Dunnet Head to intercept *Scharnhorst* and *Gneisenau*.
20 March Joined HMS *King George V* (Admiral Sir John Tovey, Commander-in-Chief Home Fleet) between Iceland and the Faeroe Islands.
21 March *Hood* ordered to steer south at maximum speed to intercept *Scharnhorst* and *Gneisenau*.
22–23 March *En route* to Scapa Flow with HMS *Queen Elizabeth* and four destroyers.
23–28 March At Scapa Flow.
28 March Departed Scapa Flow with HM destroyers *Escapade*, *Electra* and *Tartar* to act as ocean escort for convoy HX118 from Halifax.
28 March–6 April At sea.
28 March Diverted to western Bay of Biscay with HMS *Nigeria* and *Fiji* to

relieve Force H against breakout of *Scharnhorst* and *Gneisenau* from Brest.
4 April Relieved off Brest by HMS *King George V* and *London*.
4–6 April *En route* to Scapa Flow to refuel with HM destroyers *Escapade*, *Electra* and *Tartar*.
6 April At Scapa Flow.
6 April Departed Scapa Flow with HMS *Zulu*, *Maori* and *Arrow* to resume patrol in Bay of Biscay against breakout of *Scharnhorst* and *Gneisenau* from Brest.
6–14 April At sea.
13–14 April *En route* to Scapa Flow with HMS *Kenya* and destroyers *Cossack*, *Zulu*, *Maori* and *Arrow*.
14–18 April At Scapa Flow.
18 April Departed Scapa Flow with HMS *Kenya* and three destroyers to resume patrol off Brest.
18–21 April At sea.
19 April Altered course for Norwegian Sea following reports (later proved false) that the *Bismarck* had left Kiel and was heading north-west with two *Leipzig* class cruisers and three destroyers.

21 April Diverted to Hvalfjord, Iceland with HM destroyer *Inglefield* against breakout of *Bismarck* into Atlantic.
21–28 April At Hvalfjord.
26 April Assists in repair of HM destroyer *Scimitar*.
28 April Departed Hvalfjord on patrol with HMS *Suffolk*, *Norfolk* and destroyers *Echo*, *Active*, *Achates* and *Anthony*.
28 April–3 May At sea; provides distant cover for two convoys against surface attack.
3–4 May At Hvalfjord.
4 May Departed Hvalfjord for Scapa Flow escorted by HMS *Echo*, *Anthony* and two other destroyers.
4–6 May *En route* to Scapa Flow.
6–22 May At Scapa Flow.
8 May Flag of William J. Whitworth, Vice-Admiral Commanding Battle Cruiser Squadron, struck.
12 May Flag of Lancelot E. Holland, Vice-Admiral Commanding Battle Cruiser Squadron, hoisted.
13 May *Hood* carries out range and inclination exercises with HMS *King George V* in the Pentland Firth.

22 May Departed Scapa Flow with HMS *Prince of Wales*, *Achates*, *Antelope*, *Anthony*, *Echo*, *Electra* and *Icarus* to intercept *Bismarck* and *Prinz Eugen*, reported to have left Grimstadfjorden, Norway.
22–24 May At sea.
23 May *Bismarck* and *Prinz Eugen* sighted by HMS *Suffolk* in the Denmark Strait.
24 May 05.35 *Prinz Eugen* and *Bismarck* sighted by *Prince of Wales* in the Denmark Strait at a range of seventeen miles; 05.37 enemy sighted by *Hood*; 05.37 Holland turns his force 40° to starboard; 05.43 *Hood* signals enemy report; 05.49 *Hood* turns further 20° to starboard; 05.52.5 *Hood* opens fire on *Prinz Eugen*; c.05.53–4 *Hood* shifts fire to *Bismarck*; c.05.55 Holland turns his force 20° to port towards the enemy; c.05.55 *Hood* hit on boat deck by *Prinz Eugen*; 05.59–06.00 Holland turns his force another 20° to port; 06.00 *Hood* mortally hit by *Bismarck*'s fifth salvo while executing this turn; c.06.03 *Hood* sunk; c.08.00 three survivors rescued by HMS *Electra* and landed at Reykjavik later that day; HMS *Antelope* finds only wreckage.

Roll of Honour HMS *Hood*, 24 May 1941

Holland, Lancelot E., C.B.	Vice-Admiral, Battle Cruiser Squadron	
Kerr, Ralph, C.B.E.	Captain	
Abbott, Frederick	Marine	PO/X 4821
Abbott, Kenneth	Ordinary Coder	P/JX 251542
Ablett, Wallace A.	Marine	PO/X 328
Abrams, Robert G.	Marine	P/MX 64885
Acton, Percival C.H.	Able Seaman	P/JX 172597
Adams, Frank P.	Musician	RMB/X 546
Adams, Keith H.	Corporal, R.M.	PO/X 2029
Adams, Nigel N.	Midshipman, R.N.R.	
Adams, Victor E.	Ordinary Seaman	P/JX 158912
Adams, Victor H.	Leading Stoker	P/K 75215
Ainsworth, Frederick J.	Able Seaman	P/JX 234551
Akehurst, Rodney G.	Stoker 1st Class	P/KX 96072
Aldred, Gerald A.	Ordinary Telegraphist	P/JX 201132
Algate, Alfred K.	Canteen Assistant	NAAFI
Alger, Eric	Ordinary Seaman	P/JX 223041
Alland, Henry C.	Petty Officer	P/J 112089
Allcock, William S.	Boy 1st Class	P/JX 162068
Allen, Arthur F.J.	Leading Stoker	P/K 62900
Allen, Charles W.	Leading Seaman	P/J 101995
Allen, Edward B.	Ordinary Seaman	P/JX 227794
Allen, James E.	Stoker 1st Class	P/KX 100482
Allen, John G.	Marine	PO/X 2182
Allen, William E.S.	Able Seaman	P/JX 98121
Allott, George	Marine	PO/ 22532
Almond, Frederick	Able Seaman	P/JX 117643
Altham, Arthur	Stoker 2nd Class	P/SKX 625
Ambridge, Walter C.	Sergeant, R.M.	PO/ 22128
Ambrose, John	Able Seaman	P/J 94783
Amery, Thomas C.F.	Able Seaman	P/JX 173852
Anderson, Arthur D.	Able Seaman	P/JX 159545
Anderson, John	Chief Engine Room Artificer	P/M 5709
Anderson, Joseph M.	Ordinary Seaman	P/JX 157287
Andrews, Cecil V.	Ordinary Seaman	P/JX 197467
Annis, James E.	Stoker 1st Class	P/KX 98129
Applegarth, Richard	Leading Signalman	P/JX 131360
Appleyard, John A.F.	Ordinary Seaman	P/JX 22598
Ardley, Jack C.	Boy 1st Class	P/JX 162301
Arkinstall, John	Leading Seaman	P/JX 129315
Armstrong, John C.	Leading Stoker	P/KX 84345
Armstrong, Norman	Able Seaman	P/JX 158626
Arnold, William A.	Petty Officer Stoker	P/KX 80686
Ashley, Robert G.	Able Seaman	P/JX 173851
Assirati, Albert F.G.	Petty Officer Stoker	P/K 14731
Aston, John	*Alias of* André Blondel	
Atkins, William E.	Chief Petty Officer Steward	C/L 11409
Atkinson, John H.	Able Seaman	P/SSX 28511
Atkinson, Robert	Petty Officer Stoker	P/KX 83003
Austin, Albert G.L.	Able Seaman	P/SSX 21827
Avery, Albert G.	Able Seaman	P/JX 136464

Awdry, Charles D.	Lieutenant-Commander	
Ayling, Frank R.	Canteen Assistant	NAAFI
Ayling, Ronald	Able Seaman	P/JX 142821
Ayres, Henry D.	Ordinary Signalman	P/JX 216602
Badcock, John H.	Stoker 2nd Class	P/KX 110312
Baildon, Frank	Able Seaman	P/SSX 24371
Bailey, Frederick W.	Marine	PO/ 18832
Bailey, Leonard W.J.	Ordinary Signalman	P/JX 159501
Baines, Godfrey J.	Leading Seaman	P/JX 154089
Baker, Andrew L.	Ordinary Seaman	P/JX 212472
Baker, George E.	Leading Stoker	P/KX 67015
Baker, Kenneth A.	Petty Officer Telegraphist	P/JX 147862
Balch, Percy H.	Able Seaman	P/JX 126181
Baldwin, Kenneth E.G.	Stoker 1st Class	P/KX 103695
Baldwin, Phillip R.	Ordinary Seaman	P/JX 237431
Ball, Charles F.D.	Able Seaman	P/JX 174099
Ball, Phillip A.	Stoker 1st Class	P/KX 98122
Ball, William	Leading Stoker	P/KX 75116
Ballard, Arthur	Boy 1st Class	P/JX 164162
Balsdon, Ernest F.	Stoker 1st Class	P/KX 96073
Bamford, Anthony B.J.	Able Seaman	P/JX 157928
Banfield, Kenneth J.	Boy 1st Class	P/JX 171720
Banks, George H.	Stoker 1st Class	P/KX 100460
Banks, Sidney T.	Leading Cook (S)	P/MX 50364
Barclay, Alex C.	Leading Cook (S)	P/MX 59308
Barker, Thomas	Ordinary Seaman	P/JX 157016
Barnes, Thomas G.	Petty Officer Stoker	P/K 62197
Barnes, Walter J.	Able Seaman	P/J 54599
Barnet, William L.	Cook (O)	P/MX 63110
Barnett, Ivor G.	Stoker 2nd Class	P/KX 104186
Barrie, Walter R.	Able Seaman	P/JX 157059
Barringer, William H.	Marine	PO/X 4223
Bartley, Archibald E.T.	Signal Boatswain	
Barton, Kenneth C.F.	Petty Officer	P/JX 126991
Basham, Howard	Ordinary Seaman	P/JX 160189
Bassett, Charles G.	Petty Officer	P/JX 161546
Basstone, Jack	Marine	PO/X 100574
Batchelor, Arthur R.	Yeoman of Signals	P/J 54353
Bates, Frederick A.	Leading Seaman	P/JX 153715
Bates, Leonard A.	Marine	PO/X 1561
Bates, Reginald S.	Wireman	P/MX 78231
Batley, A. Roger T.	Lieutenant-Commander, R.N.V.R.	
Batten, Herbert W.L.	Ordinary Seaman	P/JX 158400
Battersby, Clifford	Able Seaman	P/JX 154410
Baxter, John K.	Petty Officer	P/J 112529
Baylis, Herbert J.	Ordinary Signalman	P/JX 224176
Beard, R. Alan	Marine	PO/X 3360
Beard, Thomas N.K.	Midshipman, R.C.N.	
Beardsley, Geoffrey V.	Joiner 4th Class	P/MX 58969
Belcher, Cyril S.V.	Electrical Artificer 3rd Class	P/MX 51470
Bell, Cyril K.	Ordinary Signalman	P/JX 216464
Bell, Ronald T.L.	Ordinary Signalman	P/JX 157978
Bell, William	Able Seaman, R.N.V.R.	P/CD/X 2532

Belsham, James R.	Able Seaman	P/J 93900
Bembridge, Percy A.	Ordinary Seaman	P/JX 161691
Bennett, Ernest	Marine	PO/X 3432
Bennett, Percival	Boy 1st Class	P/JX 162618
Benoist, Donald G.	Able Seaman	P/SSX 28581
Benton, Leonard	*Alias of* Leonard Goulstine	
Benwell, Ernest F.T.	Sick Berth Chief Petty Officer	P/M 36898
Beresford, Kenneth	*Alias of* Kenneth Radley	
Berner, Robert V.	Leading Writer	P/MX 60040
Betts, Robert	Stoker 1st Class	P/K 64411
Beveridge, Roy	Ordnance Artificer 4th Class	P/MX 62732
Biggenden, Walden J.	Chief Stoker	P/KX 88862
Binnie, John E.	Petty Officer Stoker	P/K 66612
Bird, Herbert G.A.	Ordnance Artificer 3rd Class	P/MX 50730
Bishop, Charles J.	Chief Stoker	P/K 49102
Bishop, Edward J.P.	Petty Officer (Pensioner)	P/JX 151111
Bispham, Leslie W.	Ordinary Seaman	P/JX 157878
Biss, John	Able Seaman	P/JX 135430
Blake, Harold G.	Leading Stoker	P/KX 81252
Blann, Kenneth A.F.	Able Seaman	P/JX 159936
Bleach, Arthur B.	Able Seaman	P/SSX 24656
Blondel, André	Electrical Artificer 4th Class	P/MX 72194
Bloodworth, Herbert W.	Able Seaman	P/JX 172182
Blow, Leonard	Ordinary Seaman	P/JX 158632
Blunt, William H.T.	Leading Cook (S)	D/MX 48220
Boardman, Stanley	Petty Officer	P/JX 140291
Bocutt, Alfred A.	Marine	PO/ 21632
Boncey, William L.	Petty Officer	P/JX 138206
Bond, Sidney W.	Able Seaman	P/J 114908
Boneham, Norman	Marine	PO/X 4228
Boniface, Jack	Able Seaman	P/JX 158220
Bonner, Colin A.	Able Seaman	P/JX 181870
Boone, Bernard J.	Engine Room Artificer 4th Class	P/MX 60188
Booth, George H.	Stoker 2nd Class	P/KX 116710
Borrer, Harold T.	Able Seaman	P/JX 157334
Borsberry, George	Petty Officer Cook (S)	P/MX 45410
Bosley, Frank W.	Leading Sick Berth Attendant	P/MX 46291
Bostock, Charles W.	Chief Mechanician	P/K 57520
Bower, Reginald P.	Able Seaman	P/JX 212274
Bower, Ronald	Stoker 1st Class	P/KX 104052
Bowers, Leo S.	Ordinary Seaman	P/JX 157338
Bowie, Duncan	Able Seaman, R.N.V.R.	P/CD/X 2180
Bowyer, Thomas R.	Ordinary Telegraphist	P/JX 223160
Bowyer, Walter F.	Stoker 1st Class	P/KX 96060
Bradley, Harold	Ordinary Seaman	P/JX 162374
Bradley, Kenneth J.	Able Seaman	P/SSX 25711

d'Eyncourt, Sir Eustace H.W. Tennyson, 'H.M.S. *Hood*' in *Engineering* [London], 109 (January–June 1920), pp. 423–6; also in *Journal of the American Society of Naval Engineers*, 32 (1920), pp. 374–87
_____, *A Shipbuilder's Yarn* (London: Hutchinson, 1948)
Divine, David, *Mutiny at Invergordon* (London: MacDonald, 1970)
Donald, William, *Stand by for Action* (London: William Kimber, 1956)
Dreyer, Admiral Sir Frederic C., *The Sea Heritage: A Study of Maritime Warfare* (London: Museum Press, 1955)
Duncan, Barry, *Invergordon '31: How Men of the RN Struck and Won* (Southampton: author, 1976)
Edwards, Lt-Cdr Kenneth, *The Mutiny at Invergordon* (London: Putnam, 1937)
Eller, Rear-Admiral Ernest M., U.S.N., *Reminiscences* [interview transcripts] (3 vols., Annapolis: U.S. Naval Institute, 1990)
Ereira, Alan, *The Invergordon Mutiny* (London: Routledge & Kegan Paul, 1981)
Fairbairn, Lt-Cdr Douglas, *The Narrative of a Naval Nobody* (London: John Murray, 1929)
Geary, Lt Stanley, *H.M.S. Hood* (London: Robert Ross & Co., *c*.1942)
Glover, Lt-Cdr William, 'Manning and Training the Allied Navies' in Stephen Howarth & Derek Law (ed), *The Battle of the Atlantic, 1939–1945: The 50th Anniversary International Naval Conference* (London: Greenhill Books, 1994), pp. 188–213
Godfrey, Admiral J.H., *The Naval Memoirs of Admiral J.H. Godfrey* (8 vols. in 11 tomes, privately, 1964–7)
Goldrick, Cdr James, 'The Problems of Modern Naval History' in John B. Hattendorf (ed), *Doing Naval History: Essays Toward Improvement* (Newport, RI: Naval War College Press, 1995), pp. 15–19
Grenfell, Cdr Russell, *A Cruiser Commander's Orders* (Portsmouth: Gieves, 1933)
_____, [Capt.], *The Bismarck Episode* (London: Faber and Faber, 1949)
Grove, Eric, '*Hood*'s Achilles' Heel?' in *Naval History*, 7 (1993), Summer, pp. 43–6
Gruner, George F., *Blue Water Beat: The Two Lives of the Battleship USS California* (Palo Alto, CA: Glencannon Press, 1996)
Gunnery Guide: H.M.S. Hood (restricted circulation, Admiralty, *c*.1920) [NMM, HMS *Hood*, ship's cover, II]
The Gunnery Pocket Book (restricted circulation, Admiralty, 1932)
Haines, Gregory, *Cruiser at War* (London: Ian Allan, 1978)
Halpern, Paul G. (ed), *The Keyes Papers: Selections from the Private and Official Correspondence of Admiral of the Fleet Baron Keyes of Zeebrugge* (vols. 117 & 121–2) (3 vols., London: The Navy Records Society, 1972–81)
Hill, Roger, *Destroyer Captain* (London: William Kimber, 1975)
'H.M. Battlecruiser *Hood*' in *Engineering* [London], 109 (January–June 1920), pp. 397–9
H.M.S. Hood: Notes for Visitors (*c*.1925)
H.M.S. Hood: Notes for Visitors (1931)
Hodges, Peter, *The Big Gun: Battleship Main Armament, 1860–1945* (London: Conway, 1981)
Hogg, Ian V., & John Batchelor, *Naval Gun* (Poole: Blandford Press, 1978)
Hogg, Robert S., *Naval Architecture and Ship Construction* (London: Institute of Marine Engineers, 1956)
Hore, Capt. Peter, *Sea Power Ashore* (London: Chatham Publishing, 2001)
Hoyt, Edwin P., *The Life and Death of HMS Hood* (London: Arthur Barker, 1977)
Humphries, Steve (ed), *The Call of the Sea: Britain's Maritime Past, 1900–1960* (London: BBC, 1997)
Iago, Lt John, *And Home There's No Returning: Letters Home from HMS Hood, 1939–1941*, ed. Bee Kenchington (Fleet Hargate, Lincs.: Arcturus Press, forthcoming)
James, Cdr W.M., *New Battleship Organisations and Notes for Executive Officers* (Portsmouth: Gieve's, 1916)
_____, Admiral Sir William, *The Sky Was Always Blue* (London: Methuen, 1951)
Jenson, Cdr Latham B., *Tin Hats, Oilskins & Seaboots: A Naval Journey, 1938–1945* (Toronto: Robin Brass Studio, 2000)
Johnston, David A., *H.M.S. 'Hood' on the Cards* (Fareham, Hants.: Neville Lovett Community School, 1999)
Johnston, Ian, *Beardmore Built: The Rise and Fall of a Clydeside Shipyard* (Glasgow: Clydebank District Libraries & Museums Department, 1993)

_____, *Ships for a Nation: John Brown & Company Clydebank, 1847–1971* (Glasgow: West Dunbartonshire Libraries & Museums, 2000)
Jurens, W.J., 'The Loss of H.M.S. *Hood*—A Re-examination' in *Warship International*, 24 (1987), no. 2, pp. 122–61
Jurens, William, William H. Garzke, Jr., Robert O. Dulin, Jr., John Roberts & Richard Fiske, 'A Marine Forensic Analysis of HMS *Hood* and DKM *Bismarck*' in *Transactions of the Society of Naval Architects and Marine Engineers*, 110 (2002), pp. 115–53
Kemp, Paul J., *Bismarck and Hood: Great Naval Adversaries* (London: Arms and Armour Press, 1991)
Kennedy, Ludovic, *Pursuit: The Chase and Sinking of the Bismarck* (London: Collins, 1974)
_____, *On My Way to the Club* (London: Collins, 1989)
Kent, Capt. Barrie, *Signal!: A History of Signalling in the Royal Navy* (Clanfield, Hants.: Hyden House, 1993)
Klimczyk, Tadeusz, *Hood* [Monografie Morskie, vol. 6] (Gdynia: AJ-Press, 1997)
Lambert, Andrew, 'HMS *Hood*: April–May 1936' in *Warship*, 34 (April 1985), pp. 74–9
La Niece, Rear-Admiral P.G., *Not a Nine to Five Job* (Yalding, Kent: Charltons Publishers, 1992)
Le Bailly, Vice-Admiral Sir Louis, *The Man Around the Engine: Life Below the Waterline* (Emsworth, Hants.: Kenneth Mason, 1990)
_____, *From Fisher to the Falklands* (London: Institute of Marine Engineers, 1991)
_____, 'Rum, Bum & the Lash: Some Thoughts on the Problems of Homosexuality in the Royal Navy' in *Journal of the Royal United Services Institute*, 141, no. 1 (February 1996), pp. 54–8
McMurtrie, Francis, *The Cruise of the Bismarck* (London: Hutchinson, 1942)
Manual of Instruction for the Royal Naval Sick Berth Staff (London: H.M.S.O., 1930)
Manual of Seamanship, vol. I (restricted circulation, Admiralty, 1937)
Marder, Arthur J., *From the Dardanelles to Oran* (Oxford: Oxford University Press, 1974)
Mearns, David, & Rob White, *Hood and Bismarck: The Deep-Sea Discovery of an Epic Battle* (London: Pan Macmillan/Channel 4 Books, 2001)
Moran, Lord [Charles McMoran Wilson], *The Anatomy of Courage* (London: Constable, 1945)
Moretz, Joseph, *The Royal Navy and the Capital Ship in the Interwar Period* (London: Frank Cass, 2002)
von Müllenheim-Rechberg, Baron Burkard, *Battleship Bismarck: A Survivor's Story* (2nd edn, Annapolis: Naval Institute Press, 1990)
Murfett, Malcolm H., *Fool-Proof Relations: The Search for Anglo-American Naval Cooperation during the Chamberlain Years, 1937–1940* (Singapore: Singapore University Press, 1984)
Newton, R.N., *Practical Construction of Warships* (London: Longmans, Green & Co., 1941)
Norman, Andrew, *HMS Hood: Pride of the Royal Navy* (Mechanicsburg, PA: Stackpole Books, 2001)
Northcott, Maurice, *HMS Hood* [Man O'War, vol. 6] (London: Bivouac Books, 1975)
O'Connor, V.C. Scott, *The Empire Cruise* (1st edn, London: Riddle, Smith & Duffus [for the author], 1925; there is a second printing with a foreword by Leo Amery M.P.)
O'Conor, Capt. Rory, *Running a Big Ship on 'Ten Commandments' (With Modern Executive Ideas and a Complete Organisation)* (Portsmouth: Gieves, 1937)
Owen, Cdr Charles, *No More Heroes: The Royal Navy in the Twentieth Century: Anatomy of a Legend* (London: Allen & Unwin, 1975)
_____, *Plain Yarns from the Fleet: The Spirit of the Royal Navy during its Twentieth-Century Heyday* (Stroud, Glos.: Alan Sutton, 1997)
Owen, Cdr J.H., *Mutiny in the Royal Navy*, vol. II: *1921–1937* (restricted circulation, Admiralty, 1955)
Pack, Capt. S.W.C., *Cunningham the Commander* (London: B.T. Batsford, 1974)
Padfield, Peter, *The Battleship Era* (London: Rupert Hart-Davis, 1972)
_____, *Guns at Sea* (London: Hugh Evelyn, 1973)
The Panama Canal Record, 17 (1924), no. 51, pp. 731–2
Pears, Cdr Randolph, *British Battleships, 1892–1957: The Great Days of the Fleets* (London: Putnam, 1957)
Peebles, Hugh B., *Warshipbuilding on the Clyde* (Edinburgh: John Donald, 1987)
Pertwee, Jon, *Moon Boots and Dinner Suits* (London: Elm Tree Books, 1984)

Piper, Trevor, 'HMS *Hood*' in *Warship World*, 4 (1998), no. 4, pp. 20–2
Poolman, Kenneth, *The British Sailor* (London: Arms and Armour Press, 1989)
Progress in Naval Gunnery (restricted circulation, Admiralty, 1920–39)
Pursey, Cdr Harry, 'Invergordon: First Hand—Last Word?' in *Naval Review*, 64 (1976), pp. 157–64 & 268 (erratum)
Ranft, B.McL. (ed), *The Beatty Papers: Selections from the Private and Official Correspondence and Papers of Admiral of the Fleet Earl Beatty* (Navy Records Society, vol. 128 & 132) (2 vols., Aldershot: Scolar Press, 1989–93)
Ransome-Wallis, P., *The Royal Naval Reviews* (London: Ian Allan, 1982)
Ransome-Wallis, R., *Two Red Stripes: A Naval Surgeon at War* (London: Ian Allan, 1973)
Raven, Alan, & John Roberts, *British Battleships of World War Two: The Development and Technical History of the Royal Navy's Battleships and Battlecruisers from 1911 to 1946* (London: Arms and Armour Press, 1976)
Rea, The Rev. Edgar, *A Curate's Egg* (Durban: Knox Printing Co., *c*.1967)
Rhys-Jones, Graham, *The Loss of the Bismarck: An Avoidable Disaster* (London: Cassell, 1999)
Roberts, John, *The Battlecruiser Hood* [Anatomy of the Ship] (London: Conway, 1982)
_____, *Battlecruisers* (London: Chatham Publishing, 1997)
Robertson, Lt R.G., 'HMS *Hood*: Battle-Cruiser 1916–1941' in John Wingate (ed), *Warships in Profile*, vol. II (Windsor: Profile Publications, 1973), pp. 145–72; also pubd separately as *HMS Hood* [Warships in Profile, no. 19]
_____, 'The Mighty *Hood*' in *Ships Monthly*, 10 (1975), no. 3, pp. 4–10; no. 4, pp. 22–7; no. 5, pp. 10–14, & no. 6, pp. 4–9
_____, 'H.M.S. "Hood"' in *Ships Monthly*, 16 (1981), no. 4, pp. 26–9, & no. 5, pp. 24–6
Rogers, Byron, 'H.M.S. *Hood*' in *Saga*, July 1997, pp. 38–43 and subsequent correspondence in August & September nos.
Roskill, Capt. Stephen W., *The War at Sea, 1939–1945* (3 vols. in 4 tomes, London: H.M.S.O., 1954–61)
_____, *H.M.S. Warspite: The Story of a Famous Battleship* (London: Collins, 1957; repr. Annapolis: Naval Institute Press, 1997)
_____, *Naval Policy Between the Wars* (2 vols., London: Collins, 1968–76)
_____, *Churchill and the Admirals* (London: Collins, 1977)
_____, *Admiral of the Fleet Earl Beatty: The Last Naval Hero: An Intimate Biography* (London: Collins, 1980)
Royal Navy and Royal Marines Sports Handbook 1933 (restricted circulation, Royal Marines Sports Control Board, Admiralty, 1933)
Schleihauf, William, '*Hood*'s Fire Control System: An Overview' on www.hmshood.com
Schmid, Hans, *Steuermann durch Krieg und Frieden, 1937–1946* (Berg am Starnberger See: Verlagsgesellschaft Berg, 1994)
[Shrimpton, Paymaster Lt J.T.], *H.M.S. Hood: Verses, 1932–1934* (privately, *c*.1935)
Simpson, Michael (ed), *The Somerville Papers: Selections from the Private and Official Correspondence of Admiral of the Fleet Sir James Somerville, G.C.B., G.B.E., D.S.O.* (Navy Records Society, vol. 134) (Aldershot: Scolar Press, 1995)
Smith, P.C., *The Great Ships Pass: British Battleships at War, 1939–1945* (London: William Kimber, 1977)
_____, *Hit First, Hit Hard: H.M.S. Renown, 1916–1948* (London: William Kimber, 1979)
Stephen, Martin, *The Fighting Admirals: British Admirals of the Second World War* (London: Leo Cooper, 1991)
The Stokers' Manual (restricted circulation, Admiralty, 1927)
Sturtivant, Ray, & Dick Cronin, *Fleet Air Arm Aircraft, Units and Ships 1920 to 1939* (Tonbridge Wells: Air-Britain, 1998)
Sumida, Jon Tetsuro, *In Defence of Naval Supremacy: Finance, Technology and British Naval Policy, 1889–1914* (Boston: Unwin Hyman, 1989)
Talbot-Booth, Paymaster Lt-Cdr E.C., *All the World's Fighting Fleets* (3rd edn, London: Sampson Low, 1940)
Taverner, Nixie, *A Torch Among Tapers* (Bramber, W. Sussex: Bernard Durnford, 2000)
_____, *Hood's Legacy* (Bramber, W. Sussex: Bernard Durnford, 2001)
Taylor, The Rev. Gordon, *The Sea Chaplains: A History of the Chaplains of the Royal Navy* (Oxford: Oxford Illustrated Press, 1978)

_____, *Remembrance Day Sermon, St. Giles-in-the-Fields Church, London, 12th November 2000* (privately, 2000)

Taylor, Theodore, *H.M.S. Hood vs. Bismarck: The Battleship Battle* (New York: Avon Books, 1982)

Thomas, Roger D., & Brian Patterson, *Dreadnoughts in Camera: Building the Dreadnoughts, 1905–1920* (Stroud, Glos.: Alan Sutton/Royal Naval Museum, 1998)

Thompson, The Rev. Kenneth, *H.M.S. Rodney at War: Being an Account of the Part Played in the War by H.M.S. Rodney from 1939 to 1945* (London: Hollis and Carter, 1946)

Tute, Warren, *The Deadly Stroke* (London: Collins, 1973)

Twiss, Admiral Sir Frank, *Social Change in the Royal Navy, 1924–1970: The Life and Times of Admiral Sir Frank Twiss, KCB, KCVO, DSC* (Stroud, Glos.: Alan Sutton/Royal Naval Museum, 1996)

Vian, Admiral of the Fleet Sir Philip, *Action this Day* (London: Frederick Muller, 1960)

Warden, A. Ross, 'Memories of the Battle Cruiser H.M.S. "Hood"' in *The Navy*, April 1971, pp. 82–5

Weldon, D.G., 'H.M.S. Hood' in *Warship International*, 9 (1972), no. 2, pp. 114–58

Wellings, Rear-Admiral Joseph H., U.S.N., *On His Majesty's Service: Observations of the British Home Fleet from the Diary, Reports, and Letters of Joseph H. Wellings, Assistant U.S. Naval Attaché, London, 1940–41*, ed. John B. Hattendorf (Newport, RI: Naval War College Press, 1983)

Wells, Capt. John, *The Royal Navy: An Illustrated Social History, 1870–1982* (Stroud, Glos.: Alan Sutton/Royal Naval Museum, 1994)

Williams, Leonard Charles, *Gone A Long Journey* (Bedhampton, Hants.: Hillmead Publications, 2002)

Wincott, Len, *Invergordon Mutineer* (London: Weidenfeld & Nicolson, 1974)

Winklareth, Robert J., *The Bismarck Chase: New Light on a Famous Engagement* (London: Chatham, 1998)

Winton, John, *Death of the Scharnhorst* (Chichester: Antony Bird Publications, 1983)

Wiper, Steve, *H.M.S. Hood* [Warship Pictorial, no. 20] (Tucson: Classic Warships Publishing, 2003)

Journals and Newspapers
The Globe and Laurel
The Naval and Military Review
Naval Review
The Navy
Western Evening Herald
Western Morning News

II. Unpublished Sources

Dates after names indicate period of service in ship

Applegarth School Archive, Northallerton, Yorks.
School log book for 1941 and assorted uncatalogued papers and correspondence relating to HMS *Hood*, including letters from H. Balston (1940), AB J.T. Beale (*c*.1940), the Rev. Harold Beardmore (1939–41), Rear-Admiral Irvine Glennie (1939–41), A.G. McGregor (*c*.1939–*c*.40), Tel. Leonard Taylor (*c*.1940), the Rev. James Churchill Waters (1932–4) and LS L.C. Williams (1936–41)

Churchill Archives Centre, Cambridge
DRYR boxes 3/1–2; 8/1–2; 11/1 Admiral Sir Frederic Dreyer
LEBY boxes 1–3 & 20 (boxes 16–17 closed) Vice-Admiral Sir Louis Le Bailly
ROSK boxes 4/7; 4/77–77A; 7/172; 8/27; 21/3 Capt. Stephen Roskill

The Fenhurst Society, Fenhurst, Surrey
Oral history: Cdr Keith Evans (1938–9)

Glasgow University Archives
Upper Clyde Shipbuilders 1/5/15–21; 1/86/33

HMS Hood Association Archives
Lt-Cdr A.R.T. Batley (1941)
Capt. G.C. Blundell (1922–4)
OSig. Reg G. Bragg (1922–4)
Marine 'Windy' Breeze (1920–2)
OSig. A.E.P. Briggs (1939–41)
Stoker Ken Clark (1938–40)
AB Harry Cutler (1922–4)
Cdr Keith Evans (1938–9)
S.M. Ghani (schoolboy, 1924)

LS Fred Hard (1936–9)
OD W.H.T. Hawkins (1940–1)
CERA W.L. Hudson (1923–9)
Vice-Admiral Eric W. Longley-Cook (1930–3)
OD Ernest McConnell (1938–40)
Sig. Harry Smith (1926)
OD H.D. Spence (1940–1)
Stoker W.F. Stone (1921–5)
Boy Jim Taylor (1940–1)
Boy A. Thomas (*c*.1926–9)
AB R.E. Tilburn (1938–41)
Stoker Dick Turner (1936–9)
AB Fred White (1937–8)
LS J.R. Williams (1939–40)

Imperial War Museum, London
Department of Documents
96/20/1   Mid. H.W. Acworth (1928)
90/38/1   Capt. G.C. Blundell (1922–4, 1941)
91/7/1   Boy F.B. Coombs (1935–8)
92/27/1   Boy W.M. Crawford (1939–41)
74/134–5/1 W.H. Haslam [for OD Philip X] (1941)
92/4/1   Mid. H.G. Knowles (1939)
Sound Archive
13241   AB Albert Charles Band (1937–8)
10751   OSig. Albert Edward Pryke Briggs (1939–41)
13581   AB Leo Edward Brown (1940–1)
5809   Stoker Nicholas Smiles Carr (1930–1)
794   AB Fred Copeman (*Norfolk*, 1931)
5831   Stoker Walter Roy Hargreaves (1931)
18663   Boy Tel. Ernest Kerridge (*Renown*, *c*.1934–6)
12503   Mid. John Robert Lang (*Renown*, 1935–6; *Hood*, 1936–*c*.7)
11767   Lt Charles Piercy Mills (1940–1)
22147   OA Bert Pitman (1939–41)
11951   Mid. Edmund Nicholas Poland (1935)
20817   AB Percy Thomas Price (1936–8)
18804   Noel Raymond Pugh (Royal Naval Wireless Auxiliary Reserve, 1930s)
12422   LS Joseph Frederick Rockey (1938–40)
16741   Sub-Lt (E) Brian Scott-Garrett (1940–1)
749   Plumber Ernest Henry Taylor (*c*.1926–8)
11746   AB Robert Ernest Tilburn (1938–41)
13205   Tel. James Brock Webster (*Prince of Wales*, 1941)
5818   OD Norman Wesbroom (1931–2)
5807   LS Samuel George Wheat (1931)
13240   AB Frederick William White (1937–8)
5835   Stoker Charles Edward Wild (1931)

Liddell Hart Centre for Military Archives, King's College, London
Aston 1/10 Major-General Sir George Aston (Royal Marines, 1926)

National Maritime Museum, Greenwich
Ship's cover, HMS *Hood* (3 vols.)
Chatfield/4/1–3 Admiral of the Fleet Lord Chatfield (First Sea Lord, 1932–8)
Cowan/5, 13/2, 14 & 20: Admiral Sir Walter Cowan (1921–3)
Elkins/1, 2, 11 Admiral Sir Robert Elkins (1921–3; *Valiant*, 1931)
Pursey/5, 11–16, 21: Cdr Harry Pursey (1931–3)

Naval Historical Branch, Whitehall, London
'Pink Lists', HMS *Hood* (1920–39)
Admiralty War Diary, card index (1939–41)

Naval War College, Providence, Rhode Island
Rear-Admiral Joseph H. Wellings, U.S.N. (1940–1)

Public Record Office, Kew
ADM 1/2219   Preparations for Empire Cruise (1923)
ADM 1/8662/111   Special Service Squadron, Empire Cruise (1924)
ADM 1/11726   Loss of *Hood* in action with German battleship *Bismarck* (1941)
ADM 1/30817   Loss of H.M.S. *Hood* (1941)
ADM 53 Deck logs of H.M.S. Hood, *March 1920–April 1941:*
ADM 53/78910–78966   (March 1920–December 1934)
ADM 53/97652–97675   (January 1935–December 1936)
ADM 53/104194–104217 (January 1937–December 1938)
ADM 53/109191–109202 (January–December 1939)
ADM 53/112443–112454 (January–December 1940)
ADM 53/114434–114437 (January–April 1941)

ADM 101/536   Medical Officers' Journal (1932)
ADM 101/565   Medical Officers' Journal (1940)
ADM 116/2219–2220 Empire Cruise of the Special Service Squadron (1923–4)
ADM 116/2254–2257 Special Service Squadron: Letters of Proceedings (1923–4)
ADM 116/4351–4352 Loss of H.M.S. *Hood*: Boards of Inquiry (1941)
ADM 136/13   Ship's books (11 vols.) (1916–41)
ADM 156/107   Collision between HM Ships *Hood* and *Renown* (1935)
ADM 167/83   Admiralty Minutes and Memoranda, Invergordon Mutiny (1931)
ADM 167/89   Admiralty Minutes and Memoranda, Invergordon Mutiny (1931)
ADM 178/79   Admiralty: Memoranda regarding Invergordon Mutiny (1931)
ADM 178/110   Invergordon Mutiny: Reports of Proceedings (1931)
ADM 178/114   Invergordon Mutiny: Men discharged (1931)
ADM 178/129   Invergordon Mutiny: Reports (1931)
ADM 186/797   Operations against French Fleet at Mers-el-Kebir (1940)
ADM 202/422   Operations by Royal Marines in Norway (1940)
ADM 234/317   Operations against French Fleet at Mers-el-Kebir (1940)
ADM 239/261   The Fighting Instructions (1939)
ADM 267/64   Board of enquiry into loss of H.M.S. *Hood* (1941)
AIR 15/415   Reports on loss of *Hood* and sinking of *Bismarck* (1941)

Royal Naval Museum, Portsmouth
Manuscripts Collection
1981/368-74   Paymaster Lt Robert Browne (1940–1)
1998/42   Mid. Philip Buckett (1940–1)
1999/19   AB Algernon Foster (*c*.1939–41)
1993/54   Cdr Rory O'Conor (1933–6)
1987/106   Mid. John Parker (1935)
Oral History Collection
68/1997   Mr Cavendish Morton (artist, 1930s)
27/1992   Sgt John Russell (1931–2)

The Second World War Experience Centre, Horsforth, Leeds
2001/1376   OD B.A. Carlisle (1940–1)

Author's Collection
Letter: Lt (E) Tristram Spence (1940–1)
Memoirs: Tel. R.R. Jackman (1937–9);
  Cdr R.A.C. Owen (1940–1);
  Boy Maurice Sherborne (1938–40)
Correspondence: Cdr I.W.V. Browne (1939–41); Stoker George Donnelly (1936–8); Cdr Keith Evans (1938–9); Ian A. Green (HM Dockyard, Rosyth, 1939–42); Tel. R.R. Jackman (1937–9); Vice-Admiral Sir Louis Le Bailly (1932–3, 1937–9); Cdr R.A.C. Owen (1940–1); OTel. Douglas Turner (1935–9)
Interview notes: Cdr I.W.V. Browne (1939–41); Stoker Ken Clark (1938–40); AB Harry Cutler (1922–4); Ian A. Green (HM Dockyard, Rosyth, 1939–42); Tel. R.R. Jackman (1937–9); OD Horace King (1935–8); Vice-Admiral Sir Louis Le Bailly (1932–3, 1937–9); OD Ernest McConnell (1938–40); Boy Jim Taylor (1939–40); OTel. Douglas Turner (1935–9); AB George Walker (1939–40); Surgeon Lt (D) W.J. Wolton (1936–8)
Oral history: Boy Jim Taylor (1939–40)

Private Collections
James Gordon (Boy Seaman, *Prince of Wales*, 1941): Filmed interview (*c*.2000)
Cdr David Gould:
  (i) Papers of Admiral Sir Francis Pridham (1936–8)
  Memoirs (*c*.1970)
  Lectures on Mutiny, Part I: *Prevention* (*c*.1938)
  Notes on Handling the Hood (*c*.1938)
  Notes for Newly Joined Officers (January 1938)
  (ii) Memoirs of Cdr James Gould (1921–3)
Mrs Bee Kenchington: Letters of Lt John Iago (1939–41)
Mrs E.L. Roberts: Memoirs of Cdr E.W. Roberts (1933–6)

Glossary

abaft (adv.) behind

aft, after (n. & adj.) general terms indicating something as being towards the stern of the ship or closer to the stern than another object

Aldis light *or* **lamp** a hand-held signalling lamp

'the Andrew' traditional name for the Royal Navy

athwart, athwartships across the ship, at right angles to the centreline

banyan party *or* **spree** a picnic ashore, often in foreign climes

'the Bloke' the Commander

bogie in *Hood*'s case a revolving structure in the trunking of each 15in turret used to bring shells up to the working chamber

brow ladder rigged against the ship's side giving access to and from boats lying alongside

'buffer' Bosun's Mate

cable a measurement of distance, 200 yards

caboose (*or* **'cabouche'**) an enclosed space in a ship, usually very small, unofficially taken over by a rating for his personal use

chaff banter, usually good humoured

'crusher' Regulating Petty Officer

davits cranes for lowering or hoisting the ship's boats, and from which they are suspended when not in use

deal a fir or pine wood plank about six feet long

deckhead the ceiling

divisions the grouping of a section of the crew, usually by trade, with responsibility for work and maintenance in a specific part of the ship; also the mustering or inspection of these by a senior officer

'doggie' a messenger

drifter a type of fishing boat attached to a large ship as a tender to ferry her men and keep her supplied

fanny any of several metal receptacles for food or drink which formed the culinary outfit of a mess

fathom a measurement of depth, six feet

flat a clear space below decks

forward (n. & adj.) general term indicating something as being towards the bows of the ship or closer to the bows than another object

'the Gaffer' the admiral

'gash' rubbish and waste, usually disposed of down the chutes positioned for this purpose on either side of the ship

'goffers' soft drinks provided by the canteen; by extension anything worthless or inadequate

'grog' the diluted rum ration traditionally served in the Royal Navy; see p. 86

hopper in *Hood*, the flash-tight containers for transporting cordite charges first to the working chamber and then to the gunhouse of a 15in turret

hove to (p.p. of **'heave'**) to bring a boat or ship to a standstill without anchoring or making fast

inboard the inner part of the ship

inclination exercise a gunnery exercise against another ship with a deliberate deflection or 'throw off' on the gun sights

interrupted screw the alignment of screw threads by which the hinged breech block of a gun can seal or open the firing chamber by means of a rotating movement

'Jack Dusty' Chief Petty Officer in charge of stores

jankers a punishment

'the Jaunty' the Master-at-Arms

'Jimmy the One' the First Lieutenant, in *Hood* always a lieutenant-commander

'killick' a Leading Seaman, so-called for the anchor or 'killick' device worn on his left arm

ky, kye hot cocoa made from large slabs of gritty chocolate, pounded or chipped off with a knife and melted in boiling water or under a steam main; served very thick with sugar and milk to taste

libertymen men granted temporary shore leave

Make and Mend Clothes a half-day holiday

mess properly, the grouping of men to a numbered table on a messdeck where they eat and spend much of their free time; often used to describe the entire messdeck

mess traps assorted utensils

nautical mile 6,080 feet

'oggin (hoggin) the sea

'oppo' friend; also the man in the opposite watch who performs the same duties as oneself

outboard the sea side of the ship

'the Owner' the Captain

'party' girlfriend

'pierhead jump' a rapid and unexpected draft to another ship

'pilot' a navigator

point a division of the circumference of the magnetic compass card, equivalent to 11° 15′

'pusser' corruption of 'Purser'; general term to describe anything official or issued by the Navy, and by extension a person known for always doing things by the book

rove (p.p. of **'reeve'**) to thread a rope or cable through something

'salthorse' a seaman officer without specialist training

scuttle a porthole; also a flashproof hatch in the gun-loading mechanisms

shackle a measurement of anchor cable, 75 feet (12½ fathoms); also a U-shaped iron closed with a pin and used for joining lengths of cable, etc.

'snottie' a midshipman

'stripey' a rating with some experience in the Navy, denoted by the chevrons on his left arm; usually used to refer to a three-stripe able seaman with at least thirteen years' service behind him

'tanky' a long-service able seaman charged with specific duties in the ship

'tickler' a hand-rolled cigarette; see p. 87

'tiddley' general term to describe something attractive or in first-rate condition, often with respect to uniform or other accoutrements

'tiffy' an artificer; also a general name for other rating specialists, especially Sick Berth Attendants

tompion (*also* **tampion**) a brass stopper for the muzzle of a gun, usually decorated with the ship's badge

trick a turn of duty in a watch, lasting between 30 minutes and two hours

'uckers (huckers) a form of ludo

watch one of the four-hour periods into which the naval day is divided; also the groups of men assigned to duty during this period

Places mentioned in the text

Index

Numbers in *italics* refer to photos, plans and maps. Ranks and ratings of individuals are the last under which they are mentioned in the text. Keel-laying dates are given after ship names, approval dates after ship classes, and locations after shore establishments.

Acknowledgements

To have studied a ship like the *Hood* is to have enjoyed the greatest of privileges. Not least of these has been the company, generosity and goodwill of a large number of people throughout the world. My first debt is to Frank Allen and Paul Bevand of the HMS *Hood* Association who have unstintingly supported the project from the first and generously shared not only their time and knowledge but also the resources of their website hmshood.com. A very significant part of the documentary and illustrative material on which this book is based rests in the collections of the *Hood* Association and it is thanks to the efforts of Ken Clark and now Messrs Allen and Bevand that it has been gathered and made available to an increasingly wide community of researchers. Latterly Paul and Frank have helped in the immense task of gathering the photographs which illustrate this book and in providing ready answers to those questions and problems which vex every author as his book comes full term. The debt is greater than I can possibly repay and my only hope is that they find the result an adequate tribute to their ship and their dedication to her.

Next I must thank the large number of *Hood* veterans who have taken the time and trouble to speak or correspond with me, to answer barrages of questions via phone, mail, e-mail and in person, and even to reading and commenting on lengthy chapters: Cdr Ian Browne, Ken Clark, the late Harry Cutler, George Donnelly, Cdr Keith Evans, William Hawkins, Dick Jackman, Horace King, the late Ernest McConnell, Cdr Robin Owen, Roy Pownall, Maurice Sherborne, Jim Taylor, Dick Turner, Douglas Turner, George Walker and the late Surgeon Cdr Bill Wolton; also to Ted Briggs, President of the HMS *Hood* Association, for making a vital introduction at the start of my research, and to James Gordon of *Prince of Wales* for sharing his remarkable memory of the loss of the *Hood* with me. Ian Green has provided many invaluable insights into the refit carried out in the *Hood* in the spring of 1941 and the world of the Royal Dockyards generally. George Squires recalled a visit to the ship at Hvalfjord in the spring of 1941; Mrs Mary Phillips and Mrs E.G. Wilkin generously shared their memories of the Admiralty on the morning of 24 May 1941, and Mrs Sheila Harris of life in Portsmouth after the sinking. But my greatest debt is to Vice-Admiral Sir Louis Le Bailly who has not only honoured me by writing the Foreword to this book, but has painstakingly read and commented on successive drafts of every chapter. Much of the detail of life aboard in the 1930s is owed to his phenomenal memory and it is thanks to him that I have been able to give the *Hood*'s engineering systems and personnel something approaching their due. It is not going too far to say that this book could never have assumed its present dimension without his active assistance and the debt I owe him is one for which no expression of gratitude could ever be adequate.

Then there are those who have been kind enough to give me the benefit of their knowledge, memories, contacts and information, as well as access to private documents, photographs and material; in some cases this has extended to outright donation. For this, too, I am endebted to the editors of *Ships Monthly* and *Saga* who generously published the appeals for information which led to many of the contacts listed here: Charles Arnold, Mrs Daphne Barton, Roger Batten, Sid Beckett, Jill Berelson, Mrs Margaret Berry, William M. Berry, Len Brattan, Leonard Broomfield, Adrian Burdett, Ian Bussey, Peter Cambridge, William Carrivick, Stephen Chumbley, Mrs Dinah Couchman, John Crabb, Cdr Jeff Crawford, Brian Dawson, Mrs Ruth Dawson, John England, Hugh Fulton, Mrs Brenda Glass, George Green, Eric Hall, John Haynes, Richard Hayter, Mrs Jean Jackson, Chris Judd, Mrs June Kelley, Mrs Bee Kenchington, Fred Kendall, Mrs Doris Knapman, Alistair Lorimer, Miss Nora Loxham, Mrs Jenny McIntyre-Sweet, Ted Mallett, Selwyn Maund, Mrs Doreen Miller, Mrs Thelma Miller, Trevor Moffet, Mrs Diane Morris, Phillip Morris-Jones, Ted Oldfield, Mrs Sarah Padwick, Arthur Pearsall, Langmead Pillar, Norman Pooley, Mrs Julia Roxan, Ted Senior, Geoff Smith, Mrs Sheila Smith, Mrs Mary Spence, Mrs Marjorie Sutton, Miss B. Talbot, Miss Joanna Warrand, David Weldon, Mrs Jean Winter and Jeremy Woods. The papers of Admiral Sir Francis Pridham and the reminiscences of Cdr James Gould have been made available to me through the kindness of Cdr David Gould, and those of Cdr Rory O'Conor by Mrs Nixie Taverner. Mrs E.D. Roberts has kindly supplied those of her late husband Cdr E.W. Roberts. Jeremy Whitehorn generously set aside his own research in the Public Record Office to chase up some rather voluminous references for me.

A special word of thanks is in order for Mrs Pat Astbury, Alan Procter, Gerald Granger, D.E. Cromarty, Mrs Stella Young, staff and former pupils of Applegarth School, Northallerton, Yorkshire. Mrs Astbury and Mr Procter tirelessly combed through the school archives to supply me with details of Applegarth's special wartime attachment with HMS *Hood*. Messrs Granger and Cromarty and Mrs Young kindly made available their correspondence and memories of this affiliation. My sincere gratitude to them all.

Apart from those mentioned above, chapters have been read and commented on and/or technical advice proffered by Frank Allen, Paul Bevand, Dr John Brooks, Tony Carew, Alan Dowling, Ian Johnston, Dr. Bill Jurens, Nigel Ling, Daniel Morgan, Tom O'Leary and John Roberts. A great deal of the material upon which Chapter 1 is based was provided through the kindness of Ian Johnston. Admiral of the Fleet Sir Henry Leach went to enormous trouble to find details on the *Hood*'s gunnery systems for me, while the

Rev. Gordon Taylor provided much useful information on her chaplains. To them all my sincere thanks, though it need hardly be added that, despite their best efforts, all remaining errors are mine and mine alone.

Technical assistance has been provided with saintly patience and unflagging humour by Phil Condit, Jim Feldmeier, Wojciech Gil, Patrycja Hawrylciów and Anita Maya. My thanks, too, to the following librarians and archivists for granting me access to their collections: Thomas Weis of the Bibliothek für Zeitgeschichte, Stuttgart; John Stopford-Pickering and R.W. Suddaby of the Imperial War Museum, London; Daphne Knott, Jeremy Michell and Kiri Ross-Jones of the National Maritime Museum, Greenwich; Kate Tildesley of the Naval Historical Branch, Whitehall; Evelyn Cherpak of the Naval War College, Newport, Rhode Island; John Ambler of the Royal Marines Museum, Eastney; Stephen Courtney and Matthew Sheldon of the Royal Naval Museum, Portsmouth; Patrick Osborn of the U.S. National Archives, Washington, D.C., and Paul Stillwell of the U.S. Naval Institute, Annapolis, Maryland. UCLA's Young Research Library has proved an indispensable resource for a British naval historian far from the centres of British naval history.

It is a pleasure to record here the assistance of friends old and new. Daniel Morgan has been as stalwart as ever in his support of this project, even while his co-author neglected their own. Richard and Sarah Morgan have again favoured me with their wonderful hospitality, as have Lawrence and Bee Kenchington, Guy Blanchard and Harry and Caroline Oulton, though the author's naval monologues must often have tried their patience rather. James Harris has on my account made more than one foray from the history of philosophy into that of transport. Peter Russell still gives me the great privilege of his mind and friendship. Thomas Schmid, whose plans and illustrations for this book speak for themselves, has become a trusted friend who has greatly enhanced my appreciation of the field and its possibilities. Only he and I know how frequently he has saved my bacon in technical and photographic matters. A special word also for Al Smith and Alan Dowling, 'despertadores de almas durmientes', who in their different ways have never failed to remind me of what really matters in naval history. My parents, meanwhile, have again proved the soul of patience, devotion and self-abnegation. *Les paierai-je?*

But my greatest debt is to Cynthia, Emma and Alex, not only for the love and support they give me each day but for their patience and sacrifice during the long night of work which it has taken to complete this book. I hope, glancing through its pages, they find that it's all been worth while.

B.T.
Los Angeles, April 2004